Therapeutic Recreation
An Introduction

DAVID R. AUSTIN
Indiana University, Bloomington

MICHAEL E. CRAWFORD
University of Missouri, Columbia

PRENTICE HALL, Englewood Cliffs, New Jersey 07632

Library of Congress Cataloging-in-Publication Data
Austin, David R.
    Therapeutic recreation.

    Includes bibliographical references and index.
    1. Recreational therapy.   I. Crawford, Michael E.
II. Title.
RM736.7.A96   1991   615.8′5153   90–7946
ISBN 0–13–914771–3

Editorial/production supervision and
  interior design: E.A. Pauw and Karen Buck
Cover design: Patricia Kelly
Prepress buyer: Herb Klein
Manufacturing buyer: David Dickey

© 1991 by Prentice-Hall, Inc.
A Division of Simon & Schuster
Englewood Cliffs, New Jersey 07632

Printed in the United States of America
10 9 8 7 6 5 4 3 2 1

ISBN 0-13-914771-3

Prentice-Hall International (UK) Limited, *London*
Prentice-Hall of Australia Pty. Limited, *Sydney*
Prentice-Hall Canada Inc., *Toronto*
Prentice-Hall Hispanoamericana, S.A., *Mexico*
Prentice-Hall of India Private Limited, *New Delhi*
Prentice-Hall of Japan, Inc., *Tokyo*
Simon & Schuster Asia Pte. Ltd., *Singapore*
Editora Prentice-Hall do Brasil, Ltda., *Rio de Janeiro*

Contents

Theoretical Overview

SECTION TWO
Special Areas of Practice

8. Mental Retardation   163

John Dattilo

9. Severe Multiple Disabilities   189

Stuart J. Schleien

16. Burns   333

Ann James

17. Corrections   352

Stephen C. Anderson

SECTION THREE

Professional Practice Concerns

Preface

There has been a revolution in the literature of therapeutic recreation. The first revolution took place with the "first generation" of therapeutic recreation textbooks that were published in the 1970s. These initial works offered direction to an emerging profession and fed the hunger of students and practitioners for information on which to base therapeutic recreation practice. A second revolution is now underway. We are witnessing unprecedented numbers of additions to the therapeutic recreation literature. These publications give testimony to a growing depth and breadth in the body of knowledge in the field of therapeutic recreation.

Because of the expansion of the literature of therapeutic recreation (TR), it is more and more difficult for any one or two individuals to have in-depth knowledge of the latest developments in all areas of TR practice. That is why we have asked several leading therapeutic recreation authors to join us in the writing of *Therapeutic Recreation: An Introduction*. Each of these writers brings his or her expertise to the task of providing the most current information available in his or her particular area of specialization.

All chapters in the book follow a format that begins with the listing of specific objectives for the reader and ends with reading comprehension questions and learning activities. Readers who are teaching college and university courses in therapeutic recreation should find the objectives, questions, and learning activities useful in course planning and in the evaluation of student progress. Students and practitioners should be able to use the objectives, reading comprehension questions, and learning activities to understand better the material presented.

A number of persons have contributed in many different ways to this book. Joe Heider, from Prentice Hall, was a great help to us in the conceptualization of this book. Ted Bolen, Prentice Hall's editor for health, physical education, and recreation, offered continued support and encouragement throughout the development of the book. To those authors who have joined us by providing chapters in their areas of specialization, we must offer particular thanks. Their contributions make this book a unique work, one that we hope will advance the art and science of therapeutic recreation practice.

David R. Austin
Michael E. Crawford

This book is dedicated to our students past and present.

Contributors

Teresita E. Aguilar is a faculty member at Arizona State University. She has also taught at the University of Nebraska, the University of New Mexico, and the University of North Texas, where she completed her doctorate. Aguilar's research interests include negative leisure, adolescence, leisure education, and measurement.

Stephen C. Anderson is professor and head of the Department of Recreation and Leisure Studies at the University of North Carolina at Greensboro. He served on faculties at the University of Maryland and Indiana University and as a visiting professor at the Waterloo, Southern Connecticut, and Wisconsin campuses. Anderson earned his M.S. at Indiana State University and his Ph.D. from the University of Maryland.

David R. Austin is professor of recreation in the Department of Recreation and Park Administration at Indiana University, Bloomington. Prior to gaining his master's degree at Indiana University, Austin was a therapeutic recreation specialist with the Indiana Department of Mental Health. He has held faculty positions at the University of Illinois and University of North Texas. His Ph.D. was completed at the University of Illinois. He is a Certified Therapeutic Recreation Specialist.

Andrew Chasanoff is director of recreation at Children's Specialized Hospital in New Jersey. He was a therapist at the Rusk Institute of Rehabilitation Medicine and at Blythdale Children's Hospital. Chasanoff received his B.S. from the State University of New York College at Cortland and his M.A. from New York University.

Kathleen M. Cornwall is director of therapeutic recreation for Epworth Children's Home. She holds a master's degree from the University of Nebraska, Omaha. Prior to assuming her responsibilities with Epworth, Cornwall served on the faculty at the University of Missouri, Columbia.

Michael E. Crawford is associate professor in the Department of Parks, Recreation, and Tourism at the University of Missouri, Columbia. Prior to becoming an academic, Crawford worked as a practitioner in therapeutic recreation with a wide variety of clients, including individuals with mental retardation and problems in mental health. He has an extensive background in the design of playground apparatus for children with disabilities. Crawford holds his doctorate from Indiana University.

John Dattilo is associate professor at the University of Georgia, Athens. Dattilo, a Certified Therapeutic Recreation Specialist, has experience in providing services to individuals with multiple and severe disabilities, and in documenting the effects of interventions through data-based research. He obtained his Ph.D. from the University of Illinois.

Jerry G. Dickason is professor of recreation and leisure studies at Montclair State College in Upper Montclair, New Jersey. He was a recreation therapist at Evansville State Hospital in Indiana, a recreation leader for the American Red Cross in Vietnam, the chief of activity services at Coney Island Hospital, and a research scientist at New York University, where he completed his Ph.D. and served on the faculty.

Lodene Goodwin is a certified rehabilitation counselor. Her present position is with the South Carolina Department of Vocational Rehabilitation, where she has worked for 20 years. Goodwin completed her B.S. at Presbyterian College. She holds her master's degree in counseling and guidance from Clemson University.

Barbara A. Hawkins is a member of the faculty of the Department of Recreation and Park Administration at Indiana University. In addition to her faculty appointment, Hawkins is director of the program on aging and developmental disabilities at the Indiana University Institute for the Study of Developmental Disabilities. She holds her master's degree from the University of Montana and her doctorate from Indiana University.

Ann James teaches in the therapeutic recreation program at Clemson University. She has experience as a recreation therapist in general medical and mental health facilities. James finished her M.S. at the University of North Carolina and her Ph.D. at the University of New Mexico.

Mark R. James currently is working as a therapeutic recreation consultant in the private sector. Formerly he was employed in the Department of Psychiatry at Elizabeth General Medical Center, Elizabeth, New Jersey, where he specialized in leisure counseling and relaxation training services. He completed his master's degree in therapeutic recreation at Indiana University. Previously, James was project coordinator for a state grant project providing therapy services to clients with seizure disorders.

W. B. (Terry) Kinney is chairman of the Department of Recreation and Leisure Studies at Temple University in Philadelphia. Kinney has extensive experience in the field of psychiatry and mental health and has written widely in this area. He holds his master's degree from the University of Illinois and his Ph.D. from New York University.

Robin Kunstler is coordinator of the recreation education program at Lehman College of the City University of New York. She has practitioner experience working with nursing home residents and with individuals who have psychiatric illnesses. Kunstler holds an M.S. degree from Northwestern University and an Re.D. from Indiana University.

Miriam Leahey is on the faculty of the recreation education program at Lehman College of the City University of New York. She has practitioner experience in New York City with individuals who have Alzheimer's disease and with nursing home residents. Leahey holds her Ed.D. from Columbia University.

Francis A. McGuire is associate professor at Clemson University. McGuire has worked for the Centre County Area Agency on Aging in Pennsylvania, and has held faculty posts at the State University of New York at Cortland and the University of Illinois. He earned his doctoral degree at the University of Illinois.

Stuart J. Schleien serves as associate professor in the School of Physical Education and Recreation, with a joint appointment in the Department of Educational Psychology Special Education Programs at the University of Minnesota. Schleien's research involves the integration of persons with developmental disabilities into community leisure environments. He is a Certified Therapeutic Recreation Specialist.

Judy Sottile is director of therapeutic activity services at Children's Rehabilitation Hospital in Philadelphia. She has been working in therapeutic recreation as a clinician for ten years. Although she has had experience in many service settings, her main interest and level of experience lies in psychiatry, particularly with treatment of eating disorders. Sottile holds an M.S. degree from Southern Illinois University, Carbondale.

Michael L. Teague is professor in the Department of Leisure Studies at the University of Iowa. He holds a doctorate in health, physical education, and recreation from the University of Northern Colorado. Teague's research and scholarly interests lie principally in the field of gerontology.

Judith E. Voelkl is assistant professor in the Department of Leisure Studies at the University of Illinois. She has extensive practitioner experience in psychiatric and geriatric settings. Her master's degree in therapeutic recreation was completed at Indiana University. Voelkl holds her Ph.D. from Pennsylvania State University.

Brenda Winn-Orr is director of recreation programs for the Hattie B. Munroe Foundation at Meyer Children's Rehabilitation Institute, University of Nebraska Medical Center, Omaha. She holds her master's degree in therapeutic recreation from the University of Nebraska, Omaha.

1

Introduction and Overview

DAVID R. AUSTIN

OBJECTIVES

- Conceptualize therapeutic recreation as a field.
- Understand the relationship of therapeutic recreation to a high level of wellness.
- Understand the relationship of therapeutic recreation to the stabilizing and actualizing tendencies.
- Reduce therapeutic recreation to a series of tenets.
- Identify kindred professions.
- Assess yourself in terms of competencies needed in TR.
- Know the plan for this book.

There are a number of health-related professions. Therapeutic recreation is one of these. Several health-related professions are listed, along with their areas of expertise, in Table 1.1. Each profession has a particular body of knowledge upon which to draw in providing services. It is this body of knowledge that makes the profession unique. In fact, experts (e.g., Schein & Kommers, 1972; Wilensky, 1964) have long agreed that in order to claim the title of "profession," an occupational group must have a defined area of expertise. What is the area of expertise that therapeutic recreation (TR) claims? What makes TR unique? The editors of this book believe that therapeutic recreation involves the knowledge of leisure and recreation as these phenomena relate to health.

Table 1.1
Health-Related Professions

PROFESSION	EXPERTISE
Nurse	Caring for persons
Occupational therapist	Purposeful activity
Physician	Illness, disease
Psychologist	Human behavior
Social worker	Support systems

KNOWLEDGE OF LEISURE AND RECREATION AS A BASIS FOR PROFESSIONAL PRACTICE

Inevitably, textbook authors have emphasized leisure and recreation in attempting to define the still relatively new and emerging profession of therapeutic recreation. One of the earliest conceptualizations of therapeutic recreation (referred to as recreational therapy) contained a definition of recreation within it. Davis (1936) wrote:

> Recreational therapy may be defined as any free, voluntary and expressive activity; motor, sensory or mental, vitalized by the expressive play spirit, sustained by deep-rooted pleasurable attitudes and evoked by wholesome emotional release. (p. xi)

More modern textbook authors have continued the tradition of including leisure and recreation within their definitions of TR. Examples follow:

> Therapeutic recreation is a process through which purposeful efforts are directed toward achieving or maximizing desired concomitant effects of a recreation experience. (Frye & Peters, 1972, p. 44)

> [Therapeutic recreation is] a professionally directed service that provides recreational and related activities specifically designed to meet the needs of individuals suffering from some significant degree of illness or disability. (Kraus, 1983, p. 5)

> [Therapeutic recreation is] a process wherein recreation experiences are used to bring about a change in the behavior of those individuals with special needs or problems. (O'Morrow, 1980, p. 123)

> [Therapeutic recreation is] purposeful intervention designed to improve the client's quality of life through recreation and leisure. (Iso-Ahola, 1980, p. 323)

> [Therapeutic recreation] is the provision of purposeful intervention designed to help clients grow and to assist them to prevent or relieve problems through recreation and leisure. (Austin, 1982, p. 60)

Therapeutic recreation refers to the specialized application of recreation for the specific purpose of intervening in and changing some physical, emotional, or social behavior to promote the growth and development of the individual. Therapeutic recreation may be viewed as a process of systematic use of recreation activities and experiences to achieve specific objectives. (Carter, Van Andel, & Robb, 1985, pp. 15, 16)

The unique function of therapeutic recreation is to assist the client, sick or well, in the performance of those leisure activities and experiences contributing to health or its recovery, including general recreation participation. (O'Morrow & Reynolds, 1989, p. 114)

All of the definitions of recreation presented share reference to recreation/leisure activities and experiences. Other common themes found in the definitions are (1) the purposeful nature of the use of recreation/leisure as an intervention, and (2) the personal enhancement of the client as a result of the intervention. In short, these definitions point to the purposeful use of recreation/leisure activities and experiences as a means of producing positive benefits for recipients of TR services. It follows that therapeutic recreation practice demands that TR specialists have a high level of knowledge of recreation and leisure as phenomena, as well as expertise in using recreation/leisure activities to foster growth.

Leisure and Recreation

Students in college and university departments of recreation and leisure studies are asked time and again to define the terms *leisure* and *recreation*. The purpose of the discussion within this textbook is not to cover old ground for those who have undergone the exercise of conceptualizing the meanings of leisure and recreation. Rather, the purpose here is briefly to discuss these terms as they form a basis for understanding therapeutic recreation.

Leisure. Although many views of leisure exist (Murphy, 1987), authors (e.g., Iso-Ahola, 1980; Neulinger, 1980; Smith & Theberge, 1987) commonly refer to the factors of "perceived freedom" and "intrinsic motivation" as central defining properties of leisure. Perceived freedom is typically viewed as a person's ability to exercise choice, or self-determination, over his or her own behavior. There exists an absence of external constraints. Intrinsic motivation is conceptualized as energizing behaviors that are internally (psychologically) rewarding. Intrinsically motivated behaviors are those engaged in for their own sake rather than as a means to an extrinsic reward.

Iso-Ahola (1984) has described intrinsic rewards in leisure as follows:

The intrinsic rewards that the individual pursues through leisure participation can be divided into personal and interpersonal. The personal
rewards include, in addition to self-determination, feelings of competence or mastery, challenge, learning, exploration, efforts, and relaxation. In other words, the individual participates in those leisure activities at which he/she is good, that are challenging and allow him/her to
use and develop personal talent and skills. The learning of new activities and things, acquisition of new skills, expenditure of effort, and
exploration are all intrinsic rewards that a person can achieve when
participating in leisure activities for their own sake. On the other hand,
the seeking of interpersonal rewards means that in one form or the
other, social interaction is the main intrinsic reward to be achieved. (pp.
110, 111)

Further, Iso-Ahola (1984) has argued convincingly that in addition to
allowing people to seek intrinsic rewards, leisure participation provides
escape from everyday personal and interpersonal environments. People
can temporarily set aside problems and difficulties while taking part in
leisure. Research by Iso-Ahola (with Allen, 1982) found that escape from
personal environments (everyday routines and responsibilities) and interpersonal environments (other people) was seen by participants as a benefit
of leisure. Other researchers have presented similar findings, although
they have used different terms in reporting their results. Tinsley and
Johnson (1984) reported a psychological benefit of leisure to be "expressive
compensation," which they described as occurrences different from the
everyday. Kabanoff (1982) identified "escape from routine" as a need met
through leisure participation.

Benefits of Leisure.   Tinsley and Johnson (1984), using cluster analysis
as a technique, found seven psychological benefits of leisure. In addition to
expressive compensation, they listed intellectual stimulation, catharsis, he-
donistic companionship, secure solitude, moderate security, and expressive
aestheticism. Kabanoff (1982) identified 11 needs commonly met through
leisure. Besides escape from routine, these were autonomy, relaxation,
family activity, interaction with others, stimulation, skill development and
utilization, esteem, challenge/competition, leadership/social power, and
health.

It is clear that leisure provides opportunity for people to do things
voluntarily for any number of reasons of their own choosing, including to
be with others, to seek security, to receive stimulation, or to relax. Leisure
offers freedom of choice to satisfy any number of intrinsically derived
needs.

Self-Determination and Intrinsic Motivation.   The concepts of self-
determination and intrinsic motivation, so central to leisure, deserve further consideration.

An idea deeply rooted in our Western culture is that we, as human beings, strive for control over ourselves and our environment (Grzelak, 1985; Pender, 1982). Our degree of social adjustment is related to the discrepancy that exists between our perceived and desired control (Grzelak, 1985).

Research (e.g., Langer & Rodin, 1976; Overmier & Seligman, 1967; Seligman & Maier, 1967) has found that a feeling of lack of control over adverse life situations produces a sense of helplessness. This, in turn, leads to the development of apathy and withdrawal that, in extreme cases, may ultimately end in death owing to perceived uncontrollability over a stressful environment (Gatchel, 1980). In light of this, it is unfortunate that much of what transpires in modern health care leads to feelings of helplessness. Pender (1982) has exclaimed that too often interactions with health care professionals foster feelings of helplessness in clients because of condescending behavior, paternalistic approaches, and the mystification of health care processes.

Fortunately, therapeutic recreation represents the antithesis of the controlling environment often imposed on the individual who has health problems. Rather than being repressive, therapeutic recreation provides a variety of opportunities for clients to escape the normal routines of the health facility in order to engage in intrinsically rewarding activities that produce feelings of self-determination, competence, and enjoyment.

Intrinsic Motivation. "Intrinsic motivation," according to Deci and Ryan (1985), "is based in people's needs to be competent and self-determining" (p. 58). Intrinsic motivation is inextricably tied to perceived competence in situations where competence is salient, a primary goal of taking part in an activity. The more competent a person perceives himself or herself to be at a given activity, the more intrinsically motivated he or she will be toward that activity, provided the activity is ego involving (Sansone, 1986). Self-determination plays a role as well. In order for the person to experience intrinsic motivation due to competence, he or she must feel a sense of perceived self-determination in terms of the outcome. In short, positive feedback for self-determined outcomes leads to enhanced intrinsic motivation (Deci & Ryan, 1985).

Relationship of Self-Determination and Intrinsic Motivation. Deci and Ryan (1985) have specified that a close relationship exists between self-determination and intrinsic motivation. They state:

> When people are intrinsically motivated, they experience interest and enjoyment, they feel competent and self-determining, they perceive the locus of causality for their behavior to be internal, and in some instances they experience flow. The antithesis of interest and flow is pressure and tension. (p. 34)

Connected to self-determination and intrinsic motivation is the basic human tendency toward development or the fulfillment of one's potential. Renowned psychologists Piaget and Rogers both postulated this propensity, which Rogers termed the *actualizing tendency* (Deci & Ryan, 1985). The actualizing tendency is directed toward stimulation of the organism in order to promote change, growth, and maturation within the individual. Pender (1982) has described the actualizing process of the actualizing tendency in this way:

> Motivated by the actualizing tendency, people seek to increase intensity, meaningfulness, and variation of stimuli encountered in the course of everyday living. This promotes learning, maturation, and ongoing growth through differentiation and reintegration at increasingly higher levels of complexity. Human beings find discovery both absorbing and challenging; with creative expression comes intense inner satisfaction. (pp. 14, 15)

Intrinsic motivation is seen as the energy basis or the energizer of this tendency for growth and development, according to Deci and Ryan (1985). Intrinsic motivation itself rests on the organism's innate needs for competence and self-determination. These needs, in turn, motivate us to seek and to conquer optimal challenges that stretch our abilities but are within our capacities. When we are able to achieve success, we experience feelings of competence and autonomy, along with accompanying emotions of enjoyment and excitement (Deci & Ryan, 1985).

In summary, it is clear that the two concepts of self-determination and intrinsic motivation are closely intertwined. People have a basic need to be in control of their environment so that they can exercise choices in their behavior and make autonomous decisions. Intrinsic motivation is based on self-determined behavior that results in perceiving oneself as being competent. Receiving positive feedback during a challenging activity of the person's choice leads to increased interest in the activity (i.e., greater intrinsic motivation for the activity).

Leisure, Self-Determination, and Intrinsic Motivation.   Leisure would seem to offer one of the best opportunities for people to experience self-determination because it offers a chance for individuals to be in control. The potential for control often does not occur in work or other situations where external pressure exists. Leisure also provides occasions for achieving feelings of mastery or competence as challenging activities are conquered and positive feedback is received. These occurrences bring about increases in intrinsic motivation for the activity.

Recreation.   Recreation has been viewed as activities or experiences occurring within leisure (Kraus, 1971). Recreation has also been perceived to be constructive, meeting socially accepted goals of the participant (Neulinger, 1980). Further, action and activity have been associated with recreation (Smith & Theberge, 1987). Finally, recreation has been linked with being restorative, offering refreshment or re-creation for the participant (Kelly, 1982). It is this ability to restore or refresh both mind and body that perhaps is the property that the average person most attaches to recreation.

If recreation is defined as being restorative or re-creative, the use of the term *therapeutic*, in combination with *recreation*, may appear to be redundant. If all recreation is restorative, is not then all recreation therapeutic? Perhaps a better term to describe therapeutic recreation would be *clinical recreation* because of the employment of the purposeful intervention element that promotes treatment and rehabilitative outcomes and helps define the profession.

The use of the terms *clinical* and *recreation* in combination may initially seem incongruous because of the connotation of disease and sickness associated with the term *clinical*, and the positive cognitions and emotions evoked by the word *recreation*. Clinical outcomes are serious, whereas recreation is fun. Nevertheless, the two terms *clinical* and *recreation* may be perceived to belong together. Restoration is a goal of both clinical practice and recreation. In clinical programs the object is health restoration, whereas recreation is considered to be a natural restorative phenomenon. Today the term *clinical therapeutic recreation* has come into common usage in order to interpret the field as one that employs recreation as a planned clinical intervention directed toward health restoration.

Recreation/Leisure and Therapeutic Recreation

Therapeutic recreation specialists need to have a highly developed understanding of the dynamics of recreation and leisure as they apply to practice within their profession. It is necessary to understand recreation as activity that has restorative properties, and leisure as a phenomenon that provides the individual with perceived control and the opportunity to meet intrinsically motivated needs. We will return to these concepts later in the chapter.

HEALTH

For many years the phrase *absence of disease* was synonymous with health. If you felt "okay" and your doctor did not diagnose you as having medical symptoms, you were perceived to be "healthy."

Over the years other definitions of health have evolved. These definitions stipulate a difference between the absence of symptoms of illness or abnormalities and vigorous health. The most cited definition is the one published by the World Health Organization (WHO) in 1947. The WHO defined health as "a state of complete physical, mental, and social well-being, not merely the absence of disease or infirmity."

The WHO definition has been criticized by many as being abstract, vague, simplistic, and unsuitable for scientific interpretation (Edelman & Mandle, 1986). It is difficult to deduce from the WHO definition specific criteria by which a state of health may be recognized, and the WHO definition does not recognize the phases of health people experience during their life spans (Pender, 1982).

The WHO definition does, however, offer three concepts essential to the formulation of a positive conceptualization of health (Edelman & Mandle, 1986; Pender, 1982):

1. It displays a concern for the individual as a total system rather than as merely the sum of various parts.
2. It places health in the context of both internal and external environments.
3. It relates health to fulfillment, to creative living.

Humanistic Perspective.   In the 1950s, humanistic psychology came into existence as a "third force" in opposition to Freud's psychoanalytic approach and the behavioristic approach of Watson and Skinner. This humanistic perspective recognized the uniqueness of human beings to be self-directed, to make wise choices, and to develop themselves or realize their human potentials. Humanistic psychologists proclaimed "that striving and growing are essential to human life and health" (Lindberg, Hunter, & Kruszewski, 1983, p. 70).

In general, those who embraced the humanistic perspective:

1. Took a holistic view of the person.
2. Believed that both children and adults are capable of change.
3. Saw people as being in dynamic interaction with the environment, not just reacting to the external world.
4. Viewed healthy people as those who strive for personal satisfaction yet go beyond their own needs to understand and care about others. (Austin, 1982, p. 56)

Halbert Dunn's classic definition of health grew out of the influence of the humanistic perspective. Dunn (1961) coined the term *high-level wellness*, which he defined as "An integrated method of functioning which is oriented toward maximizing the potential of which the individual is capable, within the environment where he (or she) is functioning" (p. 4).

Dunn's definition of health is centered on the wholeness of the individual and each person's actualizing tendency, which serves as a propelling force to move each human being toward the fulfillment of his or her potential. Further, Dunn's notion not only implies an absence of physical illness but positive psychological and environmental wellness as well. Mental and social well-being join the physical well-being of the total person in forming Dunn's concept of optimal health or high-level wellness (Austin, 1982).

Holistic medicine, as proposed by those who have championed high-level wellness, treats the person rather than the disease. Holistic medicine's concern lies with the "whole person" and with permitting individuals to assume self-responsibility for their own health (Austin, 1982). Ardell (1977) has identified the ultimate aim of "well medicine" (in contrast to the "traditional medicine" normally practiced by the medical community) to be that of moving individuals toward self-actualization. Whereas illness is the sole concern of traditional medicine, well medicine deals with wellness or health promotion.

Therapeutic Recreation: Illness and Wellness

Austin (1982) has compared therapeutic recreation with the concepts expressed by Dunn (1961) and Ardell (1977) on high-level wellness. There are striking similarities, as he indicates:

> Therapeutic recreation, like traditional medical practice, has long dealt with the problems of illness. Unlike traditional medicine, however, therapeutic recreation has not dealt exclusively with illness. Therapeutic recreation has historically promoted the goal of self-actualization, or the facilitation of the fullest possible growth and development of the client. Therefore therapeutic recreation may be conceived to be much like traditional, medically oriented, allied health professions in its concern for preventing and alleviating illness. At the same time, therapeutic recreation specialists join both other leisure service professionals and physicians practicing "well medicine" in their desire to bring about the self-actualization of their clients. (p. 58)

Therapeutic recreation specialists must, by necessity, take on a variety of functions, as dictated by the needs of their clients. The TR specialist initially may join other members of the treatment team in helping the client to alleviate illness. Later, the TR specialist may help the client develop leisure and social skills as a part of a growth-enhancing rehabilitation program. Still later, leisure counseling may be provided by the TR specialist to assist the client in order to assure a favorable environment during community reintegration.

Motivational Forces: The Stabilizing and Actualizing Tendencies.

Therapeutic recreation specialists therefore help clients to strive for both health protection (illness aspects) and health promotion (wellness aspects). Major human motivational forces underlie these two aspects. These are the stabilizing tendency and the actualizing tendency (Pender, 1982).

The *stabilizing tendency* is directed toward maintaining the "steady state" of the organism. It is the motivational tendency moving us to counter excess stress (i.e., distress) in order to maintain our levels of health. When faced with excessive stress we engage in adaptive behaviors in order to regain our sense of equilibrium. We attempt either to remove ourselves from the stress or to minimize the effects of the stressor on us.

The stabilizing tendency is responsible for our adapting so as to keep the level of stress in a manageable range in order to protect us from possible biophysical or psychosocial harm. It should be mentioned that potentially harmful stressors may result from internal as well as external stimuli. Negative forms of tension can come from either within us or from our surroundings. It is the stabilizing tendency that is the motivational force behind health protection (Pender, 1982).

The *actualizing tendency* is the growth-enhancement force discussed earlier in the chapter, when we considered self-determination, intrinsic motivation, and high-level wellness. It is this actualizing tendency that is the motivational force behind the achievement of optimal health.

Definitions of Health Considering both Stability and Actualization

Nursing theorist Imogene King (1971) has offered a definition of health that emphasizes both stability and actualization. King has defined health as follows:

> [Health is] a dynamic state in the life cycle of an organism which implies continuous adaptation to stress in the internal and external environment through optimum use of one's resources to achieve maximum potential for daily living. (p. 24)

Pender (1982), who, like King, is a nurse, has also provided a definition of health that similarly reflects both the stabilizing and actualizing tendencies. Pender has defined health in the following way:

> Health is the actualization of inherent and acquired human potential through satisfying relationships with others, goal directed behavior, and competent personal care while adjustments are being made as needed to maintain stability and structural integrity. (p. 37)

From her definition, Pender (1982) has derived 14 criteria for evaluating an individual's state of health. Pender's criteria offer an appropriate conclusion to this section, because they manifest the most positive aspects of the complex phenomena of health. The criteria are these:

1. Exhibits personal growth and positive change over time.
2. Identifies long-term and short-term goals that guide behavior.
3. Prioritizes identified goals.
4. Exhibits awareness of alternative behavioral options to accomplish goals.
5. Perceives optimum health as a primary life purpose.
6. Engages in interpersonal relationships that are satisfying and fulfilling.
7. Actively seeks new experiences that expand knowledge or increase competencies for personal care.
8. Displays a high tolerance for new and unusual situations or experiences.
9. Derives satisfaction from the experience of daily living.
10. Expends more energy in acting on the environment than in reacting to it.
11. Recognizes barriers to growth and deals constructively in removing or ameliorating them.
12. Uses self-monitoring and feedback from others to determine personal and social effectiveness.
13. Maintains conditions of internal stability compatible with continuing existence.
14. Anticipates internal and external threats to stability and takes preventive actions. (p. 37)

HEALTH, ACTIVITY, RECREATION, LEISURE, AND THERAPEUTIC RECREATION

Health is a complex concept that encompasses coping adaptively, as well as growing and becoming. When persons are healthy they can cope with life's stressors. Those who enjoy optimal health are free to develop themselves to the fullest. Barriers to actualization do not exist, so such persons are free to pursue personal growth and development. Health makes actualization possible.

Because of the natural progression from health protection to health promotion, Flynn (1980) has suggested that illness can be positive. The occurrence of a health problem can serve as an occasion for the client to take control over his or her life and to learn how to strive toward optimal health. An example would be an individual who has a health problem (e.g., cardiac problem or problem in mental health) because of stress. Dealing with this problem forces this person to seek the help of a health care professional. As a result of treatment, the client may not only overcome the original health concern but may learn to lead a different life-style that promotes reduced tension and increased enjoyment. By learning how to deal with stress and to take part in healthy activities that provide for growth and enjoyment (e.g., walking and swimming), the person not only is able to conquer his or her initial health problem but rises to a new level of health that might not have been experienced had the presenting problem not happened.

Therapeutic recreation specialists contribute to health by helping persons fulfill their needs for stability and actualization until they are able to assume responsibility for themselves. This is accomplished through client participation in prescriptive activities, recreation and leisure.

Prescriptive Activity

When individuals first encounter illness, they often become self-absorbed, withdraw from their usual life activities, and experience a loss of control over their lives (Flynn, 1980). For these persons, activity becomes a necessary prerequisite to health restoration. They must begin actively to engage in life in order to overcome feelings of helplessness and depression and begin to establish control over the situation. They need to become energized so that they are not passive victims of their circumstances but can take action to restore their health. Wadeson (1980) an art therapist, has described the effect of engaging in art activity. She has written:

> I don't know how to explain this observation, but I have experienced the change in energy level in myself over and over again . . . as I have become "activated" in art activity. It may be simply a matter of physical movement, but I doubt it, since often the physical activity is not that much greater than talking. I am more inclined to believe that it is a release of creative energy and a more direct participation in experience than in talking. (p. 15)

Recreation

Recreation involves activity as one component, but recreation is more than activity. As previously discussed, recreation produces restorative results. Through recreation people restore themselves. They regain their equilibrium so they can once again resume their quest for actualization.

Leisure

Leisure may be seen as a means to self-actualization. Through leisure experiences challenges are met. These leisure experiences feature self-determination, intrinsic motivation, and mastery and competence—experiences that lead people toward feelings of self-efficacy, empowerment, pleasure, and enjoyment. A unique virtue of recreation and leisure is that they are components of life free from external constraint. People are in control while experiencing recreation and leisure. There are perhaps no other parts of our lives where we, as human beings, are allowed more self-determination. During recreation and leisure we can "be ourselves." We can "let our hair down." We are allowed to be human with all our imperfections and frailties. The caring, accepting attitude the therapeutic recreation specialist assumes in creating a free and nonthreatening recreation/leisure environment allows for positive interpersonal relationships as well as for opportunities for accomplishment. Austin (1982) has asked, "In what better atmosphere than that achieved in recreation and leisure could growth be fostered and problems met?" (p. 57).

Therapeutic Recreation

Therapeutic recreation is a means, first, to restore oneself or regain stability or equilibrium following a threat to health (health protection), and second, to develop oneself through leisure as a means to self-actualization (health promotion). Additionally, therapeutic recreation may be seen as a means of preventing health problems, although the preventive function of TR has received minimal attention to date.

Therapeutic recreation has the primary goals of restoring health and helping people learn how to use their leisure in optimizing their potentials. TR provides for the *stabilizing* tendency by helping individuals to restore health, and the *actualizing* tendency by enabling persons to use leisure as a means to personal growth.

A Continuum

As illustrated in Figure 1.1, prescriptive activities, recreation, and leisure are avenues through which therapeutic recreation clients achieve health and wellness. As clients move toward optimal health, they exercise greater and greater choice, while the role of the therapeutic recreation specialist continually decreases. Clients ideally move to the point that they experience optimal health in a favorable environment. In this state of optimal health, or wellness, they are free to be self-directed and to pursue self-actualization.

Clients may enter the continuum at any point that is appropriate for their needs. Along the continuum are three broad areas. The first area is one where the stability tendency is paramount. At the extreme, the client is experiencing poor health in an unfavorable environment. Here the TR specialist helps activate the client. The client's role is relatively passive as the TR specialist provides direction and structure for the intervention.

The next area along the continuum represents mutual participation on the parts of the client and TR specialist. Here the actualizing tendency

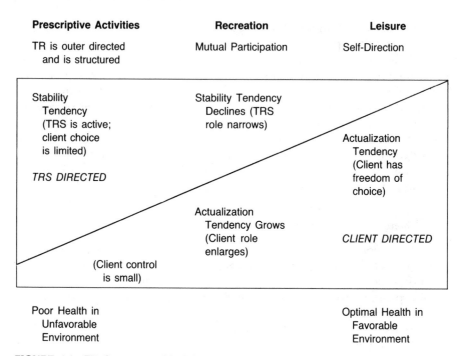

Prescriptive Activities	Recreation	Leisure

TR is outer directed
and is structured

Mutual Participation

Self-Direction

Stability
   Tendency
   (TRS is active;
   client choice
   is limited)

TRS DIRECTED

Stability Tendency
   Declines (TRS
   role narrows)

Actualization
   Tendency
   (Client has
   freedom of
   choice)

Actualization
   Tendency Grows
   (Client role
   enlarges)

CLIENT DIRECTED

(Client control
   is small)

(Client control
   is small)

Poor Health in
   Unfavorable
   Environment

Optimal Health in
   Favorable
   Environment

FIGURE 1.1   TR Continuum. *SOURCE: The above continuum was modeled after continua presented by Ball (1970), Fink (1976), and Frye & Peters (1972).*

begins to emerge as the stabilizing tendency declines. Recreation participation leads to health restoration.

In the third area the actualizing tendency enlarges as the client's health improves and he or she moves toward self-determination. The role of the TR specialist is to assist the client, who ultimately assumes primary responsibility for his or her own health.

THERAPEUTIC RECREATION AND SPECIAL RECREATION

Therapeutic recreation has been presented in this chapter as a purposeful intervention to help clients achieve as high a level of health as possible. You, the reader, may be asking yourself, "Does therapeutic recreation always involve purposeful intervention? Isn't therapeutic recreation simply providing recreation services for people who are disabled?"

Austin (1987) has indicated that therapeutic recreation has been defined in the literature in two ways. He has stated:

It is clear that two types of services operate today under the banner of therapeutic recreation. The focus of one is broad and includes the provision of recreation services for persons with disabilities who require some special accommodation in order to participate. This service has been termed "special recreation" (Kennedy, Austin, & Smith, 1987). The focus of the second is treatment and rehabilitation. It uses recreation for health enhancement, rehabilitation, and independent functioning. (p. 156)

More and more, however, contemporary authors (e.g., Austin, 1987; Bullock, 1987; Kennedy, Austin, & Smith, 1987) present therapeutic recreation and special recreation as two separate entities. These writers tend to argue that the mere provision of recreation services for members of special population groups (generally termed *special recreation*) does not constitute a therapeutic approach because it does not involve purposeful intervention aimed at accomplishing specific treatment or rehabilitation objectives.

A well-known figure in the provision of recreation for persons with disabilities has been Charles Bullock of the University of North Carolina. Bullock (1987) has written:

Recreation and special populations, or special recreation, must be distinguished from therapeutic recreation. Therapeutic recreation is the purposive use of recreation by qualified professionals to promote independent functioning and to enhance optimal health and well-being in persons with illnesses and/or disabling conditions.

Therapeutic recreation is *not* any and all recreation services for persons who are disabled. Merely being disabled does not qualify a person to receive "therapeutic" recreation services. The person who is disabled *may* receive therapeutic recreation services or he or she may simply receive recreation services. The determination is made on the basis of need and mandate for treatment rather than on disability. To call recreation services "therapeutic" because they involve a person or group of persons with a disability is doing a disservice to the person who is being served. To deny a person recreation services because of disability opposes the original philosophy of modern recreation services, which began as a social movement concerned with the needs of all persons. (p. 203)

The editors of this book agree with the position taken by Bullock. We believe that the term *therapeutic recreation* should be reserved for the clinical application of recreation and leisure. The term *special recreation* should be employed to describe the provision of recreation services for persons who require special accommodations because of unique needs they have owing to some physical, cognitive, or psychological disability.

TENETS BASIC TO THERAPEUTIC RECREATION PRACTICE

To function as promoters of health, therapeutic recreation specialists rest their practice on a belief system. The following statements provide basic tenets for therapeutic recreation practice as perceived by the editors. They are intended to further interpret the TR continuum and the purpose of therapeutic recreation (as opposed to special recreation). The beliefs listed are discussed in more detail in Chapter 3, where the therapeutic recreation process is presented. The tenets are as follows:

1. Illness (poor health) and wellness (optimal health) are dimensions of health that may be perceived to be on a continuum.

2. The higher the state of self-actualization, the more optimal is the state of health of the individual.

3. Problems in health produce needs that may be fulfilled through interactions between clients and therapeutic recreation specialists. The stability tendency motivates clients toward need fulfillment leading to health protection.

4. The actualization tendency motivates clients toward health promotion. Therapeutic recreation specialists engage in mutual participation with clients motivated by the actualization tendency, but move toward giving more and more control to clients as they become healthier.

5. Prescriptive activities initially may be used as energizing forces to engage clients with the environment. Therapeutic recreation specialists exercise the greatest amount of control at this stage, but attempt to move clients toward achieving greater health and control.

6. Client participation in recreation activities is restorative and leads to health protection. Therapeutic recreation specialists work cooperatively with clients, assisting them to move toward self-directed leisure experiences that are health enhancing.

7. Optimal health (wellness) is achieved through participation in leisure experiences that feature self-determination and competency and lead to feelings of self-efficacy, empowerment, interest, and enjoyment.

8. The basic goal of therapeutic recreation is the achievement of the highest possible level of health in clients. Illness can be a growth-producing experience for individuals who participate in therapeutic recreation.

9. The goal of therapeutic recreation (i.e., health) is achieved through purposeful intervention using the therapeutic recreation process (i.e., assessment, planning, implementation, and evaluation).

10. The client-therapist relationship is a critical element in the therapeutic recreation process. The essential role of TR specialists is that of a

catalyst who works in partnership with clients in order to help them be as self-directed as possible.

11. Therapeutic recreation specialists model healthy behavior and attitudes while helping clients develop personal competence and intrinsic motivation for participating in healthful activities.

12. Therapeutic recreation specialists focus on clients' abilities and intact strengths.

13. Therapeutic recreation is action- or experience-oriented, but the emphasis of therapeutic recreation is always on the client as a person and not on the activity.

14. Therapeutic recreation is concerned with both treatment/ rehabilitation and education/reeducation. Therapeutic outcomes emphasize enhanced functioning and the here-and-now.

15. Typical outcomes of therapeutic recreation interventions include increasing personal awareness, increasing interpersonal or social skills, developing leisure skills, decreasing stress, improving physical fitness and functioning, developing feelings of positive self-regard, self-efficacy, perceived control, pleasure, and enjoyment.

16. Therapeutic recreation specialists have a knowledge of demands inherent in specific activities. Activity analysis is employed in order to gain insights into the demands activities make on clients in order to ensure the careful selection of appropriate activities.

17. Purposeful, goal-directed behavior is an important characteristic of therapeutic recreation. Being purposeful means having a plan, which implies choice making on the part of clients. When choice is involved, clients perceive their actions to be self-determined, leading them to feelings of competence.

18. Recreation and leisure activities offer diversion or escape from personal problems, as well as from the routine of health care facilities.

19. Therapeutic recreation specialists assess causes of both client problems and client strengths. From identified problems client needs are determined. Intervention strategies are based on client strengths.

20. All client behavior is meaningful. It is motivated by personal needs and goals that can be understood only from each client's frame of reference within the context in which it transpires.

21. Every client possesses intrinsic worth and the potential for change.

22. Every client functions as a holistic being who acts on and reacts to the environment as a whole person.

23. All clients have common, basic human needs ranging from physical and safety needs to self-actualization. It is the higher-level social needs, esteem needs, and actualization needs that are the primary concerns of therapeutic recreation.

KINDRED PROFESSIONS

Therapeutic recreation specialists do not work in isolation from other health care professionals. In fact, today the use of interdisciplinary teams composed of personnel from various specializations has become widespread. The establishment of interdisciplinary teams is largely based on the notion that clients are so complex that no single profession, by itself, can be expected to be able to offer adequate health care (Howe-Murphy & Charboneau, 1987: O'Morrow, 1980). Team membership will vary as a function of the type of setting in which services are being delivered (e.g., center for physical medicine and rehabilitation or psychiatric care) and as a function of the specific problems of the client (Howe-Murphy & Charboneau, 1987).

Types of Health Care Professionals

A variety of health care professionals have been described in the therapeutic recreation literature (e.g., Avedon, 1974; Kraus, 1983; O'Morrow & Reynolds, 1989). Although no attempt is made here to discuss all possible kindred professions, major professions are covered. These include medical doctors, nurses, psychologists, social workers, play therapists, and vocational rehabilitation counselors, as well as various activity or rehabilitation therapy professions.

Medical Doctors. Medical doctors (M.D.'s) use surgery, drugs, and other methods of medical care to prevent and alleviate disease. There are over 30 different specializations of medical doctors (O'Morrow & Reynolds, 1989). Examples of these are psychiatrists (who specialize in mental and emotional disorders), pediatricians (who specialize in the care and treatment of children), and neurologists (who deal with diseases of the nervous system).

Nurses. Registered nurses (R.N.'s) have responsibility for giving nursing care to patients, carrying out physicians' orders, and supervising other nursing personnel such as licensed practical nurses (L.P.N.'s), nurses aides, orderlies, and attendants.

Psychologists. Psychologists usually hold Ph.D. or Psy.D. degrees in psychology. They engage in psychological testing, diagnosis, counseling, and other therapies.

Social Worker. Social workers use case work and group work methods to assist clients and their families in making social adjustments and in dealing with social systems. They prepare the social histories of newly admitted clients and are often the primary professionals to assist clients with community reintegration.

Play Therapists. Play therapy is a form of psychotherapy that uses play activities and toys with children to permit the expression of, and working through, emotional conflicts. Symbolic play is seen as a means for the child to surface problems so that they can be dealt with.

Vocational Rehabilitation Counselors. Vocational rehabilitation counselors (often referred to as "voc rehab" counselors) are concerned with work or career counseling of clients in treatment and rehabilitation programs. They assess client vocational interests and potentials and attempt to find appropriate training or placements to meet clients' abilities.

Physical Therapists. Physical therapists (P.T.'s) are concerned with restoration of physical function and prevention of disability following disease, injury, or loss of body part. They apply therapeutic exercise and functional training procedures in physical rehabilitation.

Occupational Therapists. Occupational therapists (O.T.'s) use purposeful mental and physical activities, prescribed by medical doctors, to enhance individuals' abilities to perform daily occupational roles. Occupational therapists rehabilitate persons who have physical injuries or illnesses, developmental problems, problems caused by aging, or social or emotional problems (*About Occupational Therapy*, 1986).

Music Therapists. Music therapists (M.T.'s) use music as a medium to reach and involve clients in treatment. Musical therapy is found primarily in psychiatric treatment programs rather than in centers for physical medicine and rehabilitation.

Art Therapists. Art therapists use art as a medium to promote self-awareness, nonverbal expression, and human interaction. Art therapy is used with both physical and psychiatric rehabilitation, although it is most widely used within psychiatric treatment.

Dance Therapists. Dance therapists use movement as a medium to work with clients. It is a nonverbal means of expression employed with both individuals and groups. Although not found exclusively in psychiatric treatment programs, it is most commonly used with people experiencing problems in mental health.

Activity Therapy and Rehabilitation Therapy Services. The terms *activity therapy* and *rehabilitation therapy* are regularly used as umbrella terms for administrative purpose in order to encompass several of the action-oriented therapies. In addition to therapeutic recreation, activity therapy and rehabilitation therapy departments commonly are comprised of occupational therapy, music therapy, dance therapy, and art therapy. Sometimes vocational rehabilitation counseling is also located within an activity therapy or rehabilitation therapy department.

RANGE AND SCOPE OF THERAPEUTIC RECREATION SERVICES

Where does therapeutic recreation take place? Whom does therapeutic recreation serve? What types of programs are conducted by therapeutic recreation specialists? What professional organizations exist to stimulate quality therapeutic recreation?

Settings for Therapeutic Recreation

At one time, practically all therapeutic recreation took place within hospitals and institutions. This is no longer true. Today therapeutic recreation is found in a variety of settings. Austin (1987) has described the situation as follows:

> While therapeutic recreation was once exclusively concerned with providing services to persons who were institutionalized, it is no longer limited to any specific type of setting. TR takes place in a wide variety of agencies, including general hospitals, psychiatric hospitals, nursing homes, rehabilitation centers, residential schools for students with disabilities, correctional facilities, outdoor recreation/camping centers, mental-health centers and other community-based health and human service agencies, and park-and-recreation departments. (p. 155)

Clients Served in Therapeutic Recreation

A therapeutic recreation client can be any person who desires to restore his or her health (engage in health protection) or to enhance his or her level of health (pursue health promotion). Persons participating in mental health programs have traditionally been therapeutic recreation's largest client group. Three other major TR client groups have been persons who are mentally retarded, physically disabled, or aged. Other types of individuals who have benefited from therapeutic recreation are those who are socially deviant or experience social disorder in their families, abuse alcohol or other chemical substances, have cognitive impairments (e.g., head injuries), are autistic, experience convulsive disorders, have multiple disabilities, are hospitalized children, are undergoing correctional rehabilitation, have experienced burns, or have cardiac conditions.

Types of Therapeutic Recreation Programs

There exist a vast array of formats for therapeutic recreation programs. These include clubs; classes; special interest groups; informal recreation opportunities; special events; leagues, tournaments, and contests; large-group activities such as dances; outdoor pursuits such as adventure/challenge activities; and individual and group leisure counseling sessions (Austin, 1982, 1987; Avedon, 1974).

Professional Organizations for Therapeutic Recreation

Two professional membership societies for therapeutic recreation specialists exist in the United States today. The largest of these, with over 3,200 members (National Recreation and Park Association, 1988), is the National Therapeutic Recreation Society (NTRS), a branch of the National Recreation and Park Association. NTRS was founded in 1966 to represent a broad-based constituency having both therapeutic recreation and special recreation concerns. The second professional membership society is the American Therapeutic Recreation Association (ATRA). ATRA was formed in 1984 by a group of clinically oriented therapeutic recreation specialists who wanted to place greater focus on therapeutic recreation intervention strategies.

COMPETENCIES NEEDED BY THERAPEUTIC RECREATION SPECIALISTS

Few would argue with the contention that the competencies needed by therapeutic recreation specialists are different from those required of park and recreation professionals who serve in park districts, municipal and county park and recreation departments, state parks, youth serving agencies, and similar leisure service delivery systems. Certainly, both therapeutic recreation specialists and professionals from the general field of parks and recreation need solid liberal arts preparation. The liberal learning dimension of professional preparation programs offers the depth and breadth of education needed for individuals to be contributing citizens of the world and provides a context for professional practice, together with a greater appreciation for the diversity of persons and environments that will be encountered in professional roles. Both those in therapeutic recreation and those in parks and recreation need understandings of the phenomena of recreation and leisure. But the therapeutic recreation professional is different from the general park and recreation professional in that the TR specialist must possess additional competencies that are specific to the practice of therapeutic recreation.

A study by Card and Rodriguez (1987) found what these researchers described as "assessment" and "leisure education" to be the primary areas of competency needed for TR specialists in clinical settings in Missouri. The choice of the term *assessment* by Card and Rodriguez is misleading, however, because this competency area included many clinical skills other than doing client assessment. A better title for this group of competencies would appear to be *treatment* because of the nature of tasks listed under the heading. These tasks included implementing treatment plans, helping clients learn to deal with problems, providing socially stimulating activities, making necessary adaptations to accommodate clients in programs, aiding clients to develop individual programs, assisting clients to examine attitudes, and developing client relationships to further treatment aims.

If the term *treatment* is accepted to describe more clearly this primary area of competency, then the two paramount areas of TR competency identified by Card and Rodriguez may be described as *treatment* and *leisure education*. This terminology is in accord with the perception of therapeutic recreation as dealing with assisting clients with health protection (i.e., treatment) and helping clients to learn to use leisure for health promotion (i.e., leisure education).

In addition to the work of Card and Rodriguez, several sources have identified competencies needed for therapeutic recreation practice (e.g., Austin, 1988; Council on Accreditation, 1986; Kelley, Robb, Wook & Halberg, 1974; National Council on Therapeutic Recreation Certification, 1988; Stumbo, 1986). These sources are the primary basis for the listing of competencies for therapeutic recreation specialists that follows. As you review this listing, think about your own preparation for doing therapeutic recreation. Are you personally gaining the competencies necessary for practice in therapeutic recreation?

Areas of competency that you as an emerging TR specialist need to evaluate include:

- theories/understandings of play, recreation, and leisure
- human development throughout the life span
- anatomy and physiology
- basic assumptions about human nature
- etiology, course, and prognosis of various diagnostic categories
- disease sequelae
- effects of stress on individuals
- perception of clients as "whole persons," not just as individuals possessing symptoms
- effects of major drugs
- health and safety information for working with clients
- medical and psychiatric terminology
- principles of rehabilitation
- concepts of health and wellness
- attitudes toward illness and disability
- self as a therapeutic agent

- leadership of various recreation/leisure activities (e.g., arts and crafts, camping, games, sports)
- theory and technique of group leadership
- community leisure resources for client involvement
- activity analysis procedures
- careful selection of activities to meet treatment aims
- interpersonal relationship skills
- interview skills
- leisure counseling theory and technique
- client assessment
- treatment goals formulation
- stating behavioral objectives
- treatment/rehabilitation planning
- theory and application of treatment/rehabilitation approaches (e.g., client-centered approach)
- learning/teaching principles
- behavior management techniques
- evaluation of intervention outcomes
- client records and documentation (e.g., charting on clients)
- referral procedures
- assistive techniques and adaptive devices for specific illnesses and disabilities
- ethical and professional standards of practice
- legal aspects of therapeutic recreation
- procedures for mainstreaming and integration
- giving and receiving clinical supervision
- role and function of health care systems
- role of TR as a component of health care
- role and function of interdisciplinary treatment teams
- role and function of kindred professionals
- current professional issues and trends (e.g., accreditation, credentialing)
- historical foundations of therapeutic recreation as they influence the philosophy of practice

It is expected that your self-assessment of the competency areas will reveal that although you have started to gain rudimentary skills and knowledge, you are still in the beginning phases of development as a therapeutic recreation specialist. This is normal, so you should not feel discouraged if you do not yet possess the competencies required for TR clinical practice.

It is important to note here that no matter which professional practice skills are learned and applied, growth-promoting relationships are at the heart of therapeutic recreation (Austin, 1982). Flynn (1980) has emphasized the significant impact the personality of the practitioner may have on the client. She has urged health care professionals to assess themselves and to consider developing further the qualities that have been identified as important to the helper-client relationship. These characteristics are listed in Table 1.2. You may wish to review these characteristics in order to conduct your own self-assessment.

PLAN FOR THE BOOK

We have attempted to make you, the reader, the focal point for this book. The book is organized with objectives at the beginning of each chapter so you will know explicitly what you should gain from your reading. Other aids to help your learning are the reading comprehension questions and suggested learning activities found at the end of each chapter.

Chapters in Section One of the book present the nature, purpose, history, and processes of therapeutic recreation. Section Two covers special areas of therapeutic recreation practice. Taken as a whole, these chapters illustrate the richness and diversity of therapeutic recreation.

We are extremely fortunate to have some of the most highly regarded authorities in therapeutic recreation as authors of the chapters in Section Two. Each of these individuals is an expert on the topic of his or her chapter.

To facilitate your learning and ensure completeness in approach, all the authors in Section Two followed a common outline. For example, in each chapter you will learn about current practices and procedures in that

Table 1.2
Characteristics Important in Helping Relationships

Sense of humor	Competence
Self-respect	Generosity
Congruence	Self-confidence
Presence	Graciousness
Acceptance	Sense of personal integrity
Balance of body-mind-spirit	Simplicity
Ability to meet with emphatic understanding	Intelligence
	Common sense
Ability to express unconditional positive regard	Genuineness
	Ability to communicate
Ability to experience the other as a person	Sense of purpose
Ability to listen	

SOURCE: From a listing in Flynn (1980, p. 20).

particular area of therapeutic recreation, and you will review a brief case study that portrays the actual application of the practices and procedures.

The chapters in Section Three cover specialized areas of professional activity and trends and issues in therapeutic recreation. These chapters, like the others, begin with objectives so you will know what to look for. They will also provide you with a means to assess your learning. It may be helpful for you to scan the objectives at the beginnings of several chapters before proceeding further.

SUMMARY

The purpose of this chapter was to provide you with an introduction to therapeutic recreation and to offer an overview of its components. Definitions of therapeutic recreation were presented, followed by an analysis of common elements found in the definitions. Leisure, recreation, self-determination, and intrinsic motivation were granted particular attention.

The relationship of therapeutic recreation to health and wellness was discussed, together with the tendencies for stability and actualization. This discussion culminated in the presentation of the TR continuum. Following a description of the continuum, therapeutic recreation was further defined first by contrasting it with special recreation, and second, by providing basic tenets that guide therapeutic recreation practice.

Remaining segments of the chapter offered information on kindred professionals, the range and scope of therapeutic recreation services, and competencies needed by therapeutic recreation specialists. The chapter ended with a brief orientation to the plan of the book.

READING COMPREHENSION QUESTIONS

1. What is the defined area of expertise for TR specialists?
2. Which of the definitions of TR do you like the most?
3. What are common themes found in definitions of TR?
4. Do you agree that perceived freedom and intrinsic motivation are the factors that define leisure?
5. Describe intrinsic rewards found in leisure.
6. Does leisure offer escape? If so, do you see any relationship to therapeutic recreation?
7. What is meant by helplessness?
8. What is the relationship between competence, self-determination, and intrinsic motivation?
9. What properties are found in recreation?
10. Is the use of the terms *clinical* and *recreation* in combination incongruous?

11. How may the WHO definition of health be criticized?

12. What positive dimensions are offered in the WHO definition?

13. Briefly describe the humanistic perspective.

14. What is high-level wellness?

15. Does TR embrace the concepts of holistic health?

16. Explain the stabilizing and actualizing tendencies.

17. What is the relationship of the stabilizing and actualizing tendencies to health?

18. Do you agree with Pender's criteria for health?

19. Can illness ever be positive?

20. What are the goals of therapeutic recreation?

21. Can you explain the TR continuum?

22. Do you agree that therapeutic recreation and special recreation are separate entities?

23. Review the basic tenets of therapeutic recreation. Do you understand each? Do you agree with each?

24. Can you describe interdisciplinary teams? Can you tell why they are widely used?

25. What are the kindred professions?

26. What are the meanings of the terms *activity therapy* and *rehabilitation therapy*?

27. In what types of settings does TR take place?

28. Does a person have to be disabled to be a TR client?

29. Who are types of clients traditionally served by TR?

30. List types of program structures for TR?

31. Name the therapeutic recreation professional organizations.

32. Do you agree with the list of competency areas?

33. How do you assess yourself in terms of moving toward becoming a competent therapeutic recreation specialist?

34. Do you understand the plan of the book?

SUGGESTED LEARNING ACTIVITIES

1. Conduct brief interviews with three or more health professionals from areas such as medicine, nursing, clinical psychology, occupational therapy, or social work. Ask each what he or she feels is the defined area of expertise for TR specialists. Bring your interview notes to class so you may share your findings with other students.

2. Interview 10 to 15 college or university students to find out if they perceive leisure participation to provide escape from everyday personal and interpersonal environments. Write a 2- to 4-page paper on your findings.

3. In a small group, with other students in your class, discuss the concepts of self-determination and intrinsic motivation. Share information about personal experiences that have provided you with opportunities to experience self-determination and intrinsic motivation.

4. Interview several faculty members or fellow students, asking them to define health in their own words. Bring your results to class to compare your findings with those of classmates and the definitions of health found in the chapter.

5. Prepare a 2- to 4-page paper on the relationship between therapeutic recreation and special recreation. Conclude the paper by stating your own position regarding the relationship.

6. Review the tenets of therapeutic recreation presented in the chapter. Pick the five you consider to be most important. Bring your list to class so your instructor can tabulate those you and your classmates have chosen. Discuss the findings in class, assessing the level of agreement.

7. As a class, visit several agencies that have extensive TR services. Later, in class, discuss the types of services provided and the types of clients served.

8. Examine the list of competencies needed for practice in TR found in the chapter. Then, in class, discuss these questions: Do you agree with the list of competencies? Does your curriculum offer the opportunity to gain competencies needed for practice in therapeutic recreation?

9. Review the characteristics in Table 1.2 in order to conduct your own self-assessment. Prepare a 2- to 4-page paper describing your findings and conclusions from your self-assessment.

REFERENCES

About Occupational Therapy. (1986). South Deerfield, MA: Channing L. Bete.

ARDELL, B. (1977). *High-level wellness: An alternative to doctors, drugs, and disease.* Emmaus, PA: Rodale Press.

AUSTIN, D. R. (1982). *Therapeutic recreation: Processes and techniques.* New York: John Wiley & Sons.

AUSTIN, D. R. (1987). Therapeutic recreation. In A. Graefe & S. Parker (Eds.), *Recreation and leisure: An introductory handbook* (pp. 155–157). State College, PA: Venture Publishing.

AUSTIN, D. R. (1988). *Therapeutic recreation education: A call for reform.* Manuscript submitted for publication.

AVEDON, E. M. (1974). *Therapeutic recreation service: An applied behavioral science approach.* Englewood Cliffs, NJ: Prentice-Hall.

BALL, E. L. (1970). The meaning of therapeutic recreation. *Therapeutic Recreation Journal, 4*(1), 17, 18.

BULLOCK, C. C. (1987). Recreation and special populations. In A. Graefe & S. Parker (Eds.), *Recreation and leisure: An introductory handbook* (pp. 203–207). State College, PA: Venture Publishing.

CARD, J. A., & RODRIGUEZ, C. (1987). Job task analysis of therapeutic recreation professionals: Implications for educators. *Journal of Expanding Horizons in Therapeutic Recreation, 2,* 33–41.

CARTER, M. J., VAN ANDEL, G. E., & ROBB, G. M. (1985). *Therapeutic recreation: A practical approach.* St. Louis: Times Mirror/Mosby.

Council on Accreditation. (1986). *Standards and evaluation criteria for recreation, park resources and leisure services baccalaureate program.* Alexandria, VA: National Recreation and Park Association.

DAVIS, J. E. (1936). *Principles and practices of recreational therapy.* New York: A. S. Barnes.

DECI, E. L., & RYAN, R. M. (1985). *Intrinsic motivation and self-determination in human behavior.* New York: Plenum Press.

DUNN, H. L. (1961). *High level wellness.* Arlington, VA: R. W. Beatty.

EDELMAN, C., & MANDLE, C. L. (1986). *Health promotion throughout the lifespan.* St. Louis: C. V. Mosby.

FINK, D. (1976). Holistic health: Implications for health planning. *American Journal of Health Planning, 1,* 17–21.

FLYNN, P. A. R. (1980). *Holistic health: The art and science of care.* Bowie, MA: Robert J. Brady.

FRYE, V., & PETERS, M. (1972). *Therapeutic recreation: Its theory, philosophy, and practice.* Harrisburg, PA: Stackpole Books.

GATCHEL, R. J. (1980). Perceived control: A review and evaluation of therapeutic implications. In A. Baum, & J. E. Singer (Eds.), *Advances in environmental psychology: Vol. 2. Applications of personal control* (pp. 1–22). Hillsdale, NJ: Lawrence Erlbaum Associates.

GRZELAK, J. L. (1985). Desire for control: Cognitive, emotional and behavioral consequences. In F. L. Denmark (Ed.), *Social/ecological psychology and the psychology of women.* New York: Elsevier Science Publishing.

HOWE-MURPHY, R., & CHARBONEAU, B. G. (1987). *Therapeutic recreation intervention: An ecological perspective,* Englewood Cliffs, NJ: Prentice-Hall.

ISO-AHOLA, S. E. (1980). *The social psychology of leisure and recreation.* Dubuque, IA: William C. Brown Company.

ISO-AHOLA, S. E. (1984). Social psychological foundations of leisure and resultant implications for leisure counseling. In E. T. Dowd (Ed.), *Leisure counseling: Concepts and applications.* Springfield, IL: Charles C. Thomas.

ISO-AHOLA, S. E., & ALLEN, J. R. (1982). The dynamics of leisure motivation: The effects of outcome on leisure needs. *Research Quarterly of Exercise and Sports, 53,* 141–149.

KABANOFF, B. (1982). Occupational and sex differences in leisure needs and leisure satisfaction. *Journal of Occupational Behavior, 3,* 233–245.

KELLEY, J. D., ROBB, G. M., WOOK, P., & HALBERG, K. J. (1974). *Therapeutic recreation education: Developing a competency-based entry-level curriculum.* Urbana, IL: Illinois Community College Project, Office of Recreation and Park Resources, University of Illinois.

KELLY, J. R. (1982). *Leisure: An introduction.* Englewood Cliffs, NJ: Prentice-Hall.

KENNEDY, D. W., AUSTIN, D. R., & SMITH, R. W. (1987). *Special recreation: Opportunities for persons with disabilities.* Philadelphia: Saunders College Publishing.

KING, I. M. (1971). *Toward a theory of nursing.* New York: John Wiley & Sons.

KRAUS, R. (1971). *Recreation and leisure in modern society.* New York: Appleton-Century-Crofts.

KRAUS, R. (1983). *Therapeutic recreation service: Principles and practices* (3rd ed). Philadelphia: Saunders College Publishing.

LANGER, E. J., & RODIN, J. (1976). The effects of choice and enhanced personal responsibility for the aged: A field experiment in an institutional setting. *Journal of Personality and Social Psychology, 34*, 191–198.

LINDBERG, J., HUNTER, M., & KRUSZEWSKI, A. (1983). *Introduction to person-centered nursing.* Philadelphia: J. B. Lippincott.

MURPHY, J. (1987). Concepts of leisure. In A. Graefe, & S. Parker (Eds.), *Recreation and leisure: An introductory handbook* (pp. 11–17). State College, PA: Venture Publishing.

National Council on Therapeutic Recreation Certification with Educational Testing Service. (1988). *Report on the national job analysis project.* Spring Valley, NY: The National Council for Therapeutic Recreation Certification.

National Recreation and Park Association. (1988). *Report by the Membership Committee* (issued in May), Alexandria, VA.

NEULINGER, J. (1980). Introduction. In S. E. Iso-Ahola (Ed.), *Social psychological perspectives on leisure and recreation* (pp. 5–18). Springfield, IL: Charles C. Thomas.

O'MORROW, G. S. (1980). *Therapeutic recreation: A helping profession.* (2nd ed.). Englewood Cliffs, NJ: Prentice Hall.

O'MORROW, G. S., & REYNOLDS, R. P. (1989). *Therapeutic recreation: A helping profession* (3rd ed.). Englewood Cliffs, NJ: Prentice-Hall.

OVERMIER, J. B., & SELIGMAN, M. E. P. (1967). Effects of inescapable shock upon subsequent escape and avoidance responding. *Journal of Comparative and Physiological Psychology, 63*, 28–33.

PENDER, N. J. (1982). *Health promotion in nursing practice.* Norwalk, CT: Appleton-Century-Crofts.

SANSONE, C. (1986). A question of competence: The effect of competence and task feedback on intrinsic interest. *Journal of Personality and Social Psychology, 51*, 918–931.

SCHEIN, E. H., & KOMMERS, D. W. (1972). *Professional education.* New York: McGraw-Hill.

SELIGMAN, M. E. P., & MAIER, S. F. (1967). Failure to escape traumatic shock. *Journal of Experimental Psychology, 74*. 1–9.

SMITH, D. H., & THEBERGE, N. (1987). *Why people recreate.* Champaign, IL: Life Enhancement Publications.

STUMBO, N. J. (1986). A definition of entry-level knowledge for therapeutic recreation practice. *Therapeutic Recreation Journal, 20*(4), 15–30.

TINSLEY, H. E., & JOHNSON, T. L. (1984). A preliminary taxonomy of leisure activities. *Journal of Leisure Research, 16*, 234–244.

WADESON, H. (1980). *Art psychotherapy.* New York: John Wiley & Sons.

WILENSKY, H. L. (1964). The professionalization of everyone? *The American Journal of Sociology, 70*, 137–158.

World Health Organization. (1947). Constitution of the World Health Organization. *Chronicles of WHO, 1*, 1, 2.

2

Formation and Organization of the Profession

MICHAEL E. CRAWFORD

OBJECTIVES

- Be able to describe the evolution of the National Therapeutic Recreation Society.
- Differentiate between the historical hospital recreation and recreation therapy movements.
- Name major enabling legislation bills that have played a major role in supporting the TR movement.
- Identify the six basic characteristics of a profession.
- Describe the relationship between therapeutic recreation's service motive and the history of organizational development.
- Describe the issues surrounding NCTRC and certification of TR personnel.

In this chapter we will explore the historical development of therapeutic recreation. Today's modern practice standards reflect a diversity of philosophies that have exerted influence on the field's development over a long period of time. In fact, some have referred to the "philosophy dilemma" of therapeutic recreation as the major stumbling block in the development of the profession (Meyer, 1980). Certainly, a great deal of the profession's efforts in the 1970s and 1980s has been devoted to the resolution of differences regarding a single, well-articulated national philosophy.

Related to the philosophical dilemma has been a rather circular history of professional organizations dedicated to providing therapeutic recreation. In this chapter we will learn how in some ways the professional organizations representing TR have come full circle, beginning first as separate organizations with conflicting philosophies, developing alliances and eventually merging into NTRS, and then finally, once again driven by conflicting philosophical and professional agendas, dividing into separate organizations.

Prior to looking closely at this contemporary history of therapeutic recreation (the majority of which has taken place in the later part of the 1900s), a brief review of ancient and historical precedents is in order. Within this review we will see how the development of TR, like the development of other human services and adjunctive therapies, has been integrally linked to the attitudes of societies in general to special populations.

HISTORICAL ROOTS

Cultural anthropologists have discovered that most ancient civilizations held beliefs and practices that relate in some way to the modern-day approach for activities to be a part of a therapeutic regimen. Although somewhat varied (Greek culture is a notable exception), most of these ancient cultural rituals and practices were tied in some way to religious beliefs. Table 2.1 provides a brief chronology of some of the more prominent historical markers.

Unfortunately, many of these ancient practices in providing more humane care and treatment for the sick and disabled were lost to post-twentieth-century Europe. In fact, many of the more brutal forms of treatment emanated from European practices, and some of the more prevalent stereotypes and dehumanizing labels in existence today can be traced to this period of time. By way of example, individuals with mental problems were frequently locked away in asylums for lunatics; many were kept in darkened cells for fear that stimulation or diversion of any kind would create aggressive or insubordinate behaviors. Similarly, many people with epilepsy were labeled as "possessed by the devil," their seizures taken as evidence of demon possession; and many were summarily burned at the stake as witches or warlocks. Also, we find the mentally retarded and otherwise congenitally disabled persons treated at best as court jesters or fools and at worst warehoused in segregated institutions.[1]

---

[1] There was a brief period of time in the United States that a more humane philosophy existed for the mentally retarded. The "happy home" movement was basically fueled by religious leaders who sought to create humane sanctuaries for the mentally retarded. Unfortunately, this philosophy of protecting the retarded from society lasted only a few decades. Later, in a wave of hysteria in which large numbers of the retarded were rounded up and institutionalized, the happy home concept was slurred to "funny farm" as society sought to protect itself from the retarded. A detailed historical accounting of the eugenic scare that triggered the end of the happy home era may be found in Wolfensburger's work (1972) on the normalization movement.

Table 2.1
Ancient Precedents for Activity Therapy

Egyptian Culture	Priests established temples to treat the sick.
	Legal codes with penalties for medical malpractice existed.
	Treatment of the ill included dances, concerts, and symbolic worship.
Greek Culture	Hippocrates, the father of modern medicine, established the oath detailing responsibilities of the medical profession, introduced the case study method as an approach to practice, and of more importance, made medicine a nonreligious art.
	Temples for the sick included libraries, stadiums, theaters, and sanatoriums.
	Treatment of mental disorders included music in conjunction with gymnastics and dancing.
Roman Culture	Physicians prescribed games that afforded relaxation to the body and mind.
	The virtues of diet and exercise were heralded as a tonic for the body.
	Circus and spectator activities were used as preventative measures for social deviancy.
	A hospital system was established. Infirmaries for the army were set up at physician homes, "nursing homes." These were forerunners of modern-day health care systems.
Chinese Culture	Activity was used to divert patients' attention from severe primary treatments.
	Deep breathing and exercise techniques were developed for sedentary older persons (tai chi).

SOURCE: Many concepts are paraphrased from Avedon, 1974, pp. 12–17, and Reynolds & O'Morrow.

Reynolds and O'Morrow's analysis of the Middle Ages, in which all science and classical learning passed into the church's keeping (a period lasting over eight centuries), provides an excellent synopsis:

> Hippocrates had freed treatment and care from religion and superstition, and had taught men that illness and disability were not sent by the gods as punishment, but rather natural phenomena to be studied. Under the church rule the view of the supernatural origin of disease was revived, partly the result of the fact that to be a physician one first had to be ordained a priest. Very little progress was made in theory and research during the Middle Ages. (Reynolds & O'Morrow, 1985, p. 89)

Not until the early 1800s did the beginnings of institutionalization with treatment (referred to at times as the so-called moral-treatment approach, which was actually a philosophical return to the same practices developed by the Greeks and Romans) begin to occur as a countermovement. Even so, the early leaders of this movement were viewed largely as being out of the mainstream of social thought. A few of the more prominent are featured in Table 2.2.

Table 2.2
Early Leaders of the Treatment with Care Era

WHO	WHEN	WHAT
Phillippe Pinel (French physician)	1700s	Used recreational activity in the form of exercise to treat the mentally ill.
Jean Itard (French physician)	1700s	Developed training techniques for the mentally retarded, using games and sport.
John Morgan (American physician)	1751	Is credited with establishing the first medical school in America.
Benjamin Rush (American physician)	1810	Advocated therapeutic values of recreation for mental-health patients.
Florence Nightingale (British nurse)	1873	Recommended recreation huts to combat side effects of soldiering as well as redesign of hospital environments to include color, music, and pets.

SOURCE: Many concepts are paraphrased from Carter, Van Andel, & Robb, 1985, pp. 35–50, and Reynolds and O'Morrow, 1985, p. 119.

The early attempts at institutional reform that advocated care and treatment fostered the beginning of the modern era of care. From the early examples set forth by Itard, Rush, and the like, refinements in institutional care took hold. We will learn in the next section that as refinements in societal methods took place (resulting in more humane institutions), the primacy of a variety of therapeutic modalities, including professional recreation services, began to develop momentum. This development, however, was not without both pragmatic and philosophic pitfalls and stumbling blocks.

THE BEGINNING OF MODERN THERAPEUTIC RECREATION SERVICES

The sudden influx of traumatic amputations and similar severe injuries to American society as a result of participation in both world wars served as a national trigger stimulus for improvement in the nation's hospital and institutional care treatment modalities. As services for returning veterans were expanded, a societal "halo," or carryover, effect in attitudes and sympathies toward special populations other than the physically challenged slowly began to emerge (emphasis should be placed on the word *slowly*, however). Along the way there were a number of important leaders, some professional, some political, who helped to champion this cause. Additionally, there were also a number of landmark legislative bills that provided both direction and funding for the modernization of human and health rehabilitation services. We will review these parallel histories briefly in order to build a chronology and a greater context that a discussion specific to the development of the therapeutic recreation profession will fit into. In Table 2.3 a brief synopsis of modern-day leaders and their contribution to the "treatment with care" movement is provided.

Collectively, these individuals (and others like them) were responsible for the expansion of recreation programs both within clinical, custodial, and community-based settings. Sometimes this support was a deliberate act of advocacy (as in the case of Haun, Menninger, and Rusk). Sometimes the recreation profession benefited indirectly from the impact that policy or organization of services had on human services in general (as in the case of Nixon). Regardless of the nature of the intent, without this kind of key support from medical and political leadership, the young field of therapeutic recreation would have had a difficult time in bringing its service mission to the attention of the consumer. Related to this personal kind of support provided by important personages was the progression in legal precedent and legislative mandate and funding that was also central to the development of the young profession.

Table 2.4 provides a brief chronology and annotation of the history of important legislative mandates as they impacted the therapeutic recreation profession.

Keeping in mind the ancillary support from professional and political leaders, as well as the more global rehabilitation laws reviewed above, we

Table 2.3
Key Proponents and Leaders of Modern Rehabilitation Services Who Influenced Therapeutic Recreation Development

Dorothea Dix	Social reformer who brought attention to the inadequate custodial care of the institutionalized in the early 1900s. She was a key figure in alleviating overcrowding and in providing enhanced resident services.
Paul Haun	Physician/advocate in the 1940s and 1950s whose writings and presentations supported recreation as a therapeutic modality able to create a desirable psychological state within the patient.
Karl Menninger	Physician/advocate, founder of the Menninger Clinic, influential advocate during the 1940s through the 1960s on the clinical effectiveness of recreation experiences as an adjunct to standard psychiatric practice.
Howard Rusk	Physician and international authority on physical rehabilitation who believed that both individual and group recreation had a direct and positive relationship upon recovery. He helped to establish the credibility of recreation as an adjunctive therapy.
Richard Nixon	President of the United States who mandated in 1967 that the mentally ill and mentally retarded population in public institutions be reduced by at least one-third, thus emphasizing a greater emphasis on community-based social services on a national scale.

SOURCE: Paraphrased from Reynolds & O'Morrow, 1985, pp. 119–121, and Carter, Van Andel, & Robb, 1985, pp. 35–50.

Table 2.4
Legislation Affecting Recreation for Special Populations

Law: Social Security Act, 1936

Impact: A compilation of law, including numerous amendments over the last several years related specifically to the elderly and disabled, including provisions for physical education and recreation through (1) formal procedure for review of professional services, (2) establishing funds to states for self-support services for individuals, (3) grants to states for providing community-based care.

Law: Vocational Rehabilitation Act, 1963

Impact: Provides training and research funds for recreation for the ill and handicapped. The first recognition by a specific federal agency of the importance of recreation services in rehabilitation.

Law: Public Law 88-29 Nationwide Outdoor Recreation Plan, 1963

Impact: Directed the formulation and maintenance of a comprehensive nationwide outdoor recreation plan. The plan was completed in 1973 and included emphasis on compliance with PL 90-480 (see below). Concerns for accessibility for the handicapped were listed as a priority area.

Law: Public Law 90-170 Education for Handicapped Children Act, 1967

Impact: Established the unit of physical education and recreation for handicapped children within the Bureau of Education for the Handicapped. Became the largest federal program for training, research, and special projects.

Law: Public Law 90-480 Architectural Barriers Act, 1968

Impact: Simply states "Any building or facility, constructed in whole or part by federal funds, must be accessible to and usable by the physically handicapped."

Law: Public Law 91-517 Developmental Disabilities Services and Facilities Construction Act, 1971

Impact: Developmentally disabled persons are specifically defined, and recreation is listed as a specific service to be included as a fundable service.

Law: Public Law 93-112 Rehabilitation Act, 1973

Impact: A comprehensive revision of the 1963 Vocational Rehabilitation Act, which included an emphasis on the "total" rehabilitation of the individual. Special provisions included: (1) personnel training, (2) special projects and demonstrations for making recreational facilities accessible, (3) powers to ensure accessibility compliance for parks and parklands, (4) states must develop a comprehensive plan which ensures that they comply under section 504 so that individuals shall not be discriminated against solely by reason of their handicap.

Law: Public Law 93-516 Rehabilitation Act Amendment, 1974

Impact: Authorized the planning and implementation of the White House Conference on Handicapped Individuals, which was conceived in 1977. Recreation was cited as one of sixteen areas of concern.

Law: Public Law 94-142 Education of all Handicapped Children Act, 1975

Impact: Requires a free and appropriate education for all handicapped children. Physical education is listed as a direct service and recreation as a related service.

Law: Public Law 99-457 Education of the Handicapped Act Amendment, 1986

Impact: Emphasized development of comprehensive statewide programs of early intervention services for handicapped infants, toddlers, and families. A multidisciplinary team must develop an individualized family services plan. Recreation is cited as a related service in these amendments.

SOURCE: Table 2.4 is a revision and update of previous work by Crawford, 1985.

can now turn our focus to the specific history of the professionalization of therapeutic recreation services. Although the vast majority of contemporary history has accumulated since the 1960s, we must begin literally at the turn of the century in order to retrieve all relevant events that have impacted the modern-day service ethic in therapeutic recreation.

THE GROWTH OF THERAPEUTIC RECREATION AS A PROFESSION

The use of the word *profession* when speaking of therapeutic recreation personnel and services is still a relatively new concept. We say relatively new in reference to more mature professions like medicine, law, or psychology. For a group of individuals and the skills they provide to qualify for the label of "profession," it is essential that what they do be distinguished from trade or semiskilled services. Most believe that a true profession has as its basis a set of characteristics, or criteria, that distinguish it as a true scientific endeavor (Thorsteinson, 1980, p. 270).

The approach of this section will be to discuss the evolution of therapeutic recreation as a profession as it relates to the key global criteria that constitute the definition of a scientific profession.

Service Motive

Truly professional people are dedicated to a particular service motive. The improvement of society is first and the betterment of their profession next. Traditionally, professionals have been viewed as altruistic, looking out for society (although in contemporary times, this has become somewhat tarnished due to teacher and nursing strikes). When groups let their own importance or well-being overshadow service, as is the case with most traditional blue collar occupations and their labor unions, then society tends to view them as nonprofessional service providers.

What is the historical case for therapeutic recreation in demonstrating a true service ethic? Most historians of therapeutic recreation point to the organization of the Boston Sand Gardens in 1885 not only as the beginning of truly professional recreation services in the United States (Bower, 1974), but also as the first true public therapeutic recreation program because of its emphasis on serving the economically disadvantaged. (Some also claim the Sand Gardens as the beginning of the American Playground Movement; see Bruya & Langendorfer, 1988). How did the public's view of the service motive build from this departure point? A brief chronology that highlights key events related to service motive will demonstrate both the diversity and relative newness of this aspect of the profession.

1893   The Industrial Home for the Blind in New York City is established to provide, among other things, recreation experiences for its clients (Avedon, 1974, p. 12).

1905   The Lighthouse (another New York association for the blind) adds the donation of theater and concert tickets as part of its services (Avedon, 1974, p. 12).

1913   The *American Journal of Insanity* details how one hospital chartered a train and took 500 patients on a picnic for curative and restorative benefits (Avedon, 1974, p. 12).

1914   The Jewish Guild for the Blind cites as one of its original purposes the provision of a recreation center (Avedon, 1974, p. 13).

1915   The director of the Vineland Institute (New Jersey) publishes an accounting of the use of games and play to help develop self-control, coordination, and manner in the mentally retarded (Avedon, 1974, p. 14).

1919   The American Red Cross formally organizes a division of recreation in hospitals (by 1930 there are 117 full-time Red Cross hospital recreation workers) (Navar, 1979, p. 88).

1932   The White House Conference on Child Health and Protection acknowledge the need for recreation as one element essential in supplementing social reform (Carter, Van Andel, & Robb, 1985, p. 47).

1938   The term *therapeutic recreation* first appears in federal legislation as part of the creation of the Works Progress Administration (WPA) (Shivers & Fait, 1975, p. 7).

1944   The first community center entirely devoted to serving older adults is started by the New York City Department of Welfare (Avedon, 1974, p. 15).

1965   The first organized attempt to develop uniform standards of practice for the delivery of therapeutic recreation gets underway via the Council for Advancement of Hospital Recreation (CAHR).

1978   Standards of practice for the delivery of therapeutic recreation in community-based programs are printed by the National Therapeutic Recreation Society (NTRS).

1979   Standards of practice in 10 specialized areas of clinical and residential service settings are formalized by NTRS.

1980   NTRS begins a dialogue with both the Joint Commission on Accreditation of Hospitals (JCAH) and the Commission on Accreditation of Rehabilitation Facilities (CARF) to see that standards of practice intended to protect the consumer become part of the standard review process of accreditation of facilities. Eventually, both bodies adopt key elements of the NTRS standards (JCAH in 1981 and CARF in 1982).

1982   The NTRS membership and board of directors formally adopt a national philosophical position statement as a declaration to the public of the mission of NTRS. It should be noted, however, that this adoption was not without controversy. Both a very low membership voting turnout and the very divided results of balloting (four different positions were voted on) contributed to postdecision divisiveness within the profession (Ollson, 1988).

Service Motive Summary.   As can be seen by this brief revisit to early beginnings of the public demonstration of the service motive, therapeutic recreation began in an unorganized fashion. Chiefly concerned with betterment of life quality for specific disability groups, private advocacy organizations developed the first delivery of services programs. Not until the formal organization of the National Therapeutic Recreation Society (1965) did more "umbrella," or inclusive, acts of advocacy take shape and push forward a well-articulated national agenda. A well-articulated national philosophy statement was not formally adopted until 1982. Even so, as we shall learn in the section of this chapter devoted to organizations, the philosophy of a therapeutic recreation service motive is still a point of controversy and division within the field.

PROFESSIONAL ORGANIZATIONS

These organizations make progress possible that individual practitioners could not on their own otherwise obtain. One of the most important aspects of professional organizations is providing a forum for the continuing education of its members. Conventions, conferences, and topical symposia enable one to keep up with the growth of the field. In a related vein, political agitation and consumer advocacy at local, state, and national levels are essential for the continued growth and upgrading of standards. In some ways, the success of a profession in following its service ethic can be either tremendously facilitated or hindered in direct proportion to the ability of its professional body to apply political clout toward the passage of important regulations, laws, and standards.

The history of the formation of professional organizations within therapeutic recreation is relatively short and, as of recent times, circular. The problem lies in a philosophical divisiveness over what really constitutes the true service motive of the profession. As we shall see, therapeutic recreation personnel have still not solved this fundamental definition of a profession, and this dilemma continues to drive deep differences. One of the ways these differences have manifested themselves has been in the formation of different professional organizations, the coalition or merger of them into a unified whole, and the eventual breakup back into separate professional groups.

1948   At the national Congress of the American Recreation Society (ARS), the Hospital Recreation Section becomes a reality. Members predominantly represent practitioners from veterans and military hospitals who espouse a "recreation for all" philosophy, also referred to as the "recreation for recreation's sake" perspective, commonly referred to today as so-called diversional programming (Navar, 1979, p. 190).

1952   A Recreation Therapy Section is established with the Recreation Division of the American Association for Health, Physical Education, and Recreation. The primary emphasis of this membership focuses on recreation and adapts physical education and sports programs in special and public schools.

1953   The National Association of Recreational Therapists (NART) is organized. This membership, comprised essentially of personnel from state hospitals and schools, is concerned with the clinical practice of therapeutic recreation. The major premise of this group is that recreation could serve as an intervention, a specific tool of treatment or rehabilitation effective in combating problems associated with primary disabilities (Austin, 1986).

1953   The Council for Advancement of Hospital Recreation (CAHR) is formed to serve as the structure for enabling all three professional organizations (NART, HRS, and RT-AAHPER) to have a common dialogue.

1959   A merger committee within CAHR is formed to discuss a plan for growth of the profession and possible merger. After four years of work, no agreement regarding direction for this field is reached.

1966   Branch status is given to the National Therapeutic Recreation Society (NTRS) by the relatively new National Recreation and Park Association (NRPA, formed in 1965). Members of NTRS constitute the combined membership of NART and the Hospital Recreation Section of ARS. The Recreation Therapy Section of AAHPER continues independently, with its focus on schools and education (a mission that eventually becomes subdivided within AAHPER among several different host organizations and professional councils). The voluntary registration plan for personnel begun by CAHR in 1956 remains intact and is administered by NTRS.

1971   The first regional training symposia for TR personnel is established—the Midwest Symposium on Therapeutic Recreation (hosted by University of Illinois). Subsequent regional symposia are developed as the NTRS front line of continuing education training for its membership.

1978   The Therapeutic Recreation Management School at Ogelby Park, Wheeling, West Virginia, is established as a formal post-degree in-service training alternative.

1978   NTRS Board of Directors approves and publishes community TR standards of practice "Guidelines for Community-Based Programs for Special Populations."

1979   Clinical Standards of practice are published by NTRS.

1981   National Council for Therapeutic Recreation Certification becomes a completely autonomous credentialing body independent of NRPA/NTRS.

1982   Residential Facility Standards of practice are published by NTRS.

1984   The American Therapeutic Recreation Association (ATRA) is founded. Key founding members and leaders include several past-presidents and board members of NTRS. The focus of the new organization is to provide for more aggressive growth of clinical practice and specialization within TR.

Professional Organizations Summary. The early organizations concerned with TR were composed essentially of different subspecialities of TR practitioners, each more or less concerned with their own constituency and service setting. After years of discussion and meetings, the failure of CAHR to find common ground and thus a more unified front for the three national organizations is symptomatic of how deep the philosophical divisions were. Then, remarkably, the number of groups concerned with TR shrank from three to one. (From a pragmatic viewpoint, RT-AAHPER did not last long as a formal group within AAHPER after the formation of NTRS, and asserted less and less influence regarding clinical practice.) (The consolidation seemed to follow the example set by the parent body of NRPA, where in 1965 five separate recreation organizations formed together into one. Within one year the three TR organizations were finally able to achieve a working alliance, and thus NTRS was established as a branch group under NRPA. Basic philosophical incompatibilities troubled NTRS, however. Most notedly, credentials and curricula served as focal points of divisiveness, resulting in frequent and radical shifts in basic services and messages to the membership. Finally, in 1984 the beginning of the unraveling of the NTRS coalition gained formal momentum with the formation of ATRA. Many of the founding members of ATRA were past-presidents and former members of the board of directors of NTRS. Impatient with the pace of change within NTRS/NRPA, these individuals decided that the subspecialty of clinical service needed a more focused organizational advocate. And so once again, the field of TR claimed more than one national organization concerned with development of the profession. In Chapter 19 on trends and issues, more of the potential concerns regarding multinational organizations is presented.

SCIENTIFIC BASIS

Simply put, scientific basis means that there is a body of knowledge related to the professional practice. Not only are the governing laws and principles of a profession supposedly guided by this body of knowledge, but also the applied and practical delivery of service is governed by certain fundamental consistencies. Consistent with the acquisition of a body of knowledge is the public display or demonstration of such. Thus, a body of literature as demonstrated through professional journals, books, and other publications is an index of the vitality and soundness of a profession. Without specific references to point to in defense of practices and skills, the individual practitioner lacks a professional stature.

When did the scientific basis for the provision of therapeutic recreation begin in this country? What evidence has accumulated in support of a scientific body of literature?

1919   The first manual concerned with recreation and illness is published: *Hospital and Bedside Games* (cited in Avedon, 1974, p. 15).

1932   The use of recreation in chronic psychiatric settings is published in a text *Emotion and Sport* (cited in Avedon, 1974, p. 15).

1932   "The Selection and Use of Games in Cases of Cardiac Insufficiency" represents the extension of recreation into the treatment of acute illness and disability (cited in Avedon, 1974, p. 15).

1932   One of the very first experimental design projects regarding recreation is completed at the Lincoln State School and Colony in Illinois. The results indicate that responses of retarded children can be significantly improved through the use of play activities (cited in Carter, Van Andel, & Robb, 1985, p. 55).

1933   The book *Psychoanalytic Theory of Play* extends the case for recreation as a part of the psychoanalytic school of psychology (cited in Avedon, 1974, p. 15).

1954   Publication of *Recreation in Treatment Centers*, an annual collection of therapeutic recreation research, is begun by the Hospital Recreation Section of the American Recreation Society and is published until 1969.

1955   One of the earliest university textbooks available is printed: *Recreation for the Handicapped*, by Valerie Hunt (cited in Carter, Van Andel, & Robb, 1985, p. 55).

1957   A quarterly journal *Recreation for the Ill and Handicapped* is developed by the National Association of Recreational Therapists and is published until 1967.

1958   The National Recreation Association commissions a study that involves more than 6000 hospitals/institutions as the first major cataloging of personnel, content, and clients served in therapeutic recreation programming (cited in Reynolds & O'Morrow, 1985, p. 129).

1959   *Recreation in Total Rehabilitation*, by Rathbone and Lucas, provides one of the first comprehensive technical manuals on provision of therapeutic recreation services (cited in Carter, Van Andel, & Robb, 1985, p. 56).

1967   NTRS begins the publication of the *Therapeutic Recreation Journal* as a replacement journal for *Recreation for the Ill and Handicapped* (publication of *TRJ* continues through to present day).

1970   NTRS begins the publication of the *Therapeutic Recreation Annual* as a replacement for *Recreation in Treatment Centers*. (However, the *TR Annual* survives only through five volumes and leaves the *TRJ* as the only professional journal published by NTRS.)

1970s   As curricula diversify, a small flurry of new academic textbooks begins with such works as: Frye and Peters (1972); Kraus (1973); Avedon (1974); Shivers and Fait (1975); O'Morrow (1976); and Gunn and Peterson (1978).

1972   Frye and Peters (1972) report that one-third of all completed studies within therapeutic recreation have been completed since 1963.

1973   Martin (1975) reports that between 1965 and 1973 a total of 210 research studies appeared either in professional journals or in conference and symposia proceedings.

1980s   Clinical specialization of textbooks begins as new titles based on specific populations and models of service appear: Austin

(1982); Teaff (1985); Carter, Van Andel, and Robb (1985); Crawford and Mendell (1987); Howe-Murphy and Charboneau (1987).

1986 The *Journal of Expanding Horizons in Therapeutic Recreation* is begun by the University of Missouri as the second contemporary refereed journal (*TRJ* being the first) dedicated exclusively to therapeutic recreation.

Scientific Basic Summary. Early technical manuals based upon a mixture of theory and case study approaches slowly gave way to more rigorous scientific inquiry in the 1950s. However, the real knowledge explosion within the field did not take place until the 1960s. As increasingly diverse clinical services documented therapeutic recreation effectiveness, the design of textbooks moved from the early comprehensive approaches of the 1970s (which attempted to deal with total knowledge organization) to client-directed or specialized-service-driven approaches of the 1980s. This evolution of textbook organization documents in part the rapid expansion of the knowledge base into more areas of client service and care. The organization of a second national journal separate from the national organization NTRS also speaks indirectly to the expanded vitality of the literature and research base of the young profession.

EXTENDED PREPARATION OF PERSONNEL

In order to ensure that the body of knowledge that constitutes the profession is properly utilized, extended years of preparation and training are required. There are two subcomponents to this process. One is the challenge of obtaining specialized skills that are unique (for example, the skills of surgery a medical doctor must acquire, or the ability to assess psychological functioning through IQ scales that the psychologist strives for). The second is to provide for the attainment of these skills under uniform standards that culminate in the awarding of a formal degree. For most contemporary professions, the baccalaureate degree is rapidly becoming inadequate or obsolete as evidence that one is a professional. Usually at least one or more graduate or professional degrees are now required for admission to truly professional ranks. (For example, although there are any number of bachelor's degrees available in psychology, one is not considered to be a "psychologist" until at least obtaining a master's or doctoral degree in the field; in fact, in most states the doctorate is required for someone to practice as and call oneself a "psychologist.")

How has the field of therapeutic recreation progressed relative to the question of extended preparation of personnel?

1909 The first known course in professional recreation is taught at an institution of higher learning (Carter, Van Andel, & Robb, 1985, p. 53).

1926   The first formal training school devoted solely to the training of professional recreation personnel is established and called the "National Recreation Association's Leadership Training School" (Navar, 1979, p. 189).

1931   New York University offers the first university curriculum in recreation.

1950   The University of Minnesota offers the first university curriculum in therapeutic recreation (Navar, 1979, p. 190).

1953   A study by the Standards and Training Committee of the Hospital Recreation Section of the American Recreation Society reports six colleges and universities with graduate or undergraduate degrees in hospital recreation (Carter, Van Andel, & Robb, 1985, p. 53).

1961   The National Recreation Association sponsors a therapeutic recreation curriculum development conference, the first nationally organized effort to identify general competencies needed by recreation personnel in hospital settings.

1963   The Rehabilitation Services Administration of the U.S. Department of Health, Education and Welfare provides funds to selected colleges and universities for graduate study in therapeutic recreation (Reynolds & O'Morrow, 1985, p. 113).

1968   A national Recreation Education Accreditation Project (begun originally in 1963) publishes therapeutic recreation emphasis criteria for both undergraduate and graduate levels of study (Carter, Van Andel, & Robb, 1985, p. 53).

1969   A national study identifies 28 undergraduate and 26 graduate programs in therapeutic recreation (Carter, Van Andel, & Robb, 1985, p. 53).

1975   The first standards for the accreditation of recreation curricula in colleges and universities are implemented by the National Recreation and Park Association in concert with the American Association of Leisure and Recreation. The first standards for therapeutic recreation are accepted by this body in 1976.

1979   A national study identifies a total of 116 undergraduate therapeutic recreation programs and another 34 master's degree programs (Carter, Van Andel, & Robb, 1985, p. 54).

1984   A national survey by the Society of Park and Recreation Educators catalogs a total of 98 undergraduate and 55 graduate programs of study in therapeutic recreation across a total of 260 responding institutions.

1987   The National Council on Post-Secondary Accreditation formally recognizes the NRPA/AALR accreditation educational standards, a kind of national "Good Housekeeping Seal of

Approval" is thus extended, and this event further legitimizes the quality of post secondary curricula in therapeutic recreation.

1988   Nationwide, a total of 63 TR curricula receives approval based on the NRPA/AALR Council for Accreditation standards.

Extended Preparation of Personnel Summary. The great span of time between the early pioneering initiatives of the 1900s through the 1930s and the flurry of expanded activity in the 1960s and 1970s demonstrates well the slow and sporadic growth of the field from a service provider to professional delivery status. The identification of content for standards was a tedious and time-consuming process spanning more than twenty years; in fact, it is ongoing. The difficulty of this process was partly because of its being a multiorganization enterprise (AALR and NRPA working together). But it was probably difficult—more because it was trying to organize statistically and definitively a very rapidly expanding field. Even so, the accreditation standards as they exist today have been criticized as being based on minimal standards that lack sufficient regulatory teeth. At a minimum, the accreditation of curricula (though still a voluntary process) has facilitated (1) improvement in the quality of professional preparation at a national level by helping to overcome in part the diversity that has existed across curricula, (2) promotion of interorganizational communication, and (3) building a more successful and positive image of the therapeutic recreation profession among the lay public (O'Morrow & Reynolds, 1989, p. 319).

AUTONOMY OF JUDGMENT

True professionals are granted by society the authority to exercise personal responsibility to practice in accord with professional standards of their field. In most cases, society has seen fit to set up licensing or certification standards for these professions in order to protect the consumer and ensure that the individual practitioner meets acceptable standards of competency. Thus, simply fulfilling the requirement for extended preparation by getting a degree or diploma—for example, graduating from medical school—is not enough; the new professional must prove his or her mastery of knowledge by passing state licensing examinations before he or she is entrusted with the authority to exercise autonomy of judgment.

In therapeutic recreation the issue of autonomy of judgment has been a relatively recent one.

1944   A publication by the National Recreation Association states that "a demand had arisen for recreation leadership personnel with proper qualifications" (cited in Navar, 1979, p. 117).

1950   The State of California Recreation Commission publishes a book of standards for recreation personnel.

1956   The Council for Advancement of Hospital Recreation (CAHR) formulates standards for qualifying hospital recreation personnel. A national voluntary registration plan with three levels: director, leader, and aide is implemented (Carter, Van Andel, & Robb, 1985, p. 52).

1961   The American Medical Association officially designates recreation service as an allied health field (Reynolds & O'Morrow, 1985).

1965   The original voluntary registration plan developed by CAHR in 1956 is taken over by NTRS.

1969   The first extensive revision of the national registry standards for therapeutic recreation personnel takes place under NTRS administration.

1969–1980   During this period of time no less than six revisions are made to the registration process. These are for the most part reactive alterations in light of curriculum improvements and employment standards of the field (cited in Carter, Van Andel, & Robb, 1985, p. 57).

1975   The State of Utah establishes a licensing procedure for therapeutic recreation personnel. All persons wishing to practice as recreational therapists must pass a state examination and be licensed to do so. This move on the part of TR leadership within Utah is taken without endorsement or consent of the national leadership. Many criticize it as premature, given the relative youth of the young profession. The State of Georgia follows suit in 1981 with a licensure law of its own.

1976   NTRS establishes the Continuing Professional Development Review Board (CPD) to review, endorse, and increase the number of therapeutic recreation training opportunities for practitioners. The goal of this board is to maintain a competent professional work force.

1981   The National Council for Therapeutic Recreation Certification (NCTRC) is formed as an independent entity (independent of NRPA and NTRS) for the sole purpose of managing and administering the certification and recertification of therapeutic recreation personnel.

1986   A model practice act for state organizations to utilize in planning licensure bills for their state court houses is endorsed by the NTRS.

1987   Formal commitment to a national certification exam is made by NCTRC via a signed contract with the Educational Testing Service to conduct a national job analysis survey with the membership (Sable, 1988).

Autonomy of Judgment Summary. From 1956 to 1969 the voluntary registration of therapeutic recreation professionals remained essentially unchanged. The confusion that followed as a result of six changes in the period from 1969 to 1980 is better understood in light of these prior 14 years of stability. Dissent among the work force from this confusion was further exacerbated by the fact that although a formal merger of the three different organizations representing TR had taken place (see professional organizations section of this chapter), a formal merger of philosophies within the new membership had not really happened (and still has not for some even today), as evidenced by the formation of ATRA (Halberg & Howe-Murphy, 1985, p. 10). Thus, from the perspective of some, the creation of the relatively new NTRS (1966) has brought about radical and seemingly unending changes in organizational and professional identity and stability that had preceded it for several decades. Further, the move from a national registry (a simple cataloging procedure) to a certification plan (with criteria/standards and requirements) served to alienate portions of the membership. Despite allowances for nondegree professionals (grandfather clauses allowing people with work experience to qualify for professional certification), many cried elitism and refused to participate in the process. The further escalation of autonomy of judgment for the field, the case of licensure acts by Utah and Georgia, was not endorsed initially by NTRS. Although in recent years NTRS has adopted a model practice act or licensure bill for states, the very issue of licensure for TR professionals (the governmental definition, monitoring, and restriction of professional practice to protect the interest of the public) is viewed by some scholars as premature (Carter, 1984) and is still hotly debated. (The issue of licensure of TR personnel can be found in Chapter 19 on trends and issues.)

What remains most significant about the creation of NCTRC is its strategy to deal definitively with the question of recertification of personnel. (The main motivation was a federal legal requirement that a professional organization cannot solely control admission to professional membership—a process considered potentially as a conflict of interest arrangement.) As the current certification plan stands, once an individual is admitted, under whatever standards are in place at the time, as long as that person maintains his or her certification there is no continuing education requirement. One can quickly realize that, given the relative youth of

TR as a profession and the rapidly expanding knowledge base, within a few years it is easy for one's knowledge to become dated or even obsolete. For example, the Leisure Diagnostic Battery (Ellis & Witt, 1986), one of the few standardized leisure assessment inventories (and thus potentially very beneficial within clinical practice), was not even in existence in the literature five years ago. Historically, other fields have dealt with the question of maintenance of a competent work force. Within many states public school teachers cannot keep their teaching credentials without accruing a specific number of hours of graduate study within a certain time frame (usually six hours within five years). In some of our sister therapies within the allied health professions, continuing education units (CEUs) are utilized to ensure that an individual has attended sufficient in-service and training hours.

Certainly, the establishment of the national certification exam in 1990 has at least set a single minimum knowledge base standard for personnel to reach. However, the mechanisms to provide in-service training of the work force through CEUs or some similar system have yet to be well articulated by the national leadership.

CODE OF ETHICS

A true professional serves his or her constituency on the basis of a set of ethical standards and practices that govern all members. Key to this code of ethics being accepted as a valid measure of professionalism by the public is a means or mechanism for ensuring compliance with the code by its practicing members. Thus, membership to the profession can not only be granted on the basis of competency, but can also be stripped from an individual based upon his or her misconduct as related to those competencies.

1953　A committee within the Hospital Recreation Section of the American Recreation Society publishes a document entitled "Basic Concepts of Hospital Recreation," which among other things asserts basic responsibilities of recreators as members of an adjunctive therapy (O'Morrow, 1976, p. 119).

1973　Following a national field study, a preliminary Code of Ethics Draft is prepared by the NRPA Code of Ethics Committee.

1976　A statement of a professional ethics is finalized for three branches of NRPA, including the National Therapeutic Recreation Society (Carter, Van Andel, & Robb, 1985, p. 55).

Code of Ethics Summary.　Unfortunately, little progress has been made in terms of formal action on the Code of Ethics since 1976. Although a joint committee of AALR/NPRA remains active, the compliance aspect of the code remains an individual, voluntary act. A formal enforcement mechanism for the code has not been enacted and remains the major problem with this aspect of professional development. Chapter 19 on trends and issues discusses the challenge that this area of professionalism presents in the future.

SUMMARY

In this chapter we have presented a snapshot in time of the professional evolution of the young field of therapeutic recreation. We have done so by first tracing the historical roots provided by ancient civilizations, where the fundamentals of specialized treatment centers, physician prescription, the case study approach, and activities applied for restorative purposes were first practiced. The leaders of the "treatment with care" era heralded not only a radical departure from the brutal treatment of medieval Europe but the beginning of the modern era of services. During the modern era, key medical and political leaders furthered the cause of therapeutic recreation. Their actions in concert with the landmark legislative acts of the 1960s and 1970s provided a rich medica for cultural change in the United States regarding the philosophy and practice of rehabilitative and habilitative care.

The current status of the TR movement as a profession was reviewed by applying a chronological approach in annotating key events against a model of professionalism. Review of the TR service motive, professional organizations, scientific basis, extended preparation of personnel, autonomy of judgment, and code of ethics, revealed a young field striving toward fulfillment of criteria to meet professional status. In Chapter 19, trends and issues that relate to further growth in these areas are addressed.

READING COMPREHENSION QUESTIONS

1. Which ancient culture was responsible for introducing the concept of medical malpractice? Which one is credited for establishing the hospital system?

2. In post–twentieth-century Europe, persons from which disability group were sometimes labeled as demon-possessed and burned at the stake?

3. What world events helped to trigger the "treatment with care" era in this country?

4. Can you name three important early leaders of the modern treatment era and briefly recount their contributions?

5. Which law required that buildings and facilities constructed with federal monies be made accessible for the handicapped?

6. In which law is recreation listed as a related service for handicapped children to receive?

7. Can you differentiate between a profession and a trade or semiskilled group? What are the six characteristics of a profession?

8. What is considered to be the first public demonstration of the TR service motive?

9. What are the two national hospital and institutional accrediting bodies that NTRS worked with to ensure that modern standards of practice were established?

10. When did the knowledge explosion in TR take place in this country?

11. Can you define the two subcomponents to extended preparation of personnel as a characteristic of a profession?

12. Can you identify positive contributions made by national accreditation standards for TR education? What is the major criticism of these standards?

13. What is the predominant assumption behind autonomy of judgment as a characteristic of a profession?

14. Which two states have licensure laws that regulate delivery of TR services?

15. What is a controversial aspect of the current approach to certification taken by NCTRC? Why was NCTRC established?

16. What philosophical connection do the old NART and modern ATRA organizations share in common?

17. Which organization has contributed the most to political agitation and consumer advocacy for the field of TR? What are the contributions?

18. Which of the six characteristics of professionalism is the most underdeveloped within TR?

SUGGESTED LEARNING ACTIVITIES

1. Write a 2- to 3-page essay entitled "My Personal Position Regarding the Licensure of Therapeutic Recreation Professionals." Within your essay discuss (1) your philosophical reason(s) for your position and (2) the pragmatic actions that have taken place or would have to take place within the field to support your position.

2. Identify which of the six characteristics of a profession you personally would like to help contribute to in the next three years. Outline a personal plan of action you will follow that will help you achieve this contribution. In discussing your plan, consider if there are any political, consumer, or practitioner agendas you should develop and pursue in making a personal contribution to the development of the field.

3. Develop a list of "Things I Would Change in the TR Profession." If you had the opportunity to become the NTRS or ATRA president and pursue some of these changes, list the potential roadblocks you would have to overcome in order to accomplish them.

REFERENCES

Austin, D. R. (1982). *Therapeutic recreation: processes and techniques.* New York: John Wiley & Sons.

Austin, D. R. (1986). The Helping Profession: You Do Make a Difference. In A. James & F. McGuire (Eds.), *Selected papers from the 1985 Southeast Therapeutic Recreation Symposium.* Clemson University Extension Services.

Avedon, E. M. (1974). *Therapeutic recreation service: An applied behavioral science approach.* Englewood Cliffs, NJ: Prentice-Hall.

Bower, E. (1974). Plays the thing. In E. Bower (Ed.), *Games in education and development* (pp. 10–11). Springfield, IL: Charles C. Thomas.

Bruya, L. D., & Langendorfer, S. J. (1988). *Where our children play: Elementary school playground equipment.* Reston, VA: American Alliance for Health, Physical Education, Recreation and Dance.

Carter, M. J. (1984). Issues in continuing professional competence of therapeutic recreators. *Therapeutic Recreation Journal, 18*(3), 7–10.

Carter, M. J., Van Andel, G. E., & Robb, G. M. (1985). *Therapeutic recreation: A practical approach.* St. Louis: Times Mirror/Mosby.

Crawford, M. E. (1985). Planning for the handicapped. In R. B. Flynn (Ed.), *Planning facilities for athletics, physical education, and recreation* (3rd ed.). Reston, VA: Athletic Institute.

Crawford, M. E., & Mendell, R. (1987). *Therapeutic recreation and adapted physical activities for mentally retarded individuals.* Englewood Cliffs, NJ: Prentice-Hall.

Ellis, G. D., & Witt, P. A. (1986). The leisure diagnostic battery: Past, present, and future. *Therapeutic Recreation Journal, 20*(4), 31–47.

Frye, V., & Peters, M. (1972). *Therapeutic recreation: Its theory, philosophy and practice.* Harrisburg, PA: Stackpole Books.

Gunn, S. L., & Peterson, C. A. (1978). *Therapeutic recreation program design: Principles and procedures.* Englewood Cliffs, NJ: Prentice-Hall.

Halberg, K. J., & Howe-Murphy, R. (1985). The dilemma of an unresolved philosophy in therapeutic recreation. *Therapeutic Recreation Journal, 19*(3), 7–16.

Howe-Murphy, R., & Charboneau, B. G. (1987). *Therapeutic recreation intervention: An ecological perspective.* Englewood Cliffs, NJ: Prentice-Hall.

Kraus, R. (1973). *Therapeutic recreation service: Principles and practices.* Philadelphia: W. B. Saunders.

Martin, F. W. (1975). Therapeutic recreation research and the recreation practitioner. In D. A. Pelegrino (Ed.), *What recreation research says to the practitioner.* Washington, DC: American Association of Leisure and Recreation of American Alliance of Health, Physical Education, Recreation and Dance.

Meyer, L. (1980). Three philosophical positions of therapeutic recreation and their implications for professionalization and NTRS. *Proceedings of the First Annual Post-Doctoral Institute.* Department of Recreation and Park Administration, Indiana University, Bloomington, pp. 28–42.

National Therapeutic Recreation Society. (1982). Philosophical position statement of the National Therapeutic Recreation Society.

NAVAR, N. H. (1979). The professionalization of therapeutic recreation in the State of Michigan. Unpublished dissertation. Bloomington: Indiana University.

OLLSON, R. (1988). A survey of southeastern therapeutic recreation specialists: Philosophy, practice and education. *JEHTR 3*, 35–40.

O'MORROW, G. S. (1976). *Therapeutic recreation; A helping profession* (3rd ed.). Reston, VA: Reston Publishing.

O'MORROW, G. S., & REYNOLDS, R. P. (1989). *Therapeutic recreation: A helping profession*. (3rd ed.) Englewood Cliffs, NJ: Prentice Hall.

REYNOLDS, R. P., & O'MORROW, G. S. (1985). *Problems, issues and concepts in therapeutic recreation*. Englewood Cliffs, NJ: Prentice-Hall.

SABLE, J. (1988, February/March). President's Report. *NCTRC Newsletter*, pp. 1, 2.

SHIVERS, J. S., & FAIT, H. F. (1975). *Therapeutic and adapted recreational services*. Philadelphia: Lea & Febiger.

TEAFF, J. D. (1985). *Leisure services with the elderly*. St. Louis: C. V. Mosby.

THORSTEINSON, W. (1980). Beyond professionalism. In T. L. Goodale & P. Witt (Eds.), *Recreation and leisure: Issues in an era of change*. State College, PA: Venture Publishing.

WOLFENSBURGER, W. (1972). *Normalization: The principal of normalization in human services*. Toronto: National Institute on Mental Retardation.

3

The Therapeutic Recreation Process

DAVID R. AUSTIN

OBJECTIVES

- Describe the TR process, including its four phases.
- Identify methods for completing client assessment.
- Understand elements of concern during the planning phase, including goals and objectives.
- Know the role of the TR specialist during the implementation phase.
- Know the purpose of evaluation in the TR process.
- Identify characteristics of therapeutic activities.

DEFINITION OF THERAPEUTIC RECREATION AND THE TR PROCESS

Therapeutic recreation is a purposeful intervention designed to help clients grow and to assist them to relieve or prevent problems through recreation and leisure. The intervention takes place through an interaction between a professionally prepared therapeutic recreation specialist and a client with whom the therapeutic recreation specialist collaborates. The therapeutic recreation process is used to achieve a higher level of health in the client.

The *therapeutic recreation process* is a systematic problem-solving procedure used by therapeutic recreation specialists to help clients improve their levels of health by meeting identified needs. During a four-phase progression, TR specialists initially assess client health status, needs, and strengths. Next, planning transpires to develop a plan of action to meet goals and objectives that flow out of the assessment phase. The planned intervention is then implemented. Finally, the effect of the intervention on goals and objectives is evaluated. The therapeutic recreation process is the essence of therapeutic recreation in that it provides a base from which all therapeutic recreation actions proceed.

The basis for therapeutic recreation practice must transcend the cognition that recreation, by its nature, is good, so it has benefit to the well-being of all persons, including those who are ill. To justify the profession of therapeutic recreation on the credo of "recreation is good for all" trivializes therapeutic recreation. As Mobily (1987) has explained, therapeutic recreation has instrumental value. Its outcomes are not "accidental and random" but rather are "purposeful and systematic." Therapeutic recreation is a means to an end—the end of health protection and health promotion. Mobily (1985) has exclaimed: "The very cognition of recreation as a means is the distinguishing feature of TR."

INTRODUCTION TO THE THERAPEUTIC RECREATION PROCESS

Purposeful intervention in therapeutic recreation is accomplished through the employment of the therapeutic recreation process. The term *TR process* may seem mysterious when first encountered. It is, however, merely a problem-solving mechanism that therapeutic recreation specialists use to help clients meet needs and thereby maintain, restore, or promote health. It involves four components: assessment, planning, implementation, and evaluation.

Therapeutic recreation specialists initially work with clients to identify their health status, needs, and strengths. This is the *assessment phase*. Possible means to meet the needs are devised during the *planning phase*. Next, the planned intervention is tried out during the *implementation phase*. Finally, outcomes are appraised during the *evaluation phase*.

Assumptions underlying the TR process are as follows:

1. The TR process provides a systematic means for organizing the delivery of therapeutic recreation services.
2. The goal of the TR process is self-actualization by maximizing human potential through the maintenance, restoration, and promotion of health.
3. Rather than emphasizing what is "wrong" with the client, the TR process allows the therapeutic recreation specialist to concentrate on client strengths.

4. The client plays as large a role as possible in the TR process. The TR specialist attempts to allow as much control as is reasonable to remain with the client. The TR specialist is the client's partner who facilitates the client's progress toward meeting his or her needs.

5. The TR process helps to define the domain of therapeutic recreation practice.

The Relationship of the TR Specialist and Client

The therapeutic recreation specialist's relationship with the client is the means for applying the TR process. The TR specialist and client work together toward achievement of the client's optimal level of health. There is a mutuality in this relationship.

The relationship between the TR specialist and client is characterized by trust, mutual respect, and positive emotional feelings. The TR specialist is a person with whom the client associates positive outcomes as he or she experiences mastery, control, personal satisfaction, and feelings of effectiveness.

Effective relationships with clients are more easily achieved once we have examined our own values, beliefs, strengths, and limitations. Knowing ourselves is helpful in many ways. It helps us identify and relate more quickly to clients' problems because we can associate their problems with ones we have personally encountered. Having an awareness of our personal values and beliefs allows us to monitor ourselves so we will not attempt to force our own values and beliefs on clients. Acknowledging our strengths and weaknesses brings us to realize that, like our clients, we have strong points and limitations. Knowing our strengths, we can exploit them in helping clients. Understanding our limitations allows us to know when we have reached the limits of our helping abilities (Austin, 1982; Yura & Walsh, 1988). In short, knowing ourselves creates an awareness so that we can consciously use ourselves in therapeutic ways.

Knowing oneself also enhances the therapeutic recreation specialist's ability to foster three aspects that facilitate therapeutic relationships. These are (1) *genuineness*, or the ability to be aware of one's feelings and to be genuine in communicating these; (2) *unconditional positive regard*, or accepting another person nonjudgmentally and without conditions; and (3) *empathy*, or the ability to understand another individual so that you can "put yourself in his or her own place" (Rogers, 1961).

The therapeutic recreation process is applied both in treatment and rehabilitation. *Treatment* follows diagnosis of illness and focuses on reduction of symptoms. *Rehabilitation* is based on assessment of disability and limitations in functioning. It emphasizes the building of a full range of skills, from basic skills (e.g., grooming) to those that are more advanced (e.g., leisure and social skills) (Gudeman, 1988). Rehabilitation follows treatment in that it prepares ("re-ables") clients to function as independently as possible in the setting in which they will eventually reside.

In both treatment and rehabilitation, therapeutic recreation specialists concentrate on strengths rather than what is "wrong" with the client. Client residual abilities are brought into focus in therapeutic recreation. Therapeutic recreation specialists also attempt to allow as much control as possible to remain with the client.

Assessment

The first phase in the TR process is assessment. It is the foundation for all that follows. A sound assessment identifies the client's health status, needs, and strengths. In so doing, the assessment provides direction for the planning phase by developing pertinent data about the client. Assessment is a critical dimension because without adequate and valid data on which to base TR interventions, much time may be lost in effecting treatment and rehabilitation programs.

The therapeutic recreation specialist gathers, organizes, and analyzes assessment data. Following this, he or she must make clinical judgments as to the appropriate application of therapeutic recreation interventions in the client's treatment or rehabilitation program.

Efforts should be made to involve the client in assessment as soon and as much as possible. Some clients obviously will be unable to participate temporarily or will be able to take part only partially. Nevertheless, it is important for the therapeutic recreation specialist to develop rapport so that the client feels comfortable in sharing personal information to the best of his or her abilities. The client needs to have confidence that the information collected is to be used in a confidential manner for the sole purpose of helping him or her toward achieving optimal health.

Even when we establish excellent rapport, client assessment is not as straightforward as it might initially seem. That is, sometimes clients tell us what they believe we want to hear or what they perceive a "good" or "rational" client might say. This occurs with some regularity with chronic psychiatric clients, as we are warned by Kanter (1985), who states that professionals may focus too much on expressed wishes for independence to the exclusion of other concerns. Kanter has written:

> While we overemphasize the expressed wishes of chronic patients for independence, we often neglect their unarticulated needs to be cared for, understood, and accepted, as well as their fear of abandonment should they actually achieve a measure of autonomy. (p. 65)

Thus, the helping professional must look past the clients' verbalizations to examine behavioral expressions of needs, as well as go beyond the client to seek other sources of assessment data. Although the client is typically a chief source of information, other data sources are interviews with family members and friends, conferences with other health professionals, the results of testing, medical records, social histories, educational records, progress notes, and team meetings.

Methods of Assessment.   Observing and interviewing are the most commonly employed methods of assessment. Observations in therapeutic recreation are often done in unstructured recreational settings. These *naturalistic observations* are recorded by anecdotal notes, photographs, film, or a combination of these techniques. *Specific goal observations* take place in structured situations where the observer sets predetermined goals for the observation. For example, the therapeutic recreation specialist may structure a situation where frustration is likely to occur in order to observe the client's reaction. *Standardized observations* are of two types. One is the standardized instrument, such as a physical fitness test. The other type is the time-interval observation where the frequency of client behaviors is recorded for predetermined times. For example, the number of aggressive acts occurring during a one-hour period could be recorded (Schulman, 1978).

Checklists and *questionnaires* are means to gain specific types of information and save time in collecting it. Clients are sometimes asked to complete checklists and questionnaires. At other times, therapeutic recreation specialists collect the data, particularly in cases where clients cannot read or write, are disoriented, or do not have the strength or inclination to fill out the forms. Even when clients complete the checklists or questionnaires, the TR specialist normally has a follow-up interview to clarify and verify the information.

The *interview* is a time to gather information about the client, clarify items not understood, and observe the client's condition and behavior. The therapeutic recreation specialist permits the client to express himself or herself freely and to have any questions answered.

The primary areas examined in interviews by the therapeutic recreation specialist are leisure interests and behaviors. The TR specialist will typically ask clients about past leisure habits, the types of activities in which they participate, with whom they usually take part, and if they can identify recreation interests they may wish to pursue in the future. Regularly used techniques to enhance the interview process are (1) open-ended questions and (2) leisure inventories (Austin, 1982).

Open-ended questions to begin conversations might include those drawn from Yura and Walsh (1988). They follow:

Activity

- What do you do in an average day?
- Do you do anything to keep in shape?
- Do you try to keep up with local, national, or world news?

Acceptance of Self and Others

- What are your personal strengths? How do you feel about them?
- Have you identified limitations? What are they, and how do you feel about them?
- Describe your acceptance by family members, friends, people with whom you work. How do you feel about their acceptance?

Appreciation

- Which of your positive qualities and accomplishments have been noticed by others?
- What type of response do you get from others in terms of their appreciation of you?

Autonomy, Choice

- Would you describe yourself as being an independent person?
- When you are confronted with choices about your leisure, how do you handle these?

Belonging

- Describe your relationship with family members, friends, co-workers.
- With whom do you have your closest relationships?
- Are you a member of any community or church groups?

Challenge

- If you had to name a challenging situation in your life, what would you say?
- Do you get satisfaction from taking on challenges?

Confidence

- In what situations do you feel most secure or sure of yourself?
- What things do you do that make you most confident? Least confident?

Leisure

- What do you do for recreation and leisure? When? How often?

- What activities are most likely to make you feel refreshed?
- Are there activities you would like to try?

Personal Recognition and Esteem

- What do you do that brings you personal recognition and esteem?
- Who are the people who provide you with recognition?

Self-control, Self-determination

- How much ability do you have to be in control of your life or be responsible for yourself?
- What within you, or outside you, gives you ability to control and determine things for yourself? What takes away control?
- How do you account for your state of health?

Self-actualization, Self-fulfillment

- Are you fulfilling your goals in life?
- What do you see in your future in terms of realizing your potential?

Wholesome Body Image

- How do you and your body appear to you?
- How would others describe your body?

Value System

- What beliefs do you hold in terms of taking part in leisure?
- Identify beliefs you hold in regard to the worth of people? In regard to experiences in your life?

Most agencies and institutions that have therapeutic recreation services will design or adopt leisure inventories appropriate for use with their clients. It is common practice for agencies and institutions to develop leisure interest checklists. Others adopt instruments. Instruments sometimes adopted for use in TR assessment include the Mirenda Leisure Interest Finder (Mirenda, 1973), the Self Leisure Interest Profile (McDowell, 1974), the Leisure Activities Blank (McKechnie, 1974), the Avocational Activities Inventory (Overs, 1970), the Leisure Diagnostic Battery (Witt & Ellis, 1985), and the Comprehensive Leisure Rating Scale (Card, Compton, & Ellis, 1986).

General Factors to Consider in Assessment.   In addition to leisure patterns and interests, a number of factors are considered in therapeutic recreation assessment. Biographical data is normally gained from the admissions report and the initial interview with the client. This data includes name, address, telephone number, date of birth, place of birth, gender, marital status, ethnic group, religious preference, primary language spoken, education, and occupation. Additional information could include socioeconomic status, developmental or life stage, physical status, emotional status, coping patterns, interactional patterns, employment status, client views of illness and wellness, client's family, and client's community (Yura & Walsh, 1988).

Conclusion on Assessment.   Thorough assessment forms the foundation for the planning phase. Both *subjective data* gained from the client and *objective data* from other sources are required to determine client needs and strengths. The *needs list* and *strengths list* are the basis for the individual program plan, treatment plan, care plan, educational plan, or whatever term is used to describe the document that contains the plan of action for each client. The term *individual program plan* has been adopted for use in this chapter because it is frequently employed in the therapeutic recreation literature.

Planning

Following the identification of the client's needs and strengths during the assessment phase, the therapeutic recreation specialist and client are ready to move to the second stage of the TR process, the planning phase. During this phase priorities are set; goals are formulated; objectives are developed; programs, strategies, and approaches are specified; and means of evaluation are determined. When this phase has been completed, the TR specialist and client have a personalized therapeutic recreation program designed to meet the client's needs.

The therapeutic recreation plan usually becomes a component part of the client's total individual program plan developed by an interdisciplinary team (often termed the *treatment team*). The TR specialist typically works closely with a variety of other health professionals in determining the overall individual program plan. Group meetings are commonly held to formulate the final plan, which is then reviewed with the client.

More specifically, in the planning phase:

• Client needs and strengths are considered.
• Priorities are stipulated.
• Specific goals and objectives are stated, including the expected time for achievement.

- Specific activities or programs are selected as means to achieve goals and objectives.
- Responsibilities for helping the client are determined.
- An evaluation plan is agreed upon so both the when and how of evaluation are made clear.

Setting priorities involves an analysis of the identified needs in order to determine which needs require the professional help of the therapeutic recreation specialist and which are most urgent. The client should be included in this determination, if possible, because it is desirable to engage the client in the planning process as soon as is practical.

Goals flow directly from the needs list. Goals reflect sought outcomes that are directed toward satisfaction of the client's needs. They are therefore stated in terms of the *client's* behavior and describe proposed changes in the individual in broad terms. Because goals describe client outcomes, they give direction to the TR specialist, client, and others in terms of knowing what results are intended from the program.

Objectives are developed to specify client behaviors related to reaching goals. Objectives enable clients to achieve goals and consequently are sometimes referred to as *enabling objectives*. Usually three to six enabling objectives are needed in order to reach a goal. Objectives therefore offer a means for the TR specialist and client to organize their efforts as they break goals down into manageable behaviors that direct program design and offer a basis for evaluation.

Because the needs list serves as the basis for the goals set, the strengths list is drawn on when objectives are formulated. That is, objectives take advantage of the strengths that the client brings with him or her. Strengths can range from possessing a particular leisure skill or ability to having the support of family and friends.

An illustration may add to a clearer understanding of goals and objectives. A need of a client might be to interact with others through verbal expression. This need could translate into a goal stated as: "Increases verbal interactions with others within one month." An enabling objective would be: "Answers questions posed by staff." This objective would provide direction so that the TR specialist would know to structure opportunities for this occurrence by scheduling a social type of activity in which the client has some amount of ability. The objective would also be readily measurable so it could be a basis for evaluation of progress toward the goal.

Programs flow out of the goals and objectives. Programs provide further specificity to the plan. The therapeutic recreation specialist, in conference with the client, prescribes programs or activities for client participation that offer opportunities for the sought outcomes of the plan (i.e., goals and objectives). As has been mentioned, the program area selected needs to be one in which the client has skills or the ability to develop skills.

Perhaps another example will be helpful in illustrating the program component. A client who has the goal of learning stress management techniques may be placed in a stress reduction group in which relaxation training techniques are learned and practiced. The strategy used may be to begin with the therapeutic recreation specialist initially working with the client in a small group so the client may become comfortable in doing relaxation training before moving to the regular stress reduction class that meets daily in the gymnasium with 15 clients taking part. One element of the plan would be for the TR specialist to be given the responsibility of determining, with the client, when the client was ready to enter the regular class.

Finally, once the programs or activities for the client's participation have been chosen, a description of *evaluation* procedures needs to be determined. The interdisciplinary team typically determines when the client's progress will be evaluated (e.g., weekly, monthly, etc.) and what documentation procedures will be followed (e.g., keeping daily progress notes). Depending on the outcome of the evaluation, the client's schedule of activities may be retained or revised to accommodate the needs of the client.

The planning phase culminates with the producing of the individual program plan. This plan serves as a "blueprint for action" (Yura & Walsh, 1988).

Implementation

The implementation phase is the action phase of the therapeutic recreation process. Implementation involves the actual execution of the individual program plan by the therapeutic recreation specialist and client. The TR specialist assumes responsibility for coordinating client-focused and goal-directed activities consistent with the proposed plan of action. He or she guides the client until the client can assume self-responsibility. The TR specialist also makes certain that the client's actions and responses are fully documented throughout the implementation phase.

Therapeutic recreation programs are tailored to the needs, capacities, and degree of readiness of each client. Programs focus on using existing strengths and interests as foundations for treatment/rehabilitation. Progressive, graded programs offer developmental sequencing for the acquisition of skills as the client progresses. The plan should stipulate the frequency and duration of the client's participation in each activity scheduled.

Most who have been acutely ill would agree that leisure is unattainable for persons who are severely ill. Initially, the client may engage in activities without any pretense of experiencing recreation or leisure. In fact, it would be naive to believe that clients who are seriously ill are ready or able to make self-determined choices. For example, clients with neurological dysfunction, Alzheimer's disease, or chronic depression may suffer from impaired functioning to the point that they cannot exercise freedom of choice (Shank & Kinney, 1987).

Shank and Kinney (1987) have portrayed this situation in a paper on clinical practice in TR. They have written:

> If leisure is a premature issue in certain clinical situations, what should a therapeutic recreation specialist do? Without abandoning service provision to individuals with these functional limitations, therapeutic recreation specialists can use recreation activity as an intervention addressing psychosocial needs associated with the stress caused by the illness or disability. In this sense, the concerns are basically "pre-leisure."
>
> The concept of "pre-leisure" behavior is an important one in understanding clinical intervention. The very notion of leisure implies . . . freedom from control. Yet freedom from control requires psychological, social, and affective functioning at a level to insure that free choice does not result in maladaptive outcomes. The basic fact that some individuals are not in control of themselves renders the question of leisure momentarily moot. Thus the central concern becomes one of helping the individual achieve or regain those pre-leisure competencies that are the necessary foundations for subsequent leisure issues addressed at another time. (pp. 68, 69)

Helplessness and despair frequently occur in clients whose coping mechanisms have been severely tested by the stress of dealing with health problems. Clients undergoing psychiatric treatment, physical rehabilitation, and nursing home care seem particularly subject to feelings of helplessness. Research by Rodin has suggested that helping people regain a sense of control over their lives offers them hope and improves their morale (Bule, 1988). Once individuals begin to experience a restoration of their morale, they develop a renewed sense of resolution or determination to conquer their health problems.

Because of the severity of the client's health condition or because of feelings of helplessness, the therapeutic recreation specialist may initially carefully select therapeutic activities that provide the structure and level of demand that can be beneficial for the client. Once the client's morale has been enhanced, he or she can move to activities that are truly recreational in nature. Recreation represents experiences that are restorative but are largely done for pleasure and enjoyment. Recreation activities are chosen by the client in close collaboration with the TR specialist. Ultimately, the client may be able to exercise perceived control by selecting leisure activities that represent growth opportunities. The highest form of therapeutic recreation participation is that which the client finds self-rewarding and is not a product of external compulsion.

The Therapeutic Recreation Specialist. Interpersonal, observational, decision-making, and technical skills are called for on the part of the therapeutic recreation specialist during the implementation phase of the therapeutic recreation process. These skills are necessary to put the program plan into action.

Interpersonal skills are particularly critical to the success of the implementation phase. Interactions need to be goal directed and purposeful within an accepting, nonthreatening atmosphere. The significance of creating a positive climate has been proclaimed by Rogers (1980), who has written:

> On the basis of experience I have found that if I can help bring about a climate marked by genuineness, prizing, and understanding, then exciting things happen. Persons and groups in such a climate move away from rigidity and toward flexibility, away from static living toward process living, away from dependence toward autonomy, away from defensiveness toward self-acceptance, away from being predictable toward an unpredictable creativity. They exhibit living proof of an actualizing tendency. (pp. 43, 44)

During interactions with clients, the therapeutic recreation specialist continually makes observations. Such observations document the progress of the client, as well as verify that the plan of action is correct. Client reactions are documented in the form of progress notes. If the plan is not working as expected, decisions need to be made in regard to modifying the goals and objectives or the approach to achieving the goals and objectives.

Technical skills relate to the therapeutic recreation specialist's knowledge of the properties of activities and leadership abilities in conducting activities. The TR specialist is action oriented in organizing activities, teaching activity skills, offering positive feedback, providing psychological support, and processing with clients on their participation following activities. In order to demonstrate the therapeutic use of an activity, the TR specialist must be familiar with the demands it makes on clients, as well as anticipated outcomes from participation.

Concluding Statement Implementation. In sum, the implementation phase of the therapeutic recreation process includes the actions of the therapeutic recreation specialist in working with clients to execute the individual program plan (IPP). In doing so, it is important that the actions of the TR specialist are consistent with the IPP. The TR specialist must remain cognizant of the goal-directed nature of his or her responsibilities in conducting activities so that they are organized and carried out in a purposeful manner and do not become "activity for the sake of activity." It is equally important to the success of the implementation phase that there is adequate documentation of client actions and responses as the plan is executed. As a result of a high level of performance on the part of the therapeutic recreation specialist, it is anticipated that positive strides will be made by the client. The direction and amount of these changes are determined during the evaluation phase.

Evaluation

Evaluation is the fourth and final phase in the therapeutic recreation process. In this phase, the goals and objectives in the individual program plan are appraised. The primary question to answer in the evaluation phase is, How did the client respond to the planned intervention?

Evaluation reveals if the plan has been effective or if it requires revision. If the planned program has not had the desired effect, it needs to be modified, reimplemented, and reevaluated. This cyclic process continues as long as it is necessary.

The same methods employed in completing the initial assessment may be used in the evaluation phase. Common means of doing evaluation are to conduct a review of progress notes, to interview the client so he or she may respond retrospectively following participation in the treatment/ rehabilitation program, and to hold an interdisciplinary team meeting to discuss the client's progress. Evaluation procedures should retrieve evaluation information from several independent sources in order to make certain that data are reliable and valid (Austin, 1982).

As has been indicated, it is essential to involve clients in all phases of the therapeutic recreation process to the fullest extent of their capacities. This principle should, of course, be followed in the evaluation phase, where clients can help the therapeutic recreation specialist to determine the effectiveness of the program in achieving sought outcomes (Austin, 1982).

SOME COMMENTS ON THE TR PROCESS

The therapeutic recreation process is an orderly, systematic means of determining a client's needs, formulating goals and objectives, establishing an action plan, implementing it, and evaluating the extent to which the plan was effective in achieving the stated goals and objectives. The basic belief that underlies the TR process is that every person has the potential for improving his or her level of health, given sound planning and proper resources.

Universal Application of the TR Process. Although the therapeutic recreation process is commonly associated with agencies and institutions that are highly clinical in nature, the TR process is not restricted to clinical settings. The use of the TR process is not confined to hospitals or treatment and rehabilitation centers. It is a systematic process that can guide therapeutic recreation in nursing homes, corrections facilities, community-based programs for persons who are disabled, or wherever recreation is used with therapeutic intent in goal-directed programs. Nor is the TR process limited to use with "special populations." It may be applied with any individual who desires to maintain or improve his or her level of health (Austin, 1982).

Direct Experience in Activities.   Bandura's (1977) self-efficacy theory deals with how people enhance their perceptions of their ability to produce intended results, or to be effective in what they do. According to Bandura, individuals derive information about themselves and their ability to produce desired outcomes, or cope with situations, from four sources. These are performance, vicarious experiences, verbal persuasion, and experiencing sensations of arousal. Of these, performance (or direct experience) plays the most important role in creating feelings of self-efficacy or effectiveness. It is through direct experience in carefully chosen activities that the majority of therapeutic benefits are derived during the therapeutic recreation process. The therapeutic recreation profession has been heavily influenced by the Gestalt therapy of Frederick (Fritz) Perls, who emphasized experiencing and learning by doing (Austin, 1982), and by Carl Rogers (1980), who in his person-centered therapy stressed staying close to "the earthiness of real experience" (p. 44) within a warm, caring, and nonjudgmental atmosphere.

Activities as Modalities for Treatment and Rehabilitation.   Almost any activity typically conceived to be a recreation or leisure activity may be used for therapeutic purpose within therapeutic recreation. Therapeutic media regularly employed in therapeutic recreation include play, games, sports, physical fitness activities, dance and movement, crafts, expressive arts, outdoor recreation activities, and social activities. Therapeutic recreation specialists also conduct individual and group leisure counseling in order to promote client self-awareness of leisure values and attitudes, as well as to prepare clients for community living.

Characteristics of Therapeutic Activities.   In order for activities to hold the potential for therapeutic outcomes, they need to be conducted so that they possess the following characteristics. Therapeutic activities:

1. *Are goal directed.* Therapeutic recreation activities are directed toward a purpose. They are not "time fillers" but rather are done for a reason. The goal may be as general as involving the client in something outside of himself or herself, thus allowing him or her less time to dwell on problems. Or the goal may be very specific, such as gaining a particular social or leisure skill.

2. *Require active participation by clients.* Self-determination is important in the sense that clients are as active as possible in both choosing activities and having a role in affecting the outcome of the activities. Clients need to be involved to the largest extent possible in determining the activity in order to exercise control. They need to feel that their participation meaningfully affects the results of the activity in order to gain feelings of self-efficacy and competence.

3. *Have meaning and value to the client.* The client needs to learn to approach activities not as a requirement but as an opportunity to achieve an end. Therapeutic recreation specialists often process (i.e., discuss) the activity with clients following participation so that clients may gain personal awareness of behaviors, feelings, and outcomes achieved as a result of taking part.

4. *Offer potential for pleasure and satisfaction.* Ideally, the primary motivation for the client lies in the pleasurable, satisfying experience gained from participation. Even where gratification is not immediate, activities should make it possible ultimately to gain pleasure and satisfaction.

5. *Provide opportunity for mastery.* Activities need to offer the opportunity for gaining and displaying mastery. Feelings of competence lead clients to feelings of self-efficacy and enjoyment with accompanying heightened interest in the activity. Clients should not be expected to participate in activities in which they are likely to be embarrassed or to fail.

6. *Are carefully selected with the guidance of the TR specialist.* As Gump and Sutton-Smith (1955) wrote years ago: "Activities have a reality and a behavior-influencing power in their own right. An activity, once entered, will exclude some potential behaviors, necessitate other behaviors, and, finally, encourage or discourage still other behaviors." Because activities make inherent demands, the therapeutic recreation specialist needs to draw on his or her professional knowledge of activities in order to help clients select activities that will possess characteristics suitable to meet the clients' needs and that are within the clients' capabilities.

SUMMARY

The purpose of this chapter was to provide an introduction to the therapeutic recreation process as an element essential to therapeutic recreation. The TR process was defined, and each of its four components was discussed.

Also covered was the relationship of the therapeutic recreation specialist with the client. This relationship was presented as the means through which the TR process is executed. Final comments in the chapter concerned the universal application of the TR process, the emphasis on direct experience in therapeutic recreation, activities as modalities for treatment and rehabilitation, and characteristics of therapeutic activities.

READING COMPREHENSION QUESTIONS

1. Do you agree with the definition of therapeutic recreation found at the beginning of the chapter?

2. Can you explain why the TR process might be termed *the essence of therapeutic recreation?*

3. What are the four phases of the TR process?

4. Do you agree with Mobily that the distinguishing feature of therapeutic recreation is that it uses recreation as a means to an end?

5. What are the assumptions on which the TR process rests?

6. Describe how the relationship between the TR specialist and client is the means for applying the TR process.

7. Do you agree that self-knowledge is important to the therapeutic use of self? If so, what things should be explored in becoming self-aware?

8. What three aspects of relationships have been emphasized by Carl Rogers?

9. Can you differentiate between treatment and rehabilitation?

10. Describe how therapeutic recreation specialists emphasize client strengths, rather than what is "wrong" with the client.

11. Why is assessment critical to the provision of treatment and rehabilitation?

12. What is the role of the client in the TR process?

13. Why should TR specialists look beyond client verbalizations in conducting needs assessment?

14. What are data sources for assessment?

15. Describe methods that may be used in TR assessment.

16. Do you believe that the open-ended assessment questions in the chapter would be helpful to a TR specialist?

17. What are some assessment instruments used in TR?

18. What biographical data are normally collected? From what sources?

19. What are subjective data? Objective data?

20. What are some names for the document that contains the action plan or blueprint for action resulting from the planning phase? In what setting do you feel each would be appropriate?

21. What transpires during the planning phase?

22. What is the relationship between goals and objectives?

23. What is the relationship between the list of client needs and goals? Between the list of client strengths and objectives?

24. Can you describe some strengths that clients might possess?

25. Why must TR activities remain "client focused" and "goal directed"?

26. Do you agree with the content of the quotation taken from Shank and Kinney's paper? Why or why not?

27. Can you differentiate between the expressions *therapeutic activities, recreation activities,* and *leisure activities?*

28. What skills are called for on the part of the therapeutic recreation specialist during the implementation phase?

29. Why the "big deal" about activities being conducted in a goal-directed, purposeful manner?

30. Explain why documentation is a major concern during the implementation phase.

31. In what respect may the TR process be cyclic?

32. Identify examples of methods of doing TR evaluation.

33. Can the TR process be applied outside of hospitals or treatment and rehabilitation centers?

34. What is the significance of direct experience in TR? How may Perls and Rogers have influenced TR?

35. What makes activities therapeutic?

SUGGESTED LEARNING ACTIVITIES

1. Interview three TR specialists regarding how each defines therapeutic recreation. In a 3- to 5-page paper, compare and contrast their definitions with definitions found in the TR literature. Conclude the paper with your own definition of therapeutic recreation that you have constructed after exploring the topic.

2. Review the literature for activities and exercises that could be used to help TR students increase self-awareness. Submit the one you like best to your instructor on a 5- by 8-inch card and/or lead it in class.

3. Working with your instructor and classmates, contact TR agencies to obtain copies of TR assessment instruments. Place these on reserve at the library so all current and future students can have access to them.

4. Invite TR specialists from several different agencies to come into your classroom to discuss (1) how they employ the TR process and (2) their perceptions of the importance of establishing and maintaining a therapeutic relationship.

5. Read over the characteristics of therapeutic activities listed in the chapter. Then, in a 3- to 5-page paper, rank these in importance and justify your ranking.

REFERENCES

Austin, D. R. (1982). *Therapeutic recreation: Processes and techniques.* New York: John Wiley & Sons.

Bandura, A. (1977). Self efficacy: Toward a unifying theory of behavioral change. *Psychological Review, 84,* 191–215.

BULE, J. (1988). Control studies bode better health in aging. *The APA Monitor, 19*(7), 20.

CARD, J., COMPTON, D., & ELLIS, G. (1986). Reliability and validity of the Comprehensive Leisure Rating Scale. *Journal of Expanding Horizons in Therapeutic Recreation, 1,* 21–27.

GUDEMAN, J. E. (1988). The person with chronic mental illness. In A. M. Nicholi (Ed.), *The New Harvard Guide to Psychiatry* (pp. 714–727). Cambridge, MA: The Belknap Press of Harvard University Press.

GUMP, P., & SUTTON-SMITH, B. (1955). Activity-setting and social interaction: A field study. *The American Journal of Orthopsychiatry, 25,* 755–760.

KANTER, J. S. (1985). Psychosocial assessment in community treatment. In J. S. Kanter (Ed.), *Clinical issues in treating the chronic mentally ill* (pp. 63–75). San Francisco: Jossey-Bass.

McDOWELL, C. F. (1974). Toward a healthy leisure mode: Leisure counseling. *Therapeutic Recreation Journal, 8*(3), 96–104.

McKECHNIE, G. E. (1974). Psychological foundations of leisure counseling: An empirical strategy. *Threapeutic Recreation Journal, 8*(1), 4–16.

MIRENDA, J. J. (1973). Mirenda Leisure Interest Finder. In A. Epperson, R. Mirenda, R. Overs, & G. T. Wilson (Eds.), *Leisure counseling kit.* Washington, DC: American Alliance for Health, Physical Education, and Recreation.

MOBILY, K. E. (1985). A philosophical analysis of therapeutic recreation: What does it mean to say "we can be therapeutic?" Part II. *Therapeutic Recreation Journal, 19*(2), 7–14.

MOBILY, K. E. (1987). A quiescent reply to Lee. *Therapeutic Recreation Journal, 21*(2), 81–83.

OVERS, R. P. (1970). A model for avocational counseling. *Journal of Health, Physical Education and Recreation, 41*(2), 28–36.

ROGERS, C. R. (1961). *On becoming a person: A therapist's view of psychotherapy.* Boston: Houghton Mifflin.

ROGERS, C. R. (1980). *A way of being.* Boston: Houghton Mifflin.

SCHULMAN, E. D. (1978). *Intervention in human services* (2nd ed.). St. Louis: C. V. Mosby.

SHANK, J., & KINNEY, T. (1987). On the neglect of clinical practice. In C. Sylvester, J. L. Hemingway, R. Howe-Murphy, K. Mobily, & P. A. Shank (Eds.), *Philosophy of therapeutic recreation: Ideas and issues* (pp. 65–73). Alexandria, VA: National Recreation and Park Association.

WITT, P., & ELLIS, G. (1985). Development of a short form to assess perceived freedom in leisure. *Journal of Leisure Research, 17,* 225–233.

YURA, H., & WALSH, M. B. (1988). *The nursing process: Assessment, planning, implementing, evaluating* (5th ed.). Norwalk, CT: Appleton & Lange.

4

Psychiatry and Mental Health

W. B. (TERRY) KINNEY AND JUDY SOTTILE

OBJECTIVES

- Understand the distinction between mental health and mental disorder within the context of our society.
- Be aware of the current classifications and characteristics of major mental disorders.
- Understand the purpose of therapeutic recreation within the context of treatment for mental disorder.
- Be aware of the relationship of therapeutic recreation to various treatment settings and to the treatment team.
- Know the process of therapeutic recreation within the context of treatment for mental disorder.

DEFINITION OF MENTAL HEALTH

Defining what constitutes mental health and its opposite, mental disorder, has always been a difficult task. In one of the classic discussions of mental health, Hartman (1939) chose to base his explanation on the process of adaptation. He states that it is the individual's adaptation to the demands of reality that determines mental health or mental disorder. Although Hartman does not elaborate on the course that adaptation may take, we can assume that it is the direction of that adaptation that decides whether we will function in a mentally healthy or mentally unhealthy manner. The crucial point to consider is that we may adapt to reality by developing mentally unhealthy behavior, such as withdrawal from reality.

The extent to which we can use our internal skills and strengths and bring to bear the various supportive elements we have at our disposal is the extent to which we can master the demands of the reality that we face. The utilization of these skills, strengths, and resources is termed *coping* (Mechanic, 1976). Coping is combined with the use of certain defenses, such as rationalization, denial, sublimation, and so on, to allow us to face challenging tasks and demands without becoming overwhelmed by anxiety. According to Mechanic (1976), "Successful application of skills and capacities [coping] requires that the individual maintain control over feelings of inadequacy and uncertainty and protect against a sense of futility" (p. 2). Through the use of defenses, the individual maintains a sense of equilibrium and esteem while attacking the demands of everyday reality in the best manner possible.

As we develop from our youngest days to our oldest days, we are faced with the issue of how we interpret and deal with reality. Part of the process of human development involves recognizing, developing, and learning how to use the judgments, skills, and internal resources we have at our disposal. These judgments, skills, and internal resources are termed *ego strengths*, and it is our use of these ego strengths that determines our success in coping.

It must be remembered that the characteristics of positive mental health are the culmination of successful human development. The course of that development involves facing a series of stages (or crises) during which we face new levels of challenges and expectations. Table 4.1 shows those levels in a developmental perspective, along with the key issues and ego strengths that need to be addressed and developed.

We all exhibit some characteristics of positive mental health and negative mental health depending on how well we have developed our ego strengths, how strong our social support system is, and the intensity of perceived stressors. Very few of us consistently operate at a very high level of positive mental health. The actuality is that we tend to vary from day to day and sometimes even from moment to moment.

How then do we determine who is mentally healthy and who is mentally unhealthy? The rather vague answer is that the broad rules and expectations of our society determine the level of mental health. Part of human development is becoming acculturated; that is, learning the expectations and rules of the culture in which we live and deciding the extent to which we wish to internalize or reject the acceptable behaviors of our society. As society changes and becomes more or less tolerant of behavior that deviates from its norms, the extent and nature of mental disorder likewise change.

If the yardstick for mental disorder is so broadly defined and ever-changing, who then needs treatment in a psychiatric program? How are people identified as requiring professional help? It must be remembered that behaviors that appear to represent mental disorder may be the result of many legitimate precipitants, for example, the side effects of medication. In such a case, bizarre or deviant behavior would not be a result of

Table 4.1
Developmental Levels and Associated Behaviors

BEHAVIORS INDICATING POSITIVE DEVELOPMENT	BEHAVIORS INDICATING NEGATIVE ADJUSTMENT

Level I: The Development of Trust

1. Invests in relationships	1. Avoids relationships
2. Has an open, nonsuspicious attitude	2. Is suspicious, closed, guarded
3. Welcomes touching	3. Is a loner and unhappy
4. Maintains good eye contact	4. Maintains poor eye contact
5. Shares self and possessions	5. Does not share self or possessions

Level II: The Development of Autonomy

1. Is independent	1. Frequently procrastinates
2. Resists being dominated	2. Has difficulty working alone
3. Stands up for self	3. Needs much structure
4. Is assertive when necessary	4. Has difficulty making decisions
	5. Is easily influenced

Level III: The Development of Initiative

1. Is a self-starter	1. Is easily depressed
2. Accepts challenges	2. Has poor self-esteem
3. Assumes leadership roles	3. Maintains poor eye contact
4. Sets goals and pursues them	4. Has low energy level

Level IV: The Development of Competence

1. Wonders how things work	1. Is timid, withdrawn
2. Brings projects to completion	2. Is overly obedient
3. Enjoys variety of projects	3. Frequently procrastinates
4. Enjoys learning	4. Is a passive observer rather than an active participant
5. Enjoys experimenting	5. Is unsure of own ability

Level V: The Development of Identity

1. Comfortable with sex-role identity	1. Has doubts about sex-role identity
2. Takes active interest in social engagement	2. Lacks confidence
3. Plans for future	3. Is overly hostile to authority
4. Appropriately challenges adult authority	4. Is overly obedient
5. Is self-accepting	5. Tends to be self-rejecting

mental disorder but of a physical, external problem. In order for behavior to be questioned as indicating mental disorder, that behavior must be in evidence for some duration and be consistently inappropriate over a period of time. Except in the case of individuals who cause serious harm to themselves or others, the question largely becomes individualized based on the input and influence of the individual exhibiting the behavior in question, the family, and sometimes significant others such as close friends, employers, teachers, or members of the clergy. As a result of the protection of individual rights, it is relatively difficult to have someone hospitalized involuntarily. Most psychiatric admissions are by voluntary means. For those individuals who make the decision to seek psychiatric treatment, there are a variety of treatment settings (e.g., inpatient, outpatient, partial hospitalization) that are available depending on the individual's needs.

CLASSIFICATION OF PSYCHIATRIC DISORDERS

Individuals undergoing psychiatric treatment, like anyone else, will exhibit a variety of behaviors that become fairly representative of their style and ability to cope with life demands and situations. Careful documentation and analysis of those particular behaviors termed *pathological*—that is, contributing to mental disorder—have enabled us to develop a classification system for diagnosing conditions of psychiatric disturbance. The consideration of both negative or pathological behavior as well as positive or behavior strengths allows clinical staff to develop approaches and plans for *clinical interventions*, such as interventions designed to further strengthen positive behaviors and reduce negative behaviors.

The *Diagnostic and Statistical Manual of Mental Disorders III, Revised* (DSM-IIIR) (1987) is the reference commonly used by clinicians in making diagnoses. The DSM-IIIR provides clear descriptions of diagnostic categories and a coding system for the assignment, treatment, and research analysis of various disorders. Each individual is assessed on five separate axes in order to give attention to various disorders, environmental concerns, and functional aspects that might otherwise be missed if the focus were on assessing a single presenting problem.

Because DSM-IIIR contains over one hundred diagnoses and categories, we will discuss only those that the therapeutic recreation specialist is most likely to encounter in various treatment settings.

Schizophrenia

Schizophrenia involves highly distorted abilities in perception, thinking, emotion, speech, and physical activity. It is an altered sense of reality displayed by inconsistency in mental functions and expected actions. For example, an individual may show remarkably *flat affect*—that is, display no emotion—or even appear happy while describing a very sad or unfortunate happening. This is the characteristic *splitting* that has led lay persons mistakenly to describe schizophrenia as "split personality."

In actuality, schizophrenia is a disturbance represented by many different causes and symptoms that result in a wide variety of clinical manifestations. This makes it an extremely difficult disorder to diagnose and requires clinicians to observe and document pathological behavior over a long period of time—at least six months.

The diagnosis may, for example, apply equally well to the hypervigilant scientist who suspects others of plotting against him, to the homemaker who believes she is controlled by her dead mother's voice, and to the withdrawn and apathetic teenager who broods incessantly on the reality of existence. (Waldinger, 1984, p. 82)

Another factor that confuses diagnosis is that individuals are not always consistent in their display of pathological behavior. The individual may be totally unable to function at one time, and a short time later, perhaps a few days or weeks later, be functioning at a fairly high level.

According to Waldinger, the classic symptoms are as follows:

1. *Hallucinations*—usually of an auditory nature consisting of sounds or voices, sometimes even continuous dialogues. It is not unusual for schizophrenic persons who commit violent crimes to be obeying the voices they hear issuing them commands.

2. *Delusions*—false beliefs that the individual clings to despite facts or logic that prove otherwise. Usually these relate to control over one's thinking, for example, that someone can read one's mind or control one's thoughts in some way. Delusions of persecution are common with some of the subtypes of schizophrenia.

3. *Emotional Disturbance*—shown by the lack of affect referred to earlier.

4. *Volitional Disturbance*—a difficulty or inability to participate in active involvement because of a belief that one can carry out great destruction and at the same time a terrible fear of doing so. The result is that the individual become "paralyzed" to do anything consequential.

5. *Disturbed Speech*—often revealed by incoherence, use of "made up" words, or thought patterns that do not logically follow one another.

6. *Disturbed Motor Activity*—may consist of extreme inactivity or overactivity; strange, repetitive behavior; mimicking; and stiff, machinelike behavior.

The DSM-IIIR identifies a number of subtypes of schizophrenia. These are the following:

1. disorganized type
2. catatonic type
3. paranoid type
4. residual type
5. undifferentiated type

Mood Disorders

Mood disorders are disorders of affect, that is, emotion; prior to DSM-IIIR they were referred to as affective disorders. They include depression and mania, and may vary from the extreme of one to the extreme of the other.

A manic episode is a markedly distinct period of elevated mood characterized by extremely high energy and activity. During this period, the individual may exhibit several of the following behaviors:

1. inflated self-esteem and grandiosity
2. decreased need for sleep
3. excessive talkativeness
4. flight of ideas, i.e., sense of fast, racing thoughts
5. distractibility
6. increased physical activity
7. increased risk taking

A depressive episode is an intense feeling of sadness, or of not caring anymore, or of discouragement. All of us at one time or another feel depressed. The difference between "everyday" depression and clinical depression is one of time, intensity, and degree of impact on our functioning.

A major depressive syndrome, according to DSM-IIIR, consists of evidence of at least five of the following symptoms that represent a change from previous functioning and are evidenced most of the day and nearly every day over at least two weeks:

1. depressed mood
2. markedly diminished interest or pleasure in activities
3. significant weight loss or gain when not dieting
4. insomnia or oversleeping
5. excessive or markedly decreased physical activity
6. fatigue or loss of energy
7. feelings of worthlessness or excessive or inappropriate guilt
8. diminished ability to think or concentrate
9. recurrent thoughts of dying or of *suicidal ideation*, that is, thoughts of committing suicide but not having a specific plan to carry it out or making an actual attempt at carrying it out

It should be remembered that many of the symptoms of depression (and other disorders as well) are common experiences in life for all of us. This points up the fact that individuals in psychiatric treatment are just like us—human beings, albeit ones who are having difficulty dealing with the stresses of reality at a particular time in their lives. The difference, according to Waldinger (1984) may be pointed out by examining the following questions:

1. How intense is the mood, and how long does it last?
2. Do physical symptoms accompany the mood change?
3. Does the mood disrupt normal daily activities?
4. Is the person's capacity to view reality appropriately disturbed?
5. Does the mood put the person or other individuals in danger?

In some cases, individuals may experience both manic and depressive episodes—not at the same time, but as wide swings in behavior and feelings ranging from extremely manic to extremely depressed. These are called bipolar disorders, or more commonly, manic-depressive disorders. Other individuals may swing less widely in their affective shifts and exhibit the symptomatic behaviors in a much less extreme fashion. Mood swings may last for several days or months. Bipolar disorders tend to respond quite well to medication; however, a frequent problem is that individuals start feeling better and think they no longer need their medication, thereby starting the cyclical process over again.

Anxiety Disorders and Phobic Neuroses

Anxiety is a commonly used term to describe "nervousness," an emotion experienced by everyone at various times. Clinically, however, anxiety takes on a much sharper focus. Anxiety can be better described as intense fear or panic and clinically it appears where it is not justified, where there is no real reason for fear or panic. Panic attacks may result in the individual's feeling a shortness of breath, dizziness, trembling, sweating, and perhaps nausea. Other feelings may be a sense of depersonalization (a strange sense of unreality about one's self or the environment), chest pains, a fear of dying, or a fear of "going crazy" or losing control.

In psychiatric settings, panic disorders are frequently associated with phobias. Phobias are continuous, unrealistic fears about an object, situation, or event that come to dominate an individual's thinking. Individuals become obsessed with avoiding that object, situation, or event, and go to extraordinary steps to do so. Many of us experience unrealistic fears, for example, a fear of flying or a fear of snakes. Such a fear becomes a phobia when it causes panic to the extent that an individual becomes almost unable to function.

DSM-IIIR provides three general types of phobias: *agoraphobia*, a fear of being caught in an open place (for example, outside the home) where one feels he or she cannot escape or get help in the event of a panic attack; *social phobia*, a fear of not being able to perform appropriately in social situations; and *simple phobia*, a fear of a generally specific object or situation, such as snakes or flying.

Obsessive compulsive disorders are an interesting subtype of the anxiety disorders (not to be confused with obsessive compulsive personality disorder). As an anxiety disorder, the obsessive compulsive person experiences persistent thoughts (an obsession) that are extremely discomforting and cause a great deal of anxiety. For example, the individual may have thoughts about killing his or her own child, something that he or she recoils from in horror but cannot stop thinking about. The compulsion is a particular behavior or routine that helps the individual control the unpleasant obsession. Compulsions tend to reflect fairly rigid, time-consuming behaviors that serve to "cleanse" the individual of those terrible thoughts. Continuous cleaning of a house or apartment for hours on end or a long and tedious ritual of hand washing are examples. Of course, the compulsions do not completely control the obsession, and the individual becomes locked into a frightening cycle of increased compulsive, ritualistic behavior.

Personality Disorders

Many behaviors associated with this category bear a resemblance to other categories discussed. Obsessive compulsive behaviors, paranoid behaviors, and mood-related behaviors are part of personality disorders as well as other categories. The primary difference is one of level and degree of dysfunction. The personality disorders are lifelong patterns of maladaptive behaviors. Although many people suffering with psychiatric problems are truly suffering (they know something is very wrong with them), the person with a personality disorder tends to view his behavior as healthy, not deviant. Thus, the problems he creates are someone else's, not his. Individuals with personality disorders do not tend to seek help voluntarily. Instead, they usually are coerced into treatment by family members and become very reluctant clients. These individuals typically behave in ways that make people very angry. They always know what "buttons to push" and seem to be masters at manipulating others. Obviously, they are very difficult to treat, and the failure rate with them is extremely high.

DSM-IIIR describes the following personality disorders:

paranoid personality
schizoid personality
schizotypal personality
antisocial personality
borderline personality
histrionic personality
narcissistic personality
avoidant personality
dependent personality
obsessive compulsive personality
passive aggressive personality

Only one disorder, borderline personality, will be described in any detail, because that particular disorder appears to be significantly increasing in incidence. Borderline individuals have a number of strengths that make them, initially, appear to be high functioning. As you become more familiar with the true character of the individual, however, a number of typical problem behaviors emerge. The most typical pathological defense used by the borderline is splitting. As a result of "a developmental failure to integrate and to accept positive and negative feelings about himself, [the individual] divides his world into either good and nurturing objects or punitive and rejecting objects" (O'Brien, Caldwell, & Transeau, 1985). Borderline individuals see the world and themselves in all good or all bad terms. In order to protect themselves internally, they project the bad parts of themselves onto others and react to those now externalized bad things with tremendous anger. Borderline persons frequently do not feel alive and constantly seek stimuli to reassure themselves of their existence. Borderline persons also have a tremendous need to control their environment, develop tremendous manipulation skills, and become involved in destructive "people games," pitting staff against staff or patient against patient. Slashing—the act of cutting oneself purposely but not seriously enough to be considered suicidal—is a frequent behavior of some borderlines. This cutting is both a manipulative behavior and an attempt to affirm that one is alive by seeing one's own blood and feeling the wound. Other characteristics may include being impulsive in a self-destructive manner (e.g., engaging in frequent, inadvisable sexual involvements without considering the consequences), a fear of being alone, engagement in stormy interpersonal relationships that are intense and unstable, and marked shifts in mood.

Because the borderline personality engages in such manipulation, it is very difficult for staff to form the type of relationship needed to create clinical progress. Consequently, treatment is frequently unsuccessful, with the client leaving the program feeling as though he or she is the victim of an uncaring and incompetent staff. The borderline individual typically experiences many repeated hospitalizations, with intermittent times of relatively stable functioning.

Prevalence of Mental Disorders

The most ambitious attempt to determine prevalence rates has been made by the Epidemiologic Catchment Area (ECA) program, which has been surveying individuals in five communities across the country. Although still underway, data from the first three communities (New Haven, Baltimore, and St. Louis) is available. ECA surveyors in each of the communities randomly interviewed individuals regarding the prevalence of symptoms from 15 of the major diagnoses of DSM-IIIR. Findings revealed that from 29–38% of the people interviewed had experienced at least one of the 15 disorders during their lifetime. An average of the three sites yields a prevalence rate of 33%, which indicates that one in three individuals has experienced such disturbance. Alcohol and/or drug abuse was the most common disorder (16.7%), followed by anxiety disorders (15.5%), mood disturbances (7.8%), and personality disorders (2.6%) (Robins et al., 1984). Given the difficulties in determining accurate recall of symptoms, it can be assumed that these prevalence rates are on the conservative side. Although specific symptomatology will vary from region to region, it can be seen that the total number of individuals experiencing psychological disturbance is a distressingly high number.

Lest these numbers mislead the student into thinking that everyone in his or her classroom belongs in a psychiatric hospital, it should be pointed out that these figures do not reflect level of functioning. That is, the presence of psychiatric symptomatology does not automatically necessitate treatment. As pointed out at the beginning of this section, almost everyone has problems of one nature or another, but it is the degree of impairment that really precludes outside assistance.

PURPOSE OF THERAPEUTIC RECREATION

Within the realm of psychiatric rehabilitation, therapeutic recreation reflects the characteristics of the three levels of service delivery defined by Peterson and Gunn (1984): rehabilitation, education, and participation. A comprehensive therapeutic recreation program would direct attention to those three levels, depending on the level of staff resources, agency expectations, and client needs.

The recreation participation component provides clients with the opportunity to participate in freely chosen activities that are similar to activities and opportunities outside the treatment setting. This experience duplicates all the beneficial outcomes of recreation participation for anyone. It is fun, enjoyable, makes us feel better about ourselves, and provides the opportunity to feel in control; that is, you choose whether to participate, with whom, when, and how much. There are other benefits of a more therapeutic nature also. Clients get to try out new behaviors or ways of interacting with others in a relatively safe environment, and they get to "be themselves" in a setting where everything is not always clinically examined for its significance and meaning. Recreation participation has the potential to improve the client's currently perceived quality of life. It can make him or her feel better about being in the treatment program and thus more accepting of the clinical interventions of other areas of treatment.

The leisure education component serves to address leisure-related skills, attitudes, and knowledge (Peterson & Gunn, 1984). Whereas the role of the therapeutic recreation specialist in the participation component is one of organizer and activity leader, the role in the leisure education component is one of educator and group facilitator. Both the participation and education components are geared toward somewhat less tangible and observable outcomes. Attitudes and values are difficult to observe and measure directly. The nature of their benefits tends to be largely internal and very much under the control of the client.

For this and other reasons there is a great deal of emphasis within psychiatric treatment on the rehabilitation, or therapy, component of therapeutic recreation service delivery. This is what Shank and Kinney (1987) refer to as the clinical context. It is a situation where the client experiencing disturbed mental processes is recognized as an individual involved in a health crisis, a situation where clinical interventions are required to help the individual free himself or herself from the constraints that are limiting his or her personal growth.

The health crisis is a result of an individual's coping style's being inadequate or inappropriate for the demands of a particular situation. Disorganization or disequilibrium results, with consequent increased stress placed on coping resources. This disorganization means that the individual is now dealing with reality at a lower level of effectiveness than previously. As further crises develop, the individual, with reduced effectiveness, experiences increased stress and disequilibrium. For some individuals, this cycle represents a continuing downward cycle until some sense of stability prevails. At the total extreme, stability may be maintained by withdrawal from reality. It is the purpose of the therapy component to work with the entire treatment team to disrupt this downward spiral, reinforce those effective coping behaviors that are working, develop new coping behaviors, and help the individual become more effective in dealing with life crises.

Treatment in therapeutic recreation may be individual or small-group oriented, depending on the needs of the client and the resources of the agency. Most of these interventions tend to be group oriented. If these therapeutic recreation groups are to be effective as clinical interventions, it is necessary for them to meet certain requirements.

1. The group must be conceptualized to meet the specific needs of particular clients.

2. Specific referral criteria for admission to the group must be clearly identified, along with the purpose of the group, objectives and/or planned outcomes, and a description of how the group will function.

3. The group typically has a specific beginning, course, and end (usually over a period of weeks or months) and generally consists of the same individuals who are expected to attend systematically scheduled meetings (i.e., once/week, twice/week, etc.).

4. The functioning of the group is supported by the clinical milieu; that is, it is accepted by other therapies as a legitimate and important part of the treatment environment, clients are encouraged to attend, and nonparticipation becomes a concern for all staff to explore with the client.

This type of clinical group differs from the purely recreational group in that it allows for the principles of group process to evolve. In other words, the group, through natural evolution (and the therapist's interventions) takes on a life and characteristics that reflect its members' typical interactions with other elements of life. To make a contrast, a recreation participation group—for example, a library discussion group that meets periodically with attendance dependent only upon interest—may have a completely different set of individuals at each meeting. Consequently, there is little opportunity for intense group process to occur. Although this library group may meet some of the purely recreational needs of clients, it stands little chance of serving as a therapy group.

COMMON SERVICE SETTINGS

The individual experiencing disturbed mental processes has a variety of alternatives for treatment. The choice of alternative depends on a number of factors, including finances (or health insurance), family and work concerns, and the degree to which the individual is able to function or not function in his or her current environment. Typical settings include inpatient, outpatient, partial or day settings, transitional settings, and individualized settings with one's own counselor or therapist. The significant aspect of these settings is one of structure. The individual who is experiencing psychological discomfort but remains functioning at a reasonable level probably requires only periodic meetings with a psychologist, psychiatrist, or other licensed and certified therapist. As individuals regress in functional abilities, the choice becomes settings with increased structure and number of staff. Inpatient, day settings, and transitional settings are those most likely to employ therapeutic recreation specialists.

Within those settings, the preferred approach is some variation of the team-treatment concept whereby representatives from various disciplines meet as a group to plan an integrated treatment program. Typically, a treatment team consists of representatives from nursing, psychiatry, psychology, social work, and therapeutic recreation (or one of the other activity therapies). This team is responsible for an assigned group of clients and coordinates the various therapies in an individualized fashion. Often the team meets several times each week and discusses the progress of various clients. Team meetings provide the opportunity to review clients on a routine basis as well as on an "as needed" basis, particularly when difficulties arise.

Information is taken back by the therapeutic recreation specialist to be shared with relevant workers in therapeutic recreation staff meetings. Thus, each staff member may be a representative to a different treatment team as well as a member of the therapeutic recreation staff. This information sharing is a two-way process, with staff who interact with the client providing information to the primary therapeutic recreation specialist who, in turn, provides information to the treatment team. Conversely, thoughts and direction about the best way to interact with a client come down from the treatment team and back to the many individual staff who see the client. It is this coordination that is the heart of the milieu therapy concept whereby everything in the client's environment becomes oriented to a consistent treatment approach (Gunderson, 1978).

Within psychiatric settings, many agencies have opted to combine administratively a number of therapies that incorporate similar modalities into one activities therapy department. Such departments may house specialists from art, dance/movement, music, occupational therapy, and therapeutic recreation. The way such departments function varies a great deal. Some function as discrete subunits and attempt to hang on to their unique identities, whereas some merge into one cohesive group and attempt to use each individual's unique talents in a way that best serves the total unit.

CURRENT BEST PRACTICES AND PROCEDURES

Assessment

Assessment is the initial determination of a client's strengths and weaknesses regarding optimal leisure functioning, and is used to establish treatment objectives within therapeutic recreation and to provide data to the treatment team for the establishment of overall treatment goals. It needs to be made very clear that although the purpose of therapeutic recreation assessment is relative to optimal leisure functioning, many of the elements of that assessment will be concerned with the same aspects of mental status that most other disciplines consider. This is not a redundancy. When different assessments look at similar behaviors, they are looking at them under different conditions and expectations. The environments of a psychiatrist's office and a recreation workshop are very different. Consequently, the sharing of this data allows for the treatment team members to validate (confirm) their own thoughts regarding the client or to question their own findings regarding the client. Given the difficult nature of defining exactly what is psychological disorder, this consensual process is very important.

Because of this, there are a number of universal characteristics of psychological process that the therapeutic recreation specialist wants constantly to monitor. These are relevant to the *mental status examination*, which is (1) the process of gathering information regarding a client's state of mind during observations and interactions with that client, and (2) a standard section of the client's medical chart. Waldinger (1984) provides an excellent discussion of these assessment concerns.

Waldinger asserts that therapeutic recreation specialists need to differentiate between thought content and thought process. *Thought process* is the manner in which a client puts ideas and thoughts together; *thought content* is the ideas the client projects; and a *thought disorder* "is a disturbance of content or process, or of both" (Waldinger, 1984, p. 63).

Relative to *thought process*, Waldinger identifies the following for assessment concern:

1. *Rate and flow of ideas.* This includes racing thoughts—a feeling of being flooded with thoughts; retarded or slow thought; circumstantiality—delayed, indirect thoughts; blocking—an interruption in the flow of thought; and perseveration—the repeating of the same verbal responses over and over.

2. *Associations.* These are the connections between various ideas. Various disturbances with associations may include loose associations—switching subjects in discussion where there appears no logical connection between the subjects; flight of ideas—rapid switching from one idea to another; and tangentiality—answering questions in a very roundabout manner.

Concerning *thought content*, Waldinger identifies the following for assessment concern:

Delusions. These are false beliefs that the person tenaciously hangs on to despite all evidence to the contrary. They may include *delusions of grandeur* (exaggerations of one's importance); *delusions of persecution* (thinking that one is the target of planned abuse or oppression); *delusions of control* (thinking that one's thoughts are somehow being controlled by someone or something else); *somatic delusions* (beliefs that involve some part of the body—e.g., that a particular mark on the body means that the person is of some cosmic importance); *thought broadcasting* (the belief that others can read one's mind); *ideas of reference* (beliefs that unrelated events bear some special meaning specifically for the individual—e.g., that an actor in a movie is giving you a personal message); *depersonalization* (a strong sense of unreality about the environment and the self); *morbid preoccupations* (obsessive thinking regarding death); and *suicidal and homicidal ideation* (thoughts of physical injury or death to one's self or someone else).

Other aspects of mental status that the therapeutic recreation specialist should be concerned about include various hallucinations: strange and inappropriate perceptions the client experiences, including auditory, visual, olfactory (smell), and gustatory (taste) hallucinations; level of consciousness, that is, alertness; orientation to time, place, and person; concentration; memory; judgment; and insight, that is, the client's awareness of his or her own disturbed thought and reasons for that disturbed thought.

Table 4.2 presents an outline recommended for assessments by therapeutic recreation specialists. It should be noted that there are few standardized instruments available for assessment in therapeutic recreation. The principal approach is to design activities and tasks that will require the client to demonstrate the skill or behavior to be assessed. As the specialist views those behaviors of concern, he or she makes a judgment as to the degree of function or dysfunction of those behaviors. Finally, the specialist seeks to validate or deny his or her interpretations through input from the client and other treatment team members.

Table 4.2
Therapeutic Recreation Assessment Format

I. Personal Presentation

Appearance	Relative orientation
Physical mannerisms	Motor behavior
Eye contact	Impulse control
Quality of speech	Affect
Comfort level	Insight
Thought pattern	

II. Task Performance (Includes individual and group, structured and unstructured)

Ability to follow directions	Problem solving/Decision
Organization	making
Attention span	Task completion
Follow-through	Quality of effort

III. Interpersonal Skills

Reaction to authority figures	Resistance/Compliance
Competitiveness and reaction	Assumption of group role
to competition	Dependence/Independence
Cooperation and sharing	Responsibility
	Interpersonal space

IV. Physical Skills

Fine motor	Endurance
Gross motor	Mobility
Balance	Coordination
Strength	Flexibility
Agility	Aerobic fitness

V. Leisure Pattern

History	Motivations
Knowledge	Barriers
Interests and involvement	Life-style organization
Attitudes and values	

SOURCE: Developed from Kinney (1980, pp. 42–45) and Carter, Van Andel, & Robb (1985, p. 236).

Planning

Results of the assessment and input from other sources, including the client, become the basis for selecting the goals and objectives to be addressed. Ideally, this is a process that is done with the client; however, in some cases a client's functioning may be so impaired that planning will have to be done for the individual. In many cases the focus of the treatment plan will include targets of change other than the client. Maladaptive behavior may be the legitimate result of an unhealthy environment. To change an individual's behavior and send that person back into the same environment is attacking only part of the problem.

The treatment plan, therefore, should consider and address, where appropriate, goals relevant to the individual, the physical environment, and the social environment (Howe-Murphy & Charboneau, 1987). Goals targeted within therapeutic recreation will vary, depending on the mission of the agency and the perspective of therapeutic recreation as a treatment modality. Another important factor affecting goal planning is the length of time the client is expected to be affiliated with the agency. Third-party insurers dictate the length of time they are willing to cover, and that time constraint becomes a very important factor in treatment planning.

Implementation

Figure 4.1 illustrates how the clinically designed group becomes treatment. Beginning at the innermost level, the group consists of a number of clients (selected for some particular reason relevant to the anticipated outcomes) and a therapeutic recreation specialist. Each client relates to the group on three levels reflected by the triangle: (1) *individual level*—the thoughts and behavior regarding the self, (2) *interpersonal level*—the thoughts and behavior reflected through interactions with two or more individuals, and (3) *group level*—the thoughts and behaviors that reflect the collective thoughts and behaviors of the group (Ward, 1985). These individuals function within the structure of a specific recreational activity selected to help the group address its ultimate purposes. This activity serves as a stimulus that elicits behaviors at all three levels, sometimes at the same time. This group and recreational activity occurs within a particular environment that also affects thoughts and behaviors.

Within this mix, the therapeutic recreation specialist introjects his or her group process skills, which are targeted at one or more of the three levels and are designed to help the group evolve and overcome identified problem areas. Examples of a therapeutic recreation specialist's verbal comments at each level might be the following:

> *Individual level:* "Bill, you continue to picture yourself as an incompetent person, yet your contributions to the group project today were invaluable."

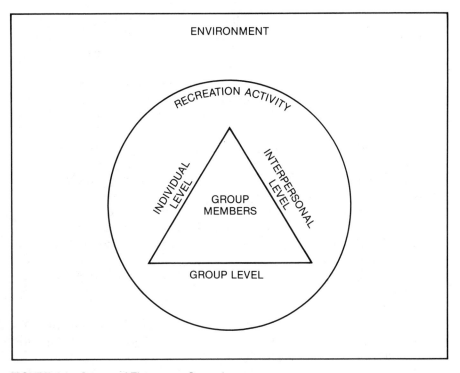

FIGURE 4.1   Context of Therapeutic Group Activity

Interpersonal level: "You know, Bill and Mary, the two of you have become increasingly supportive of each other in your attempts to reach out to others more. To what do you attribute that?"

Group level: "I sense quite a lot of tension over the fact that we are planning to move on to a project that will involve a lot more commitment from each of us. How do you think that tension reflects how we feel about ourselves as a group?"

The careful planning of interventions and their settings and the "on the spot" group process skills of the therapeutic recreation specialist allow the group to become more cohesive and more willing to confront each other or support each other as the need requires. As a group becomes cohesive, there are a number of naturally occurring therapeutic factors that the therapeutic recreation specialist wants to attempt to enhance. Yalom (1985) has identified eleven therapeutic factors that exist in cohesive treatment groups. These are the following:

1. *Instillation of hope*—the belief that we can get better and that no matter how bad the situation, there is hope for a better life.

2. *Universality*—the recognition that we are not alone, other people have similar problems, and we do share much in common with each other.

3. *Imparting of information*—the teaching of skills, giving of advice, and other events of an instructive nature.

4. *Altruism*—the giving to others and the sense of positive esteem that results from helping someone else.

5. *Corrective recapitulation of the primary family group*—In many respects, a cohesive group represents a family, and the interactions of group members tend to reflect somewhat the similar interactions they experienced with their first and primary group, their own family. The exploration of those pathological interactions within the cohesive group allows for corrective action to occur.

6. *Development of socializing techniques*—the learning through role playing, observing others, or through feedback from others the effects that one's social behaviors have on others, and learning how to improve social interactions.

7. *Imitative behavior*—seeing how others in the group behave in certain situations and picking up some of those behaviors to "try out" in one's own interpersonal interactions.

8. *Interpersonal learning*—the reconstruction and examination of relationships and interactions within the group that typify relationships and interactions outside the group. The interventions of the group leader and members allow individuals to realize how they have been contributing to their problems and how they can subsequently change their behavior (Waldo, 1985).

9. *Group cohesiveness*—the "togetherness" of the group; also, the recognition of group norms and conformance to those norms.

10. *Catharsis*—the good or "cleansing" feeling that results from expressing some emotion that one has had difficulty previously expressing.

11. *Existential factors*—a broad group of factors that generally result in an acceptance of life as it is and the recognition that each person is ultimately responsible for his or her own life.

It is these therapeutic factors that determine how the therapeutic recreation specialist designs and guides the therapeutic recreation group toward its goals. Clearly, the therapeutic recreation specialist must have an excellent grasp of group dynamics and group process as well as an understanding of the psychodynamics of human thinking and functioning.

Evaluation Procedures

Evaluation is the analysis of data to determine the extent to which an individual or group of clients have progressed toward their identified goal(s). Although evaluation is typically an ongoing process, it involves several levels of input. The therapeutic recreation specialist, in working with groups, helps members set individual as well as group goals. It is helpful to the group process periodically to have the group spend time discussing progress and providing feedback to each other. Thus, client self-evaluation is an important source of input.

Information from others is extremely valuable in gathering evaluation data. Such information may come from other staff working with the client (this information is usually transmitted through treatment-team meetings), from family or other significant individuals in the client's life, and from the client's medical chart (Posavac & Carey, 1985).

Within the psychiatric setting there is an additional form of evaluation that is particularly helpful to the specialist. This is the practice of *clinical supervision*. Clinical supervision is a process whereby one therapist (usually of senior standing and experience) helps another therapist develop his or her clinical skills through an intensive, interpersonal approach (Critchley, 1987). Whereas one focus of clinical supervision is to analyze difficulties that the therapist may be having with a particular client (Platt-Koch, 1986), another may be to help a therapist recognize the progress a client is making in the interventions the therapist is structuring. Thus, clinical supervision can be a helpful process of evaluating client movement and the appropriateness of certain interventions.

APPLICATION OF THE TR PROCESS

The following case study is provided as an illustration of the TR process.

CASE STUDY

Wilbur is a 27-year-old white male with a diagnosis of schizophrenia, further complicated by diabetes. Psychological evaluation indicates delusions of grandeur and paranoia. His IQ is normal to high normal. He has had numerous psychiatric admissions at other facilities, but this is his first admission to this facility. His activities of daily-living skills are poor; his appearance is disheveled; he wears multiple-layered clothing; and he bathes infrequently. He does not follow his diabetic diet, which has led to several health crises (i.e., insulin shock, rehospitalization, etc.).

The therapeutic recreation evaluation revealed a poor work history, a pattern of severe isolation, poor interpersonal skills, a short attention span, and little insight into his illness or how others perceive him. His goal in life was to be a rock star.

One goal for treatment focused on building social interaction skills. This group placement emphasized tolerating other people in a group; speaking to others in a group setting, giving suggestions and/or opinions; and learning to make compromises.

Progress was slow and often delayed. In the initial stages of participation, he was unable consistently to attend groups; he was resistant to suggestions and unwilling to participate in activities; and he quit when frustrated. He eventually progressed to the point where he met the criteria for discharge from the group. His treatment was initially designed with his input. His progress included the following:

1. He was able consistently to attend the group for four weeks.
2. He could verbally express a minimum of two suggestions per group for a week.
3. He initiated conversation with another group member (not staff).
4. In stressful situations, he discussed the problem and made compromises two out of three times.
5. He was able to encourage other group members to participate in an activity when they were refusing to be involved.

Six months after Wilbur was in the recreation therapy group and demonstrated the ability to tolerate working with others and was somewhat consistent in attending, he was referred to the work skills program, the next step in his rehabilitation.

TRENDS AND ISSUES

Rather than attempt to discuss the multitude of issues in a field as complex as mental health, we have chosen to focus on eating disorders as a trend that has significant implications for therapeutic recreation. The section that follows details this trend.

We live in a society that emphasizes youth and physical fitness. We see slogans, such as "lean is mean," and advertisements with gorgeous slim models for fitness centers that promise "we'll get you there." There is pressure, whether real or perceived, to be thin—especially for women. Research has shown that females tend to be more dissatisfied with their bodies than males, and, although both sexes tend to distort their image of what they look like, women's image is negative whereas men's is positive (Coleman, 1985).

With the above societal expectations and facts in mind, it should be of no surprise to the reader that the majority of people diagnosed with these illnesses are women. In fact, 90% of those diagnosed are women. This statistic holds true for both types of eating disorder—anorexia nervosa and bulimia (Andersen, 1979). As with all psychological disorders, it is difficult to identify the exact prevalence rates of eating disorders. However, it has been estimated that as many as 10% of college women are presently exhibiting one of the eating disorders (Thompson & Schwartz, 1982).

Anorexia Nervosa

The age of onset is typically before age 25 and may start as early as age 12. Families often describe their child as being a model child at home and an excellent student. The parents report being unable to understand the change in behavior that can drastically change the interactions between parent and child: they report the child's becoming angry, negativistic, and/ or suddenly mistrustful. Signs for potential problems include:

1. *Change in weight goals.* Suddenly the individual determines that she should weigh much less than she does presently. Weight has not previously been a problem.

2. *Dieting that leads to increased criticism about one's body.* Instead of being pleased about the results of dieting, the person does not feel satisfied with the results.

3. *Dieting that leads to increased social isolation.* As one tends to lose weight and improve in appearance, the logical outcome is to become more active socially. Paradoxically, as the individual loses weight, she becomes more and more isolated.

4. *Amenorrhea.* The individual experiences loss of the menstrual cycle.

It is important to remember that an eating disorder is not really a disturbance of eating; it is a psychological problem. Prior to onset, the individual often feels helpless and lacking in control over her life. To begin to gain control, she refuses to eat as a solution to personality difficulties that are manifested through eating (Garner & Garfinkel, 1985). These are a result of underlying deficits in the development of the personality, including low self-esteem/self-worth, trust, and autonomy. Bruch (in Garner & Garfinkel, 1982) states that developmentally, the anorectic does not adequately master the stage of formal operations whereby she learns to think abstractly and perfects problem solving.

With increased weight loss, the anorectic creates a sense of control and effectiveness in one aspect of her life. Contrary to popular belief, the anorectic is hungry. She does not lose her appetite. In fact, the individual becomes obsessed with thoughts about food; however, the fear of losing control while eating becomes so powerful that rigid restrictions are put on the amount of food she is allowed to eat. This severe discipline over her body indicates a desperate effort to ward off panic about being completely without power (Bruch, 1982). There is also an unrealistic fear of becoming obese. Although she may be severely emaciated, in her own mind she imagines her body to be grossly overweight.

Treatment is initially difficult with anorectics because they are convinced that they are not sick. Anorectics often appear defiant, and power struggles are frequent. This is a defense against feeling that they don't have a core personality of their own, and a feeling of being powerless and ineffective. They also operate on "all or nothing" thinking, which is very difficult to deal with and often carries over into other areas of living—exercise, relationships, attitudes towards self, and interactions with others.

DSM-IIIR (1987) has outlined the following criteria for diagnosis:

1. Refusal to maintain body weight over a minimal normal weight for age and weight. A loss of more than 15% of total body weight.
2. Intense fear of gaining weight even though underweight.
3. Disturbance in the way in which one's body weight, size, or shape is experienced.
4. In females, absence of at least three consecutive menstrual cycles, when they are otherwise expected to occur.

Bulimia

Often the two diagnoses of anorexia and bulimia are intertwined. Differences do occur, however. Bulimics usually have been overweight prior to symptoms, and behaviors begin as a way to control weight by relying on artificial means. Behaviorally, bulimics are more impulsive. The age of onset is from the teens to over age 30. Again, this is predominantly a female disorder, and individuals are generally well groomed, bright, and high achievers. Outwardly they present a very successful appearance, often perfectionistic; however, they often suffer from a deflated self-image and inadequate ego development.

As stated in the previous paragraph, the individual begins dieting as a means to control her weight. Most of us (especially women) have experienced dieting at one point in our lives. A common difficulty experienced during the dieting process is reaching a plateau and being unable to lose more weight. Another difficulty is remaining on the diet. Most dieting individuals build in breaks or rewards, indulging in fattening goodies that are avoided during a diet. This is very typical, but it is a frequent downfall for the bulimic.

At this point in the bulimic's cycle, intense hunger leads the person to overeat. Guilt from overeating generates self-induced vomiting to avoid weight gain. This results in an addictive cycle of gorging (binging) and self-induced vomiting (purging). The self-induced vomiting allows an escape from the stress and reality caused by overeating. Soon the individual becomes a victim of these impulsive urges. Purging includes one of the following: self-induced vomiting, severely restricted dieting, fasting, cathartics, or exercise.

The binge/purge cycle can be as infrequent as one to two times per week or as many as dozens of times per day. The cycle often takes place during the late evening or night after restricting during the day. It also increases in times of stress and during unstructured time. As the disorder progresses, the individual becomes more isolated from others out of fear of being discovered.

There is a definite difference between overeating and a bulimic binge episode. The quantity of food eaten must be excessive (often 5,000–10,000 calories in one session), and the eating is *not* controllable. The individual has the capacity to consume vast quantities of food in a short time. Remember, the bulimic is overly concerned with weight and appearance; therefore, she is greatly distressed by her lack of control over eating.

Bulimics tend to be much more resistant to treatment and have more complications than anorectics. Bulimics often experience depression, may be cross addicted (substance abuse), and may engage in sexual promiscuity and/or self-destructive behavior. They also experience low self-esteem, obsessions of being thin, social isolation, and have difficulty establishing a firm identity.

DSM-IIIR (1987) has identified the following diagnostic criteria:

1. Recurrent episodes of binge eating (rapid consumption of a large amount of food in a discrete period of time).
2. A feeling of lack of control over eating behavior during the eating binges.
3. Engaging in either self-induced vomiting, use of laxatives or diuretics, strict dieting or fasting, or vigorous exercise to prevent weight gain.
4. A minimum average of two binge-eating episodes a week for at least three months.
5. Persistent overconcern with body shape and weight.

Therapeutic Recreation Programming

Working with eating disorder clients is very difficult. They tend to be highly controlling, verbal overachievers who are difficult to satisfy and who have successfully manipulated their environment for some time. It is important to remember several facts discussed earlier. These clients have ego-functioning deficits. They are at a stage where rebellion against authority is at its peak, and defiance is a defense against feeling powerless and ineffective. It is therefore important to give options to clients whenever possible.

Physical Exercise

The most difficult adjustment to be made by the therapeutic recreation specialist is one of philosophy. We are trained to get people involved in activities. When working with eating disorder patients, the therapeutic recreation specialist has to shift gears. Many clients want to be involved and active, but there is a need to restrict them because of severe malnutrition or medical instability. As can be expected, this can evoke a sense of conflict between the client and therapist. Emphasizing self-responsibility for their behavior by restricting exercise can be effective. Once the client has been allowed some supervised exercise, the job becomes more difficult. It is vital to educate the importance of moderation of exercise and how to exercise correctly. Limit setting will be at its height during this time. During the course of treatment, the client will eventually earn the right to unsupervised exercise. This will become one test that determines the effectiveness of treatment.

Social Skills

As described earlier, the nature of anorexia and bulimia often isolates the individual because he or she fears being detected. Also, ego deficits prevent the individual from functioning successfully in groups. The ability to make compromises is poor (remember the "all or nothing" thinking), and problem-solving abilities are also often poor, resulting in rigid viewpoints. Therefore, activities that focus on group problem-solving skills can be highly effective.

Food-Related Activities

Goals should focus on difficulties surrounding food: planning, shopping, food preparation, and eating. Anorectics enjoy feeding others while denying themselves food; some are even involved in food-related professions. Bulimics are often threatened by food; it is seen as a temptation.

Planning. Planning is difficult, especially with four or more clients in the group and if they are of mixed diagnoses. In spite of the fact that they have their own rigid eating patterns, they are forced to make compromises that require all to agree on a plan for eating. The process of planning a meal must be structured by the therapist, and time limits of planning must be strictly enforced. Because one of the goals might be for the clients to learn to eat new foods, some food selections may have to be limited or eliminated from the selection process, such as "safe foods"—salads, tofu, chicken.

Shopping. Shopping for food items selected during planning is an important component of the group and brings out different stressors. Avoidance is at its highest peak for some individuals, and they will have excuses not to attend. Some bulimics have put grocery stores off limits; others have to go through several ritualistic behaviors prior to entering a store. This a traumatic time, and support from the therapist is needed. Structuring the trip has proven helpful. Making out a shopping list prior to shopping and then sticking to that list is important. Some clients become insistent that other items be bought or that the amount of food will not be enough to feed the group.

Food Preparation. It is important to keep the group as normalized as possible, but precautions for a safe environment should be taken. It is a calculated risk to allow the use of knives and other sharp instruments. Expectations of group behavior should be clearly identified.

Eating. Eating family style is very difficult. Even with close supervision, oftentimes a client is able to achieve her goal of limiting her intake to almost nothing, while the therapist is convinced that the person has eaten the required amount. As the group becomes more cohesive through familiarity with the routine and with verbal processing, the group becomes a supportive element for each individual member.

Time Management/Leisure Counseling

It is best to approach a leisure counseling group from a time management concept. Eating disorders affect all aspects of life, and denial of the impact of the disorder on clients' lives is a common defense. Instead of focusing on just leisure time, explore all aspects of time—work, leisure and maintenance (sleeping, eating, grooming), and the importance of creating a balance between these three aspects. Utilization of exercises such as the "pie of life" can bring about recognition that the disorder has impacted every aspect of their lives. Leisure/free time is a very threatening entity; it is one of the clients' most vulnerable times. Looking at alternative patterns of leisure time is important.

The most important fact is that the clients must recognize that they have a problem and then have a desire to change their present patterns of coping. Therapeutic recreation through these and other groups can be very effective in helping individuals recognize their problems and become invested in their own growth and change.

SUMMARY

This chapter has described the difficult task of defining what constitutes mental disorder. In a sense, we define it as not having mental health. If one looks at mental health as having the ability to cope with the life stresses of reality, it becomes easier to see what specific characteristics are involved. Individuals learn to cope by using various defense mechanisms to protect the psychological self from stress. At the same time, individuals bring to bear the cognitive and emotional skills they have either to adapt to stress and crisis or to reach out and change things so that their stress is reduced.

People experiencing mental disorder are overwhelmed by the stress of their situations because their defenses and ego strengths cannot meet the demands of those situations. Consequently, they experience psychological pain, much as we feel physical pain, and sometimes develop behaviors that put them further at odds with society's accepted behavior.

The *Diagnostic and Statistical Manual of Mental Disorders III, Revised* (DSM-IIIR, 1987) provides a basis for examining behaviors associated with mental disorders and categorizing them for purposes of understanding. This chapter has discussed only those most prevalent that the therapeutic recreation specialist may encounter: schizophrenia, mood disorders, anxiety disorders and phobic neuroses, personality disorders, and eating disorders.

Individuals experiencing mental disorders have a variety of alternatives in seeking treatment. The setting in which the therapeutic recreation specialist is most likely to be involved is where a team of health care professionals design and supervise the various treatment interventions. The therapeutic recreation specialist may be involved in services that are primarily oriented to either recreation participation, education, or rehabilitation (therapy).

When engaged in delivering therapy services, the specialist usually is involved in the development of therapeutic recreation groups. The specialist uses his understanding of individual psychodynamics, group process, and various activities to help the group become cohesive and engage in a level of interaction that is appropriate for the individuals in the group. Through the processing of interactions and feelings, group members learn how their behavior affects themselves and others, and gradually recognize that their behaviors within the group are typical of their behaviors outside of the group.

READING COMPREHENSION QUESTIONS

1. What is the distinction between mental health and mental illness?
2. What is coping?
3. How does coping contribute to positive and negative mental health?
4. What are the developmental steps (levels) involved in becoming a mentally healthy person?
5. Give examples of each one of the developmental levels of behaviors indicating positive development and behaviors indicating negative adjustment.
6. How does our society determine just who is mentally healthy and who is mentally unhealthy (ill)?
7. Define clinical interventions in psychiatric treatment.
8. What are the classical symptoms of schizophrenia?

9. What are the three types of mood disorders?

10. What is the difference between obsessions and compulsions in obsessive compulsive disorders?

11. Why do individuals with personality disorders tend not to seek help?

12. Within the context of mental health, how is a health crisis defined?

13. What are the criteria for effective groups within the treatment context of therapeutic recreation?

14. Describe how a therapeutic recreation clinical group differentiates from a recreation participation group.

15. What are the distinctions between the various common service settings for treating mental health problems?

16. In what way does the therapeutic recreation specialist contribute to the goals of the entire treatment team?

17. Why should therapeutic recreation assessments be concerned with some of the same behaviors as those assessed in other disciplines?

18. What are the assessment components regarding thought processes with which the therapeutic recreation specialist should be concerned?

19. What are the factors that affect goal planning once the assessment is completed?

20. Describe the three levels of interaction within which a therapeutic recreation group can function.

21. Describe how an activity can elicit responses from a client on all three levels of interaction.

22. Give examples of how therapeutic recreation can contribute to each of Yalom's therapeutic factors that exist in cohesive treatment groups.

23. What are the typical signs for identification of anorexia nervosa?

24. What are the diagnostic criteria for bulimia?

25. How is the philosophy toward physical activity with eating-disorder clients different from that of other types of clientele in therapeutic recreation?

26. How can leisure counseling be an effective method of treatment with eating disorders?

SUGGESTED LEARNING ACTIVITIES

1. Pick an activity to focus on, such as eating in a restaurant or playing volleyball. Identify possible behaviors that might be exhibited in that activity by a depressed individual, a very passive individual, and an aggressive individual.

2. Debate, within a group, whether deinstitutionalization has helped or hindered the cause of mental health advocacy.

3. Research how different societies and cultures deal with mentally ill individuals. What are the similarities and differences to our societal approach?

4. Visit different settings that treat mental illness (e.g., a state hospital, private inpatient hospital, day care hospital, etc.), and discuss the differences in approaches.

5. Draw a time line 10 inches long; mark it off into one-inch intervals. Now draw a "high point line" three inches above your time line and a "low point line" three inches below your time line. You should have three parallel lines. Label the one-inch spaces on your time line by years, going back over your previous ten years. Now graph your own emotional highs and lows for the previous ten years. Take selected spots and examine what was going on in your life at the time; how were you contributing to the feelings? What kind of environmental or external support did you have at the time? What behaviors did you utilize, particularly at the low points, to help yourself through those difficult times? Was your overall behavior different between the high spots and the low spots?

6. Interview someone else who understands the time line process, using a technique similar to the one described in activity 5. Use helpful questions to attempt to understand their behavioral profile and the internal and external things that contributed to the situation.

REFERENCES

ANDERSEN, A. E. (1979). Anorexia nervosa: Diagnosis and treatment. *Weekly Psychiatry Update Series 3*, Lesson 1.

BRUCH, H. (1982). Anorexia nervosa: Therapy and theory. *American Journal of Psychiatry, 139* (12), 1531–1538.

CARTER, M. J., VAN ANDEL, G. E., & ROBB, M. (1985). *Therapeutic recreation: A practial approach.* St. Louis: Times Mirror/Mosby.

COLEMAN, D. (1985, March 19). Dislike of own body found common among women. *New York Times*, C1.

CRITCHLEY, L. (1987). Clinical supervision as a learning tool for the therapist in milieu settings. *Journal of Psychosocial Nursing, 25* (8), 18–21.

Diagnostic and statistical manual of mental disorders III, Revised (DSM-IIIR). (1987). Washington, DC: American Psychiatric Press, Inc.

GARNER, D. M., & GARFINKEL, P. E. (Eds.). (1985). *Handbook of psychotherapy for anorexia nervosa and bulimia.* New York: The Guilford Press.

GUNDERSON, J. G. (1978). Defining the therapeutic processes in psychiatric milieus. *Psychiatry, 41*, 327–335.

HARTMAN, H. (1939). Psychoanalysis and the concept of health. *International Journal of Psychoanalysis, 20*, 308–321.

HOWE-MURPHY, R. & CHARBONEAU, B. G. (1987). *Therapeutic recreation intervention: An ecological perspective.* Englewood Cliffs, NJ: Prentice-Hall.

KINNEY, W. B. (1980). Clinical assessment in mental health settings. *Therapeutic Recreation Journal, 14*(4), 39–45.

MECHANIC, D. (1976). Stress, illness, and illness behavior. *Journal of Human Stress, 3*, 2–6.

O'BRIEN, P., CALDWELL, C., & TRANSEAU, G. (1985). Destroyers: Written treatment contracts can help cure self-destructive behaviors of the borderline patient. *Journal of Psychosocial Nursing, 23*(4), 19–22.

PETERSON, C. A., & GUNN, S. L. (1984). *Therapeutic recreation program design: Principles and procedures* (2nd ed.). Englewood Cliffs, NJ: Prentice-Hall.

PLATT-KOCH, L. M., (1986). Clinical supervision for psychiatric nurses. *Journal of Psychosocial Nursing, 26*(1), 7–15.

POSAVAC, E. J., & CAREY, R. G. (1985). *Program evaluation methods and case studies.* Englewood Cliffs, NJ: Prentice-Hall.

ROBINS, L. N., HELZER, J. E., WEISSMAN, M. M., ORVASCHEL, H., GRUENBERG, E., BURKE, J. D., & REGIER, D. A. (1984). Lifetime prevalence of specific psychiatric disorders in three sites. *Archives of General Psychiatry, 41*, 949–958.

SHANK, J., & KINNEY, T. (1987). On the neglect of clinical practice. *Philosophy of therapeutic recreation ideas and issues.* Alexandria, VA: National Therapeutic Recreation Society of the National Recreation and Park Association.

THOMPSON, M. & SCHWARTZ, D. (1982). Life adjustment of women with anorexia nervosa and anorexic-like behavior. *International Journal of Eating Disorders, 2*, 47–60.

WALDINGER, R. J. (1984). *Psychiatry for medical students.* Washington, DC: American Psychiatric Press.

WALDO, M. (1985). A curative factor framework for conceptualizing group counseling. *Journal of Counseling and Development, 64*, 52–57.

WARD, D. D. (1985). Levels of group activity: A model for improving the effectiveness of group work. *Journal of Counseling and Development, 64*, 59–63.

YALOM, I. D. (1985). *The theory and practice of group psychotherapy* (3rd ed.). New York: Basic Books.

5

Social Deviancy

TERESITA E. AGUILAR

OBJECTIVES

- Understand the meaning of social deviance.
- List and describe four types of negative consequences resulting from deviant behavior.
- Name at least seven examples of deviant behaviors and explain potential leisure-related problems for each.
- Describe six types of settings or organizations that provide treatment for persistent norm violators or victims of social deviance.
- Describe two intervention techniques that are conceptually appropriate for the treatment of deviant, leisure-related behavior.
- Identify and explain three limitations to the treatment of norm violators or victims of deviancy.

The very notion that a society has social norms or rules ensures the existence of deviance. There can be no deviance without social rules (and, as far as we know, there can be no society without rules and norms, either). (Conrad & Schneider, 1980. p. 5)

DEFINITION OF SOCIAL DEVIANCY

Social deviance is defined as behavior that violates a group's norms (Douglas, 1984). The group may be a collective of individuals with similar interests or characteristics, or it may encompass an entire society. Generally, a group has norms that define a range of acceptable behaviors. Individuals who are dissatisfied with a group's norms are most likely to deviate from or violate selected norms (Pavlos, 1979).

The cause(s) of deviant behavior remain unclear. Sociologists attempt to explain deviancy in terms of social structure (Liska, 1981), whereas psychologists suggest mental or emotional disorders as causes. Riemer (1981) suggests that we acknowledge the "fun" dimension of deviancy to better understand many deviant behaviors. That is, some deviant behaviors may provide entertainment and challenge to the deviant actor.

The medical perspective implies that "the problem" lies with the individual who engages in deviant behavior (Conrad & Schneider, 1980). The deviant actor is seen as ill, imbalanced, and in need of prescriptive remediation. The medical model virtually ignores environmental factors that encourage deviancy. Further, this viewpoint ignores the victims of deviant behavior who, in many cases, are affected on a long-term basis.

Rather than attempt to explain and discuss all possible deviant behaviors, this chapter will focus on frequent violations of social norms that can be related to leisure time, activity, or experience. In addition, the role of therapeutic recreation intervention in selected areas of social deviance will be described. Attention will be given to the treatment of both victims and actors of deviant behaviors.

CLASSIFICATION OF DEVIANT BEHAVIOR

Social norm violations can be grouped according to the following consequences: physical harm to self or others, emotional harm to others, addiction, and social disorder. There is clearly overlap among the categories, yet each division is based on the *primary consequence* of the norm violation or deviant behavior. A primary consequence is the major and immediate result of deviant behavior. The consequential classification system below illustrates specific outcomes of various deviant behaviors.

Physical Harm to Self or Others

Physical abuse results in direct physical harm to others. Victims are generally children, women, and older adults. Child, spouse, and elder abuse are examples of physically abusive situations. The seriousness of *child abuse* lies in the long-term effects on the child. It may encourage delinquency, social isolation, or future abusive behaviors when the abused child becomes an adult. *Spouse abuse* generally involves physically aggressive attacks by the husband on his wife. Such attacks are often denied by both the husband and the wife.

More recent research has introduced the occurrence of *parent* or *elder abuse* (Kosberg, 1985). This abuse may take the form of physical attacks, maltreatment, or substandard health care of older adults. The elderly are especially vulnerable to physical abuse because of their decline in physical strength, endurance, and overall health.

Another type of physical abuse is *rape* or *sexual assault*, which occurs when one or more individuals force themselves upon an unwilling person in a sexual act (Brownmiller, 1975). Date rape has received increased recognition as a serious problem, especially on college campuses. The rapist is often an acquaintance of the victim. Gang rape is yet another type of sexual assault and has been described as analogous to a team sport (Scully & Marolla, 1984). Interviewed rapists described having feelings of control that were associated with a challenging situation.

One example of physical abuse resulting in harm to self is *suicide*. This deviant behavior is increasing among adolescents, older males, and among the economically stressed. The suicide victim cannot be helped, but does provide a valuable source of information for identifying suicidal tendencies. Recent investigations on teen suicide have suggested that popular music and movies that glorify suicide might somehow be linked to increased incidence.

Emotional Harm to Others

Similar to physical abuse, emotional abuse is often directed toward children, a spouse, or parents. Emotional abuse occurs when an individual of significance to the victim constantly subjects the victim to stressful situations. Examples of emotionally abusive behaviors include verbal insults, ignoring behaviors, extreme intolerance, and lack of emotional or financial support.

Emotional abuse also may result from sexual activities such as child pornography, juvenile prostitution, incest, and other forms of sexual molestation that violate social norms (Eve, 1985; Nees, 1988). Emotional abuse carries with it feelings of guilt, anger, isolation, insecurity, or low self-esteem. These feelings might certainly be expected to interfere with the victims' leisure experiences and general quality of life. Emotional abuse, then, can be considered a barrier to leisure.

Addictive Behaviors

Several deviant behaviors may result in habitual or addictive use. A conceptual model illustrating the developmental stages of (drug) addiction is provided by Van Dijk (1986). In his model, five stages leading to addiction include (1) initial contact, (2) experimentation, (3) integrated use, (4) excessive use, and (5) addiction. At each stage, the person has the option to discontinue use, maintain use, or move to the next stage. This model identifies steps leading to the final addictive stage and appears applicable to addiction to a variety of substances or behaviors (i.e., alcohol, gambling, eating disorders).

Legal drugs such as tobacco, alcohol, and prescribed medications are potentially addictive substances. These substances may be perceived as being central to social situations, status symbols, or pleasure-seeking/escape mechanisms. *Illegal drugs* such as marijuana, cocaine, crack, and heroin are often consumed for recreational purposes (Etherington, 1987). Whether the substance is legal or illegal, the experience provided by the substance will certainly influence future use or abuse.

Compulsive gambling is another example of addictive behavior. Gambling activity is certainly not limited to casinos and racetracks. It may include "office pools" in conjunction with professional or collegiate sporting events, lotteries, bingo, card games, pool, and so on. Gambling is a form of leisure activity (McGurrin, Abt, & Smith, 1984). However, what begins as a form of entertainment may eventually lead to some rather serious and detrimental social problems (Livingston, 1984), such as stealing or neglecting financial obligations in order to continue the gambling habit.

Eating disorders constitute another type of addictive behavior. This includes compulsive eating, anorexia nervosa, and bulimia. There is no doubt that food is associated with social experiences in our society. We are constantly reminded of food in magazines, on billboards, and on television. Unlike the past, prepared food today is readily available on virtually every street corner in America. For the compulsive eater, this alone may present a temptation and a problem.

Despite its availability and promotion, food may also be interpreted as "the enemy." A multitude of people (usually women) have been socialized to believe that slim and trim is beautiful. The fear of gaining weight often leads to one of two deviant eating behaviors: anorexia nervosa (intentional starvation) and bulimia (binging and purging).

Of these behaviors, bulimia is considered to be the more deviant (Huon, Brown, & Morris, 1988). Kaufman, McBride, Hultsman, and Black (1988) found initial support for a link between bulimia and negative perceptions of leisure. Bulimics tend to experience fewer benefits from leisure than nonbulimics. Further research with eating disorders and leisure functioning will help clarify the direction for therapeutic recreation intervention.

Social Disorder

A fourth category of consequences of deviant behavior is social disorder. Deviant behaviors that are in violation of a law or ordinance are included in this group. These behaviors contribute at least temporarily to social disorder.

Delinquent and criminal behaviors often occur during free time and in some cases provide leisure experiences for the participants (Aguilar, 1987; Csikszentmihalyi & Larson, 1978). Delinquent behaviors are generally associated with adolescents, whereas adult (18 years and older) offenses are labeled as criminal. Common delinquent behaviors include offenses against other persons, property offenses, drug offenses, or public disorder. The most frequently reported delinquent behaviors in 1987 were property offenses, including burglary, arson, auto theft, and larceny (Allen-Hagen, 1988). Engaging in delinquent and criminal behaviors clearly illustrates an abuse of free time, and an implication is that therapeutic recreation intervention should be designed to promote more responsible and acceptable forms of leisure activity.

DESCRIPTION OF LIMITATIONS

Three potential limitations in the treatment of deviant behaviors are described. First, there is the potential *denial by the deviant actor*. When the rapist, abuser, addict, or criminal blatantly denies engaging in deviant behavior, it is difficult to provide treatment. Another tactic parallel to denial by the actor is the actor's persuasion of the victims that he or she (the abuser) is ill and that the behavior is uncontrollable and therefore excusable.

A second limitation exists when there is *denial by the victim* that the deviant act ever occurred. This is common in situations of rape, incest, spouse abuse, and molestation, which require that the victim report the norm violation. In abusive situations, the abuser may threaten the victim who considers reporting the abuse.

A third possible limitation to treatment is *failure ever to come into contact with the deviant actor*. Many deviant acts are private in nature. Unless direct harm is done or a law has been blatantly violated, it may be extremely difficult to identify a deviant actor. For example, the frequent consumer of pornography who may need treatment for social or psychological problems may never be identified unless engaged in other, more obvious deviant behaviors.

Another illustration is the adolescent who engages in delinquent behavior but is "protected" by parents or others. Essentially, these adolescents avoid the system that would introduce them to treatment for their problem behavior.

PURPOSE OF THERAPEUTIC RECREATION

The purpose of therapeutic recreation services, in the case of social deviancy, is not to "cure" the problem. That mission, if at all possible, is the task of psychologists, psychiatrists, social workers, or counselors. A major role of therapeutic recreation is to promote socially acceptable leisure pursuits that might substitute for the deviant behavior(s). A secondary function of therapeutic recreation is to enhance the treatment or rehabilitative efforts of other disciplines within the treatment setting.

Two specific treatment approaches suggested in the literature on deviancy, delinquency, and related social problems are leisure education and leisure counseling. Both of these approaches are described as they contribute to promoting socially acceptable leisure for deviant actors. Additionally, these approaches are applicable to enhancing the victims' leisure appreciation, awareness, and opportunities.

Leisure Education Programs

Recreation specialists and educators generally have agreed upon the mission of leisure education—to enhance knowledge and skills for leisure. Within the rehabilitative process, leisure education programs should be designed to promote healthy, socially acceptable leisure pursuits (Aguilar, 1986a). This is true for the rehabilitation of substance abuse, criminal, delinquent, and other socially deviant behaviors.

The promotion of acceptable or positive leisure requires an understanding of existing barriers to positive leisure and sources of motivation for negative pursuits. These components are illustrated in Figure 5.1. Essentially, leisure education programs are especially appropriate for individuals who consistently engage in negative leisure activity such as delinquency, compulsive gambling, and drug abuse.

Leisure education programs may focus on such content areas as awareness of leisure resources, knowledge of resource utilization, and acquisition of specific activity skills (Aguilar, 1986a). Other leisure education program components may include social interaction skills (Peterson & Gunn, 1984), self-awareness, and decision-making skills (Mundy & Odum, 1979). Recreation specialists must design their leisure education program's content areas on the basis of recipients' needs or deficiencies. Such needs are determined by assessment procedures.

Leisure Counseling

Leisure counseling is a therapeutic intervention designed to address leisure-related problems directly. This intervention is used to facilitate an individual or group toward self-responsibility and leisure well-being (McDowell, 1984). Following an extensive review of the leisure counseling literature, McDowell (1984) identified four leisure counseling orientations: leisure-related behavior problems, leisure life-style awareness, leisure resource guidance, and leisure skills development. In the leisure-related behavior problems orientation, the counselor assists the consumer in problem-solving abilities associated with leisure environment coping skills. In leisure life-style awareness, the counselor presents a comprehensive view of leisure and other life-style components. Resource guidance includes matching personal and community resources with individual desired interests. The skills development orientation is used to help the consumer identify, plan, and initiate activity to develop skills in desired

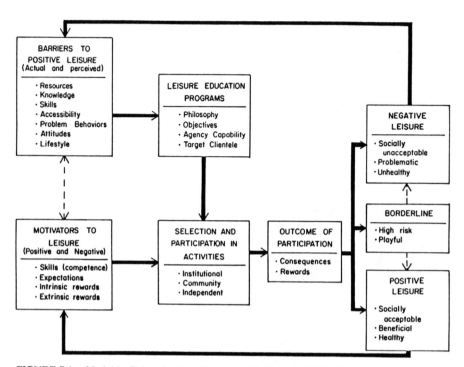

FIGURE 5.1. Model for Enhancing Socially Acceptable Leisure. SOURCE: From "Leisure Education Program Development and Evaluation" by T. E. Aguilar, 1986, *Journal of Expanding Horizons in Therapeutic Recreation, 1*, p. 16. Copyright 1986 by the University of Missouri Board of Curators. Reprinted by permission.

leisure pursuits. The selection of the appropriate counseling orientation depends on the specific needs of the consumer.

The leisure counseling process must utilize appropriate stages of progression, as identified in counseling techniques. This progression is based on the counselor-consumer interaction and is frequently determined by the sensitivity of the subject matter.

Potential outcomes of leisure counseling include a better understanding of the environment in which deviant behaviors occur, an acceptance of responsibility for leisure choices, an awareness of leisure alternatives, and an increased understanding of the role and significance of leisure in the individual's life.

The effective leisure counselor must have a solid foundation in leisure behavior theory, behavioral change theory, and counseling techniques. The counselor must be able to contend with the consumer's thoughts, feelings, behaviors, and total situation. Among the desired counseling conditions are empathy, genuineness, respect, and concreteness (Munson, 1984). Most therapeutic recreation specialists, however, are untrained for leisure counseling because counselor training usually takes place at the graduate level.

COMMON SERVICE SETTINGS

Because of the uniqueness of deviant behavior, the provision of therapeutic recreation is often appropriate on two levels. On one level, treatment for the deviant actor is essential. On the other hand, the victims of deviant behavior are often in need of therapeutic recreation services, especially if the deviant behavior can in any way affect their leisure behaviors. Thus, the following settings or organizations that can provide therapeutic recreation services to either the deviant actor or the victim are briefly described.

Correctional Institutions

The correctional system includes detention centers, prisons, jails, probation services, diagnostic centers, farms and camps, and release centers (Travisono, 1985). Although recreation services are provided at most facilities, the purpose of such programs is often limited to the provision of diversionary services (Aguilar, 1986b). However, some facilities do provide recreation programs designed to teach new leisure skills to the inmates and therefore fulfill a rehabilitative purpose. Inasmuch as these recreation programs are committed to rehabilitation and leisure education, they may qualify as therapeutic recreation services.

Community Mental Health Settings

Community mental health settings provide services to both victims and deviant actors. Therapeutic recreation in these settings often includes large group diversionary programs, special events, and leisure education. Few TR practitioners in these settings are given the opportunity to provide individualized treatment such as leisure counseling, which could directly address individual leisure-related problems.

Drug and Alcohol Rehabilitation Settings

These settings generally provide inpatient, outpatient, and residential services to individuals who have or are abusing various substances. One purpose of therapeutic recreation services is to encourage substitution of drugs with acceptable leisure pursuits. A second purpose of TR is to provide recreation opportunities to enhance other institutional treatment efforts by reinforcing other treatment plans, contributing to institutional adjustment, or balancing between medical/behavioral treatment and educational or enjoyable activity.

General Hospitals

Hospital settings include private, public, and quasi-public facilities. Many hospitals offer short-term and outpatient services related to deviant behaviors such as substance abuse, eating disorders, emotional and physical abuse. These settings serve both the victim and the deviant actor. Among the largest systems are the Veterans Administration Medical Centers, which recognize therapeutic recreation as a viable service within their rehabilitative efforts. Therapeutic recreation is often provided through leisure education and diversionary services.

Mental/Psychiatric Hospitals

These settings specialize in the treatment of psychological disorders. When persistent involvement in deviant behaviors is directly attributed to emotional or psychological disorders, treatment for deviant actors is provided. These settings often provide long-term treatment. The provision of TR in mental and psychiatric hospitals is often designed according to the continuum model of clinical TR services (Peterson & Gunn, 1984), which includes treatment, leisure education, and recreation participation.

Self-Help Groups/Organizations

Within urban communities, several self-help groups are often organized to support individuals with various addictions. Examples of such organizations include Alcoholics Anonymous, Gamblers Anonymous, and Overeaters Anonymous. In general, these organizations do not offer or recognize therapeutic recreation services. However, such organizations could enhance their programs by acknowledging the need to promote leisure pursuits as substitutes for addictive, free-time behaviors.

Community Social Services

Victims of deviant behavior are often assisted via crisis counseling, support groups (such as spouse abuse survivors, incest survivors, and sexual assault survivors), and shelters for abused victims. The deviant actors are also likely to find assistance within the community through programs such as anger control groups. Similar to the self-help groups previously described, many of these community social service settings are not concerned with leisure issues of the client. Yet the need for therapeutic recreation services, especially leisure education, seems evident.

CURRENT BEST PRACTICES AND PROCEDURES

A primary purpose of therapeutic recreation intervention is to encourage both deviant actors and victims to participate in socially acceptable, rewarding leisure pursuits. Two specific programmatic approaches were previously described: leisure education and leisure counseling. These two approaches are useful in addressing leisure problems, resources, skills, and opportunities. Specific practices and procedures for the delivery of therapeutic recreation interventions, including assessment, planning, implementation, and evaluation, are presented.

Assessment

Assessment is the systematic collection of information necessary for diagnosing needs and determining interventions. It is necessary to assess thoroughly the consumer's leisure situations (skills, patterns, attitudes, etc.). From this assessment, the specialist should identify leisure behaviors or attitudes for which change would be beneficial. A secondary area of assessment includes potential outcome measures of selected psychological variables. For example, if an intervention is designed to enhance an individual's perception of himself or herself, the therapist would initially assess the client's self-concept or self-esteem. This latter assessment represents an outcome measure of a psychological variable.

Several assessment procedures are suggested for both leisure issues and outcome measures. Suggested leisure assessments are presented in Table 5.1. These assessments address leisure interests, functioning, and participation.

Although the leisure assessments are critical to the design of treatment content and techniques, outcome assessments are useful measures to determine effectiveness of the intervention. Two studies in the TR literature illustrate the process of using outcome measures to determine the effectiveness of treatment programs (e.g., Gibson, 1979; Hunter, 1984). Several assessments are recommended for measuring program impact (see Table 5.2).

Table 5.1
Recommended Leisure Assessments

TITLE	AUTHOR(S)	MEASURES
Leisure Activities Blank (LAB)	McKechnie (1974)	Past and future leisure interests
Leisure Interest Inventory (LII)	Hubert (1969)	Preferred leisure activities
Brief Leisure Rating Scale (BLRS)	Ellis & Niles (1985)	Helplessness in leisure
Boredom-in-Leisure Scale	Iso-Ahola & Weissinger (1987)	Leisure as boredom
Leisure Ethic Scale	Slivken (1978)	Affinity toward leisure
Leisure Diagnostic Battery (LDB)	Witt et al. (1982)	Leisure functioning; subscales: perceived control, perceived competence, playfulness, motivation, depth of involvement, barriers, knowledge, preferences

Table 5.2
Examples of Supportive Assessments (Outcome and/or Initial Measures)

TITLE	AUTHOR(S)	MEASURE	TARGET	NO. OF ITEMS	ADM. TIME	AVAILABILITY
Family Environment Scale	Moos (1979)	Family interactions and activities	Youth & adults	92 (long) 24 (Rec. only)	(N. R.)*	Consulting Psychologists Press, 577 College Ave., Palo Alto, CA 94306
Coopersmith Self-Esteem Inventories (3 forms: A, B, C)	Coopersmith (1981)	Overall self-esteem	Youth (A & B) Adult (C)	50 (A) 25 (B & C)	10–15 min	Consulting Psychologists Press, 577 College Ave., Palo Alto, CA 94306
Life Event Scale—Adolescents	Coddington (1981)	Environmental stress	Adolescents	51	5–10 min	Stress Research Co., St. Clairsville, OH 43729
Self-Consciousness Scale	Fenigstein, Scheier, & Buss (1975)	Private/public self-consciousness; social anxiety	Adults	23	(N. R.)*	American Psychological Association, Washington, DC 20015
Hopelessness Scale	Beck, Weissman, Lester, & Trexler (1974)	Pessimistic expectations	Adults	20	5–10 min.	American Psychological Association, Washington, DC 20015

*N. R. = Not Reported.

Planning

In addition to leisure education (Aguilar, 1987) and leisure counseling techniques (Kaufman et al., 1988; Munson, Baker, & Lundegren, 1985), other types of programs have been suggested and implemented within the scope of social deviancy. Selected examples include the following:

Outdoor/Adventure Programs. Wilderness, adventure, and outdoor programs have been implemented frequently with youth and adults with psychological or emotional disorders. Another related technique is the use of ropes courses. The length of such programs may vary from one day to several months.

Prevention/Educational Programs. Programs designed to prevent deviant problems through educational techniques are also common. Examples include drug prevention or drug education programs, and sex education (including prevention of sexual abuse) programs. The target audiences for such programs are generally populations that are considered to be at greatest risk to engage in or be a victim of the identified social problems.

Wellness Programs. In an effort to promote a more balanced and healthy life-style, several agencies have responded with wellness, well-being, or similarly entitled programs. The populations served include those with specific problems (i.e., poor health, problem behaviors, etc.) and individuals without such limitations (i.e., employee or work-site wellness). These programs often address physical fitness, nutrition, stress management, and leisure life-styles.

Implementation

The implementation procedures for various intervention programs may include individual, small group, or large group techniques. An individual interaction approach is recommended when severe deviant problems exist. Small group techniques are useful when the group members have similar needs and are willing to address their problems in a group setting. Small groups are also recommended for educational programs.

Large group techniques are appropriate in educational programs when the material is not too sensitive. For example, a wellness program focusing on leisure life-styles and activities could be implemented using a large group technique.

In the delivery of educational or prevention programs targeted for social deviancy, it is important to consider several issues that may affect the program's impact. These issues are the following:

- reading level of participants
- writing ability of participants

- biased materials (gender, race, age, occupation)
- sensitive topics/materials (especially for victims)
- generalizability of program content (consider participants' social environment upon completion of the program)

Evaluation

As previously stated, the major role of therapeutic recreation is to encourage socially acceptable leisure pursuits that might substitute for deviant behavior. A secondary purpose of enhancing other treatment efforts was also suggested. These purposes should serve as the bases for program evaluation.

To evaluate the TR program, input should be sought from a variety of sources. For example, information should be collected from the program participants during and after the program, from staff members, from participants' significant others, and other potential informants. The effectiveness of the program delivery and impact should be evaluated on the basis of the information acquired from multiple sources. This approach is known as a triangulation approach to evaluation.

Examples of the types of information that might be useful for program evaluation include pre- and post-treatment skill level, skill acquisition, recreation participation following treatment, attitudinal changes, emotional or psychological changes, or recidivism rates. Recidivism rates indicate the percentage of participants who return to treatment following completion of the treatment program. These rates are frequently used as a measure of program effectiveness in the treatment of social deviancy.

APPLICATION OF THE TR PROCESS

The following case study is provided as an illustration of the TR process.

CASE STUDY

Maurice is a 29-year-old single white male. He has been a compulsive gambler since age 22 and has a poor employment record. He completed two years of junior college. He is currently employed as an apartment complex maintenance worker. He took several junket trips to casinos and racetracks, and is heavily involved in betting on sporting events. He was forced to file bankruptcy at age 27. His parents and two siblings refuse to provide further financial assistance. Maurice has realized the need for help to eliminate, decrease, or find a substitute for his gambling behavior.

Assessment

Maurice is given a battery of assessments including the Leisure Diagnostic Battery (short form), the Boredom-in-Leisure Scale, and the Leisure Interest Inventory. In addition to these instruments, the TR specialist completes an in-depth interview to determine Maurice's current and past leisure participation. Information also is gathered to assess his leisure resources and opportunities.

Results of the comprehensive leisure assessment indicate that Maurice has a low perception of freedom in leisure and a sense of boredom with traditional leisure pursuits. His interests in leisure include risky and challenging pursuits, with little interest in highly social activity. Maurice has had minimal experience in physical or intellectual leisure pursuits, and his social interactions in leisure are generally limited to other gamblers. His financial resources for leisure are restrictive, and his knowledge of acceptable leisure opportunities is also minimal.

Planning

As with other addictive behaviors, gambling has become the center of Maurice's attention and existence. This behavior is more than an abuse of free time. Therefore he is not ready for mere substitution of behaviors; he needs to acknowledge and understand the role of gambling in his life. Given this situation, the TR specialist has selected leisure counseling as the most appropriate treatment approach. An expected outcome is for Maurice to have a better understanding of the environment or stimuli to his gambling behaviors. Other goals will be an increased awareness of his leisure alternatives and an acceptance of responsibility for his leisure choices.

Implementation

To understand the impact of gambling on his life and others, a small group technique will be utilized in treatment. The process will include the following stages: understanding gambling behaviors in general, identifying steps leading to compulsive gambling, describing specific gambling activity on an individual basis, describing feelings associated with gambling, paralleling feelings associated with socially acceptable leisure experiences, identifying specific problems associated with gambling behavior, and addressing substitutions for gambling activity. It also would be beneficial to complement the leisure counseling technique with recreation participation opportunities in which Maurice and other members of the group could acquire new skills in recreational activities.

Evaluation

In order to determine the effectiveness of the leisure counseling approach, the TR specialist will consult the progress notes of each counseling session. A final summary of the group session should address whether Maurice did, in fact, increase his understanding of the stimuli that preceded his gambling behavior. This evaluative summary also should acknowledge whether he increased his awareness of leisure alternatives and understands his responsibility for his leisure choices. As further supportive evidence, the TR specialist should reassess Maurice's leisure status, using the same leisure assessments that were used to determine his treatment program. These data could indicate a change that might be attributed to his treatment.

TRENDS AND ISSUES

One area of controversy in the treatment of social deviancy is whether to adopt a medical approach to treatment. Many therapeutic recreation specialists perceive themselves as medical personnel. Other TR specialists identify more closely with social service personnel. Although the division is not clear-cut, the social service approach is perhaps more appropriate than is the medical approach.

Parallel to the argument of specialists' identification is the debate on the professional's perception of the deviant. Is the deviant ill? Does the deviant freely and consciously choose to engage in deviant behavior? Do genetics, the environment, or socialization *cause* deviant behavior? Beliefs about the deviant actor will determine the type of treatment provided to deter future deviant behaviors. Just as these perceptions vary, so too will the types of treatment provided.

Research on the relationships between such social elements as television, music, and other forms of entertainment, and increases in violent or criminal behaviors may shed some light on our understanding of some forms of social deviancy. Research using time budgets might illustrate uses and abuses of free time, and the amount of participation in acceptable forms of leisure. These issues would be useful in increasing our understanding of social deviancy. Therapeutic recreation specialists will need to keep abreast of research efforts relevant to social deviancy and leisure.

The educational preparation of therapeutic recreation specialists should demand skill acquisition in counseling techniques. If therapeutic recreation services are to be used as a treatment for an individual's leisure-related problems, then the specialist will need to focus on service delivery at the individual level. In many cases, this individualized service would best be served via leisure counseling.

SUMMARY

This chapter provided an introduction to social norm violations that relate to leisure time, activity, and experience. Following a brief definition of social deviancy, four categories of primary consequences of social norm violation were presented and illustrated: physical harm to self or others, emotional harm to others, addiction, and social disorder. Three limitations to the treatment of deviant behaviors were identified.

The role of therapeutic recreation was described as the promotion of socially acceptable leisure pursuits that might substitute for deviant behaviors. Leisure education and leisure counseling processes were suggested as appropriate treatment approaches. Several settings or organizations that could provide therapeutic recreation services were briefly described. The therapeutic recreation processes of assessment, planning, implementation, and evaluation were briefly described. A case study of a compulsive gambler was provided to illustrate the therapeutic recreation process. The case study specifically addressed the processes of assessment, planning, implementation, and evaluation.

A brief overview of anticipated trends and issues relevant to therapeutic recreation and social deviancy identified areas of professional debate or controversy, and suggested changes in the educational preparation of therapeutic recreation specialists.

The reader is invited and challenged to understand how social deviancy problems are actually leisure problems. For those who intend to pursue a professional career in leisure services, a further challenge is to accept the role as a human service provider committed to reducing social problems and enhancing socially acceptable leisure behaviors.

READING COMPREHENSION QUESTIONS

1. Who determines whether a behavior or activity is considered socially deviant?

2. Identify three schools of thought that attempt to explain social deviance.

3. What are four primary and negative consequences to deviant behaviors? Give examples for each of the consequences.

4. Illustrate the stages of addiction, using one of the following substances or behaviors: jogging, desserts, caffeine, cigarettes, alcohol.

5. Name three possible limitations to the treatment of problems related to social deviancy.

6. What is the primary purpose of therapeutic recreation in the area of social deviancy?

7. Name and briefly describe the two recommended treatment approaches for deviancy-related problems.

8. List five settings or organizations available for the treatment of social deviancy problems.

9. What two types of assessments were recommended for designing and delivering TR services?

10. List several guidelines that should be considered before implementing a TR program.

SUGGESTED LEARNING ACTIVITIES

1. Read the local newspaper carefully over a one-week period. Collect articles that are directly related to social deviance. Categorize the articles (1) by region (local, state, national, and international); (2) by consequences listed in the chapter; or (3) by age groups (i.e., child, adolescent, adult, older adult). Summarize and discuss your findings in class.

2. Visit one of the service settings/organizations described in the chapter. Determine the prevalence of clientele who are victims/actors of deviant behaviors. Determine the role and priorities of recreation in that setting or organization. Develop a brief summary of this experience.

3. An annotated bibliography consists of a selection of readings (usually journal articles) on a single topic. Each article in the bibliography is briefly summarized. Develop an annotated bibliography of 10–15 journal articles on any topic presented in this chapter (e.g., child abuse, pornography, leisure education with a deviant group, eating disorders). The annotated bibliography consists of three parts: introduction to your topic, presentation of article summaries, and a conclusion that highlights themes, consistencies, or contradictions in the articles read.

4. Select an article from a recent issue of one journal from the following list. Read the article carefully. As you read it, think about leisure-related issues you consider relevant to the topic of the article. Summarize the article and your connection(s) to leisure. Prepare to present this summary in class.

Selected Journals Related to Social Deviance:

> *Addictive Behaviors: An International Journal*
> *International Journal of the Addictions*
> *British Journal of Addiction*
> *International Journal of Eating Disorders*
> *Journal of Studies on Alcohol*
> *American Journal of Drug and Alcohol Abuse*
> *Journal of Drug Abuse*
> *Deviant Behavior*
> *Victimology: An International Journal*
> *Crime and Delinquency*
> *Social Problems*

REFERENCES

Aguilar, T. E. (1986a). Leisure education program development and evaluation. *Journal of Expanding Horizons in Therapeutic Recreation, 1*, 14–21.

Aguilar, T. E. (1986b). Recreation—An untapped resource. *Corrections Today, 48*(2), 173–175, 178.

AGUILAR, T. E. (1987). Effects of a leisure education program on expressed attitudes of delinquent adolescents. *Therapeutic Recreation Journal, 21*(4), 43–51.

ALLEN-HAGEN, B. (1988). Children in custody. *Juvenile Justice Bulletin.* U.S. Department of Justice.

BECK, A. T., WEISSMAN, A., LESTER, D., & TREXLER, L. (1974). *Hopelessness scale.* Washington, DC: American Psychological Association.

BROWNMILLER, S. (1975). *Against our will: Men, women, and rape.* New York: Bantam Books.

CODDINGTON, R. D. (1981). *Life Event Scale—adolescents.* St. Clairsville, OH: Stress Research.

CONRAD, P., & SCHNEIDER, J. W. (1980). *Deviance and medicalization: From badness to sickness.* St. Louis: C. V. Mosby.

COOPERSMITH, S. (1981). *Self-esteem inventories.* Palo Alto, CA: Consulting Psychologists Press.

CSIKSZENTMIHALYI, M., & LARSON, R. (1978). Intrinsic rewards in school crime. *Crime and Delinquency, 24,* 322–335.

DOUGLAS, J. D. (1984). *The sociology of deviance.* Boston: Allyn & Bacon.

ELLIS, G. D., & NILES, S. (1985). Development, reliability and preliminary validation of a brief leisure rating scale. *Therapeutic Recreation Journal, 19,* 50–61.

ETHERINGTON, T. (1987, January). People use drink/drugs to make life "interesting." *The Journal* (Toronto), p. 1.

EVE, R. A. (1985). Empirical and theoretical findings concerning child and adolescent sexual abuse: Implications for the next generation of studies. *Victimology: An International Journal, 10,* 97–109.

FENIGSTEIN, A., SCHEIER, M., & BUSS, A. (1975). *Self-Consciousness Scale.* Washington, DC: American Psychological Association.

GIBSON, P. M. (1979). Therapeutic aspects of wilderness programs: A comprehensive literature review. *Therapeutic Recreation Journal, 13*(2), 21–31.

HUBERT, E. E. (1969). The development of an inventory of leisure interests. Unpublished doctoral dissertation, University of North Carolina, Chapel Hill.

HUNTER, I. R. (1984). The impact of voluntary selection procedures on the reported success of outdoor rehabilitation programs. *Therapeutic Recreation Journal, 18*(3), 38–44.

HUON, G. F., BROWN, L., & MORRIS, S. (1988). Lay beliefs about disordered eating. *International Journal of Eating Disorders, 7*(12), 239–252.

ISO-AHOLA, S. E., & WEISSINGER, E. (1987). *The Leisure Boredom Scale: Internal consistency and construct validation data.* Manuscript submitted for publication.

KAUFMAN, J. E., McBRIDE, L. G., HULTSMAN, J. T., & BLACK, D. R. (1988). Perceptions of leisure and an eating disorder: An exploratory study of bulimia. *Therapeutic Recreation Journal, 22*(1), 55–63.

KOSBERG, J. I. (1985). Victimization of the elderly: Causation and prevention. *Victimology: An International Journal, 10,* 376–396.

LISKA, A. E. (1981). *Perspectives on deviance.* Englewood Cliffs, NJ: Prentice-Hall.

LIVINGSTON, J. (1984). From adventurous to compulsive gambling. In J. D. Douglas (Ed.), *The sociology of deviance* (pp. 191–198). Boston: Allyn & Bacon.

McDOWELL, C. F. (1984). Leisure: Consciousness, well-being, and counseling. In E. T. Dowd (Ed.), *Leisure counseling: Concepts and applications.* Springfield, IL: Charles C. Thomas.

McGURRIN, M., ABT, V., & SMITH, J. (1984). Play or pathology: A new look at the gambler and his world. In B. Sutton-Smith & D. Kelly-Byrne (Eds.), *The masks of play* (pp. 88–99). New York: Leisure Press.

McKECHNIE, G. E. (1974). *Manual for the Leisure Activities Blank.* Palo Alto, CA: Consulting Psychologists Press.

Moos, R. H. (1979). *Family Environment Scale*. Palo Alto, CA: Consulting Psychologists Press.

Mundy, J., & Odum, L. (1979). *Leisure education: Theory and practice*. New York: John Wiley & Sons.

Munson, W. W. (1984). Helping: Multimodal leisure counseling with delinquent youth. In G. L. Hitzhusen (Ed.), *Expanding horizons in therapeutic recreation* (pp. 185–213). Columbia, MO: Curators University of Missouri.

Munson, W. W., Baker, S. B., & Lundegren, H. M. (1985). Strength training and leisure counseling as treatments for institutionalized juvenile delinquents. *Adapted Physical Activity Quarterly, 2*, 65–75.

Nees, H. (1988). Tackling the ultimate taboo. [Review of *The sexual trafficking in children*]. *Law Enforcement News, 14*(268), 13–14.

Pavlos, A. J. (1979). *Social psychology and the study of deviant behavior*. Washington, DC: University Press of America.

Peterson, C. A., & Gunn, S. L. (1984). *Therapeutic recreation program design: Principles and procedures* (2nd ed.). Englewood Cliffs, NJ: Prentice-Hall.

Riemer, J. W. (1981). Deviance as fun. *Adolescence, 16*(61), 39–43.

Scully, D., & Marolla J. (1984). Convicted rapists' vocabulary of motive: Excuses and justification. *Social Problems, 32*(3), 530–544.

Slivken, K. E. (1978). *Development of a Leisure Ethic Scale*. Unpublished master's thesis. University of Illinois, Champaign-Urbana.

Travisono, D. N. (Ed.). (1985). *Directory of juvenile and adult correctional departments, institutions, agencies and paroling authorities*. College Park, MD: American Correctional Association.

Van Dijk, W. K. (1986). *Addictive Behavior*. Englewood, CO: Morton Publishing.

Witt, P. A., Ellis, G. D., Compton, D. M., Howard, G., Aguilar, T. E., Forsyth, P., Niles, S., & Costilow, A. (1982). *The Leisure Diagnostic Battery: Background, conceptualization, and structure*. Denton: North Texas State University, Division of Recreation and Leisure Studies.

6

Substance Abuse

ROBIN KUNSTLER

OBJECTIVES

- Define terms used to describe drug and alcohol abuse.
- Comprehend the effects and scope of drug and alcohol abuse.
- Understand the purposes and benefits of TR programs.
- Know typical treatment approaches used with this population.
- Know how the TR process is used with this population.
- Evaluate social and economic trends and issues as they impact on drug abuse and alcoholism and their treatment.

DEFINITION OF TERMS

A drug can be defined as any nonnutritional chemical substance that can be absorbed into the body. It can be either a prescribed medicine or something taken voluntarily (usually) to produce a temporary, pleasurable (usually) effect.

Most *psychoactive drugs* are used for the changes they produce in how a person feels. Psychoactive drugs affect the brain directly by changing one's perceptions of how the brain interprets the messages it receives. The drug causes the brain to read "painlessness" for "pain," for example. Abuse of drugs is a major health problem for millions of users, their families, and their friends, and it affects society as well.

The following are commonly used terms to describe problems with drug and alcohol use:

1. *Substance or drug abuse* is the repeated use of any drug to the point where it seriously interferes with health, economic status, or social functioning.

2. *Chemical dependency* involves developing a reliance on one or a combination of drugs that alter moods to achieve pleasure and happiness. The body adapts to the presence of the drug (this can occur without addiction).

3. *Addiction* is a chronic disorder characterized by compulsive use of a substance. It results in physical and/or psychological danger to the individual and involves continued use of the substance despite its harmful effects. Addiction is an irresistible compulsion to use a drug at increasing doses and frequency, even in the presence of severe physical or psychological side effects and the extreme disruption of the user's personal relationships and system of values.

Drug and alcohol abuse is a major health problem in the United States. The most prevalent form of drug abuse is alcoholism. Some estimates of alcohol addiction go as high as 20 million Americans over age 18. Their alcohol problems affect an additional 56 million people, half of whom are children of alcoholics. Of these children, 12–14 million are dependent children of female alcoholics. One in three families is affected by a problem drinker. Additionally, alcohol is the most widely used drug by youth. Almost one in three youths can be classified as a problem drinker.

For most problem drinkers under age 35, alcohol is used in combination with other drugs. It is often used after cocaine. Of the 22 million Americans who have tried cocaine at least once, almost 6 million are regular users and 1 million are addicted. "Crack," an extremely addictive, inexpensive, and readily available form of cocaine, became a severe problem in the cities in the mid-1980s.

Three and a half million Americans have reported occasional use of heroin; between 500,000–700,000 are heroin addicts. This number has been fairly constant since the early 1970s.

Seven million Americans use sleeping pills once a week or more. Although these drugs are medically prescribed, taking a tranquilizer for more than four to six weeks carries the risk of dependency. In fact, more people die from prescription drugs each year than from all illegal substances combined (Gold, 1986).

CLASSIFICATION OF DRUGS

Drugs can be classified as depressants, such as narcotics (opiate derivatives: opium, morphine, heroin, and methadone), alcohol, and barbiturates; and stimulants, including cocaine and amphetamines. These drugs are referred to as "hard addictions" because of the quickness with which they affect many aspects of behavior and adversely influence many people around the user. Addiction can occur to one or a combination of several drugs that affect the central nervous system.

Some drugs, such as caffeine, are freely available. Nicotine and alcohol are considered more harmful, and their use is discouraged but not prohibited. Barbiturates, amphetamines, and tranquilizers have legitimate medical uses as well as significant potential for harm. Marijuana and heroin are considered to be harmful to individuals and society, and their medical use is largely unexplored.

When does use become abuse? According to the American Psychiatric Association, substance abuse is distinguished from normal use by three criteria: (1) a pattern of pathological use (lack of control over how much of the substance is used and when it is used), (2) impairment in social or occupational functioning caused by the pattern of pathological use, and (3) a pattern of abuse that continues for at least one month (DSM-IIIR).

The following chart depicts the progression of drug use/abuse:

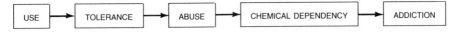

USE → TOLERANCE → ABUSE → CHEMICAL DEPENDENCY → ADDICTION

An individual who uses a drug may not necessarily go beyond any one of the stages. Progress depends on several factors: (1) predisposition to a drug problem, based on heredity, physiology, psychology, and/or socioculture; (2) the drug itself (which drug, the dosage, potency, availability, and how it's used—orally, intravenously, etc.); and (3) the enabling system of one's own attitudes and the attitudes of family, friends, and society. Successful treatment of addiction requires understanding why a drug is more addictive in one society than another, for one individual and not another, and for the same individual at one time and not another (Peele, 1985).

DESCRIPTION OF LIMITATIONS

All drug abusers may be victims of their own neglect in terms of personal health and self-care. Disorientation, confusion, and fear of drug withdrawal often characterize their condition when they enter treatment.

Alcoholics may suffer blackouts, seizures, and chest pains. They may have brain damage from injuries sustained in falls or from banging their heads. Some alcoholics may be taking Antabuse, a medication that causes violent illness if alcohol is ingested.

Chronic heroin users can be suffering from malnutrition, high blood pressure, or diabetes. They may have a history of hepatitis, broken bones, and various infections. Cocaine abusers often suffer from exhaustion.

The therapeutic recreation specialist must be aware of the possible medical and/or physical complications that may affect clients' recreation participation.

PURPOSE OF THERAPEUTIC RECREATION

Therapeutic recreation has an important role in drug abuse treatment and rehabilitation because of the emphasis on treating the whole person and changing his or her life-style. Most drug abusers have passive and sedentary life-styles that they need to change in order for them to be successful after their drug abuse has ended. According to Berg and Neulinger (1976), "The importance of helping the individual live meaningfully during his non-working hours has been recognized as a critical aspect of rehabilitation programs."

Therapeutic recreation can contribute to overall treatment by creating an atmosphere that is positive and therapeutic, offering an avenue for developing stress management techniques and social skills, and providing leisure education. A primary function of the TR specialist is to help the client find healthy means to satisfy the needs previously met through drug taking. The abilities to experience fun and pleasure and feel capable and in control of their lives are often lacking in the drug abuser. A well-planned TR program provides opportunities to develop these abilities and experience them in personally satisfying and meaningful leisure pursuits. Clients need to develop interests that they can pursue post-treatment that do not involve contact with drugs, drug users, and the drug-abusing environment.

Providing a nonpunitive and confidential atmosphere in which clients are treated with dignity and respect, and in which staff serve as positive role models of effective functioning without the use of drugs, is the first objective of the TR program. As a TR professional, you should be straightforward and nonjudgmental in your concern. However, addicts are known to be manipulative. Exercise control and set limits on acting-out behaviors while allowing clients to express their feelings in a safe context. Community meetings and client responsibility to monitor the environment for drugs are recommended. Addicts have a need for structure that can be provided by a comprehensive program that allows for choice within the restrictions imposed by the treatment setting. For example, if clients must attend all programs, including TR, allow them choice by having them (1) select the specific game or craft for the group, (2) select an individual quiet activity to do in the same room, or (3) be a spectator. Contract with them (have them make an agreement with you) that they can choose this alternative for a period of time, such as three days or two consecutive sessions. In this way, they are given control over their own behavior within the structured setting but are being supported and shown that they can eventually make a positive, healthy decision.

In order to present himself or herself as a role model, it is essential for the TR specialist to develop a trust relationship with the client. The TR specialist should be able to participate in recreation with joy and a sense of fun. Addicts may feel guilty about having fun if they do not feel they deserve it. Activities that allow them slowly to shed their inhibitions, such as holiday activities, contests, and games from childhood, are nonthreatening choices.

Clients need to develop feelings of competence and control through learning social skills, coping techniques, and decision-making processes. Addicts' behaviors often include impulsivity, low frustration tolerance, a tendency to place blame for their situation on persons and circumstances outside of themselves, denial, rationalization, and manipulativeness. To change these behaviors involves development of self-awareness, personal efficacy, and satisfying alternatives to drug abuse. Therapy works best when it requires clients to change attitudes, practice skills, and make life changes, and when it attributes these changes to the client (Peele, 1985). Sessions in relaxation techniques, assertiveness training, social skills training, exercise and other fitness activities, as well as participating in the planning, organizing, and operation of the activities can help addicts learn more about themselves and acquire methods to function without drugs. Honest, supportive feedback is essential to helping them identify their gains in these areas. They can build their self-esteem through completion of success-oriented recreation experiences for which they receive praise. Addicts function in the here and now, so they need to plan for today and work on today's goals, not for a distant future (even tomorrow) that is out of their control. Encourage them to receive feedback from their peers as well as from staff.

Developing a satisfying leisure life-style through assessment of leisure interests, acquiring leisure skills, and engaging in leisure pursuits are essential to successful functioning post-treatment. Addicts improve when their relationships to work, family, and other aspects of their environment improve. They can give up rewards they get from their addiction when they believe they will find superior gratification from other activities in their regular lives (Peele, 1985). A leisure education program that includes daily enjoyable recreation participation can demonstrate to the addict that there are healthy sources of gratification available *everyday*. Discussion of reasons why clients drink or take drugs, the results of substance abuse, and alternative coping mechanisms can help clients choose healthy outlets. Identifying barriers to leisure participation, discussing societal expectations of behavior, clarifying personal values, and choosing among alternatives are particularly suitable leisure education activities. Determining leisure interests through self-assessment and activity inventories, developing leisure participation skills, and participating in a variety of realistic activities to be pursued alone, at home, and with one's family are components of leisure education. The TR program can provide an environment in which to try out these newly acquired behaviors.

The goal of all treatment for drug abuse, dependence, and addiction should be sobriety, a state beyond abstinence, because it involves reshaping of life-styles and values as well as not using the problem substance(s). Sobriety demands that an addict find new ways to have fun, relax, deal with stress, and experience satisfaction. Too often, not enough effort goes into developing new forms of recreation for clients. This process requires practice and energy. However, it is essential to successful recovery and should be the primary purpose of therapeutic recreation with this population.

COMMON SERVICE SETTINGS

Scientists are still debating how best to treat substance abuse. The National Institute on Alcohol Abuse and Alcoholism began a research program in 1987 to compare effectiveness of inpatient and outpatient treatment, especially in light of increasing drug abuse and rising treatment costs.

Treatment can take place in a variety of settings. The severity of addiction should be considered in choosing a treatment setting. Schnoll (1986) describes four treatment settings:

1. An *acute-care hospital program*, often in a major medical center, provides assessment through observation and use of diagnostic tests, stabilization of patients' conditions, and a safe, medically approved method of withdrawal from the drug. Patients are helped to realize the severity of their problem, are educated about the nature of addiction, and are encouraged to continue treatment. Individual and group therapy, vocational rehabilitation, and peer support are offered. The length of stay is typically 3–30 days.

2. *Residential care* is less intensive than acute care and provides less medical care, but it offers maximum structure and more counseling. There are five types of residential care: (1) The first is hospital-based, offering three to four weeks of standardized treatment. (2) Freestanding facilities, the second type, are independent of hospitals and have a positive, retreatlike atmosphere, vocational and educational counseling, and a length of stay of over one month. (3) The first therapeutic community, Synanon, was established in 1959. This is a long-term (6–24 months) residential program with a self-help and psychological focus on restructuring the addict's personality and character. Usually staffed mostly by recovering addicts, it offers a rigidly structured program with punishments and rewards and an emphasis on confrontation. (4) Halfway houses are communal living situations that provide a transition between a 24-hour-a-day treatment environment and independent living. (5) Detoxification centers provide food, clothing, shelter, and medication for a 1- to 5-day period.

3. *Partial hospitalization* is for those clients needing structure but who can live at home, work, or attend school. Services include self-help, education, and individual, family, and group therapy.

4. *Outpatient services* offers a wide variety of programs. They can provide methadone maintenance, medication, milieu therapy, self-help,

psychotherapy, and relaxation training. About 80% of addiction treatment is on an outpatient basis.

CURRENT BEST PRACTICES AND PROCEDURES

Historically, treatment for drug abusers began with two federal hospitals: Lexington, Kentucky (1935) and Fort Worth, Texas (1938). Those convicted of the "crime" of addiction (officially, the drug addict was viewed as a criminal) were sent to these hospitals for detoxification and prolonged isolation from the environment in which the addiction occurred. But this approach was not successful because patients had severe difficulty readjusting to their communities. Most addicts returned to addiction after discharge. The need for preparation to return to the community was finally recognized in 1952, when Riverside Hospital in New York City began a program to treat juvenile drug addicts, with an emphasis on readjustment to the home community.

In the 1960s reports that heroin addicts could be treated successfully with methadone, a synthetic morphine substitute, led to the establishment of methadone treatment programs in many cities. These provided alternatives to the mostly unsuccessful treatment programs that emphasized abstinence. It was hoped that the rise in urban street crime committed by heroin addicts, "junkies," could be reduced by methadone treatment. However, federal officials were reluctant to be supportive because many saw it as substituting one addiction for another. The advantage of methadone use was that clients appeared more alert, energetic, and motivated. Methadone can be taken orally, and its effects last up to 24 hours.

In the early 1970s drug treatment programs were expanded, in great part because of the returning Vietnam veterans, who reportedly had high levels of drug addiction. The Veterans' Administration expanded its programs. However, the fears of large numbers of addicted veterans trained in warfare returning to the United States did not materialize. In the late 1970s, President Jimmy Carter called for programs to treat abusers of barbiturates, amphetamines, and combinations of drugs, including alcohol.

Treatment always begins with detoxification and medical care to restore physical health. Detoxification is the metabolism and excretion of drugs from the body, which can take from hours to weeks. Although therapeutic programs may be offered, their intensity increases after "detox."

A popular treatment model is the milieu therapy approach, in which all aspects of the treatment environment contribute to the client's care. This usually includes group therapy, individual psychotherapy, an emphasis on social skills development, and availability of support groups such as Alcoholics Anonymous (AA) and Narcotics Anonymous (NA). Other services, such as vocational rehabilitation, social services, occupational therapy, therapeutic recreation, creative arts therapy, and family therapy have become more popular as rehabilitation philosophy takes the holistic view of client needs. Frequently, treatment is delivered by an interdisciplinary team. The community reinforcement approach recognizes the importance of providing help from a clinician in the community to assist clients in finding employment, improving family and marital relationships, and enhancing social skills.

Alcoholics Anonymous (AA) is the most famous form of treatment for drug abusers. Begun in 1935, there are 1.5 million members worldwide. In New York City alone there are 1,826 weekly meetings. About 60% of those who attend AA stay as members. Anyone can join by just walking into a meeting. Philosophically, members recognize they cannot refrain from drinking on their own and need to talk about it with others. Meetings are loosely structured, and members provide support to each other to stay sober. Today, more and more members are addicted to other drugs in addition to alcohol, or just to other drugs alone. But they feel AA provides the support to refrain from substance abuse. Alcoholics Anonymous is a fellowship of alcoholics (and others) who believe that maintaining a life of sobriety depends on admitting that they no longer have control over alcohol. They find help in surrendering to a power (spiritual or personal) that is greater than themselves. Some experts point out that there is no empirical evidence to prove AA is effective. However, many members feel AA and NA are significant factors in maintaining their recovery from substance abuse.

Assessment

Assessment procedures for drug abusers follow the same basic principles and guidelines used for other groups. Techniques of observation and interview, as well as reports from family, friends, and other treatment staff, are utilized. During their initial assessment, drug abusers may be in poor health owing to their life-style. Their reactions and reflexes are slower than normal, and their coordination is poor. Therefore, TR specialists should plan to reassess the client after detox and when his or her health status stabilizes. Particular attention should be given to the client's stress management and social and leisure skills.

The first observation is usually of the client's physical appearance. What is his or her level of self-care and grooming? Adjustment to the treatment environment and program is frequently difficult. Is the client familiar with any stress management techniques, such as yoga, relaxation, exercise, or other fitness activities that he or she can practice? How developed are his or her verbal and nonverbal communication skills? How does he or she relate to peers and to authority figures? To what degree does he or she exhibit motivation and tolerate frustration? How is his or her impulse control? What is the client's ability to express feelings and make decisions? Does he or she possess a repertoire of cooperative, competitive, and solitary play skills?

Addicts tend not to have well-defined interests and take a passive approach to leisure participation. They see leisure as empty. Assessment of leisure functioning can include prior interests, availability of persons to recreate with, activity skills, awareness of leisure, perception of leisure time, and knowledge of community resources. Try to determine what needs the drug satisfies in order to use recreation instead to satisfy those needs. Clients should participate actively in the definition of the problem, goal setting, selection of intervention strategies, and evaluation of progress.

Planning

Activities in therapeutic recreation programs for drug abusers should be planned based on the client's needs, behaviors, and personality. The client's own statement of his or her problem should be of utmost consideration. By addressing the issue with which the client is most preoccupied, progress moves faster, and the client is more willing to participate in treatment. For the drug abuser, a new way of life is necessary, one that encompasses new skills and abilities.

An unpublished paper "Alternatives to the High Life" (Neves, Beck, & Lawrence, 1974) presented some of the following approaches to drug rehabilitation. Addiction is a coping mechanism that is not necessarily an escape, but a way of survival and a way of life. Treatment can provide opportunities to practice normal, daily activities such as household living, family recreation, and having fun. Through role playing, for example, addicts can view their needs and behaviors in different ways and try out new skills and methods of interacting.

Addicts have a great need for acceptance and attention. Provide this with a smile, a touch, or praise about their involvement or participation. At times, redirect this need toward interaction with their peers or toward continuing their work on a project on their own. Activities such as New Games, which emphasize cooperation instead of competition, offer group emotional support and trust. Working collectively on a group project, such as a mural painting, music performance, or play production, can also promote trust and cooperation.

Addicts need to build enjoyable and creative activities into their daily routine. Programs such as exercise, yoga, relaxation, and fitness exercises should begin almost immediately because they aid in treatment as well as have long-term benefits.

One study found that college students who were heavy drinkers were able to reduce their alcohol consumption by 30–40% when they either did aerobic exercise or practiced meditation. Those who did both regularly reduced alcohol intake by 50–60% (Kutner, 1987).

Other beneficial activities are walking, swimming, bike riding, weight lifting, sports such as basketball, assertiveness training, group brainstorming, and discussion groups. Women substance abusers particularly need discussion groups led by women.

Outdoor activities seem to enhance feelings of freedom and enjoyment. Organizations such as Outward Bound stress the natural highs that come from rock climbing, mountaineering, and wilderness survival, which can contribute to the development of self-esteem and feelings of self-worth. These and other high-risk and challenge activities provide excitement through nondrug means. Addicts' drug-oriented life-style provided them with excitement and dreams that must now be experienced in other ways. Trips, parties, the arts, and nature are possible choices.

Outlets for inner anger and hostility can be released through volleyball, Ping-Pong, bowling, woodworking, and clay work. Discussions that follow these activities can focus on clients' feelings and the means of expressing them. If clients feel an activity has worked for them, they can then learn more about the resources necessary to incorporate it into their leisure life-style.

Addicts are often noted for their impulsivity. This can be controlled through activities that take time to complete, such as candle making and relay races, so the clients can slowly experience delayed gratification. For those who never put impulses into action, beginning to act is a form of control.

Leisure education is of course an essential part of the addict's TR program. Exploring the addict's perception of and attitude toward leisure and free time, examining personal barriers to leisure participation and developing strategies to overcome these barriers, identifying interests, and building activity skills are important components of leisure education. Family recreation can provide a positive, healthy form of family interaction.

Without predischarge counseling and the development of referrals for the continuation of satisfying leisure activities, the effectiveness of TR treatment is diminished. The TR specialist should follow the client into the community, providing counseling, evaluation, and cooperation with community agencies.

Implementation

In implementing the TR program, as with overall treatment and rehabilitation, a multimodality approach is more efficient than a one-dimensional approach (Craig, 1985), because there is no one strategy or technique that works best with *all* patients. Therapy succeeds when it increases people's sense of their strength to withstand uncertainty and discomfort as well as to generate positive rewards for themselves (Peele, 1985). Opportunities to explore possible rewards and feedback given in a supportive, structured environment should be provided. Clients should participate in conducting activities as well as planning them. This gives them more of an investment in the program, makes them aware of problems, involved in programming, and gives them opportunities to do something worthwhile by assisting the TR specialist (Earle, 1981).

Implementation begins with the initial contact between the TR specialist and the client. This meeting is the first step in establishing a relationship that may prove to be a factor in clients' staying in treatment. Encourage clients to use recreation activities as stress reduction aids and to identify realistic, constructive leisure pursuits in which they can participate immediately. Promote group cohesiveness and trust in the relaxed atmosphere of the recreation setting. In this setting, clients can be encouraged to take responsibility for their own behavior and to monitor the behavior of their peers. Set limits, but be sure they understand the rules and why they exist, or they may not follow them. Offer realistic praise and reinforcement in order to aid them in the development of a healthy leisure life-style.

Evaluation

Evaluation is an especially critical function of the TR specialist with this population, because the TR specialist is monitoring changes in the course of the illness as well as treating leisure dysfunction. Careful observation of clients' behaviors and recording of their expressed feelings is necessary. The TR specialist is responsible for providing input at interdisciplinary team meetings, revising clients' care plans according to their changes and progress, and doing accurate, explicit documentation. It is also important to use clients' self-reports on their drug use, their leisure participation, and their feelings and reactions to these experiences. The clients should be made aware of the TR specialist's evaluation of their progress as well as be asked to reflect on their own perceptions of their progress.

APPLICATION OF THE TR PROCESS

The following case will be used to illustrate the application of the TR process with a drug abuse client. The four steps in the process are assessment, planning, implementation, and evaluation. Following the presentation of the case, each step will be discussed as applied to the case.

CASE STUDY

The client, David, is a 26-year-old single white male admitted for detoxification from cocaine. He was employed as an accountant until three months ago. He lives with two male roommates in a rental apartment in New York City. Both parents and a 23-year-old brother live nearby. His medical doctor referred him for admission to this 30-day inpatient treatment unit.

Assessment

Prior to meeting the client for the assessment interview, the TR specialist should review the following information from the client's chart: physical and mental status, duration of addiction, functional limitations resulting from addiction, family social history, results of neurological and psychological tests, educational and occupational background, purposes and results expected from treatment, and general treatment goals that have been established.

During the initial client contact, the TR specialist should begin developing a rapport with the client. Building a trust relationship is the key to successful involvement of the client in the TR programs, as well as an important factor influencing his or her attitude toward overall treatment. The TR specialist should display warmth, genuine interest, and concern when greeting the client, but not be overwhelming. The TR professional should state his or her name, offer a nonthreatening handshake, and explain the purpose of the visit. At this time the TR specialist can begin to observe the client's physical appearance, body language, and communication skills. Other key areas to assess are the client's leisure history, including past and present leisure interests and recreational pursuits, participation patterns (with whom did he or she participate in recreation, how often, where, etc.), attitude toward leisure, and attitude toward and feelings about self and treatment. The client should be encouraged to explore what he or she could gain from the TR program.

In David's case, the TR assessment yielded the following information. During the interview, the client was very talkative but rambling, and then would lapse into silence. He would then begin talking abruptly, his eyes darting around the room. He did not look at the TR specialist, although he welcomed the TR specialist into his room and invited the TR specialist to sit down. He complained of fatigue and could not focus on the discussion. The TR specialist terminated the interview after ten minutes, after obtaining the client's agreement to meet again in five days.

David was seen a second time for reassessment as scheduled. He was subdued, sat in a chair, spoke slowly, and answered the TR specialist's questions. Although eye contact was still poor, the client's eyes were downcast rather than darting. He was neat and well groomed, although he appeared fatigued (an occasional stifled yawn, slowed speech). He told the TR specialist that he was socially active in college, attending parties and dating casually within a large group of friends. He volunteered the information that he dabbled in smoking marijuana and drinking. He did not perceive that behavior as a problem at the time. His family recreated together, playing tennis and taking summer vacations, but each member also pursued independent interests. After college graduation, the client moved in with roommates, got a job as an accountant, attended night school for an MBA, and became active in a late-night social life. His experimentation with cocaine led to increased involvement, he stopped attending school, and his work behavior was affected. His roommates finally convinced him to seek help.

Planning

Following assessment, the TR specialist draws up an individualized plan of treatment for the client that includes goals and an activity program. David's treatment goals are these:

1. Establish a trust relationship with the TR specialist.
2. Use personal relaxation techniques.
3. Improve physical fitness.
4. Find an outlet for self-expression.
5. Identify a satisfying leisure interest.
6. Develop cooperative relationships with others.

To attempt to meet these goals, the following schedule is made for David and presented to him by the TR specialist for his agreement to participate:

- Daily A.M.—yoga (for relaxation and fitness)
- Tues. A.M.—bowling (for fitness, leisure, and interest development)
- Thurs. A.M.—swimming (for fitness, leisure, and interest development)
- Mon. and Wed. P.M.—leisure education (focus on perceptions of leisure and alternative recreation choices)
- Evenings—social recreation such as word games, New Games, parties (for relaxation and cooperation)
- Weekend—camping trip on third weekend (for trust, cooperation, self-expression, and leisure interests)
- Client's choice—daily arts and crafts, coffee hour, and weekly sing-along as desired

Implementation

David has agreed to and signed the TR care plan. As treatment progresses, feelings of anger and hostility may surface. Intervention techniques include limit setting, redirecting dependency needs toward the task at hand or peer interaction, encouraging taking responsibility during activities, and offering praise, support, and constructive feedback. The client's motivation may lag. He should be reminded that he has agreed to this plan of care. Encourage him to discuss feelings about treatment. Offer creative arts as a means to express feelings. This is not "required" in the care plan because the client should experience the freedom to express self in this way.

The client's self-image is badly shaken. Keeping score in bowling and word games and planning for the camping trip are responsibilities that build on his previous skills. He needs to restore his emotional strength. His previous interests included sports, dining out, TV, movies, and reading. Explore his perception of leisure as an opportunity to express and fulfill self. Encourage experimentation with various media such as painting, ceramics, poetry, singing, and musical instruments. He needs to identify "healthy" friends with common interests. Invite his family to the unit party after three weeks.

Evaluation

Evaluation is made during and at the termination of treatment. Observations of David during treatment revealed that he was becoming more stable but was still quiet in groups and slightly suspicious of others' intentions. Although his recreation interests were more individual, such as painting daily, he participated in a group sing-along on Friday nights and was helpful to other patients, especially elderly alcoholics who were less physically capable. During leisure education sessions he expressed that his life-style needed changing so he could avoid stressful situations. During the weekend camping trip he participated in New Games and cooperative cooking and clean-up tasks. Upon return to the unit he seemed more relaxed and laughed a few times.

David is making progress toward goals; he is responsive to the TR specialist and open about feelings within the context of a professional relationship. To relax, he uses deep breathing learned in yoga. His physical health has improved as a result of hospital care; swimming and bowling have contributed to this. He has developed a strong interest in painting as a means of self-expression. Several of these activities can become part of his new leisure life-style. He is cooperative with others. However, he still appears to have feelings that need to be expressed verbally and a need to develop more trusting relationships with others.

Discharge Plan

The discharge plan is critical to maintaining and building on the progress made in treatment. On the recommendation of the treatment plan, David is being referred to an outpatient day program for 30 days. He has agreed to attend Narcotics Anonymous meetings and wants to seek a new job in a smaller company. He plans to buy painting supplies and continue some form of aerobic exercise. He wants to spend more time with his brother. Values clarification will be part of his outpatient treatment. He says he will use yoga as a relaxation tool. He hopes to explore his feelings toward his parents and family dynamics during individual psychotherapy sessions.

David's case represents one type of drug-abusing client. The poor, inner-city, poly-drug abuser would not have the same educational, occupational, or family background and would need longer treatment, job skills training, and schooling programs. Some TR goals and programs could be similar and other activities substituted, based on available resources.

The life-style of the addict includes not only the habit of drug use, but patterns of language, ethics, and behavior. Restructuring of the life-style could include stress management, values clarification, and assertiveness training. Awareness of one's problem and the necessity of change are crucial, as are learning to accept and understand one's own feelings and appropriate nondrug coping mechanisms.

TRENDS AND ISSUES

Most of the trends in the areas of drug abuse, including alcoholism, are not reassuring. Drug dependency among youth, women, and individuals in the inner cities is on the rise. Although use of one substance may decrease, abuse of another takes its place. In addition, poly-drug abuse and dual diagnosis of psychiatric illness and alcoholism or another drug addiction is rising. (There are reportedly very few "pure" alcoholics under age 35.) Use of crack, a relatively cheap and extremely addictive form of cocaine, often followed by alcohol to counteract the severe letdown of a crack high, is widespread in poor urban areas. Crack use is also increasing among young professionals.

Many intravenous (IV) drug users also have the disease AIDS (acquired immune deficiency syndrome) contracted from sharing needles with an infected person. They are often poor, with little family or social service support available. Babies are being born with AIDS, fetal alcohol syndrome, or addiction to cocaine or heroin because their mothers are drug abusers or alcoholics.

Although the number of treatment programs appears to be increasing, many have waiting lists of several years. Most addicts continue their drug abusing behavior while waiting for treatment, which has a 40–50% failure rate, regardless of treatment philosophy (Mast, 1987). No single approach has been shown to be effective in the treatment of alcoholism and chemical dependency (NIAAA, 1986). It is generally accepted that Alcoholics Anonymous and Narcotics Anonymous are significant factors in maintaining a drug-free existence for those who have recovered. The group-meeting format provides support and sharing. Standing up at a meeting and saying "I am an alcoholic" continually fights the denial of drug dependency that interferes with recovery.

More attention is being focused on the needs of women alcoholics, for whom there is a shortage of treatment programs nationwide. Day care for their children, vocational rehabilitation for job skills training, and women role models and counselors to encourage frank discussion of issues such as sexuality are needed.

Drug use and alcoholism among youth are widespread. Although marijuana use had declined in 1987 among high school youth, alcohol use increased. Young people's drug taking is not done in isolation, but is part of their group social life. Therefore, particular concern should be given to how youth groups can be formed that do *not* regard drug taking or drinking as an "in thing." Any prevention program must have personal meaning for its participants if it is to succeed. The program should provide them with a sense of identity and acceptance. Young people need to receive feedback about their competencies from adults they esteem if they are to better define their futures in non–drug-involved ways. The focus should be on life-style commitment, rather than on substance use per se (Dembo, et al., 1978).

One approach to treatment is family therapy, which is becoming a regular facet of many rehabilitation programs. Most families with an adolescent drug abuser see the adolescent as the only or the main problem in the family, rather than that the whole family is dysfunctional or disturbed. A central concept of family therapy is to work with and attempt to change the family system rather than the individual family members (Beschner & Friedman, 1986).

A view that is gaining acceptance in alcoholism rehabilitation is that psychological and environmental factors precipitate heavy drinking, but a person's biological makeup is responsible for susceptibility to alcoholism. A new approach to alcoholism treatment is offered at Pace Health Services in New York City. This outpatient program remains open at night and offers a regimen as intensive as a residential program, without interrupting careers and home life, and without the high cost of inpatient care (Franks, 1985).

Community-based recreation services may also take on a significant role in providing recreation to those who have been in treatment and now need a positive place to go and activities to do. The Parks and Recreation Department of Eugene, Oregon, offers an extensive community-based recreation program for alcoholics (Earle, 1981) that could be a model for other departments.

Although drug and alcohol abuse continues to be a major health and social problem in the United States, some of the above methods, if utilized, do offer hope.

SUMMARY

Drug and alcohol abuse is a serious social and health problem in the United States. Drug use by youth, women, and individuals in the inner cities is increasing. Millions of Americans are adversely affected by the consequences of drug abuse. Unfortunately, there is a severe shortage of treatment services for addicts.

Therapeutic recreation has an essential role in the treatment of addiction. Treatment focuses on life-style changes, including social skills, stress management, and leisure skills. The TR specialist can help the client identify healthy means of satisfying needs previously met through drugs. Experiencing feelings of fun and achievement through leisure participation is a goal for all addicts in treatment.

READING COMPREHENSION QUESTIONS

1. Define addiction.
2. Describe the scope of drug and alcohol abuse in our society.
3. What is meant by the term *hard addictions*? Give examples.
4. What are the possible physical problems of a drug abuser or alcoholic upon admission to a treatment setting?
5. Explain the objectives of TR in the holistic treatment approach. What types of activities can be used to meet these objectives?
6. Describe the types of settings for delivery of TR to this population.
7. Explain milieu therapy, methadone maintenance, and the therapeutic community.
8. How does AA benefit recovering alcoholics and drug addicts?
9. What behaviors should be assessed in implementing the TR process?
10. Give specific examples of client behaviors and needs, and types of TR programs that address these behaviors and needs.
11. What types of evaluation should be done with this population?
12. What are the special problems and needs of youth, women, and inner-city drug abusers?
13. What new treatment approaches are seen as successful with this population?

SUGGESTED LEARNING ACTIVITIES

1. Invite to class a TR specialist working with drug abuse and alcoholic clients to speak on needs and behaviors of clients and types of TR programs that are effective in their treatment.

2. Attend an Alcoholics Anonymous or Narcotics Anonymous meeting. Discuss your observations and reactions in class.

3. In small groups of students, discuss how you feel about recreational drug use and drinking. When does use become abuse? Do you think drug abuse and alcoholism are crimes or diseases?

4. Define the following in your own words: social drinker, heavy drinker, problem drinker, alcoholic. Compare with other students.

5. Reflect on your personal stress management techniques. Do you drink or take drugs, including nicotine and caffeine, to cope? What other means can you use instead?

6. What problems do you see with drug and alcohol abuse on your campus and in your community? Write a short paper on the role of school and community recreation services in addressing these problems.

7. Develop a community resource file of recreation programs that can serve as alternatives to drug abusing behavior by teenagers and adults.

8. Brainstorm societal factors that might affect the level of drug and alcohol abuse, both positively and negatively, and the role of the therapeutic recreation profession in preventing and alleviating abuse.

REFERENCES

BERG, C., & NEULINGER, J. (1976). Alcoholics' perception of leisure. *Journal of Studies on Alcohol, 37*(11), 1625–1632.

BESCHNER, G., & FRIEDMAN, A. (EDS.). (1986). *Teen drug use.* Lexington, MA: D. C. Heath.

CRAIG, R. (1985). Multimodal treatment package for substance abuse treatment programs. *Professional Psychology: Research and Practice. 16*(2), 271–285.

DEMBO, R., BURGOS, W., BABST, D., SCHMEIDLER, J., & LaGRAND, L. (1978). Neighborhood relationships and drug involvement among inner city junior high school youths: Implications for drug education and prevention programming. *Journal of Drug Education, 8*(3), 231–250.

Diagnostic and statistical manual of mental disorders III, Revised (DSM-IIIR) (1987). Washington, DC: American Psychiatric Press, Inc.

EARLE, P. (1981). *A leisure education notebook for community alcohol programs.* Eugene, OR: Parks and Recreation Department.

FRANKS, L. (1985, October 20). A new attack on alcoholism. *The New York Times Magazine,* pp. 47–66.

GOLD, M. (1986). *The facts about drug and alcohol.* New York: Bantam Books.

KUTNER, L. (1987, December 10). Parent and child. *The New York Times,* p. C8.

MAST, E. (1987). Sobriety—An elusive concept. *Therapy 'N' Games, 1*(1), 1–4.

National Institute on Alcohol Abuse and Alcoholism. (1986). *A guide to planning alcoholism treatment programs.* Rockville, MD: U.S Department of Health and Human Services.

National Institute on Alcohol Abuse and Alcoholism. (1987). *Sixth special report to the U.S. Congress on alcohol and health.* Rockville, MD: U.S. Department of Health and Human Services.

NEVES, B., BECK, N., & LAWRENCE, K. (1974). *Activities: Alternatives to the high life.*

Paper presented at the First Annual National Drug Abuse Conference, Eagleville Hospital and Rehabilitation Center, Eagleville, PA.

PEELE, S. (1985). *The meaning of addiction: compulsive experience and its interpretation.* Lexington, MA: D. C. Heath.

SCHNOLL, S. (1986). *Getting help: Treatments for drug abuse.* New York: Chelsea House Publishers.

7

Autism

BARBARA A. HAWKINS

OBJECTIVES

- Describe the DSM-IIIR diagnostic criteria applied in the identification and assessment of autism.
- Recognize behavioral characteristics of persons having autism.
- Identify state-of-the-art procedures used in the assessment of autism for programming purposes.
- Describe the impact of autism on and the scope of services needed by families of persons with autism.
- Discuss intervention procedures and the role of therapeutic recreation services in the social and behavioral habilitation of persons with autism.
- Describe community preparation and in-service training strategies necessary to support community integration of persons with autism.
- Recognize best practices in program implementation and evaluation for persons with autism.

DEFINITION OF AUTISM

Autism, a little understood and highly perplexing developmental disability, is most accurately described as a collection of symptoms that, when taken as a group, describe a syndrome. Autism is a complex disability that affects the individual, his or her family, care givers, and professionals who seek to provide appropriate diagnosis and interventions in the treatment of this lifelong, pervasive developmental disorder.

Until the early 1940s when Leo Kanner first systematically observed and described the autistic syndrome, little was known about the disorder, and even less information was available regarding the treatment or management of autism. Kanner described children with autism as primarily exhibiting the following qualities: inability to develop normal social relationships, delay in speech development, noncommunicative use of speech (echolalia), insistence on sameness, stereotypical play, lack of imagination, pronominal reversal, strong rote memory, normal physical appearance, and the appearance of the disorder's symptoms in infancy (Rutter, 1978). In the 1950s, the common mistaken approach to the diagnosis of autism was to confuse the disorder with psychological disturbances (i.e., schizophrenia). At that time, the treatment of choice was rooted in psychotherapy. Most current research, however, supports the theory that autism is a pervasive developmental disability related to the central nervous system, rather than a psychological illness. Throughout the past five decades, many names have been given to autism, including Kanner's syndrome (Kanner, 1943), childhood autism (Wing, 1980), infantile autism (Rutter, 1978), and childhood psychosis (Fish & Ritvo, 1979).

Autism is difficult to diagnose because of the complexity of the syndrome coupled with the lack of specific tests for the disorder (Freeman & Ritvo, 1981). The American Psychiatric Association's *Diagnostic and Statistical Manual of Mental Disorders, Revised* (1987), is the foremost reference utilized in describing the criteria that are applied in a diagnosis of autism. The DSM-IIIR criteria are as follows:

overhead

- Onset during infancy or childhood.
- Qualitative impairment in reciprocal social interaction.
- Qualitative impairment in verbal and nonverbal communication and in imaginative activity.
- Markedly restricted repertoire of activities and interests.

The Autism Society of America, Inc. (ASA) offers a similar description of the definitional criteria for autism:

- Onset before 30 months.
- Disturbance of response to sensory stimuli.
- Disturbance of speech, language, cognition, and nonverbal communication.
- Disturbance of capacity to relate appropriately to people, events, and objects.
- Disturbance of developmental rates and sequences (Dalrymple, 1987).

Children diagnosed as having autism exhibit a profound inability to develop appropriate or normal social relationships with other people.

overload

Distinct to the syndrome of autism is the delay or deviance in language development, as well as an "insistence on sameness" and stereotypical behavior patterns (Rutter, 1978). Other symptoms commonly associated with autism are hyperactivity, compulsive behaviors, sleep problems, food obsessions, ritualistic behaviors, abnormal perceptual responses (hyposensitivity and hypersensitivity), self-stimulation, and self-destructiveness (Coleman, 1985; Coleman & Gillberg, 1985). Symptoms are unevenly distributed across individual cases and development such that, although all the symptoms reflect the syndrome, they rarely all exist in every person having autism.

As frequently found in other syndromes, autism can occur concurrently with other disabilities. Approximately 75% of the population with autism also have mental retardation (Rutter, 1978; Wing, 1978). About half of the individuals with autism and mental retardation have cognitive functioning at or less than 50 IQ and, therefore, are considered severely mentally retarded (Coleman & Gillberg, 1985). In addition, one quarter to one third of all children with autism will develop epileptic seizures by adolescence (Coleman & Gillberg, 1985).

overload

Autism is a disorder that occurs in approximately four to five cases per 10,000 people (Coleman & Gillberg, 1985). Autism occurs more frequently in males than females, at a ratio of 1 girl to every 4 boys (Coleman & Gillberg, 1985). Other than these incidence patterns, there appears to be no other significant pattern to its occurrence. Autism is found throughout the world among individuals of all socioeconomic and racial strata (Paluszny, 1979). Although there is no known cure for autism, people with autism do not get worse. Properly designed intervention programs can reduce the severity of the disorder on functional behavior.

CLASSIFICATION OF AUTISM

Along with general agreement on the overall definitional criteria for autism, a system of classification of the disorder has recently been developed. This classification entails a multiaxial system of various elements used in the diagnosis of autism (Rutter & Schopler, 1978). For research and clinical purposes, independent axes are used to clarify the differential diagnosis of autism from other disabilities or conditions. Application of the multiaxial coding system will indicate a diagnosis of the behavioral syndrome of autism on one axis and the description of intellectual impairment (mental retardation) on a second axis; a third axis will indicate factors associated with medical conditions (such as phenylketonuria); and a fourth axis will describe the psychosocial situation. This system reduces ambiguity and enhances clarity of different elements (axes) in diagnosis.

Investigators (Schopler, 1966) have found autism to be related to specific deficits in cognition that involve central coding processes and language. Therefore, the application of a multiaxial approach to classification and diagnosis differentiates autism from the presence or absence of mental retardation.

Autism also has been previously confused with childhood schizophrenia; however, the multiaxial system provides clarification to this potential point of confusion. Research evidence (Rutter, 1968, 1971, 1972) substantiates important distinctions regarding the course of autism and schizophrenia such that they should be regarded as separate disorders. The same differentiation has been determined for autism and neurosis; therefore, the multiaxial system is useful in distinguishing between the two conditions.

In summary, significant progress has been made in the definition of autism and the development of a multiaxial system for distinguishing autism from other, often concomitantly occurring disorders such as schizophrenia, mental retardation, or other psychosocial conditions.

DESCRIPTION OF LIMITATIONS

As with all people, individuals with autism have their own strengths and limitations. There are limitations that are inherent in the disability, such as deficits in social behavior, communication, and learning skills. Table 7.1 illustrates common behaviors related to these limitations as they appear in people with autism (Dalrymple, 1987).

In addition to these limitations, people with autism often experience other factors that inhibit normal activity. Two of these factors are seizure disorders and pharmacologic treatments.

As mentioned previously, one quarter to one third of all autistic children develop epileptic seizures before adolescence. Although there is little research in this area, various types of seizures have been documented in individuals with autism (Coleman & Gillberg, 1985). Seizures can be of the generalized motor type or sudden episodes, as in periods of blank staring or as associated with abnormalities in specific behavior (Dalldorf, 1983).

Although there is no evidence that medication can reduce or reverse the symptoms of autism, many individuals with autism are on medication to treat associated problems (Gualtieri, Evans, & Patterson, 1987). These difficulties include hyperactivity, withdrawn states, sleep disturbances, aggression, agitation, self-injurious behaviors, and seizure disorders (Dalldorf, 1983; Gualtieri, Evans, & Patterson, 1987). Several classifications of medications have been used with people with autism. These groupings include neuroleptic drugs to control overactive and aggressive behaviors, and anticonvulsant drugs to control seizures (Gualtieri, Evans, & Patterson, 1987). A number of side effects can be associated with each of these types of medication, including cognitive impairment and tardive dyskinesia from

Table 7.1
Common Behaviors Associated with Autism

SOCIAL BEHAVIOR	COMMUNICATION BEHAVIOR	UNUSUAL BEHAVIORAL CHARACTERISTICS	LEARNING CHARACTERISTICS
Relates to people with difficulty	Develops and understands gestures poorly	Acts deaf and/or very sensitive to some sounds	Develops unevenly within and across skills areas
Has strange fears	Speaks infrequently or not at all for 50% or more of the time	Resists change in routine	Resists change in learning environment; perseverates
Lacks understanding of social cues	Has difficulty understanding abstract concepts	Lacks fear of real danger	Has difficulty with unstructured time and waiting
Avoids or has odd use of eye contact	Has problem answering even simple questions	Exhibits repetitive body movements such as rocking, pacing, hand flapping	May not generalize skills to other areas and places
Wants to be alone frequently	Lacks comprehension of content and timing of communication	May stare or fixate on objects	Has difficulty with abstract concepts
Develops strong inappropriate attachment to objects	Perseverates on one topic; rambles	Explores environment by inappropriate methods such as licking, smelling, handling	Overselects one or more stimuli with failure to understand the whole
Giggles, laughs, screams inappropriately	Follows a line of exchange with difficulty	Perseverates on or has short attention to task	Exhibits impulsivity and inconsistency
Lacks imaginative play	Has difficulty communicating socially	Uses peripheral vision rather than straight on vision and/or avoids looking	Needs to be taught to make choices, decisions, and plans
Often uses toys in odd ways such as lining up, spinning, etc.	Initiates communication infrequently	May avoid human contact in favor of touching objects	Relies on cues and learned routines often
Lacks understanding of how others feel	May run, aggress, or be self-injurious to express frustration		Usually is not competitive
Expresses emotions inappropriately and has narrow range			
Lacks social/sexual understanding			

SOURCE: Reprinted with permission from N. J. Dalrymple: Introduction to Autism; 1987. Bloomington, IN: Institute for the Study of Developmental Disabilities.

the neuroleptic medications, and negative cognitive and behavioral effects from anticonvulsants (Gualtieri, Evans, & Patterson,1987).

Gualtieri and his colleagues (1987) point out that few physicians have adequate training or knowledge to administer these types of medications properly to people with autism because of the complexity and low incidence of the disorder. Additionally, little research has been done with autistic people in such areas as long-term and interactive effects of multiple medications. Therefore, careful monitoring of medications must be considered when programming for the person with autism to ensure proper health and to determine whether specific behaviors are associated with the medication, with the disability, or with the intervention that is being introduced.

Strengths

Although the preceding list of limitations may have the service provider wondering just what the person with autism *can* do, there are a number of strengths that, with proper motivation, can be used to improve programming with the autistic person. These strengths include stamina, well-developed gross and fine motor skills, enjoyment of routines, good long-term memory, accuracy, and "splinter skills" (Dalrymple, 1987). Frequently observed in autistic persons are qualities that are both identifiable with the syndrome and, under certain circumstances, are considered as assets. The ability to stay on task until it is completed, to withstand constant monotonous routines, and to perform the same task repeatedly with accuracy (once it is learned) may be a consequence of the disorder that can be a great strength. In addition, many people having autism display unusual talents, such as facility with numbers, calendar skills, music abilities, art, and fine motor precision skills. These talents must not be overlooked in gaining a more complete understanding and appreciation of the person with autism.

PURPOSE OF THERAPEUTIC RECREATION

Since Kanner's historic case study work in which he detailed salient attributes of the autistic syndrome, a large new body of work has been proliferated about children with this developmental disability. Most recently, concern has begun to extend beyond childhood autism and to confront the changes in young adults.

Typically, physicians, psychologists, speech clinicians, educational consultants, social workers, and other allied health professionals (i.e., nurses, occupational therapists, physical therapists) have been the primary professionals to come in contact with, diagnose, and treat children with autism. Therapeutic recreation specialists have had minimal roles heretofore; however, it may be expected that their professional involvement in the care and treatment of persons with autism will expand as an increasing number of these individuals are assisted in remaining in the community as opposed to being institutionalized. As residents in institutions, historically people with autism have had opportunities to participate in recreation services but probably not as a significant part of their written treatment plan. The role of a variety of disciplines, including therapeutic recreation, in the interdisciplinary treatment process is greatly needed and will continue to expand as clearer definition of the contribution these services make to habilitation is drawn out.

General Approaches to the Treatment of Autism

Lifelong habilitation is the ongoing mission of intervention programming for persons with autism. Habilitation can be simply described as a process of gaining the necessary skills required to function as independently as possible, given the constellation of individual strengths and deficits. As a consequence of a significant amount of research on program design in the area of autism, general habilitation areas have emerged to include behavior management, socialization, communication, and learning (Dalrymple, 1983; Donnellan, 1980; Koegel, Rincover, & Egel, 1982; Lovaas, 1981). Because of profound deficits and anomalies in the sequence of normal development, several disciplines join together to design and implement the intervention program. Each discipline focuses on a common set of goals to enhance habilitation. The preferred treatment strategy involves an *integrated triad approach*, which combines the utilization of the behavioral, functional, and developmental approaches to skill development (Donnellan & Kilman, 1986).

The *behavioral approach* to intervention (Lovaas, 1981; Koegel, Rincover, & Egel, 1982) provides the methodology (or "how to") needed to affect skill development. Important characteristics of the behavioral approach include the following:

1. Definable, observable, and measurable responses that are predicated on goals and objectives that indicate present as well as postintervention levels of functioning.
2. Accountability through objective and reliable evaluation procedures that are amenable to modification and revision as needed in order to support educational efforts and success.
3. Flexibility in terms of the variety of data that can be meaningfully applied and used.
4. Power and effectiveness in teaching a variety of skills to persons with autism (i.e., the application of incidental teaching, time delay, and the technique of shaping).

5. Power and effectiveness in managing behavior (i.e., nonaversive technology for managing social behaviors) (Donnellan & Kilman, 1986).

The *functional approach* (Donnellan, 1980; Brown et al., 1979; Brown, Nietupski, & Hamre-Nietupski, 1976) provides the content to be taught (otherwise known as the "what" to teach). The functional skills approach to intervention programming is predicated on the question, What does this individual need to know in order to function in his or her current environment or in preparation for functioning in a subsequent environment? A functional skills approach safeguards against persons with autism being taught meaningless tasks in relationship to the skills that are needed for the particular age, residential setting, family/care giver situation, and community context (Donnellan, 1980). The functional approach focuses on the skills needed to function in a particular context and teaches them in that context rather than in an artificial learning environment. For example, riding the bus is not taught in a classroom using a prop bus; rather, it is taught using the actual bus and bus route on which the client is to develop competency. A functional skills approach reduces problems associated with task generalization, which is typically problematic for the person with autism, while capitalizing on the requisites, cues, and consequences of the natural context for the skill being taught (Brown, Nietupski, & Hamre-Nietupski, 1976).

The *developmental approach* (Wood, 1975) focuses on the individual's present ability repertoire as applied to the task to be taught. Information about the person's abilities in relation to the developmental continuum (Piaget, 1960; Schopler, Reichler, & Lansing, 1980) provides a base to determine what the person already knows as well as how to accommodate the environment to enhance learning of other tasks through use of present skills.

The combined triad-based approach (behavioral, functional, developmental) is the preferred methodology for planning and implementing treatment programs for persons with autism. The application of the triad approach will enhance the potential for success in habilitation programming throughout the life course and across the varied settings in which services are delivered to autistic persons.

Common Habilitation Objectives

Habilitation objectives designed for persons with autism are usually established based on a set of primary needs (cognitive, social, behavioral, and communicative) for this population. It is important to emphasize that specialized programming will not cure autism; it is a severe disability that requires lifelong treatment and support. In spite of the severity of the disability, people with autism can learn functional skills, and higher-functioning (intellectually) people can learn to live independently as adults. Each person with autism is distinct, so programs must be designed to meet individual needs ranging from specialized, individualized programming to generic programs (in the case of public school, regular classes).

Common treatment objectives include the development of interactive social and communication skills, appropriate social behavior, and community living skills (e.g., leisure, vocational, and home-life skills). Opportunities to participate in programs with social peers and in programs that are age appropriate are important considerations in the treatment of autism. Because nearly all persons with autism exhibit difficulty in generalizing, treatment programming should be designed for implementation in the actual context in which the autistic person is expected to perform the skill (Olley, 1986).

Planning for behavior management is a particularly important aspect of treatment programming for persons with autism (Dalrymple, 1983; Favell, 1983). Frequently, failure to learn or function appropriately is due to behavioral interference. The selection of the appropriate behavior management strategy in any given situation also should take into consideration environmental modifications to support the person's ability to behave accordingly (Amado, 1988). Frequently, the manner in which the environment is designed will reduce behavior problems. The environment should offer consistency and structure, and should focus on a functional skills program.

The Role of the Family in Intervention

Mesibov (1983) noted the need to define more clearly the family's role in the treatment of persons with autism. The value of family involvement has been demonstrated with some concern noted regarding the abilities of families to sustain their involvement throughout the lives of their children (Schopler & Reichler, 1971; Sullivan, 1977). Therefore, although families may be more involved when their autistic children are young, other avenues for their participation in treatment should be delineated as their children mature to adulthood (Mesibov, 1983). These avenues might include advocacy for needed services, self-help support network building, long-range financial planning for their autistic child, and other legal concerns.

DeMyer and Goldberg (1983) have noted the primary adverse effects of autism on family life to be first and foremost a total loss of family recreation because of the totality of demand in caring for a child with autism. This situation does not ease with time, and families often express fatigue and burnout by the time the son or daughter reaches adolescence. Financial drain, along with strain in the emotional/mental health status of parents, is another adverse outcome of caring for an autistic son or daughter.

Illustrative of a contributing factor to financial loss is the mother's inability to work outside of the home to supplement income. Being able to find care for children with autism is difficult at best and usually impossible. When mothers can manage to work outside of the home, most of the extra income is dispensed in the care and treatment (including private residential placement) of the autistic son or daughter. Feelings of depression, grief, and burnout are common among families with an autistic member.

Additional adverse effects for parents include diminished physical health, difficulty managing housekeeping in the face of destructive behaviors, difficulty meeting the needs of siblings, loss of friendships and neighbor relationships, increased tensions among siblings, and strained marital relationships. It is an accepted fact that the family life-style will alter markedly in the presence of a son or daughter with autism in order to accommodate the range of symptoms associated with the disorder (DeMyer & Goldberg, 1983).

The treatment strategy used with families entails the provision of social and emotional support services, services to assist with the autistic child's growth and development, and services to enable the family to experience growth. Approaches that have been successful in meeting family needs include parent training, parent and sibling support groups, and accessible respite care programs.

The Role of TR in Social and Behavioral Treatment

Deficits in appropriate social and behavioral skills in persons with autism have been described as a major contributor to failure in family life, school life, and vocational placements (Henning & Dalrymple, 1986). Social skill deficits alone are characteristic and pervasive attributes of the syndrome and thus require special attention in programming (Schmidt, McLaughlin, & Dalrymple, 1986; Henning et al., 1982). Mesibov (1986) noted the paucity in specific programs for addressing sociability in persons with autism. Based on the widely accepted role of leisure and recreation in social development, it is appropriate to apply therapeutic recreation as a treatment modality in the development of social skills by autistic persons (Wehman, 1977, 1983; Wehman & Schleien, 1980, 1981).

Therapeutic recreation programs designed to address social skill and behavior deficits should first establish overall program priorities. Commonly, these priorities will emerge from an interdisciplinary team assessment of the client's strengths and needs as well as known priorities generally associated with autism. Targeted deficits should be responsive to remediation. Other considerations when selecting priority social and behavioral skills for programming should include sensitivity to age appropriateness, family preferences, learning style, sensory considerations, current developmental level, program resources, and community resources (Henning & Dalrymple, 1986).

The role of therapeutic recreation, therefore, will be to support global treatment goals in behavior management, socialization/social skill development, and leisure skill development. An emphasis should be placed on those social, behavioral, and leisure skills that are age appropriate and will be used throughout the life course (Schleien, Kiernan, & Wehman, 1981; Wuerch & Voeltz, 1982).

Treatment objectives (Henning & Dalrymple, 1986) that are applicable in therapeutic recreation programming include the following:

1. Teaching functional academic skills such as money skills, time skills, reading, and giving/requesting information.
2. Teaching self-care skills such as personal grooming, socially appropriate manners, appropriate sexual behavior, and care of personal belongings.
3. Teaching interpersonal skills such as cooperation, appropriate ways of interacting socially with others within situational context (handshake, hugs, etc.).
4. Teaching social communication skills such as proper greetings, use of personal names when greeting or requesting attention, requesting permission to borrow others' possessions.
5. Teaching specific leisure skills such as playing games following rules and etiquette, choosing independently from three leisure activity options, recognizing and distinguishing picture cues of leisure activities and work activities.
6. Teaching community living skills such as ordering food and eating properly at a restaurant, shopping skills, and using public transportation.

Therapeutic recreation can make its greatest contribution in the treatment of autism when the focus is on social and behavioral skills development, using leisure activities as the modality for goal attainment. In some ways, therapeutic recreation services offer a superior avenue for supporting social and behavioral skill development because usually leisure activities are recognized as fun and pleasurable experiences (Wehman & Marchant, 1978; Schleien & Ray, 1988). Most people with autism have recreation activity preferences, and involvement in these activities can supplant less stimulating ways of achieving skill development.

COMMON SERVICE SETTINGS

Probably one of the most noteworthy advancements in the area of autism is the movement toward community integration of persons with this disability. Describing common service settings for persons with autism is problematic at best. Mesibov (1983) noted the lack of appropriately designed community-based program alternatives that meet the habilitation needs of this population. Unfortunately, this situation has made little progress in recent years. Children and adults with autism have difficulty finding residential alternatives outside of the family and institutional contexts. Vocational training programs and employment options also present limited capacity to meet the social, behavioral, communicative, and cognitive needs of autistic persons. Children with autism are entitled to educational services under Public Law 94-142, but teachers with knowledge and skills in teaching children with autism are not commonly available.

Probably the most useful way of conceptualizing service settings for persons with autism is to focus on the major settings in which the habilitation plan is implemented. Individual educational or habilitation plans will be implemented across home (residential context), school or work, and play or recreation. The variety of settings in which the individual client will have habilitation goals and objectives implemented in programmed activities will be dependent upon whether the basis of residential placement is with the family, in a community-living alternative, or in an institution. Probably the most critical of issues for persons with autism is the preparation of community programs and environments in understanding and accepting the behaviors commonly associated with the disability.

Because knowledge about autism and development of appropriate programming strategies for persons with autism is still relatively new, it is understandable that progress in the evolution of common service settings is less well developed than in other areas (e.g., geriatric services, substance abuse). There are contemporary curriculum materials and teaching environments, such as the Treatment and Education of Autistic and related Communication handicapped Children (TEACCH) program at the University of North Carolina (Mesibov, Schopler, & Sloan, 1983), that demonstrate effective strategies for teacher and learner education. Benhaven (Lettick, 1983) offers the example of the specialized day and residential school facility that provides an intensive program for children and adults.

Parent advocacy efforts also have impacted the development of program and treatment options for autistic persons. For example, the Jay Nolan Center (LaVigna, 1983) in Newhall, California, was developed from the consumer-based activities of the Los Angeles chapter of the National Society for Autistic Children. This center is committed to the development of a continuum of residential, recreational, vocational, and educational services for persons with autism and their families. These services and programs are provided based on normalization and community integration principles. As parents and professionals gain better understanding and skills in the treatment of autism, it is hoped that future strides in the availability and use of community-based programs will evolve.

CURRENT BEST PRACTICES AND PROCEDURES

The diagnosis of autism has had a history of confusion because of misinterpretation of symptoms with other disorders (e.g., schizophrenia, mental retardation). Today, a differential diagnosis can be made through the application of criteria and instruments that have significantly enhanced the identification of clients with autism. The ASA, through its detailed definition of autism, provides criteria for making a diagnosis. These criteria are (1) onset before the age of 30 months; (2) disturbance of response to sensory stimuli; (3) disturbance of speech, language, cognition, and nonverbal communication; (4) disturbance of capacity to relate appropriately to people, events, and objects; and (5) disturbance of developmental rates and sequences (Dalrymple, 1987). Although the ASA's definition is useful in the process of making a diagnosis, problems associated with distinguishing autism from mental retardation, schizophrenia, other psychosocial conditions, and medical conditions may require a multiaxial approach as previously discussed. The Childhood Autism Rating Scale (CARS) (Schopler, Reichler, DeVellis, & Daly, 1980), which is comprised of 15 scales, can be widely applied for determining the diagnosis of autism.

Assessment

Current best practices in the identification, assessment, and treatment of persons with autism rely heavily on the use of an interdisciplinary approach. This approach incorporates the expertise of several professionals in the assessment of functioning, the formulation of the diagnosis of autism, and the development of an individual program plan. Maximum benefits for the person with autism and his or her family have the greatest potential when the interdisciplinary approach is pursued. Typical disciplinary areas represented in the interdisciplinary approach include education, social work, audiology/speech and language, medicine, recreation therapy, occupational/physical therapy, and psychology. Each of these disciplinary areas relates closely with characteristics of the autistic syndrome.

Illustrations of the different disciplinary roles are as follows. Based on deficits in cognition that affect learning, it is appropriate that education play a role in identification, assessment, and treatment of cognitive function. Social work will assist with family education and adjustment. Audiology, speech, and language will be interested in total communication development of the individual. The physician may be the first professional to recognize problematic development that suggests the autistic syndrome in the young patient, as well as provide pharmacologic interventions when indicated. The psychologist will supply important evaluative information on social and cognitive development as compared to normal developmental markers. The therapeutic recreation specialist can assess functional social skills and recreational interests that will enhance participation in community-based activities. And the occupational/physical therapist will provide more complete information on perceptual problems and motor function. It is readily apparent from this sampling of disciplinary involvement that the interdisciplinary approach will provide greater depth and breadth in understanding the needs of persons with autism.

Currently, assessment instruments and procedures for young children through to adolescence and young adulthood are available. Unfortunately, very few middle-aged or older adults are likely to be living in community-based residential alternatives; thus, little assessment information exists that is applicable to older adult development, nor is there certainty of its value at this time in the life course.

Illustrative of an appropriate assessment instrument for young children with autism is the PEP (Psycho Educational Profile) developed at the Division for TEACCH at the University of North Carolina (Schopler & Reichler, 1979). The instrument is a behaviorally based tool for application with autism or related communication handicaps that produces highly useful information for individual program planning. Using a Pass-Fail-Emerging scoring system, the PEP assesses 10 areas of functioning: perception, imitation, fine motor skills, gross motor skills, eye-hand integration, expressive language, cognitive performance, self-help skills, behavior problems, and social skills (Mesibov, Schopler, & Sloan, 1983). The PEP has demonstrated its success in the identification and assessment of autism because it minimizes the use of language, it provides the needed time for completing all tasks, it presents materials in an attractive manner for young children, and it allows for flexible administration. Worldwide use of the PEP has produced test results for children who were previously reported to be untestable (Schopler & Reichler, 1979).

Whereas the PEP was specifically designed for young children, an assessment process appropriate to the needs of autistic adolescents and young adults was also developed at TEACCH. The Adolescent and Adult Psycho Educational Profile (AAPEP) applies more relevant tasks to the needs and goals of adolescents and young adults (Mesibov, Schopler, & Schaffer, n.d.). AAPEP is divided into six overlapping functional areas encompassing vocational, independent functioning, leisure, functional communication, and interpersonal behaviors that are assessed on three scales. A Direct Observation Scale is administered clinically by a therapist, and the Home Scale and the School/Work Scale are based on behavioral reports made by primary people in each context. The AAPEP uses the same Pass-Fail-Emerging scoring system as does the PEP and is targeted for use with the presence of moderate to severe retardation. The integrated results of the three scales formulate the basis of individual program plan development.

Important features of both the PEP and the AAPEP are the minimal use of verbal language-based directions, the significant application of the "emerging" score for identifying the possession of some skills necessary to complete a task, flexible administration, and the allotment of adequate time to complete test items. A significant difference between PEP and AAPEP is that the former is based upon developmental levels and the latter on criterion reference.

It is important to note that members of the interdisciplinary assessment team will, by choice, implement a variety of assessment instruments associated with their individual disciplinary areas. Thus, the PEP and AAPEP are illustrative of one methodology in the assessment and evaluation of program needs and progress of persons with autism.

Planning

The basis for program design for autistic people focuses upon the characteristic deficits associated with the disorder as they appear for individual clients based upon the interdisciplinary team assessment. These characteristics fall under the following four areas:

- behavioral
- communication
- learning
- social and interpersonal skills

The unusual behavior generally exhibited by autistic persons is one of the most notable characteristics of the syndrome and thus requires special program planning. The success or failure of programming in other areas often depends upon the effectiveness of the behavior management plan for the client. People with autism do not perceive the world in the same manner in which nondisabled people respond. Therefore, sensory stimuli can often evoke unusual behaviors in persons with autism. Behaviors most often encountered with autism include ritualistic and compulsive behavior, staring or visual fixation on objects, perseveration, avoidance of human contact, aggression, lack of self-control, insensitivity or oversensitivity to sounds, and inappropriate interaction with environment (e.g., licking) (Mesibov, 1983; Dalrymple, 1987).

Communicative skills are central to the autistic person's ability to relate to those around him or her; therefore, the individual plan will probably contain programmatic accommodations and objectives targeted at the development of communicative skills. Common deficits include poor or no spoken language skills; perseveration on words or topics; infrequent initiation of communication; exhibited difficulty in comprehending abstract concepts, in following a line of exchanges, and in answering questions even when they are simple (Dalrymple, 1987).

Learning difficulties for persons with autism are compounded by the simultaneous presence of mental retardation. Typical deficits in learning skills include the inability to generalize skills, difficulty with unstructured or extra time, difficulty changing learning environments, tendencies to perseverate, overselection of stimuli, uncompetitiveness, impulsivity, inconsistency, difficulty with the abstract, and reliance on routine, prompts, and cues (Dalrymple, 1987).

The social and interpersonal skills of persons with autism are foremost areas in which therapeutic recreation services can make a contribution. Persons with autism relate poorly to people. They have strange fears, tend to avoid eye contact or use it oddly, often want to be alone, demonstrate strange and inappropriate social behavior (giggling, screaming), and lack empathy or an understanding of how another feels. The use of toy and play materials often will be odd. Emotive expression is either inappropriate or within a very narrow range. Difficulty with social and interpersonal behavior is present for all persons with autism (Dalrymple, 1987). Leisure activities and therapeutic recreation have the potential, therefore, to occupy a significant place in the planned intervention strategy that addresses social skills.

Implementation

People with autism have difficulty generalizing skills across settings and materials. Therefore, the development of a leisure and social skills program that is based upon the overall functional life skills of the client is the preferred implementation strategy. This strategy will be enhanced through the selection of skills that consider (1) age appropriateness and frequency of involvement by nondisabled age cohorts, (2) family preferences, (3) community resources, and (4) client's characteristic strengths and needs (Wuerch & Voeltz, 1982; Henning & Dalrymple, 1986).

An important element in program implementation for this population is the need to include a behavior management plan based on the presence of aggressive or unacceptable behaviors. The program implementation plan should include client-specific behavior management strategies and contingencies so that managing behavior does not overshadow the original intent of the program and habilitation objectives. Examples of behavior management considerations include identifying the antecedent to behavioral problems, understanding how to make environmental modifications, understanding the use of natural consequences, being capable of helping clients manage behavior with prompts and cuing, and identifying client reinforcers for appropriate behaviors (Favell, 1983; Amado, 1988; Dalrymple, 1983).

Wehman (1983) identified the characteristics of an appropriately designed leisure skills program for autistic persons as including (1) normalization and social integration as a philosophical base; (2) the capacity to modify equipment, facilities, rules, and skill sequences as needed; (3) a behavioral base to skill training; and (4) teaching skills where they will be used. The optimal service delivery model will be one in which the community is prepared to accept the autistic person's participation. A skilled therapeutic recreation specialist will act as a consultant on the treatment team in relation to assessment, selection of age-appropriate skills, adaptation of the environment and/or skill, instruction, community preparation, and evaluation.

Evaluation

Evaluation of client progress is a difficult process in regard to documenting the effects of treatment programming for severely handicapped individuals. Gains often take a long time to produce in terms of measurable change, yet even the smallest success may be a very important statement toward attaining individual potential.

Brookhiser and Dalrymple (1987) have produced a computer-based model for tracking the behaviors and capabilities of the individual with autism based on each individual's educational (habilitation) plan goals and objectives. Through this sophisticated system, client behaviors and capabilities can be monitored and evaluated across all program environments (home, school/work, recreation, and community living). A system of data documentation and management that can track behaviors and performance across time and all program components has the greatest promise for providing useful evaluation data in the treatment of complex disabilities such as autism.

APPLICATION OF THE TR PROCESS

The uniqueness of each individual with autism is a noteworthy aspect of this class of developmental disability. It is inappropriate, therefore, to draw generalizations for all people with autism from an individual characterization other than providing reinforcement for the general characteristics of the syndrome. Specifically, these characteristics include profound disturbances in the development of appropriate social, behavioral, and communicative skills. The following case study provides illustration of the manifestation of these disturbances, as well as glimpses of splinter skills that may also be present in persons with autism.

CASE STUDY

Joan is a 23-year-old female who is presently residing in an acute care mental health facility. She previously has been living at home while waiting for a group home placement. Her parents live in the same community as the facility. Her father is employed at a local retail firm, and her mother has been the primary homemaker for the family. Joan has two older siblings—a married brother and a sister with a professional career.

Assessment

Joan was reported (by mother) to be a good baby in that she did not frequently cry for attention. She walked independently at 11 months and babbled a few single words between the first and second birthday. At age 5 Joan was putting two words together. She was a head banger, crib rocker, and slept less than other children as a young child.

Joan has a history of biting herself and shows a particular interest in whirling objects. At 5½ years of age, she was formally evaluated and identified as having autism and mild to moderate mental retardation. She also developed seizure disorder shortly after the diagnosis of autism was made. The seizure disorder has been controlled with medications since its onset. During early adolescence, Joan's self-injurious behaviors were extinguished, whereas functional communication skills and vocational skills were developed.

Joan suffers from constipation and seems to like salty foods. Often, she eats enormous amounts of food.

Since Joan's eligibility for public educational programming ended, she has been employed in several sheltered workshops. Each of these placements has ended in her removal from the program because of interfering and aggressive social behaviors. She was unable to work continuously without direct adult supervision and cuing.

Joan has other skills that should be developed in regard to their potential for vocational placement. She demonstrates a remarkable ability to participate in a variety of housekeeping chores, including cooking and cleaning.

Joan's special talent is music; she can play the piano quite well and likes listening to the radio. Past history records show that her behavior management is assisted by engaging in activities such as rug hooking and music.

Present behaviors: Joan is on a focused program to bring her behavior under control. Little else can be accomplished until she is settled down regarding residential and vocational placement. She has been preoccupied with self-injurious behaviors and with pronounced regression to past behaviors (i.e., biting herself). This period in Joan's life is one of the most turbulent and distressing because of the lack of community residential alternatives and suitable vocational placements that match her needs and strengths.

Current pharmacologic intervention is the use of Haldol to reduce agitation and activity level, and Tegretol for seizure disorder. Previous medications include Stelazine and Mellaril.

Planning

Long-term goal: To seek stable daily leisure activities that are independent of the residential location and that support Joan's needs for restorative leisure behaviors.

Short-term goals: (1) To assist Joan in using leisure interests to cope with present mental distress. (2) To assist Joan in using past leisure skills to add predictability and routine to the present situation.

Objectives: Joan will participate in daily therapeutic recreation programming to (1) provide an expected routine to each day, (2) assist in releasing tensions associated with the temporary nature of the current residential situation, and (3) provide opportunities to demonstrate acquired leisure skills successfully.

Opportunities to take Joan into the community for leisure activities will be sought as reinforcers to community living skills she has previously demonstrated.

Content: Joan will verbally indicate leisure activities she enjoys and will be encouraged to plan ahead for the next therapeutic recreation session. Her awareness of the pleasure and satisfaction derived from leisure participation will be observed and recorded.

Process: (1) To sensitize mental health facility staff to the leisure needs, interests, and skills that Joan possesses. (2) To encourage facility direct care staff to use relaxation activities to calm and focus Joan's attention on positive skills. (3) To request direct care staff to schedule daily routine times for independent leisure activity beyond those associated with therapeutic periods.

Implementation

Joan will participate in daily recreation therapy as well as have opportunities to participate in activity preferences during unscheduled free or downtime. Recreation therapy will focus on providing reinforcement for skill performance and daily routines in leisure activity. Participation and anecdotal records will be maintained by the TR specialist and direct care staff.

Evaluation

Behavioral data will be maintained on a daily basis for Joan. Targeted interfering behaviors (e.g., self-biting), situational antecedents, and consequences will be observed and recorded. Progress on therapeutic recreation interventions for controlling interfering behavior will be reviewed and evaluated for change or modification in the individual treatment plan. As residential and vocational placement is identified for Joan, her therapeutic recreation program will be reviewed as part of the development and implementation of her overall individual habilitation plan.

TRENDS AND ISSUES

The current trend in services to persons with severe handicapping conditions is to support programming within the community and thus advance the concept of normalization. However, as Schleien et al., (1987) point out, persons with severe handicaps such as autism have yet to be fully and effectively socially integrated into community, school, vocational, and recreational program settings. For persons with autism, the process of social integration is one that requires careful planning, systematic implementation, and sustained effort in order to ensure success for both the autistic person as well as other community members. One clear goal that is necessary in advancing social integration is the availability of systematically planned and implemented age-appropriate experiences with chronological age peers (Schleien & Ray, 1988; Schleien et al., 1987; Wuerch & Voeltz, 1982). It is important to note that research (Reynolds, 1981) does support the positive influence of normalized, community-based settings on improved recreational functioning of severely handicapped persons.

In therapeutic recreation service, as with other professional services, there are numerous issues related to successful community integration of people with autism. A primary issue is the limited level of training in the treatment of autism that is available to community-based service providers. In addition to having a basic knowledge of behavior management techniques in order to provide effective motivation and reinforcement, the community-based professional will need training in the use of alternative communication techniques. People with autism often have severe limitations in expressive and receptive communication skills, as well as in language comprehension skills. Even when speech develops, the pattern of communication may not be like that of the nonhandicapped population. Some training in communication strategies will be necessary in order to provide effective programming in support of community and social integration goals.

As community-based recreation program opportunities expand for persons with autism, the potential arises for new roles in service delivery to emerge (Reynolds, 1981). These roles encompass the following:

- Decreasing the number of special events that reach large groups and increasing individualized programming.
- Moving away from the clinical medical model of service delivery.
- Using behavior management techniques that are commensurate with normalization practices.
- Adopting advocacy roles and providing liaison with community programs to ensure access.
- Transferring training and skills from the specialist to the general community recreation leader and family members.

Although these changing roles seem far off in the distance for professionals serving individuals with autism, the intent of enabling the community to accept people with severe disabilities lies at the heart of the community integration trend, a trend that is here to stay. Preparing the service delivery system, as well as other constituents who use leisure services, to understand, accept, and assist in meeting the needs of autistic persons perhaps is the greatest challenge awaiting the field of autism.

SUMMARY

Perhaps one of the most frustrating aspects of dealing with autistic people is the continual perplexing nature of the disorder. Designing interventions that eventually produce habilitative results, but only after long periods of programming, often leaves care givers with a sense of burnout and exhaustion. Meeting the needs of persons with autism across the life span will bring a myriad of professionals in contact with the disabled individual and his or her family. The pervasive nature of this developmental disability will necessitate professional fortitude. Thus, only a select few will probably choose to become key professionals working with the autistic client. For the few who do opt to work with these clients, a cycle of in-service training will be needed to fortify energies in the face of rising feelings of burnout. People with autism need extra special care givers who are open to change and growth, and who demonstrate adaptability.

For those therapeutic recreation specialists working with the autistic client and his or her family, the rewards may be greater than in other areas of human service. Persons with autism are capable of learning and participating in a wide variety of leisure activities that bring both habilitative functions and moments of joy and pleasure in an otherwise confusing world of demands and disorder. In this respect, the opportunity to develop socially appropriate and fun-oriented behavior through therapeutic recreation may be the single most important contribution of therapeutic recreation in the treatment of autism.

READING COMPREHENSION QUESTIONS

1. Describe the American Psychiatric Association's current (DSM-IIIR) criteria that are applied in the identification and diagnosis of autism.
2. What are six disciplines that might cooperate to complete an interdisciplinary assessment of a person suspected of having autism?
3. Explain why there is a lack of understanding about the syndrome of autism.
4. Describe common behavioral characteristics that are often associated with autism.

5. Explain the role that therapeutic recreation can play in the treatment of persons who have autism.

6. Describe the potential impact that the trend in community integration for persons with severe handicapping conditions may have on therapeutic recreation services to autistic persons.

SUGGESTED LEARNING ACTIVITIES

1. Invite a parent of a child with autism to visit your class and discuss his or her experiences of living with an autistic son or daughter. Follow up the parent-visit class session with a separate class discussion period to explore students' perceptions of parent adjustment, grief, guilt, and family life dynamics that are a consequence of the presence of the autistic family member.

2. Prepare a short analytical paper on the role of leisure in the development of social skills in persons with autism.

3. Hold a small group discussion in which you identify and review the primary issues associated with normalization and community integration for autistic people.

4. Develop a list of behavioral characteristics of persons with autism. Visit a large public area (e.g., shopping mall) and there apply your checklist randomly to people you observe in the setting. Share your findings in class.

5. Visit an agency that serves clients who have autism and assist the TR process. Give a report in class on your experience.

REFERENCES

AMADO, R. S. (1988). Behavioral principles in community recreation integration. In S. J. SCHLEIEN & M. T. RAY *Community recreation and persons with disabilities: Strategies for integration* (pp. 79–90). Baltimore: Paul H. Brookes.

American Psychiatric Association. (1987). *Diagnostic and statistical manual of mental disorders* (3rd ed., rev.). Washington, DC: American Psychiatric Association.

BROOKHISER, J. K., & DALRYMPLE, N. J. (1987). A microcomputer-based system for profiling behaviors and capabilities of individuals with autism or severe learning and behavioral handicaps. In K. L. Mayfield & G. G. Yajnik (Eds.), *Proceedings of the Second Annual National Symposium on Information Technology as a Resource to Health & Disability Professionals, 1,* 205–220. Columbia, SC: University of South Carolina.

BROWN, L., BRANSTON, M. B., HAMRE-NIETUPSKI, S., PUMPIAN, I., CERTO, N., & GRUENEWALD, L. (1979). A strategy for developing chronological age-appropriate and functional curricular content for severely handicapped adolescents and young adults. *Journal of Special Education, 13,* 81–90.

BROWN, L., NIETUPSKI, J., & HAMRE-NIETUPSKI, S. (1976). The criterion of ultimate functioning and public school services for severely handicapped students. In M. A. Thomas (Ed.), *Hey, don't forget about me: Education's investment in the severely, profoundly and multiply handicapped* (pp. 2–15). Reston, VA: Council for Exceptional Children.

COLEMAN, M. (1985). The autistic syndromes. In A. M. DONELLAN (Ed.), *Classic readings in autism* (pp. 370–382). New York: Teachers College Press.

COLEMAN, M., & GILLBERG, C. (1985). *The biology of the autistic syndromes.* New York: Praeger.

DALLDORF, J. S. (1983). Medical needs of the autistic adolescent. In E. Schopler & G. B. Mesibov (Eds.), *Autism in adolescents and adults* (pp. 149–168). New York: Plenum Press.

DALRYMPLE, N. J. (1983). *Helping children with autism manage their behavior.* Bloomington, IN: Indiana University Developmental Training Center.

DALRYMPLE, N. J. (Ed.). (1987). *Introduction to autism.* Bloomington, IN: Institute for the Study of Developmental Disabilities.

DeMYER, M. K., & GOLDBERG, P. (1983). Family needs of the autistic adolescent. In E. SCHOPLER & G. B. MESIBOV (Eds.), *Autism in adolescents and adults* (pp. 225–250). New York: Plenum Press.

DONELLAN, A. M. (1980). An educational perspective of autism: Implications for curriculum development and personnel development. In B. Wilcox & A. Thompson (Eds.), *Critical issues in educating autistic children and youth* (pp. 53–88). Washington, DC: U.S. Department of Education, Office of Special Education.

DONELLAN, A. M., & KILMAN, B. A. (1986). Behavioral approaches to social skill development in autism. In E. SCHOPLER & G. B. MESIBOV (Eds.), *Social behavior in autism* (pp. 213–236). New York: Plenum Press.

FAVELL, J. E. (1983). The management of aggressive behavior. In E. Schopler & G. B. Mesibov (Eds.), *Autism in adolescents and adults* (pp. 187–222). New York: Plenum Press.

FISH, B., & RITVO, E. R. (1979). Psychoses of childhood. In V. Noshpitz (Ed.), *Basic handbook of child psychiatry* (Vol. 2, pp. 249–303). New York: Basic Books.

FREEMAN, B. J., & RITVO, E. R. (1981). The syndrome of autism: A critical review of diagnostic systems, follow-up studies, and the theoretical background of the behavior observation scale. In J. E. Gilliam (Ed.), *Autism: Diagnosis, instruction, management, and research* (pp. 17–63). Springfield, IL: Charles C. Thomas.

GUALTIERI, T., EVANS, R. W., & PATTERSON, D. R. (1987). The medical treatment of autistic people: Problems and side effects. In E. Schopler & G. B. Mesibov (Eds.), *Neurobiological issues in autism* (pp. 373–388). New York: Plenum Press.

HENNING, J., & DALRYMPLE, N. J. (1986). A guide for developing social and leisure programs for students with autism. In E. Schopler & G. B. Mesibov (Eds.), *Social behavior in autism* (pp. 321–350). New York: Plenum Press.

HENNING, J., DALRYMPLE, N. J., DAVIS, K., & MADEIRA, S. (1982). *Teaching social and leisure skills to youth with autism.* Bloomington, IN: Indiana University Developmental Training Center.

KANNER, L. (1943). Autistic disturbances of affective contact. *Nervous Child, 2,* 217–250.

KOEGEL, R. L., RINCOVER, A., & EGEL, A. L. (Eds). (1982). *Educating and understanding autistic children.* San Diego: College Hill Press.

LaVIGNA, G. W. (1983). The Jay Nolan Center: A community-based program. In E. Schopler & G. B. Mesibov (Eds.), *Autism in adolescents and adults* (pp. 381–410). New York: Plenum Press.

LETTICK, A. L. (1983). Benhaven. In E. Schopler & G. B. Mesibov (Eds.), *Autism in adolescents and adults* (pp. 355–379). New York: Plenum Press.

LOVAAS, O. (1981). *Teaching developmentally disabled children.* Baltimore: University Park Press.

MESIBOV, G. B. (1983). Current perspectives and issues in autism and adolescence. In E. Schopler & G.B. Mesibov (Eds.), *Autism in adolescents and adults* (pp. 37–53). New York: Plenum Press.

MESIBOV, G. B. (1986). A cognitive program for teaching social behaviors to verbal autistic adolescents and adults. In E. Schopler & G. B. Mesibov (Eds.), *Social behavior in autism* (pp. 265–283). New York: Plenum Press.

MESIBOV, G. B., SCHOPLER, E., & SCHAFFER, B. (n.d.). *Adolescent and adult psychoeducational profile.* Chapel Hill, NC: University of North Carolina.

MESIBOV, G. B., SCHOPLER, E., & SLOAN, J. L. (1983). Service development for adolescents and adults in North Carolina's TEACCH program. In E. Schopler & G. B. Mesibov (Eds.), *Autism in adolescents and adults* (pp. 411–432). New York: Plenum Press.

OLLEY, J. G. (1986). The TEACCH curriculum for teaching social behavior to children with autism. In E. Schopler & G. B. Mesibov (Eds.), *Social behavior in autism* (pp. 351–373). New York: Plenum Press.

PALUSZNY, M. J. (1979). *Autism: A practical guide for parents and professionals.* Syracuse, NY: Syracuse University Press.

PIAGET, J. (1960). The definition of states of development. In J. Tanner & B. Inhelder (Eds.), *Discussions on child development* (pp. 116–135). New York: International Universities Press.

REYNOLDS, R. P. (1981). Normalization: A guideline to leisure skills programming for handicapped individuals. In P. Wehman & S. J. Schleien, *Leisure programs for handicapped persons* (pp. 1–13). Baltimore: University Park Press.

RUTTER, M. (1968). Concepts of autism: A review of research. *Journal of Child Psychology and Psychiatry, 9,* 1–25.

RUTTER, M. (1971). The description and classification of infantile autism. In D. W. Churchill, G. D. Alpern, & M. K. DeMyer (Eds.), *Infantile autism.* Springfield, IL: Charles C. Thomas.

RUTTER, M. (1972). Childhood schizophrenia reconsidered. *Journal of Autism and Childhood Schizophrenia, 2,* 315–337.

RUTTER, M. (1978). Diagnosis and definition of childhood autism. *Journal of Autism and Childhood Schizophrenia, 8,* 139–161.

RUTTER, M., & SCHOPLER, E. (Eds.). (1978). *Autism: A reappraisal of concepts and treatment.* New York: Plenum Press.

SCHLEIEN, S. J., KIERNAN, J., & WEHMAN, P. (1981, February). Evaluation of an age-appropriate leisure skills program for mentally retarded adults. *Educational Training of the Mentally Retarded,* pp. 13–19.

SCHLEIEN, S. J., KROTEE, M. L., MUSTONEN, T., KELTERBORN, B., & SCHERMER, A. D. (1987). The effect of integrating children with autism into a physical activity and recreation setting. *Therapeutic Recreation Journal, 21*(4), 52–62.

SCHLEIEN, S. J., RAY, M. T. (1988). *Community recreation and persons with disabilities: Strategies for integration.* Baltimore: Paul H. Brookes.

SCHMIDT, G., MCLAUGHLIN, J., & DALRYMPLE, N. J. (1986). Teaching students with autism: A sport skill specialist's approach. *Journal of Physical Education, Recreation, and Dance, 57*(7), 60–63.

SCHOPLER, E. (1966). Visual versus tactual receptor preference in normal and schizophrenic children. *Journal of Abnormal Psychology, 71,* 108–114.

SCHOPLER, E., & REICHLER, R. J. (1971). Parents as co-therapists in the treatment of psychotic children. *Journal of Autism and Childhood Schizophrenia, 1,* 87–102.

SCHOPLER, E. & REICHLER, R. J. (1979). *Individualized assessment for autistic and developmentally disabled children: Psychoeducational profile,* Vol. I. Baltimore: University Park Press.

SCHOPLER, E., REICHLER, R. J., DEVELLIS, R. F., & DALY, K. (1980). Toward objective classification of childhood autism: Childhood autism rating scale (CARS). *Journal of Autism and Developmental Disorders, 10,* 91–103.

SCHOPLER, E., REICHLER, R. J. & LANSING, M. (1980). *Individualized assessment and treatment for autistic and developmentally disabled children: Teaching strategies for parents and professionals,* Vol. II. Baltimore: University Park Press.

SULLIVAN, R. C. (1977). Parents speak. *Journal of Autism and Childhood Schizophrenia, 7,* 287–288.

WEHMAN, P. (Ed.). (1977). *Recreation programming for developmentally disabled persons.* Baltimore: University Park Press.

WEHMAN, P. (1983). Recreation and leisure needs: A community integration approach. In E. Schopler & G. B. Mesibov (Eds.), *Autism in adolescents and adults* (pp. 111–132). New York: Plenum Press.

WEHMAN, P., & MARCHANT, J. (1978). Improving free play skills of severely retarded children. *American Journal of Occupational Therapy, 32*(2), 100–172.

WEHMAN, P., & SCHLEIEN, S. J. (1980). Assessment and selection of leisure skills for severely handicapped persons. *Education and Training of the Mentally Retarded, 14*(3), 36–42.

WEHMAN, P., & SCHLEIEN, S. J. (1981). *Leisure programs for handicapped persons: Adaptations, techniques, and curriculum.* Baltimore: University Park Press.

WING, L. (1978). Social, behavioral, and cognitive characteristics: An epidemiological approach. In M. Rutter & E. Schopler (Eds.), *Autism: A reappraisal of concepts and treatment.* New York: Plenum Press.

WING, L. (1980). *Early childhood autism* (2nd ed.). Oxford: Pergamon Press.

WOOD, M. M. (Ed.). (1975). *Developmental theory.* Baltimore: University Park Press.

WUERCH, B. B., & VOELTZ, L. M. (1982). *Longitudinal leisure skills for severely handicapped learners: The Ho'onanea curriculum component.* Baltimore: Paul H. Brookes.7

8

Mental Retardation

JOHN DATTILO

OBJECTIVES

- Understand the following terms and phrases: mental retardation, significantly subaverage intellectual functioning, intelligence quotient, adaptive behavior, developmental period, and developmental disability.
- Describe ways of classifying persons with mental retardation and the implications of these classifications on their lives.
- Describe the importance of treatment in providing comprehensive therapeutic recreation services to persons with mental retardation.
- Understand the components of leisure education and their relevance to persons with mental retardation.
- Explain the concepts of least restrictive environment, deinstitutionalization, normalization, and their role in determining the most appropriate setting for administering therapeutic recreation services to persons with mental retardation.
- Understand the procedures of preference analysis, activity analysis, environmental analysis, and task analysis, and their role in the assessment and planning phases of therapeutic recreation services.
- Discuss the importance of partial participation, cooperation and competition, behavior modification, instructional prompts, practice and repetition, and generalization.

When relating to people who have been grouped together, for whatever reasons, it is important to consider these individuals as people first and then, if relevant, consider their group affiliation. It is much easier to interact with a person if we initially concentrate on the similarities we share with this person rather than the differences. Therefore, as you read this chapter, as much as possible try to avoid the tendency to make stereotypic generalizations about people who, in addition to many of the other characteristics that affect their humanity (i.e., sense of humor, reliability, honesty), happen to be identified as having mental retardation.

DEFINITION OF MENTAL RETARDATION

According to the American Association on Mental Deficiency, mental retardation refers to significantly subaverage general intellectual functioning, resulting in or associated with concurrent impairments in adaptive behavior, and manifested during the developmental period (Grossman, 1983). Identification of "significantly subaverage intellectual functioning" occurs when a person receives a score on standardized measures of intelligence quotient (IQ) that is below the score of the average person taking the test to such a degree (two standard deviations) that society has determined that this person requires assistance in development beyond what is typically provided by the family and community. The average IQ has been determined to be a score of approximately 100, and a score below approximately 70 results in a significantly subaverage intellectual functioning. Although IQ and intelligence are frequently used interchangeably, it is important to remember that these concepts are not synonymous. The IQ score is only an estimate of an individual's rate of intellectual development as compared with the average rate for same-age peers (Gottlieb, 1987). According to Gottlieb, the concept of intelligence is often clouded by terminology confusion, highly specialized classification systems, varying methods of assessment and data interpretation, heterogeneity of population samples, and limited practical application assessment of information to life situations.

Although various instruments have been developed that attempt to compensate for particular disabilities (i.e., Peabody Picture Vocabulary Test), a person's lack of performance on a particular standardized measure of IQ can be the result of many factors other than actual intelligence. For instance, some people may not have been exposed to the items presented on the test because of cultural and environmental differences. Perhaps other people may have difficulty communicating their responses due to physical or neurological impairments. Other individuals could be experiencing pain and sickness. In addition, the attitudes of the examiner and examinee can also influence test scores (Zigler & Butterfield, 1968). The aforementioned situations may reduce the performance of a person on an intelligence test and perhaps bring into question the reported scores. The reader is referred to the text by Jensen (1980) entitled *Bias in Mental Testing* for an extensive review of the debate focusing on the validity and utility of intelligence testing.

According to Gunn (1975) "adaptive behavior" relates to the effectiveness with which individuals meet the standards of personal independence and social responsibility expected of their age and cultural group, including maturation, learning, and social adjustment. The focus of adaptive behavior is on the ability of an individual to function as others within the same age and cultural group (Deutsch et al., 1982). Therefore, impairments in adaptive behavior are defined as significant limitations in an individual's effectiveness in meeting standards of maturation, learning, personal independence, and/or social responsibility (Grossman, 1983). Adaptive Behavior Scales are used to determine individuals' independence relative to maturation, learning, and social adjustment. The extent of difficulty that a person with mental retardation experiences related to expressing adaptive behavior is primarily related to the degree of intellectual impairment. However, Baroff (1986) reminds us that adaptive behaviors are also strongly affected by both society's general attitudes toward persons with limited intelligence and the services they receive.

The "developmental period" refers to the time after conception when growth and change occur at a rapid rate. This rate of development typically begins to slow as the person enters adulthood (identified as age 18, 21, or 22). Mental retardation is one particular type of developmental disability. A developmental disability, as reported in Public Law 95-602 enacted in 1978, refers to a severe, chronic disability that (1) is attributable to a mental and/or physical impairment, (2) is manifested before age 22, (3) is likely to continue indefinitely, and (4) results in substantial functional limitations (Grossman, 1983).

The definition of mental retardation established by the American Association on Mental Deficiency is based on the following assumptions that should alert the reader to some possible interpretation problems:

1. Retardation is a general phenomenon.
2. Intelligence, as defined by tests, is permanent.
3. Defined intelligence is sufficiently general to describe all functioning and imply potential.
4. Adaptive behavior includes both spontaneous and trained adaptation.
5. There is a specific developmental period for all people.
6. It is meaningful to catalog people according to their tested intelligence and adaptive behavior.

7. Retardation is more meaningfully conceptualized as a phenomenon existing within individuals rather that the context in which they exist.

As a result of these assumptions, Gold (1978) has proposed an alternative definition that refers to mental retardation as a level of functioning that requires from society significantly above-average training procedures and superior assets in adaptive behavior, manifested throughout life. Therefore, the person with mental retardation is characterized by the extent of training required for the person to learn and not by limitations to what the person can learn. The height of a person's level of functioning is determined by the availability of training technology and the amount of resources society is willing to allocate and not by significant limitations in biological potential. Gold's proposed definition of mental retardation contains the following underlying assumptions:

1. Mental retardation is not a general phenomenon.
2. Intelligence, as defined by tests, has limited use.
3. No behavior clearly defines potential.
4. Adaptive behavior can be assumed.
5. Development is lifelong.
6. Educate people and avoid testing them.
7. Mental retardation is most meaningfully conceptualized as a phenomenon existing within the society, which can be observed only through the depressed performance of some of the individuals in that society.

Therefore, although the phrase *mental retardation* is used throughout this chapter, the label alone means very little. The unique profile of cognitive, adaptive, educational, and recreational ability, as well as the biomedical status associated with each person, is critical for appropriate planning and implementation of effective services (Wodrich & Joy, 1986).

When therapeutic recreation specialists are working with persons with mental retardation, they may examine the results of these persons' scores on standardized measure of IQ and adaptive behavior scales and determine that the person with mental retardation has significant problems as well as limited potential for growth and development. If this conclusion has been drawn, with the focus of the problem on the individual with mental retardation, the specialist's work has ended. However, if therapeutic recreation specialists view people with mental retardation as having the potential for growth and development, then these specialists have before them a lifetime of challenges as they continuously attempt to determine the most effective and efficient procedures to assist these individuals in achieving their maximum potential.

CLASSIFICATION OF MENTAL RETARDATION

Although the current American Association on Mental Deficiency definition of mental retardation contains three major components, the classification of people, once they are labeled "mentally retarded," is based primarily on the scores obtained from an intelligence test. The current definition identifies the following four levels of mental retardation: mild, moderate, severe, profound. The levels are segmented according to the score that people receive on different intelligence tests. For example, those people receiving a score on the Stanford-Binet Intelligence Scale of 52 through 67 are identified as having mild mental retardation; those between 36 through 51 are considered to have moderate mental retardation; people are identified as having severe mental retardation if they score within a range of 20 to 35; and individuals scoring less than 20 are considered to have profound mental retardation. These scores will vary slightly depending on the specified intelligence test that was administered.

Another form of classification of persons with mental retardation is by mental age. The practice of classifying individuals according to mental age has been drastically reduced in recent years. The Stanford-Binet Intelligence Scale, developed by Terman (1916), calculated IQ scores by dividing the "mental age," derived from the test, by the chronological age and multiplying by 100. It has been strongly suggested that practitioners avoid using the phrase *mental age* because the label tells the practitioner nothing about the particular pattern of the person's cognitive strengths and weaknesses (Baroff, 1986).

Frequently, practitioners mistakenly treat a person who receives a low score on a standardized measure of IQ as a child. A problem occurs when an adult who happens to have mental retardation is compared to a child, because that adult has many more years of experience at living and as a result has developed a variety of skills. Therapeutic recreation specialists must avoid viewing adults with mental retardation as children and instead give them the respect provided to other adults in our society. This view of people with mental retardation will encourage specialists to develop therapeutic recreation programs that are appropriate for the age of the participants and do not require persons with mental retardation to compromise their dignity.

Information related to definitions and classifications associated with mental retardation has been presented. For a more detailed description of terminology related to mental retardation, the reader is encouraged to consult the text *Classification in Mental Retardation*, edited by Grossman (1983). To obtain historical information about the development of mental retardation, refer to Scheerenberger (1987), who has developed the text *A History of Mental Retardation*, which provides an in-depth history of mental retardation by examining major decisions, events, and personages of time that resulted in the author's interpretation of a quarter century of

promise. In addition, Accardo and Capute (1979) present a concise historical description of mental retardation.

DESCRIPTION OF LIMITATIONS

Mental retardation is associated with more than 200 known medical entities, including genetic defects, chromosomal disorders, infections during
pregnancy, accidental poisonings and injuries, metabolic disorders, and
central nervous system infections (Gottlieb, 1987). However, Carter, Van
Andel, and Robb (1985) identified research indicating that the present
known number of causes, nearly 300, represents only one third of those
possible. According to the authors, there is rarely one cause or simple
explanation of mental retardation.

Mental retardation occurs as a result of biological occurrences and
environmental conditions, or, for the majority of the cases, the cause is
idiopathic (unknown). There are instances of mental retardation that are
determined at conception due to hereditary disorders (i.e., phenylketonuria) or to chromosomal abnormalities (i.e., Down's syndrome). In
addition to these two forms of biological causes, mental retardation may be
biologically developed after conception during the prenatal period (before
birth), perinatal period (immediately preceding or during birth), or postnatal period of development (following birth). Approximately 90% of
people who acquire mental retardation through biological reasons develop
their disability during the prenatal period of development and manifest
the condition at birth or early infancy (Grossman, 1983). The following are
problems that can occur during the prenatal period of development that
may result in mental retardation: diseases (e.g., syphilis, rubella); nutritional deficits; infections (e.g., encephalitis); toxemias (i.e., poisonous drugs
such as alcohol or lead); and radiation in large doses. Many of the conditions that can occur during the prenatal period may result in prematurity
and low birth weight. In addition to prematurity and low birth weight,
other possible perinatal conditions causing mental retardation may include
trauma, infection, anoxia (oxygen deprivation), and the development of
antibodies by the mother (RH incompatibility). Following birth, mental
retardation appears primarily to occur as a result of malnutrition, trauma
(i.e., automobile collisions, child abuse), or poisoning (i.e., lead encepha-
lopathy). A variety of conditions that can contribute to the occurrence of
mental retardation have been identified; however, the majority of reasons
for the development of mental retardation are yet unknown.

Persons with mental retardation are at significant risk for concomitant
disabilities, and the more severe the mental retardation, the greater the
probability of an associated disability (Accardo & Capute, 1979). Because
people with mental retardation have different biological deficits and environmental experiences resulting in differing levels of cognitive function-

ing, it is difficult to make generalizations about individuals with mental retardation (Browman et al., 1987). For a detailed description of etiology associated with mental retardation, the reader is referred to the chapter developed by Gottlieb (1987) entitled "Major Variations in Intelligence."

PURPOSE OF THERAPEUTIC RECREATION

The purpose of therapeutic recreation is to facilitate the development, maintenance, and expression of an appropriate leisure life-style for the person with physical, mental, emotional, or social limitations (National Therapeutic Recreation Society [NTRS], 1982). The phrase *leisure life-style* refers to the day-to-day behavioral expression of one's leisure-related attitudes, awareness, and activities revealed within the context and composite of the total life experience (Peterson, 1981). Therapeutic recreation places special emphasis on the development of an appropriate leisure life-style as an integral part of independent functioning (American Therapeutic Recreation Association [ATRA], 1984). According to Peterson and Gunn (1984), the most essential aspect of the definition is the focus on day-to-day behavioral expression, in that it implies that leisure life-style is a routine engaged in as a part of the individual's daily existence. Therefore, specialists should provide comprehensive therapeutic recreation services for persons with mental retardation to develop leisure-related skills that allow them to enhance the quality of their life each day. Three specific areas of professional service are used to provide this comprehensive leisure ability approach that facilitates appropriate leisure life-styles: therapy (treatment), leisure education, and recreation participation (NTRS, 1982).

Treatment

Because people with mental retardation have impaired intellectual functioning, it is extremely important for therapeutic recreation specialists to develop interventions and treatments that assist these individuals in developing functional skills necessary for participation in leisure pursuits. Therapeutic recreation involves the application of appropriate leisure intervention strategies to promote independent functioning for persons with a variety of disabling conditions (ATRA, 1984). It is apparent that interventions encouraging the development of cognitive skills such as understanding and remembering rules and procedures, concentrating on the task, maintaining scores, and following directions should be the focus of therapeutic recreation treatment for persons with mental retardation. However, it is also important for therapeutic recreation specialists to remember to develop strategies that increase physical, social, and emotional development related to leisure participation.

Leisure Education

Leisure education provides a vehicle for developing an awareness of leisure activities and resources and for acquiring skills requisite for participation throughout the life span (Howe-Murphy & Charboneau, 1987). As a result of leisure education, individuals will be able to enhance the quality of their lives in leisure; understand the opportunities, potentials, and challenges in leisure; understand the impact of leisure on the quality of their lives; and have knowledge, skills, and appreciations that enable broad leisure skills (Mundy & Odum, 1979). An effective leisure education program for persons with mental retardation should include, but is not limited to, the following components: awareness of self, perception of leisure competence, awareness of leisure, knowledge of leisure resources, decision-making skills, and social interaction skills.

Recreation Participation

Wehman and Schleien (1981) asserted that the ultimate goal of any leisure education program is to facilitate self-initiated independent use of free time with chronologically age-appropriate recreation activities. Therefore, the importance of recreation participation in the lives of persons with mental retardation relative to having opportunities to make choices and decisions as well as being able to participate in age-appropriate recreation activities will be presented.

Choice.   As previously discussed, when providing therapeutic recreation services to people with mental retardation, it is important to develop functional skills through therapy or treatment and to teach leisure skills and knowledge through leisure education. Although these actions are important, they are not sufficient when attempting systematically to enhance the leisure life-styles of individuals with mental retardation (Wuerch & Voeltz, 1982). Dattilo (1986) noted that a person may not encounter the freedom of choice associated with the leisure experience when involved in therapy or structured leisure education. Therefore, opportunities for choice, often associated with recreation participation, must be systematically provided (Dattilo & Rusch, 1985).

Decision Making.   If one of the goals of therapeutic recreation is to foster independence, it is imperative that the ability to make appropriate decisions regarding specific tasks be encouraged during recreation participation (Dattilo & Murphy, 1987a). According to Dattilo and Murphy, an intended benefit of recreation participation is an increase in personal effectiveness that can result from the making of timely and correct decisions. Persons with mental retardation who do not possess the appropriate appraisal and judgment skills needed for activity involvement will be more likely to acquire these skills if they participate in actual recreation activities.

Age-Appropriate Participation. It is extremely important for individuals with mental retardation to develop age-appropriate, community-based leisure skill repertoires that facilitate successful integration into the community (Schleien, Tuckner, & Heyne, 1985). Ford and colleagues (1984) suggested that leisure skills should be developed in a wide variety of integrated community environments, on the basis of those activities performed by individuals who are not disabled. Therefore, therapeutic recreation specialists should encourage persons with mental retardation to acquire leisure skills that are age appropriate and comparable to their peers. Practitioners should teach only those leisure skills that have the potential of being performed in the presence of, or in interaction with, peers without disabilities (Schleien & Ray, 1988). Because some people with mental retardation may have inaccurate perceptions of their own capabilities, Kennedy, Austin, and Smith (1987) suggested that therapeutic recreation specialists assist participants in selecting activities that are age appropriate.

COMMON SERVICE SETTINGS

The majority of persons with mental retardation reside either in residential training centers, in group homes within the community, with their families at home in their community, or on their own in the community. Regardless of where the person lives, there are important concepts that therapeutic recreation specialists must consider when determining the best environment for the provision of leisure services. The following concepts are presented to encourage therapeutic recreation specialists to establish the most appropriate service setting for persons with mental retardation: least restrictive environment, deinstitutionalization, normalization, and integration.

Least Restrictive Environment

It is important that therapeutic recreation specialists support efforts encouraging persons with mental retardation to reside and receive services in an environment that is as least restrictive to their life as possible. The concept of "least restrictive environment" involves people with mental retardation living as normally as possible and receiving appropriate services in the least separate or most integrated setting. To determine the least restrictive recreation environment for persons with mental retardation, Brown and colleagues (1979) encouraged practitioners to delineate the current and subsequent chronological age-appropriate recreation community environments that are (1) currently available and used in the community by persons both with and without disabilities, (2) available and used in other communities by persons both with or without disabilities, and (3) used by peers without disabilities that are potentially available and usable in the community for persons with disabilities. Once these three steps have been completed, the therapeutic recreation specialist can access the environments that best represent the least restrictive environment for a person with mental retardation residing in a specific community.

Deinstitutionalization

The philosophy of least restrictive environment has led to the deinstitutionalization of persons with mental retardation. Deinstitutionalization as a concept affecting persons with mental retardation gained recognition during the sixties, acquired greater support during the seventies, and has now become a national professional goal (Scheerenberger, 1987). Scheerenberger described the philosophy of deinstitutionalization as seeking greater emphasis on freedom, independence, individuality, mobility, personalized life experiences, and a high degree of interaction in a free society. Although for at least a decade our rhetoric has called for deinstitutionalizing persons with mental retardation and the creation of community-based services, the development of these services has lagged (Baroff, 1986). Therefore, every attempt should be made to provide recreation services for persons with mental retardation in an integrated fashion within the community.

Normalization

The introduction of the principle of normalization by Nirje nearly two decades ago has become the primary philosophical orientation guiding the development and delivery of community-based services for persons with disabilities (Schleien & Ray, 1988). Normalization is defined as the process that involves making available for persons with mental retardation patterns and condition of everyday life that are as close as possible to the norms and patterns of the mainstream of society (Nirje, 1969). Wolfensberger (1972) broadened Nirje's definition of normalization to include the use of means that are as culturally normative as possible, and to establish and/or maintain personal behaviors and characteristics that are as culturally normative as possible. Therefore, normalization involves placing a high value on the life, rights, and dignity of citizens with disabilities (Lakin & Bruininks, 1985). The integration of persons with disabilities into community recreation programs is essential if the process of normalization is to be completed (Schleien & Ray, 1988).

Integration

When people are grouped together and then separated from others, for whatever reason, the differences between the groups, rather than their similarities, appear to become the focus of attention. In effect, when people are separated from other people in a society, they do not experience equal opportunities to receive services. Although integration has been described as consisting of those practices that maximize a person's participation in the mainstream of society, integration is only meaningful if it involves social integration and acceptance, and not merely physical presence (Wolfensberger, 1972). Hutchison and Lord (1979) described integration of persons with disabilities into recreation activities as involving: (1) experiencing participation and enjoyment similar to peers who do not possess disabilities, (2) upgrading skills and confidence, (3) participating in community activities of their choice, and (4) encouraging self-confidence and the perception of dignity. Schleien and Ray (1988) encouraged practitioners to set the stage for integrated recreation by implementing the following strategies: (1) develop communication linkages between persons and agencies concerned about community leisure services, (2) conduct surveys of architectural accessibility of leisure service settings, and (3) provide comprehensive staff in-service training.

The potential advantages of integration of persons with mental retardation into recreation activities in the community are not limited to the people with disabilities (Howe-Murphy & Charboneau, 1987). After participating in experiences involving systematic interaction with people who possess disabilities, individuals without disabilities have demonstrated an increase in positive attitudes toward people with disabilities (Donder & Nietupski, 1981; Fenrick & Petersen, 1984; McHale & Simeonsson, 1980).

CURRENT BEST PRACTICES AND PROCEDURES

The remediation of learning difficulties associated with mental retardation necessitates the use of a spectrum of educational strategies (Gearheart, 1987). Austin (1982) described therapeutic recreation as being characterized by eclecticism, or the utilization of approaches and techniques drawn from several sources. Therefore, therapeutic recreation specialists are encouraged to use a variety of assessment, planning, implementation, and evaluative strategies in order to facilitate leisure participation resulting in enjoyment and satisfaction for persons with mental retardation.

Assessment and Planning

Kennedy, Austin, and Smith (1987) observed that the wide range of behaviors and abilities of people with learning impairments, such as mental retardation, necessitates careful consideration of each person's recreation abilities and the avoidance of assumptions of the individual based on categorical designation. Gearheart (1987) stated that significant improvement is often observed when a combination of approaches are employed based on valid assessment data and reasonable planning. To encourage therapeutic recreation specialists working with persons with mental retardation to plan comprehensive assessment procedures, the following areas of analysis will be presented: preference, activity, environment, and task.

Preference Analysis.   An initial step in providing opportunities for individuals with mental retardation to participate in chosen leisure experiences is the assessment of an individual's preferences (Dattilo, 1986). These preferences should be of major concern in the development of recreation programs for persons with mental retardation. Although the literature contains numerous examples of successful training programs for individuals with mental retardation (Pace et al., 1985), Favell and Cannon (1977) observed that practitioners frequently find the usual methods for determining preferences (i.e., verbal interviews) ineffective for persons with mental retardation, especially those with more severe mental retardation. The limited response repertoires of individuals with severe disabilities often result in unreliable assumptions about their preferences (Wacker et al., 1985). It is important to develop strategies to recognize the exhibition of preferences for people who are unable to indicate choices through conventional means (Guess, Benson, & Siegel-Causey, 1985; Houghton, Bronicki, & Guess, 1987). Once assessment of their preferences has occurred, individuals with mental retardation can experience enjoyment and control through participation in a preferred activity (Dattilo, 1988).

Activity Analysis.   After assessment information concerning the abilities of persons with mental retardation has been collected, it is important for the therapeutic recreation specialist to analyze the recreation activities. This analyzation will permit the specialist to match the appropriate activity with the individual participants. If there is a discrepancy between the requirements of the activity and the skills of the individual, the therapeutic recreation specialist will be able to determine activity modification procedures or instructional strategies to teach the individual the necessary participatory skills. The procedure for breaking down and examining an activity to find inherent characteristics (physical, mental, affective, and social) that contribute to program objectives is termed *activity analysis* (Peterson & Gunn, 1984). The reader is referred to the text by Peterson and Gunn (1984), *Therapeutic Recreation Program Design*, for an example and description of an activity analysis rating form.

Environmental Analysis.   It is useful for the therapeutic recreation specialist to examine the total environment in which the person with mental retardation will attempt to participate in a recreation activity. Environmental analysis inventories provide the therapeutic recreation specialist with a systematic approach to analyze the leisure context and facilitate leisure involvement for persons with mental retardation (Certo, Schleien, & Hunter, 1983). Use of the inventory helps heighten public awareness and increases the level of sensitivity of all persons involved in the process of integrating community leisure services (Schleien & Ray, 1988). The reader is referred to the text by Schleien and Ray (1988) entitled *Community Recreation for Persons with Disabilities* for a detailed description and examples of environmental analysis inventories.

Task Analysis. Wuerch and Voeltz (1982) defined tasks analysis as the identification of all the necessary participant responses or component skills and the sequence in which these responses or skills must occur for appropriate interactions with the activity. The use of task analytic assessment procedures has been suggested as an alternative approach for assessing performance of individuals with mental retardation (Vallet, 1972). Task analysis is not a statement of how to assess but rather a statement of what is to be assessed (Williams & Gotts, 1977). The task analysis procedure involves the description of the tasks associated with a recreation activity to be performed during the testing procedure and allows the therapeutic recreation specialist to analyze critically the content of the skills used during the assessment process (Dattilo, 1984). Once a task has been described in observable and measurable terms, identification and sequencing of component skills of the task should occur. Following the delineation of the component skills, the client is encouraged to perform the task associated with the recreation activity. Assistance may be provided by the therapeutic recreation specialist to allow the person with mental retardation to complete the task. However, Knapczyk (1975) suggested that the assistance provided by the practitioner should be provided only when the person has made an unsuccessful attempt at performing the task in the specified time. It is critical when using this assessment procedure that the therapeutic recreation specialist record the type and degree of assistance that was needed for the person with mental retardation to complete the task associated with the recreation activity.

Implementation

In general, when comparing persons with mental retardation to those individuals not identified as having a disability, individuals with mental retardation tend to perform well on practical and concrete types of tasks and less well on those that require primarily verbal reasoning and judgment (Baroff, 1986). Mental retardation is observed when individuals attempt to complete developmental tasks expected of their same-age peers. These age-appropriate developmental tasks require demonstration of maturation, learning, and social adjustment. Baroff observed that in the earlier years of development, a slower rate of maturation is reflected by lags in the development of skills related to motor performance, communication, cognition, self-help, and socialization. As a result of these delays, people with mental retardation may encounter a greater number of failures than their same-age peers when attempting to participate in recreation activities. The following strategies appear useful when attempting to implement therapeutic recreation services for persons with mental retardation that foster success and development: partial participation, cooperation and competition, behavior modification, instructional prompts, practice and repetition, and generalization training.

Partial Participation.   Individuals with mental retardation are often excluded from participating in a wide range of recreation activities because it is assumed that they cannot perform complete sequences of skills independently (Ford et al., 1984). Therefore, it should be emphasized that a person who is currently unable to engage in a particular activity independently should not be denied the opportunity for "partial participation" (Brown et al., 1979). Brown and colleagues provided suggestions for adaptations that enhance or make participation possible: (1) provide personal assistance; (2) adapt activities by changing materials, modifying skill sequences, altering rules, and using adaptive devices; and (3) adapt physical and social environments. Through partial participation, individuals are provided the opportunity to experience the exhilaration and satisfaction associated with actively responding to the challenge present in a particular recreation activity (Dattilo & Murphy, 1987a). Partial participation involves the use of adaptations and the provision of necessary assistance to the individual to facilitate recreation participation. Baumgart and colleagues (1982) stated that the principle of partial participation affirms the rights of persons with mental retardation to participate in environments and activities without regard to degree of assistance required.

Cooperation and Competition.   In an attempt to provide persons with mental retardation with recreation activities that encourage success, the therapeutic recreation specialist should include those activities that encourage cooperation and indirect competition. According to Fait and Billing (1978), competition against a record or previous achievement is termed *indirect competition* as opposed to *direct competition*, which requires a rivalry between opposing forces in which the interests of both are not mutually obtainable. Based on these definitions, Dattilo and Murphy (1987b) recommended the redirection of an emphasis from direct competition and winning to learning and development fostered by indirect competition. In this way, participants will be encouraged to "celebrate" their abilities and skills rather than compare them with others (Farrington, 1976). The challenge that therapeutic recreation specialists should instill in the participants with mental retardation is to develop and grow through indirect competition and cooperation rather than defeat or destroy through direct competition.

Behavior Modification.   Behavior modification is a systematic, evaluative, performance-based method for changing any observable and measurable act, response, or movement by an individual (Dattilo & Murphy, 1987b). The authors contend that an understanding of introductory techniques of behavior modification can provide therapeutic recreation specialists and other professionals with helpful facilitation procedures in the provision of leisure services. Therapeutic recreation services incorporating behavior modification techniques promote a hopeful view that emphasizes the learning capabilities of persons with mental retardation and recognizes possibilities for growth and development in recreation (Raw & Errickson, 1977). Trap-Porter and Perry (1982) suggested that therapeutic recreation specialists, especially those providing services to persons with mental retardation, should receive comprehensive training in behavior modification principles. The reader is referred to the text by Dattilo and Murphy (1987a) entitled *Behavior Modification in Therapeutic Recreation* for additional information.

Instructional Prompts.   Instructional prompts refer to information provided before an action is performed (Wuerch & Voeltz, 1982). Falvey and colleagues (1980) stated that instructional cues are an addition to information naturally provided by the environment. Frequently, those prompts that are concrete have been found to be useful for persons with mental retardation. Therefore, the specialist may attempt to demonstrate or model the appropriate leisure behavior. If direct physical guidance is needed, Donnellan and colleagues (1986) suggested a physical prompt-fade strategy that can involve a hand-over-hand procedure. The therapeutic recreation specialists should allow the participant with mental retardation to perform as much of the task as possible, and only provide light physical assistance as needed. This procedure also has been described as a graduated-guidance technique that involves the fading of more restrictive physical cues and replacing them with less assistance. Additional prompts such as verbal, gestural, and visual also may be used by the therapeutic recreation specialist. Visual cues can be in the form of symbols, colors, or words positioned within view of the participant to permit the individual to learn or remember the proper procedure for participation. Finally, the therapeutic recreation specialist can provide assistance to the person with mental retardation simply by arranging the environment to remind the person of necessary steps for activity involvement.

Practice and Repetition.   Baroff (1986) identified problems in acquisition of information by people with mental retardation that results in the need for greater repetition of experiences and more frequent explanations of the principles being presented. Therefore, therapeutic recreation specialists may wish to incorporate numerous opportunities for persons with mental retardation to practice leisure skills. Additional opportunities to practice the leisure skills could be facilitated by providing longer time segments for acquisition of skills. In addition, the task analysis procedure, previously discussed, will provide sufficient information to allow the therapeutic recreation specialist to teach persons with mental retardation small concrete steps.

Generalization Training.   Dattilo and Murphy (1987a) defined the term *generalization* as the display of a specified behavior over time, in a variety of situations and settings, across different people, or with similar materials. According to Dattilo and Murphy, generalization also can involve the exhibition of various related behaviors that are similar to the target behavior. Frequently, the knowledge that persons with mental retardation acquire tends to be specific to the situation in which it was learned rather than generalized to related environments.

The more similar two situations, people, or materials are, the more likely it is that the behavior will generalize (Dattilo & Murphy, 1987a). According to the authors, one way for therapeutic recreation specialists to encourage generalization is to conduct training and practice sessions in an environment that is as similar as possible to the environment where the behavior is ultimately performed. Once a person with mental retardation has learned a leisure skill, the therapeutic recreation specialist should then gradually decrease the amount and rate that a particular reward is being administered. Therefore, as the specialist decreases the reward, the participants will be required to exhibit more of the desired leisure skill for a longer period of time to receive the same reward. In addition, it is important for the therapeutic recreation specialist to use rewards that are naturally occurring within the environments where the leisure skill is intended to be performed, because if the rewards used during the teaching of the skill are not available in other situations, the likelihood of generalization is reduced.

Evaluation

The process of collecting and analyzing information about people and programs is a critical task of the therapeutic recreation specialist. In response to the unique problems created by the application of therapeutic recreation programs in a variety of settings and situations, the specialist should possess an assortment of evaluation skills. Observational strategies appear to be the most reliable method of evaluation for individuals with mental retardation. Pelegrino (1979) stated that observational procedures are the primary method to obtain information on what is actually happening in a situation.

Therapeutic recreation specialists should employ an individualized evaluation strategy to examine accurately the impact of services on participants. One methodology that allows practitioners to evaluate the effect of interventions on the individual is the application of single-subject designs (Dattilo & Nelson, 1986). Single-subject evaluation requires an extensive examination of each individual, using multiple measurements to verify the functional relationship between a therapeutic recreation program and its effect on the individual with mental retardation. However, Dattilo (1987) reported that single-subject designs provide a feasible procedure for therapeutic recreation specialists to implement. According to Dattilo and Nelson (1986), single-subject evaluation represents a viable method for making informed decisions about the quality of a therapeutic recreation program and provides the context for understanding the behavioral dynamics of individuals.

APPLICATION OF THE TR PROCESS

CASE STUDY

James is a 33-year-old man who enjoys spending his free time socializing with his friends and family. Although James has an excellent sense of humor, he needs to develop more social interaction skills. In addition, he has encountered difficulty in attempting to initiate participation in preferred recreation activities. As a result of his severe mental retardation, James has limited expressive communication skills. James's parents have been extremely supportive of him; however, at times they have tended to be somewhat overprotective.

James has registered to participate in a leisure education class offered by the community recreation and parks department. The therapeutic recreation specialist has developed the following comprehensive leisure education program that will provide James with long-range leisure instruction intended to allow him to participate with his family and friends in integrated recreation programs within his community.

Self-Awareness. In order for James to make appropriate choices about recreation participation, it is vital that he possess knowledge of himself relative to his preferences (Montagnes, 1976). It is important for James to gain a realistic view of his abilities as well as his limitations. It is also helpful for him to examine his preferences and desires relative to leisure participation. Reflecting on past leisure pursuits may permit James to gain insight into his skills. Analyzation of his current leisure involvement should assist him in identifying activities he enjoys as well as determining barriers he would like to overcome. To enhance motivation to participate in leisure education, the therapeutic recreation specialist will encourage James to look beyond his past and present leisure participation patterns and begin to consider areas for future discovery.

Leisure Competence.   Witt, Ellis, and Niles (1984) emphasized the need for therapeutic recreation specialists to provide leisure education services that promote an individual's perception of leisure control, leisure competence, and intrinsic motivation to facilitate the person's sense of freedom of choice. This recommendation was based on the arguments presented by many contemporary theorists for the inclusion of choice in definitions of leisure (Csikszentmihalyi, 1975; Iso-Ahola, 1980; Neulinger, 1982). Therefore, the therapeutic recreation specialist will attempt to incorporate the notion of choice into the leisure education program designed for James. It is hoped that the demonstration of choice through selection will encourage James to initiate activity spontaneously, interact with elements of the environment, and assert a degree of control over his surroundings (Dattilo & Barnett, 1985). In an attempt to address the unmet leisure education needs of adolescents with severe mental retardation, Wuerch and Voeltz (1982) developed a leisure training project designed to provide people with opportunities to learn and make choices during their free time. The specialist will implement portions of the program described in the text by Wuerch and Voeltz (1982) entitled *Longitudinal Leisure Skills for Severely Handicapped Learners.*

Leisure Awareness.   To gain an awareness of leisure, it is useful for James to develop an understanding of the concepts of leisure and leisure life-style. If James begins to understand these concepts, his ability to participate in recreation activities that result in satisfaction and enjoyment will be enhanced. Because James has been overprotected, his ability to take personal responsibility for his own leisure involvement has been reduced. Therefore, the leisure education for him will be designed to teach James to take responsibility for his leisure life-style. By focusing on leisure awareness, James should begin to develop a sensitivity for the uniqueness of leisure. In addition, it is important for him to understand the outcomes of his leisure participation. Finally, it is useful for James to be aware of the numerous possibilities that can facilitate the leisure experience.

Decision Making.   James has encountered difficulty in making decisions related to many aspects of his life. This problem is evident in relation to his leisure life-style. Based on observations that persons with mental retardation frequently fail in their attempts to adjust to community living as a result of inappropriate use of their free time, Hayes (1977) recommended that therapeutic recreation specialists teach the decision-making process and encourage the selection and participation in appropriate recreation activities. Therefore, the therapeutic recreation specialist will teach James the decision-making process.

Knowledge of Leisure Resources. According to Overs, Taylor, and Adkins (1974), difficulty in making appropriate leisure choices may result from people's lack of knowledge of leisure resources. Knowledge of leisure resources and the ability to use these resources appears to be an important factor in the establishment of an independent leisure life-style (Peterson & Gunn, 1984). Therefore, Dattilo and Murphy (1987a) recommended that therapeutic recreation specialists teach participants not only how to participate in an activity but also how they can answer questions such as (1) where can one participate, (2) are there others who will participate, (3) how much will participation cost, (4) what type of transportation is available, and (5) where could a person learn more about a particular recreation activity. The therapeutic recreation specialist will implement the leisure education program described in Joswiak's (1979) text entitled *Leisure Counseling Program Materials for the Developmentally Disabled* and will teach James to become more aware of the leisure resources available to him.

Social Interaction Skills. One of the major deficits experienced by James that prevents him from developing a satisfying leisure life-style is related to social interaction skills. In fact, a defining characteristic of mental retardation has become a deficiency in social skills (Knapczyk & Yoppi, 1975). Frequently, James has been identified as being mentally retarded, not because people observed his inability to perform some cognitive or physical skill but as a result of his display of inappropriate social behaviors. The absence of social skills is particularly noticeable during leisure participation (Marlowe, 1979) and frequently leads to isolation and an inability to function successfully (O'Morrow, 1980). Therefore, the development of social skills used in leisure situations appears to be important to James because the acquisition of these skills facilitates integration (Keogh et al., 1984). The development of meaningful friendships and effective social interaction skills can be taught to James through a systematic leisure education program.

TRENDS AND ISSUES

The trends and issues related to leisure services for persons with mental retardation are as follows:

- Focus on individual's similarities as opposed to differences.
- Implementation of services including treatment, leisure education, and recreation participation.
- Provision of opportunities to make leisure choices and decisions.
- Development of age-appropriate recreation activities.
- Support for the provision of leisure services in the person's least restrictive environment.

- Encouragement of the deinstitutionalization movement.
- Provision of leisure programs demonstrating the normalization principle.
- Development of strategies that facilitate integration into community recreation activities.
- Incorporation of assessment, planning, implementation, and evaluation into programming.
- Implementation of preference, activity, environmental, and task analysis assessment procedures.
- Facilitation of the opportunity for partial participation.
- Provision of recreation activities that involve cooperation and indirect competition.
- Use of behavior modification in applied settings to facilitate positive leisure involvement.
- Systematic administration of instructional prompts to develop a repertoire of leisure skills.
- Provision of opportunities for practice and repetition of leisure participation.
- Development of procedures to encourage generalization of leisure behaviors.
- Use of observational strategies to evaluate performance in recreation activities.
- Implementation of single-subject research designs to examine the impact of leisure services.

SUMMARY

This chapter was developed with the intent of encouraging the reader to gain an understanding of mental retardation, significantly subaverage intellectual functioning, intelligence quotient, adaptive behavior, developmental period, and developmental disability. Ways of classifying persons with mental retardation and the implications of these classifications on their lives were also highlighted. The reader was presented with information on the causes of the limitations associated with mental retardation. Therapeutic recreation and leisure life-style were described in relation to people with mental retardation. The importance of treatment in providing comprehensive therapeutic recreation services to persons with mental retardation was emphasized. The chapter also contained information describing the components of leisure education (self-awareness, leisure competence, leisure awareness, decision making, knowledge of leisure resources, and social interaction skills) and their relevance to persons with mental retardation. Strategies for incorporating opportunities for choice and decision making as well as encouraging age-appropriate involvement in recreation participation for persons with mental retardation were presented. The reader was introduced to the concepts of least restrictive environment, deinstitutionalization, normalization, and integration, and their role in determining the most appropriate setting for administering therapeutic recreation services to persons with mental retardation. Specific techniques such as preference analysis, activity analysis, environmental analysis, and task analysis, and their role in the assessment and planning phases of therapeutic recreation services for persons with mental retardation were described. A major portion of the chapter was devoted to identifying and describing the procedures of partial participation, cooperation and competition, behavior modification, instructional prompts, practice and repetition, and generalization training when implementing therapeutic recreation programs for persons with mental retardation. The chapter also contained a description of the value of behavioral observation and single-subject designs when evaluating therapeutic recreation services designed for persons with mental retardation. A specific application of the therapeutic recreation process for an individual with mental retardation was subsequently provided in the chapter. Finally, the chapter concluded with the identification of trends and issues affecting therapeutic recreation services for persons with mental retardation.

READING COMPREHENSION QUESTIONS

1. What is meant by mental retardation?

2. What is the difference between the phrases *developmental disability* and *mental retardation*?

3. What is Gold's alternative definition of mental retardation? Why did Gold develop this definition? What are the advantages associated with the alternative definition?

4. Why is the practice of classifying people with mental retardation based on mental age a problem?

5. What are some conditions that may cause mental retardation?

6. What are the three specific areas of professional service that are used to provide a comprehensive leisure ability approach for people with mental retardation?

7. Why is it important to incorporate opportunities for people with mental retardation to demonstrate choices, make decisions, and learn age-appropriate skills when participating in recreation participation programs?

8. What is meant by the following: least restrictive environment, deinstitutionalization, normalization, and integration? Why are these principles important to consider when providing recreation services for people with mental retardation?

9. Why should you encourage the integration of people with mental retardation into community recreation programs? Who benefits from the integration of people with mental retardation into community programs?

10. Why is it useful to conduct a preference analysis when providing comprehensive leisure programs for people with mental retardation?

11. What is meant by the phrase *task analysis*? Why is it useful to employ task analytic assessment procedures prior to providing leisure services for people with mental retardation?

12. Why is it valuable to adopt the philosophy of partial participation that encourages people with mental retardation to participate actively in recreation activities?

13. What is meant by the phrase *indirect competition*? Why should indirect competition and cooperation be incorporated into recreation programs for people with mental retardation?

14. What is meant by the word *generalization*? Why is it useful systematically to promote the generalization of leisure skills acquired by individuals with mental retardation?

15. What are some components of a comprehensive leisure education program that should be addressed when developing lifelong leisure skills for people with mental retardation?

SUGGESTED LEARNING ACTIVITIES

1. Attend a meeting of your local chapter of the Association for Retarded Citizens. Take notes at the meeting and write a brief report describing what you learned.

2. Contact your community recreation and parks department to determine if any individuals with mental retardation participate in an integrated recreation event. If so, participate in the activity and attempt to get to know the persons.

3. Develop an outline of a comprehensive leisure education program that you would develop if you were planning to teach a variety of people, including those with mental retardation.

4. Choose a friend, family member, or acquaintance. Attempt to communicate to the person the advantages associated with integrating people with mental retardation into community recreation programs.

5. Practice using appropriate terminology when talking about people with mental retardation. Remember: (1) Use a label only when necessary. (2) If it is relevant to use a label, use the label only as a noun referring to a condition (e.g., "a person with mental retardation"). (3) Do not use a label as a noun referring to the person (e.g., "the retard"). (4) Do not use a label as an adjective (e.g., "the mentally retarded person").

6. Interview a person with mental retardation and determine his or her leisure interests and desires. Discuss ways that the person may be able to meet the identified needs by accessing community recreation resources.

REFERENCES

ACCARDO, P. J., & CAPUTE, A. J. (1979). *The pediatrician and the delayed child.* Baltimore: University Park Press.

American Therapeutic Recreation Association. (1984). *ATRA.* Washington, DC: American Therapeutic Recreation Association.

AUSTIN, D. R. (1982). *Therapeutic recreation: Processes and techniques.* New York: John Wiley & Sons.

BAROFF, G. S. (1986). *Mental retardation: Nature, cause, and management* (2nd ed.). Washington, DC: Hemisphere.

BAUMGART, D., BROWN, L., PUMPIAN, I., NISBET, J., FORD, A., SWEET, M., MISSINA, R. & SCHROEDER, J. (1982). The principle of partial participation and individualized adaptations in educational programs for severely handicapped students. *Journal of the Association for the Severely Handicapped, 7*(2), 17–27.

BROWMAN, S., NICHOLS, P. L., SCHASUGNESSY, P., & KENNEDY, W. (1987). *Retardation in young children: A developmental study of cognitive deficit.* Hillsdale, NJ: Lawrence Erlbaum Associates.

BROWN, L., BRANSTON, M. B., HAMRE-NIETUPSKI, S., WILCOX, B., & GRUENEWALD, L. (1979). A rationale for comprehensive longitudinal interactions between severely handicapped and nonhandicapped students and citizens. *AAESPH Review, 4*(1), 3–14.

CARTER, M. J., VAN ANDEL, G. E., & ROBB, G. M. (1985). *Therapeutic recreation: A practical approach.* St. Louis: Times Mirror/Mosby.

CERTO, N. J., SCHLEIEN, S. J., & HUNTER, D. (1983). An ecological assessment inventory to facilitate community recreation participation by severely disabled individuals. *Therapeutic Recreation Journal, 17*(3), 29–38.

CSIKSZENTMIHALYI, M. (1975). *Beyond boredom and anxiety.* San Francisco: Jossey-Bass.

DATTILO, J. (1984). Therapeutic recreation assessment for individuals with severe handicaps. In G. L. Hitzhusen (Ed.), *Expanding horizons in therapeutic recreation* (Vol. 11, pp. 146–157). Columbia, MO: Curators University of Missouri.

DATTILO, J. (1986). Single-subject research in therapeutic recreation: Implications to individuals with limitations. *Therapeutic Recreation Journal, 20*(2), 76–87.

DATTILO, J. (1987). Encouraging the emergence of therapeutic recreation research-practitioners through single-subject research. *Journal of Expanding Horizons in Therapeutic Recreation, 2,* 1–5.

DATTILO, J. (1988). Assessing music preferences of persons with severe disabilities. *Therapeutic Recreation Journal, 22*(2).

DATTILO, J., & BARNETT, L. A. (1985). Therapeutic recreation for persons with severe handicaps: An analysis of the relationship between choice and pleasure. *Therapeutic Recreation Journal, 21*(3), 79–91.

DATTILO, J., & MURPHY, W. D. (1987a). *Behavior modification in therapeutic recreation.* State College, PA: Venture Publishing.

DATTILO, J., MURPHY, W. D. (1987b). Facilitating the challenge in adventure recreation for persons with disabilities. *Therapeutic Recreation Journal, 21*(3), 14–21.

DATTILO, J., & NELSON, G. (1986). Single-subject evaluation in health education. *Health Education Quarterly, 13*(3), 249–259.

DATTILO, J., & RUSCH, F. (1985). Effects of choice on leisure participation for persons with severe handicaps. *Journal of the Association for Persons with Severe Handicaps, 10,* 194–199.

DEUTSCH, H., BUSTOW, S., WISH, C. W., & WISH, J. (1982). *Developmental Disabilities: A training guide.* Boston: CBI.

DONDER, D., & NIETUPSKI, J. (1981). Nonhandicapped adolescents teaching playground skills to their mentally handicapped peers: Toward a less restrictive middle school environment. *Education and Training of the Mentally Retarded, 16,* 270–276.

DONNELLAN, A. M., LA VIGNA, G. W., NEGRI-SCHOULTZ, N., & FASSBENDER, L. (1986). *Progress without punishment: A staff training manual of non-aversive behavioral procedures.* Madison, WI: University of Wisconsin.

FAIT, H. F., & BILLING, J. E. (1978). Reassessment of the value of competition. In R. Martens (Ed.), *Joy and sadness in children's sports* (pp. 98–105). Chapaign, IL: Human Kinetics.

FALVEY, M., BROWN, L., LYON, S., BAUMGART, D., & SCHROEDER, J. (1980). Strategies for using cues and correction procedures. In W. Sailor, B. Wilcox, & L. Brown (Eds.), *Methods of instruction for severely handicapped students.* Baltimore: Paul H. Brookes.

FARRINGTON, P. (1976). Games. In A. Fluegelman (Ed.), *The new games book* (p. 10). Champaign, IL: Doubleday.

FAVELL, J., & CANNON, P. R. (1977). An evaluation of entertainment materials for severely retarded persons. *American Journal of Mental Deficiency, 81,* 357–362.

FENRICK, N., & PETERSEN, T. K. (1984). Developing positive changes in attitudes towards moderately/severely handicapped students through a peer tutoring program. *Education and Training of the Mentally Retarded, 19,* 83–90.

FORD, A., BROWN, L., PUMPIAN, I., BAUMGART, D., NISBET, J., SCHROEDER, J., & LOOMIS, R. (1984). Strategies for developing individualized recreation and leisure programs for severely handicapped students. In N. J. Certo, N. Haring, & R. York (Eds.), *Public school integration of severely handicapped students: Rational issues and progressive alternatives* (pp. 245–275). Baltimore: Paul H. Brookes.

GEARHEART, B. R. (1987). Educational strategies for children with developmental disabilities. In M. I. Gottlieb & J. E. Williams (Eds.), *Textbook of developmental pediatrics* (pp. 385–397). New York: Plenum Medical.

GOLD, M. W. (1978). An adaptive behavior philosophy: Who needs it? In W. Coulter & H. Morrow (Eds.), *Adaptive Behavior* (pp. 234–235). New York: Grune & Stratton.

GOTTLIEB, M. I. (1987). Major variations in intelligence. In M. I. Gottlieb & J. E. Williams (Eds.), *Textbook of developmental pediatrics* (pp. 127–150). New York: Plenum Medical.

GROSSMAN, H. J. (1983). (Ed.). *Classification in mental retardation.* Washington, DC: American Association on Mental Deficiency.

GUESS, D., BENSON, H. A., & SIEGEL-CAUSEY, E. (1985). Concepts and issues related to choice-making and autonomy among persons with severe disabilities. *Journal of the Association for Persons with Severe Handicaps, 11,* 79–86.

GUNN, S. L. (1975). *Basic terminology for therapeutic recreation and other action therapies.* Champaign, IL: Sites.

HAYES, G. A. (1977). Professional preparation and leisure counseling. *Journal of Physical Education and Recreation, 48*(4), 36–38.

HOUGHTON, J., BRONICKI, G. J., & GUESS, D. (1987). Opportunities to express preferences and make choices among students with severe disabilities in classroom settings. *Journal of the Association for Persons with Severe Handicaps, 12,* 18–27.

HOWE-MURPHY, R., & CHARBONEAU, B. G. (1987). *Therapeutic recreation intervention: An ecological perspective.* Englewood Cliffs, NJ: Prentice-Hall.

HUTCHISON, P., & LORD, J. (1979). *Recreation integration: Issues and alternatives in leisure services and community involvement.* Ottawa, Ontario: Leisurability.

ISO-AHOLA, S. E. (1980). *The social psychology of leisure and recreation.* Dubuque, IA: William C. Brown.

JENSEN, A. R. (1980). *Bias in mental testing.* New York: The Free Press.

JOSWIAK, K. F. (1979). *Leisure counseling program materials for the developmentally disabled.* Washington, DC: Hawkins & Associates.

KENNEDY, D. W., AUSTIN, D. R. & SMITH, R. W. (1987). *Special recreation: Opportunities for persons with disabilities.* Philadelphia: Saunders College Publishing.

KEOGH, D. A., FAW, G. D., WHITMAN, T. L., & REID, D. H. (1984). Enhancing leisure skills in severely retarded adolescents through a self-instructional treatment package. *Analysis and Intervention in Developmental Disabilities, 4,* 333–351.

KNAPCZYK, D. R. (1975). Task analytic assessment of severe learning problems. *Education and Training of the Mentally Retarded, 10,* 74–77.

KNAPCZYK, D. R., & YOPPI, J. O. (1975). Development of cooperative and competitive play responses in developmentally disabled children. *American Journal of Mental Deficiency, 80,* 245–255.

LAKIN, K. C., & BRUININKS, R. H. (Eds.). (1985). *Strategies for achieving community integration of developmentally disabled citizens.* Baltimore: Paul H. Brookes.

MARLOWE, M. (1979). The game analysis intervention: A procedure to increase the peer acceptance and social adjustment of a retarded child. *Education and Training of the Mentally Retarded, 14,* 262–268.

McHALE, S. M., & SIMEONSSON, R. J. (1980). Effects of interaction on nonhandicapped children's attitudes toward autistic children. *American Journal of Mental Deficiency, 85,* 18–24.

MONTAGNES, J. A. (1976). Reality therapy approach to leisure counseling. *Journal of Leisurability, 3,* 37–45.

MUNDY, J., & ODUM, L. (1979). *Leisure education: Theory and practice.* New York: John Wiley & Sons.

National Therapeutic Recreation Society. (1982). *Philosophical position statement of the National Therapeutic Recreation Society.* Alexandria, VA: National Recreation and Park Association.

NEULINGER, J. (1982). *The psychology of leisure: Research approaches to study of leisure* (2nd ed.). Springfield, IL: Charles C. Thomas.

NIRJE, B. (1969). The normalization principle and its human management implications. In R. Kugel & W. Wolfensberger (Eds.), *Changing patterns of residential services for the mentally retarded.* Washington, DC: President's Committee on Mental Retardation.

O'MORROW, G. S. (1980). *Therapeutic recreation: A helping profession.* Reston, VA: Reston.

OVERS, R. P., TAYLOR, S., & ADKINS, C. (1974). Avocational counseling for the elderly. *Journal of Physical Education and Recreation, 48*(4), 44–45.

PACE, G., IVANCIC, M., EDWARDS, G., IWATA, B., & PAGE, T. (1985). Assessment of the stimulus preferences and reinforcer values with profoundly retarded individuals. *Journal of Applied Behavior Analysis, 18,* 249–255.

PELEGRINO, D. A. (1979). *Research methods for recreation and leisure: A theoretical and practical guide.* Dubuque, IA: William C. Brown.

PETERSON, C. A. (1981, September). *Leisure lifestyle and disabled individuals.* Paper presented at Horizons West Therapeutic Recreation Symposium, San Francisco, CA.

PETERSON, C. A., & GUNN, S. L. (1984). *Therapeutic recreation program design: Principles and procedures* (2nd ed.). Englewood Cliffs, NJ: Prentice-Hall.

RAW, J., & ERRICKSON, E. (1977). Behavioral techniques in therapeutic recreation. In T. Thompson & J. Grabowski (Eds.), *Behavior modification of the mentally retarded* (pp. 379–395). New York: Oxford University Press.

SCHEERENBERGER, R. C. (1987). *A history of mental retardation: A quarter century of promise.* Baltimore: Paul H. Brookes.

SCHLEIEN, S. J., & RAY, M. T. (1988). *Community recreation and persons with disabilities: Strategies for integration.* Baltimore: Paul H. Brookes.

SCHLEIEN, S. J., TUCKNER, B., & HEYNE, L. (1985). Leisure education programs for the severely disabled student. *Parks and Recreation, 20,* 74–78.

TERMAN, L. M. (1916). *The measurement of intelligence.* Boston: Houghton Mifflin.

TRAP-PORTER, J., & PERRY, W. J. (1982). Moving from a medical to a behavioral model: Can therapeutic recreation learn from special education? *Education and Training of Children, 5*(3), 297–301.

VALLET, R. E. (1972). Developmental task analysis and psycho-educational programming. *Journal of School Psychology, 10,* 127–134.

WACKER, D., BERG, W., WIGGINS, B., MULDOON, M., & CAVANAUGH, J. (1985). Evaluation of reinforcer preferences for profoundly handicapped students. *Journal of Applied Behavior Analysis, 18,* 173–178.

WEHMAN, P., & SCHLEIEN, S. J. (1981). *Leisure programs for handicapped persons: Adaptations, techniques, and curriculum.* Baltimore: University Park Press.

WILLIAMS, W., & GOTTS, E. A. (1977). Selected considerations on developing curriculum for severely handicapped students. In E. Sontag (Ed.), *Educational programming for the severely and profoundly handicapped.* Reston: VA: The Council for Exceptional Children.

WITT, P. A., ELLIS, G. D., & NILES, S. H. (1984). Leisure counseling with special populations. In T. E. Dowd (Ed.), *Leisure counseling: Concepts and applications.* Springfield, IL: Charles C. Thomas.

WODRICH, D. L., & JOY, J. E. (1986). *Multi-disciplinary assessment of children with learning disabilities and mental retardation.* Baltimore: Paul H. Brookes.

WOLFENSBERGER, W. (1972). *The principle of normalization in human services.* Toronto: National Institute on Mental Retardation.

WUERCH, B. B., & VOELTZ, L. M. (1982). *Longitudinal leisure skills for severely handicapped learners: The Ho'onanea curriculum component.* Baltimore: Paul H. Brookes.

ZIGLER, E., & BUTTERFIELD, E. C. (1968). Motivational aspects of changes in IQ test performance of culturally deprived nursery school children. *Child Development, 39,* 1–14.

9

Severe Multiple Disabilities

STUART J. SCHLEIEN

OBJECTIVES

- Understand the definition of the term *severe multiple disability* and the problems in defining this population.
- Identify typical repertoires and needs of persons with severe multiple disabilities.
- Identify and provide a rationale for specific goals of the therapeutic recreation process as they relate to persons with multiple needs.
- Understand the importance of selecting age-appropriate and functional leisure skills for instruction.
- Recognize leisure-related support skills necessary for participation in select activities.
- Understand the various behavioral techniques for systematic leisure skills instructional programming.
- Understand the rationale for integrated recreation programs.

DEFINITION OF SEVERE MULTIPLE DISABILITIES

To what group of individuals does the term *severe multiple disability* refer? This question is not easily answered and requires an analysis of the factors influencing such a definition.

Note: The author wishes to thank Cheryl Light and Cheryl Baldwin, graduate assistants in the Division of Recreation, Park, and Leisure Studies at the University of Minnesota, for their assistance in the development of this chapter.

A review of the terms currently being used by professionals reveals an inconsistency in defining a specific population (Fredericks, 1987). Perhaps the single greatest factor influencing this inconsistency is the process of definition. Definitions have been created based on the interests of the particular agency serving the individual with a severe multiple disability. This type of influence has resulted in an abundance of terms, all somewhat workable but limited by an unclear variation in who exactly is being included or excluded.

The components of this definition problem are displayed in Figure 9.1 Two types of descriptive terms have emerged. There are generic descriptions that attempt to describe the population in a broad sense. These terms include such descriptions as persons with dual sensory handicaps and profound handicaps. The second type of terms used are those that describe by referring to a specific disability. Examples of this kind of

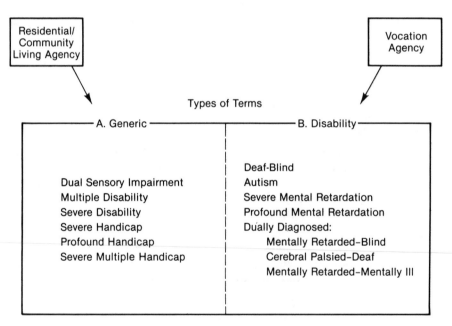

FIGURE 9.1   The Definition Problem and the Four Types of Influencing Agencies that Adopt Their Own Definition

description include persons who are profoundly mentally retarded and cerebral palsied–deaf. The abundance of terms is created by four types of influencing agencies, each of which adopts its own definition. These agencies are categorized as residential/community living, vocational, recreational, and educational.

The problem of definition is made apparent by comparing the definition of *severely handicapped* as determined by the Rehabilitation Services Administration and the Office of Special Education Programs. Both agencies describe an individual with a disability that seriously limits functional ability, but this functional ability is assessed in regard to the intensive support needed to meet either vocational objectives or educational objectives, respectively. Defined in this way, two distinctly different definitions are created. The result is that a person with a severe handicap is categorized by the type of service the agency provides (Bellamy, 1985).

A definition problem also arises when the population is described by the individual's specific disability. This method may exclude some individuals from service by being too limited as to who is included under that disability. For example, the assessment label *deaf-blind* refers not only to those individuals who are deaf and blind, but to those who are visually and auditorially impaired. This includes those individuals categorized as blind/ severely hearing impaired or severely hearing impaired/severely vision impaired. Another factor entering into this characterization is that many individuals who are deaf-blind are either mentally retarded or are functioning in the range of mental retardation. Through this example it becomes evident that the term *deaf-blind* may not accurately reflect the dynamics of this population (Barrett, 1987; Fredericks & Baldwin, 1987).

This definition problem establishes the need for a definition that can include the numerous low incidence populations and all their variable characteristics. The following definition attempts to satisfy this need by being general enough to include the variance of this population, yet specific enough to be a viable definition for those servicing this population. Severe multiple disability refers to those individuals with a profound disability or with a combination of disabilities that so limit their daily activities that they require services and programming that is more innovative, extensive, and intensive than common programming for individuals with disabilities provides. This population is characterized as but is not exclusively nonambulatory, nonindependently mobile, needing to be fed, needing assistance in toileting, and needing daily occupational or communication therapy (Covert, 1987; Fredericks, 1987).

Recreation Participation: Current Repertoires and Needs

Participation in leisure/recreational/social activities is an important aspect of life in our society. When such activities meet individuals' needs, the activities promote physical health and conditioning, provide opportunities to develop social relations, and lead to the development of new skills. Unfortunately, leisure services have had relatively low priority in programs for persons with severe multiple disabilities until recently, when specific leisure skill training techniques and curricula incorporating behavioral training procedures, in conjunction with purposeful environmental arrangements, were developed. The neglect of relevant programming and services for this population is particularly unfortunate because appropriate participation in leisure activities is an important aspect in the participants' successful community adjustment (Cheseldine & Jeffree, 1981), and is associated with the development of collateral skills (Schleien, Kiernan, & Wehman, 1981) and the reduction of maladaptive behaviors (Adkins & Matson, 1980; Flavell, 1973; Voeltz & Wuerch, 1981).

Unfortunately, a discrepancy exists between what is known about the short- and long-term benefits of participation in leisure activities and the current status of services to persons with severe multiple disabilities. For these individuals to participate maximally in community leisure/recreation activities alongside their nondisabled and less-disabled peers, specific leisure and recreation skill training in home, school, and community environments, and specific provisions by communities to incorporate them into recreational activities are necessary.

Before any attempts are made to design, deliver, and evaluate appropriate therapeutic recreation services, it is necessary to describe common characteristics of persons with severe multiple disabilities. In any investigation into their community adaptation and overall wellness, it is necessary to understand their current participation in leisure and social activities, their ability to occupy themselves during discretionary time, and make choices, and the other primary variables that seem to influence leisure participation.

A brief review of typical repertoires and skill deficits in persons with severe multiple disabilities, as they concern therapeutic recreation service delivery, could include the following variables: (1) leisure skill repertoires, (2) choice making and self-initiated behavior, (3) social skills and other leisure-related support skills, (4) maintaining and generalizing skills, and (5) community integration. It is important to recognize that different individuals within the broad category of severe multiple disabilities (persons who are often grouped homogeneously) have separate programming needs. Individuals will differ markedly in their motor, social, cognitive, and affective abilities. For example, an individual who is moderately retarded and uses a wheelchair has abilities and needs substantially different from those of an individual who is labeled autistic with a visual impairment. Therefore, it is necessary to approach service delivery in an individualized manner in order to satisfy personal needs and preferences. Because of the risk of thinking stereotypically, one is cautioned not to overgeneralize when designing programs for person with severe multiple disabilities.

Leisure Skill Repertoires. A major factor for the relatively little attention given to teaching leisure skills for home and community settings to persons with severe multiple disabilities is their serious skill deficits. Skill deficits could include two general skill areas of interaction—with objects and with people. Current habilitative and educational technology has not yet advanced to the point where professionals can determine reliably how many skills can be acquired or environments accessed. Professionals engaged in leisure skill instruction with persons with severe multiple disabilities face a variety of challenges in expanding their repertoires. Barriers center around three basic concerns: (1) specific skill deficits, (2) limited instructional materials, and (3) environmental barriers/resistance (Wehman, 1979; Wehman & Schleien, 1981). Although a totally independent leisure life-style, including independent functioning in community leisure environments, may be unrealistic, these individuals are capable of considerably more complex skills than they typically have performed.

Lagomarcino and colleagues (1984) demonstrated a method of training an intermediate community living skill to institutionalized teenagers who were severely and profoundly retarded. Appropriate dancing performance of noninstitutionalized persons who were mildly and moderately retarded served as the empirical norm for their training programs. By using behavioral training procedures, other attempts to remediate play problems and address leisure education needs have been successful. Procedures such as contingent reinforcement, task analysis, careful selection of activities, cooperatively structured activities, skill modifications, and pairing individuals in environments with nondisabled peers have recently been successfully used in teaching a variety of age-appropriate leisure skills to children and adults with severe multiple disabilities. Examples include miniature golf (Banks & Aveno, 1986), pinball (Hill, Wehman, & Horst, 1982; Horst et al., 1980), video games (Powers & Ball, 1983; Sedlak, Doyle & Schloss, 1982), darts (Schleien, Wehman, & Kiernan, 1981), photography (Wehman, Schleien, & Kiernan, 1980), and functional use of a community recreation center (Schleien & Larson, 1986).

Choice Making and Self-Initiated Behavior. Recreational activities, generally, are considered to involve the performance of particular behaviors that are not work related, are enjoyable, and are ones that the individual chooses to do. Dattilo and Barnett (1985) suggested that the omission of choice in the participation process actually prevents individuals from genuine leisure experiences. Recreational activities are often selected by therapeutic recreation specialists, special education teachers, and care providers on behalf of persons with severe multiple disabilities. Common practice is to identify the chronological age, physical characteristics, and current functioning level of the individual, and subsequently select an activity for instruction based on this information only (Wehman & Schleien, 1981;

Wuerch & Voeltz, 1982). Designers of leisure skills curriculum are accustomed to making decisions in the planning process and, consequently, may lack the inclination or skills to honor preferences of the participant (Putnam, Werder, & Schleien, 1985).

Persons with severe multiple disabilities present very few functional preferences (Dattilo & Mirenda, 1987). Selecting leisure skills for instruction based on the present leisure preferences of the individuals could result in nonfunctional activities such as increasing rates of stereotypic behavior and participation in age-inappropriate activities. This highlights a frequent problem encountered by therapeutic recreation specialists, teachers, and care providers attempting to select skills or activities for instruction. Individuals with severe multiple disabilities generally demonstrate few activity or object preferences reliably. Of the preferences that are reliably demonstrated, few can be incorporated into functional, age-appropriate, and socially appropriate leisure skills. In addition, because very few individuals possess extensive formal communication skills, determining whether particular leisure skills are enjoyable becomes even more subjective and suspect than it is with verbal individuals.

From a slightly different perspective, there are persons with severe multiple disabilities who frequently smile and laugh, and, as an example, seem to enjoy holding hands and "dancing" in a circle around a phonograph playing an archaic folk song sung in an unfamiliar language. As a result of their supposed expression of enjoyment, we become complacent, believing we have identified an appropriate leisure skill. Teaching this same group of individuals to use a local nightclub in a socially appropriate manner may produce an equivalent amount of smiles and laughs. Questions that need to be answered include: Why are these age-appropriate correlated leisure skills so infrequently attempted? and, Why are these age-inappropriate and nonfunctional skills so frequently encountered? Interestingly, Matthews (1980) found many similarities in recreational preferences of children with and without mental retardation, suggesting that chronologically age-appropriate and integrated activities are feasible. Others have discovered that persons with developmental disabilities have interests in the same general outdoor activities as nondisabled persons. West (1981) found activities of hiking, camping, and other outdoor education pursuits to be preferred over the typical indoor activity offerings. Indeed, many activities that have typically been associated with persons with severe multiple disabilities have been stereotyped, including inaccurate ideas of what these individuals might be able to participate in or enjoy.

If we attend to factors such as potential for integration, age appropriateness of the skill, adaptability, and nondisabled performance standards when selecting activities, it will become easier to refrain from the shortsighted selections that often accrue from too close an adherence to enjoyment or convenience factors.

A primary focus of any leisure skill program is to provide the participant with as many alternatives as possible. This outcome will become realistic only when the individual has acquired the necessary skills to exercise meaningful choices and when materials and activities are made available.

Social Skills and Other Leisure-Related Support Skills. Persons with severe multiple disabilities rarely act on play materials in self-initiated or constructive ways without large amounts of instruction and prompting. This lack of spontaneous play may be attributable to not having previously experienced the reinforcing characteristics of play. Also, a lack of sensory awareness or a failure to respond or attend to the materials presented may result in passive and stereotypic behavior. By acquiring a variety of play skills that require the same basic types of fine and gross motor movements, the individual's general development would be enhanced, and he or she would concurrently be gaining a larger repertoire of leisure skills (Wehman, 1977). Also, such a positive experience and the development of a leisure repertoire can have a positive influence in the areas of cooperation, social skills and social adjustment, and, ultimately, development of friendships and integration into the community.

Maintaining and Generalizing Skills. Even those individuals who successfully acquire leisure skills often have a difficult time generalizing these skills to other environments. Transfer of training is an area in which most people with developmental disabilities require additional programming or systematic transitioning. Research indicates that older individuals with developmental disabilities and those persons who are more severely disabled have an even more difficult time generalizing to other nontrained environments and situations (Wehman, 1979). The greater the alteration of the environmental conditions from the original training site, the less transfer of training that will occur. For example, an individual who has acquired electronic pinball game skills at a video arcade may not exhibit similar competencies on another pinball machine that makes different sounds.

In addition to generalization being of primary concern, it should not be assumed that the individual will continue to engage in the newly acquired activity after formal training has been terminated. Unless the recreational activity itself is highly preferred and the individual can maintain appropriate play behavior, it is unlikely that the individual will continue to select and participate in the activity in the future. An ideal way to promote maintenance of recreational activities is to provide an individual with experiences that are so enjoyable that he or she is eager to engage in these activities without external prompting or encouragement (Wehman, 1979; Wehman & Schleien, 1981). Also, it is suggested that by varying the training conditions (e.g., using different instructors or settings) and encouraging the involvement of parents or care providers who are knowledgeable of the training procedures, transfer of training and the durability of the skill could be enhanced (Wuerch & Voeltz, 1982).

Community Integration.   A historical look at the kinds of community recreation programs that have generally been made available to children and adults with severe multiple disabilities reveals a substantial gap between the services needed and those available. The recreation programs offered for school-age children, for example, have focused on a small set of activities so predominant in this area that they have become stereotyped. These include bowling, swimming, arts and crafts, and field trips (Schleien & Werder, 1985). Summer programs offer a similarly restricted range of options. Most typically, children and youth with severe multiple disabilities may attend a handicapped-only camp (which itself is labeled with a "handicappism" such as "Camp Hope") for from one to two weeks during summer vacation. Finally, even those recreation events that might be available in community settings require that persons with disabilities be segregated from those who are not disabled or, when interactions with nondisabled persons do occur, that they participate in integration experiences characterized by strictly hierarchical role relationships. In these relationships, the nondisabled person is the helper and the individual with severe disabilities receives the help (Schleien & Meyer, 1988).

Just as community integration involves mastering certain skills and activities in the vocational and domestic living domains, the ability to deal constructively with leisure time has been considered an important predictor of successful community adjustment (Gollay, 1981; Intagliata, Willer, & Wicks, 1981). There is evidence that difficulties in dealing positively with free time—such as a coffee break at work or evenings in a group home—will impede the success of a community placement, even when the individual has otherwise mastered specific job and domestic living skills (Birenbaum & Re, 1979). Additionally, persons with severe multiple disabilities who are living in a community facility have minimal contact with nondisabled people in their neighborhoods (Salzberg & Langford, 1981) and may actually decrease their involvement in community activities over time (Birenbaum & Re, 1979). Thus, despite the fact that a community-based residential facility could provide increased potential for the development of a more normalized life-style, it by no means guarantees one.

Various authors have emphasized the importance of providing systematic instruction to address leisure education needs, and have argued that the learning characteristics of persons with severe disabilities require that this instruction focus directly on criterion activities and situations as they actually occur in community environments (Ford et al., 1984; Voeltz, Wuerch, & Wilcox, 1982; Wuerch & Voeltz, 1982). Within the last few years, human service professionals have attempted to provide services to individuals with severe disabilities in community and other noninstitutional settings. The least restrictive environment (LRE) is commonly used to describe this service emphasis. The LRE doctrine as applied to leisure and discretionary time use is defined as the acquisition and performance of leisure skills by persons with severe multiple disabilities in normalized community environments.

This overview of the typical characteristics and behavioral repertoires of persons with severe multiple disabilities was intended as a preface to a comprehensive discussion of "best practices" in therapeutic recreation. It is important to remember that the capabilities and learning potential of children and adults with severe multiple disabilities far surpass the traditional levels of competencies that have been reached in the past. If leisure skill programs are designed and implemented carefully, and if they incorporate sound behavioral principles and occur throughout the individuals' life span, there is little doubt that these persons will demonstrate that they, too, can participate successfully in many leisure environments and activities.

PURPOSE OF THERAPEUTIC RECREATION

Because persons with severe multiple disabilities have traditionally received little attention in the area of leisure, there happens to be an abundance of "dead time," or unoccupied time (Schleien & Wehman, 1986; Voeltz, Wuerch, & Wilcox 1982), in their daily lives. Many individuals participate in passive and sedentary activities throughout the day, such as watching television or listening to music (Powers & Ball, 1983). Unfortunately, many of these individuals lack the means, skills, and opportunities to participate in more active leisure pursuits and a greater variety of them. Inappropriate behaviors are often exhibited excessively by these individuals during this unoccupied time (Voeltz & Wuerch, 1981; Voeltz, Wuerch, & Wilcox, 1982; Wehman, 1979).

Therapeutic recreation offers persons with severe multiple disabilities opportunities to learn appropriate, functional, and normalizing leisure skills that will expand their leisure repertoires and help them become more independent. The therapeutic recreation specialist must consider individualized needs and preferences of participants while implementing systematic instruction that will promote acquisition, maintenance, and generalization of lifelong leisure skills. Therapeutic recreation goals for persons with severe multiple disabilities are developed with the concept of normalization in mind and may include the following:

Increased Exploration and Manipulation of Environment.   Limited mobility or deficits in one or more sensory areas prevent many individuals from actively becoming involved in and familiar with their environment. For individuals who are severely motorically impaired, exploration and manipulation can often be facilitated by using computer and microswitch technology that can be individualized according to an individual's abilities (Dattilo & Barnett, 1985).

Increased Range of Lifelong Leisure Skills.   Expanding one's leisure repertoire can provide opportunities to enjoy a greater variety of chronologically age-appropriate activities that could lead to a better quality of life and increased involvement with peers who are both disabled and nondisabled.

Increased Independent Leisure Behavior.   It may be true that persons with severe multiple disabilities may never be totally independent; however, interdependence is also a normalizing principle. The therapeutic recreation specialist can help an individual become more independent while learning appropriate ways of becoming interdependent. Once an individual has acquired a leisure skill, he or she can then learn to identify and initiate preferred activities. Adaptive equipment and strategies for partial participation could be helpful in facilitating interdependent and independent participation.

Increased Socialization and Cooperation Skills.   A majority of people with severe multiple disabilities do not have well-developed interaction and socialization skills. Cooperatively structured leisure activities can help individuals learn to interact appropriately and effectively with people around them (i.e., parents, care providers, neighbors or other persons in the community, and peers who are both disabled and nondisabled).

Increased Collateral or Support Skills.   Developing collateral or support skills is essential for maintaining almost any leisure skill. Few leisure skills are performed in isolation without the use of leisure-related support skills. Some interconnected areas include self-care, money-management, communication, motor, and cognition/attention span skills. An individual's affect (i.e., enthusiasm shown through facial expressions and vocalizations) can also be positively influenced and facilitative during participation in recreational activities (Kibler, 1986; Powers & Ball, 1983). Several authors have found that as leisure-related support skills are developed, inappropriate behaviors often decrease in frequency (Alajajian, 1981; Flavell, 1973; Schleien, Kiernan, & Wehman, 1981).

Increased Self-Concept and Self-Esteem.   A low self-concept or low self-esteem is often attributable to a feeling of helplessness due to repeated failures and lack of choice. Leisure skills should be taught in such a manner as to help the participant experience success often, especially during the initial stages of skill acquisition.

Increased Opportunities to Perform Acquired Skills.   Following skill acquisition, it is essential that the learner be able to practice those skills frequently. Horner, Williams, and Knobbe (1985) found that individuals with severe disabilities needed at least two opportunities per month to maintain performance of newly acquired skills. Increased opportunities in slightly different settings could also enhance generalization to nontrained environments and prepare the individual for a more normalized community adjustment (Voeltz, Wuerch, & Wilcox, 1982; Goetz, 1987).

COMMON SERVICE SETTINGS

Traditionally, individuals with developmental disabilities, especially those with severe multiple disabilities, were generally ignored by society and not considered worthy of membership. Prior to 1800, society did little in the way of systematic study, treatment, or care of these individuals. The real beginnings of therapeutic treatment and services took place in the early 1800s when education and political reform became widespread. The first successful public residential institutions serving persons with developmental disabilities were established, and schools throughout Germany, France, and the United States were created.

With the exception of an occasional after-school recreation program sponsored by a municipal park and recreation department, therapeutic recreation services in hospitals and state institutions, or a handicapped-only camp that offered individuals with severe multiple disabilities an opportunity to participate, few programs have been made accessible to this population over the years. It was not until the 1970s (i.e., the Decade of the Disabled) that monumental civil and human rights advances by people with severe disabilities were achieved. The 1973 Rehabilitation Act (PL 93-112), one of the most significant landmarks in the struggle for equality for all individuals, made it illegal for any agency or organization that receives federal funds to discriminate against persons with severe disabilities solely on the basis of his or her disability. Also, the Education for All Handicapped Children Act of 1975 (PL 94-142) mandated equal educational opportunity for all children who have disabilities. It also addressed the use of related services, including therapeutic recreation, in least restrictive environments.

During the past 15 years, residential services for people with severe multiple disabilities have undergone a substantial shift in direction. Several thousand individuals each year have moved from large, public residential facilities to smaller residential programs in community settings. These smaller community facilities have experienced dramatic decreases in numbers of residents, averaging approximately 16 residents per agency as compared to a mean of 25 residents in 1978 (Hill, Lakin, & Bruininks, 1984). If these trends toward smaller numbers and movement to community settings continue, then community programs will be offering services to increasing numbers of people with severe and profound disabilities, because these people constitute the majority of those still residing in the large public and private facilities (Hauber et al., 1984). The next section of this chapter discusses the best practices in the therapeutic recreation process that promote a continuing movement of persons with severe multiple disabilities toward less restrictive living, learning, and recreational environments.

CURRENT BEST PRACTICES AND PROCEDURES

Needs/Preference Assessment

A needs assessment is vitally important when working with individuals who are severely multiply disabled. The assessment provides information that helps the therapeutic recreation specialist identify activities and materials that will best meet the participant's lifelong leisure needs. Many authors (Crawford, Griffin, & Mendell, 1978; Orelove & Sobsey, 1987; Schleien & Ray, 1988; Voeltz & Wuerch, 1981; Wehman & Schleien, 1980; Wehman & Schleien, 1981; Wuerch & Voeltz, 1982) have identified key areas to address within a needs assessment. The first area includes general background information (e.g., age, abilities, physical characteristics) about the individual. An assessment of the appropriateness and functionality of the targeted activities should be part of the second component. The third area could feature an environmental analysis that helps identify component tasks required to complete an activity and the individual's current level of proficiency relative to those tasks.

First, it is useful to gather information concerning the participant from a variety of sources. Care providers, family members, teachers, related services personnel, and other support staff can contribute pertinent information concerning (1) the individual's family background, physical and medical needs (e.g., physical/motor characteristics and limitations, sensory disorders, seizure disorders, lung and breathing control), (2) educational needs (e.g., appropriate handling and positioning techniques, methods of communication), (3) social/emotional needs (e.g., types of reinforcers that are effective, preferences, means of selecting items), (4) family and individual leisure preferences and activities that family members commonly engage in during their discretionary time, and (5) information regarding client resources (e.g., activities and materials that are available to the participant on a regular basis, and agencies and activities in the community that are used by the family) (Wehman & Schleien, 1981; Wuerch & Voeltz, 1982). Specific needs assessment inventories available include the "Client Home Environment Checklist" (Wehman & Schleien, 1981), "Home Leisure Activities Survey" (Wuerch & Voeltz, 1982), and the "Student Interest Survey" (Wuerch & Voeltz, 1982).

A second area of assessment should address the appropriateness and functionality of activities relative to the needs of the client with regard to the principle of normalization. Functional skills are those that an individual is frequently asked to demonstrate in daily life, whether it be in the home, job site, or community environment. A nonfunctional skill is one that has a "low probability of being required by daily activities" (Brown et al., 1979). The age appropriateness of an activity is assessed by determining whether nondisabled peers of the same chronological age typically engage in that activity.

Voeltz and Wuerch (1981) developed a checklist that allows for the systematic evaluation of activities "in relation to the handicapped person's characteristics and needs" (p. 27). Three elements make up the "Leisure Activity Selection Checklist." The first element, *normalization*, addresses concerns for socially appropriate or socially valid activities. Questions in this area focus on whether nondisabled peers would be interested in and engage in the activity, how many people could use this activity, and whether the activity is potentially lifelong in nature. The second element, *individualization*, addresses the adaptability of the activity as it relates to the participant's specific needs and preferences. The third and final component of the checklist addresses *environmental aspects* of the activity, including availability, durability, safety, noxiousness, and expense (Voeltz & Wuerch, 1981).

A third area to be addressed in a needs assessment inventory concerns an individual's level of proficiency when engaged in a particular activity. An ecological assessment or an environmental analysis inventory (Belmore & Brown, 1976; Certo, Schleien, & Hunter, 1983; Schleien & Ray, 1988; Voeltz & Wuerch, 1981) can be conducted to determine the specific components of the activity that the individual has already mastered and those requiring additional training. Certo, Schleien, and Hunter (1983) stated that this inventory is "a systematic method of conducting an observation of an event as it occurs in a natural setting under typical conditions" (p. 33). The environmental analysis inventory is helpful in developing instructional sequences and identifying their component tasks. Also, it identifies the client's proficiency relative to the targeted task and highlights further training needs. The inventory could be instrumental in identifying appropriate teaching strategies as well as adaptations/modifications that enhance participation.

Skill Selection Guidelines/Functional Curriculum

Following the initial needs assessment, the therapeutic recreation specialist must select the most important skills to be targeted for instruction as part of the leisure/recreation program. Most professionals agree that the skills selected must be functional and chronologically age appropriate (Certo, Schleien, & Hunter, 1983; Fardig, 1986; Wuerch & Voeltz, 1982).

As explained earlier, functional skills are those needed daily for routine tasks and are natural to an individual's environment. These skills help an individual function as independently as possible in normalized settings. When developing a leisure skills curriculum, one can assess its worth or validity by determining the functionality of the curricular activities. For example, a nonfunctional skill could be the development of the participant's palmar grasp and voluntary release skills by instructing the individual to push a medicine ball, an activity not commonly performed by nondisabled peers. A functional alternative could be to teach the individual to grasp and turn a doorknob to help him access other rooms and environments. Another example of a nonfunctional activity frequently incorporated into a prevocational or recreational curriculum would be placing pegs into pegboards to increase a child's pincer grasp and release skills. A functional alternative could be teaching the child to play with a Lite-Brite (by Hasbro) game. Both activities have identical topography, but the Lite-Brite game provides additional sensory stimulation and reinforcement and is an age-appropriate activity that could be practiced and enjoyed at home. It is essential to understand, however, that functional curricular materials themselves are insufficient if the skills are not chronologically age appropriate as well (Brown et al., 1979).

Collateral Skill Development/Infusion Chart

One of the principal outcomes of leisure skills instruction may be its contribution to collateral skill development. In addition to providing pleasurable activity and entertainment, participation in recreational activities enhances development in social, emotional, psychological, communication, problem solving, motor, and other collateral skills because it allows for continued practice of newly acquired skills in positive and naturally occurring contexts. Vandercook (1987) reported that as persons with severe handicaps became more proficient in two recreational activities (i.e., pinball, bowling), their social repertoires became more sophisticated. A likely hypothesis for this phenomenon is that greater skill with the mechanics of a recreational activity allows individuals more freedom to expend greater efforts monitoring their social behavior. If social competencies can be improved "incidentally" within the context of age-appropriate recreational activities, valuable intervention time could be saved and social competencies could accrue within the context of activities in which they are expected to be expressed.

Although few empirical investigations supporting the development of skills in other curriculum areas through play by persons with severe multiple disabilities are conclusive or exist at all (Voeltz, Wuerch, & Wilcox, 1982), these potential outcomes are compelling. For example, in a well-designed play setting, a child is able, and encouraged, to perceive himself or herself in positive ways. Research has shown that play experiences enable the child to perceive a more positive body image and self-image (Verhoven, Schleien, & Bender, 1982). As self-image is cultivated and grows, social and personal security increases. Possibly for the first time in this individual's life he or she is perceiving himself or herself as more competent. This type of environment could provide a setting for accomplishment to balance the feelings of learned helplessness or inferiority, which many persons with severe disabilities experience through repeated failure (Dattilo & Rusch, 1985; Seligman, 1975).

Other collateral skills that could be acquired within the context of a leisure program include increased communication and language skills (Rogow, 1981; Bates & Renzaglia, 1982), various social skills such as cooperation, and relationship building (i.e., making friends), taking turns and sharing materials (Kibler, 1986; Schleien & Wehman, 1986), and appropriate manipulation of materials and motor skills (Orelove & Sobsey, 1987; Sherrill, 1986). Other life domains could also be addressed during leisure/recreation activities. For example, if an individual with severe multiple disabilities was to participate in a horseshoe activity, he or she would need to learn about appropriate clothing (i.e., activity of daily living), necessary motor skills involved in grasping and pitching horseshoes (i.e., gross and fine motor skills), and a method of scoring and measuring (i.e., functional academics/math).

Undesirable behaviors have been known to decrease following an individual's acquisition of appropriate object manipulation skills or functional leisure skills (Alajajian, 1981; Flavell, 1973). Alajajian (1981) discovered that an added advantage to a jogging program that focuses on physical fitness in students with severe sensory impairments and cognitive deficits was a noticeable decrease in their self-abusive and self-stimulatory behaviors.

Instructional Programming

Following the critical processes of assessment and skill selection, the therapeutic recreation specialist must decide on a systematic method of instructing the targeted leisure skills.

Task Analysis.   Numerous authors (Schleien & Ray, 1988; Wehman & Schleien, 1979; Wehman & Schleien, 1981; Wuerch & Voeltz, 1982) have supported the use of task analysis when teaching leisure skills to persons with severe multiple disabilities. By depicting component steps of an activity that are easily teachable and observable, task analysis instruction has several advantages. First, it serves as an assessment tool that provides skill proficiency information. Second, a task analysis individualizes a program, allowing for adaptations to be made based on the learner's needs and abilities. Third, it provides a teaching sequence that can be used consistently by multiple trainers.

Schleien, Ash, Kiernan, and Wehman (1981) taught a woman who was profoundly retarded three cooking skills (i.e., uses of an oven—boiling, baking, broiling) using a task-analytic approach. Using a similar procedure, Storey, Bates, and Hanson (1984) taught coffee-purchasing skills across several community environments to adults who were severely disabled.

Shaping and Chaining. A task analysis approach is usually implemented through a variety of behavior-shaping and chaining procedures. Shaping consists of the instructor reinforcing approximations toward the desired or final behavior rather than reinforcing the final response itself. For example, the learner could purchase a snack from a vending machine by using extensions on the push buttons. This adaptation could gradually be reduced as the response becomes more accurate until the participant is manipulating standard size buttons on the vending machine. At this time, previously reinforced approximations are ignored. Chaining, on the other hand, involves the sequencing of the responses within the task. In a forward chain, the learner is initially instructed on the first step of the task analysis (i.e., locate vending machine) and then guided through the remainder of the steps. In a backward chain, instruction is initially provided on the final step in a response sequence (i.e., consume snack item) until that step is mastered. The remaining steps are then taught in reverse order, one at a time, always including the previously instructed step in the teaching sequence. In this manner, the student enjoys the naturally reinforcing consequences of the activity early on in the instructional process, which enhances the learning process.

Cue Hierarchy and Prompting System. Cues and prompts are intricate parts of instructional programs that attempt to elicit behaviors before they are mastered. Prompts (usually arranged in a hierarchy of least-to-most intrusiveness) are used to develop new behaviors or correct undesirable ones. Cues and prompts may include physical guidance, modeling appropriate behaviors, gestures, and verbal direction. They should be faded shortly after the learner masters a specific response so that dependency on the instructor does not become a problem. Fading requires the gradual removal of the guidance as the learner becomes more competent. A desirable outcome of instruction is to have the play materials become the natural or environmental cues that elicit appropriate and independent leisure behavior.

When comparing two different prompting procedures (i.e., antecedent and correction procedures), Day (1987) and McDonnell (1987) found that prompting strategies were more effective when delivered prior to (i.e., antecedent procedure) an erroneous response (similar to an "errorless learning" approach) rather than when they were presented following an incorrect response (i.e., correction procedure).

Prompting strategies have been major components of behavioral packages that are effective in teaching persons with severe multiple disabilities a variety of skills, including communication skills and leisure behaviors (Meehan, Mineo, & Lyon, 1985), coffee-purchasing skills in community environments (Story, Bates, & Hanson, 1984), and reciprocal social interactions between siblings with and without disabilities (James & Egel, 1986).

Reinforcement.   A reinforcement component is usually included in leisure skill instructional procedures. Reinforcers are events that occur following a desired response, which increase the likelihood that the behavior will occur again. Individuals with severe multiple disabilities characteristically do not find many events reinforcing. Using effective reinforcers contingently and more frequently may be necessary to promote learning (Wehman, 1977). Commonly used and effective reinforcers are learner specific and may include food items, praise, attention, switch-activated buzzers, vestibular reinforcers, and access to favorite recreational materials (Sandler & McClain, 1987; Sobsey & Reichle, 1986). Reactive recreational materials such as Simon, cameras, remote control vehicles, and vending machines that result in sensory feedback provide participants with natural reinforcers. Secondary reinforcers (i.e., those not necessarily associated with the activity) could also be effective when used contingently in a behavior-specific manner.

Adaptations/Modifications

Individuals with severe multiple disabilities often have difficulty exploring and manipulating their environments because of physical, cognitive, or sensory limitations. Oftentimes, selecting materials and activities that are reactive in nature (i.e., producing sound, motion, visual, tactile sensations) facilitates manipulation of recreational materials (Bambara et al., 1984; Rogow, 1976). Therefore, it is an important task to identify materials and activities that are optimal for leisure instruction. In most instances, it is possible to adapt existing materials and activities (Dixon, 1981; Garner & Campbell, 1987) to increase participation and independence. Different methods of adapting materials and activities are discussed below.

Materials and Equipment Adaptations.   Common recreational activities that have been adapted and made accessible for persons with severe multiple disabilities include bowling (using handle-grip bowling balls, bowling ramps, and bowling ball pushers) (Wehman & Schleien, 1981), basketball (using larger or softer balls and adjustable backboards), and camera operation (using extended shutter release buttons and color codings) (Wehman & Schleien, 1981). Individuals with severe multiple disabilities have been successfully taught to play miniature golf using adapted golf clubs (Banks & Aveno, 1986), video games using head wands and alternative control devices (i.e., adaptive switches) (Hughes, 1981; Powers & Ball, 1983; Sedlak, Doyle, & Schloss, 1982), board games using exaggerated materials initially, with gradual reductions to normal proportions as acquisition occurred (Kibler, 1986), and battery-operated toys (Meehan, Mineo, & Lyon, 1985).

Rules and Procedural Modifications.   Because of the complexity of certain games and activities, it is often necessary to alter the procedures or rules slightly so that an individual can participate more readily. Schleien, Certo, and Muccino (1984) adapted several procedures when teaching a young adult who was severely retarded to use a bowling alley in a functional manner. Among them, the participant was not required to locate his lane independently, but instead was escorted to his lane by the bowling alley staff. Another procedural modification was to teach him to select the first bowling ball that his fingers fit into and slid out of easily, instead of selecting a ball according to ball weight.

Skill Sequence Changes.   In some instances, a simple rearrangement of the skill sequence can promote increased participation by an individual with multiple needs. Skill sequences have been successfully rearranged for activities such as swimming (i.e., dressing in swim gear prior to leaving for pool or beach) (Ray et al., 1986) and cooking (i.e., placing eggs in pan of cold water before boiling) (Schleien et al., 1981).

Environmental Modifications.   There are numerous ways of modifying the environment to meet the needs of persons with severe multiple disabilities. Examples include changing the lighting, reducing extraneous noise, and making certain the area is architecturally accessible (e.g., ramps, curb cuts, paved paths).

Lead-up Activities.   Lead-up activities are often helpful when attempting to teach more complex leisure skills. Wehman and Schleien (1981) found that initial training activities such as practicing phone skills using a tape recorder, playing kickball prior to instruction in softball, and catch-throw newcomb before engagement in volleyball, served as effective lead-up activities. Kibler (1986) used a homemade game to teach the necessary skills for playing commercially available games. Lagomarcino and colleagues (1984) taught young adults who were severely and profoundly retarded specific dance maneuvers in preparation for participation in community nightclubs.

Partial Participation. Partial participation is a proposed way of assuring that persons with severe multiple disabilities will participate in activities that require skills beyond their abilities (Baumgart et al., 1982). Partial participation could be achieved when individuals are assisted by non-disabled peers, including volunteer advocates (Ray et al., 1986) and "Special Friends" (Voeltz et al., 1982), and when cooperative grouping arrangements and cooperative learning activities (Rynders et al., 1980) are implemented.

Maintenance and Generalization

A desired outcome of leisure skills instruction is for the newly acquired skills to remain part of the learner's repertoire over long periods of time following instruction. Also, it is important that the learner have the ability to transfer these across several environments, people, and materials.

Numerous researchers (Banks & Aveno, 1986; Crawford, 1986; Horner, Williams, & Knobbe, 1985; James & Egel, 1986; Schleien, Ash, Kiernan, & Wehman, 1981; Schleien, Certo, & Muccino, 1984; Sedlak, Doyle, & Schloss, 1982; Singh & Millichamp, 1987; Storey, Bates, & Hanson, 1984) have demonstrated that even though persons with severe multiple disabilities have difficulty maintaining and transferring skills, it is possible to promote the maintenance and generalization of skills by implementing particular instructional methods.

Performance repetition of the acquired skill affects skill maintenance. Horner, Williams, and Knobbe (1985) discovered that maintenance of a skill required at least two performance opportunities per month following acquisition training. Skills can be maintained when networking transpires between families/care providers, professionals, and key servicing agencies. As parents and residential staff assume more active roles in leisure skills instruction, there is greater likelihood that individuals will be provided with additional opportunities to practice and perform these skills in non-trained and integrated community settings.

Another method of promoting skill generalization and maintenance is to use naturally occurring reinforcers during instruction. Reactive recreational materials (e.g., Lite-Brite, Simon, remote control vehicles, video games) and activities (e.g., bowling and purchasing a snack from a vending machine, jumping on a minitrampoline, activating a switch to turn on a cassette recorder) contain naturally occurring reinforcers that promote and maintain independent leisure behavior.

A third method to enhance skill generalization and maintenance is to vary the conditions of skill performance. Coffee purchasing (Storey, Bates, & Hanson, 1984), bowling (Schleien, Certo, & Muccino, 1984), and cooking skills (Schleien et al., 1981) were instructed using task analyses and graduated prompting. The participants were offered opportunities to perform the acquired skills in multiple environments with less intrusive prompts as they acquired the skills. This set of procedures resulted in successful generalization to nontrained environments. Lagomarcino et al. (1984) manipulated the training conditions by using multiple trainers. The participants learned to perform the dancing skills in the presence of several individuals.

Networking and Integration

It is necessary that persons with severe multiple disabilities have strong support systems if they are to learn and maintain leisure skills throughout their lifetimes. The interdisciplinary approach to programming has been successfully used in our educational system (Rainforth & York, 1987). We cannot afford to provide exemplary services to persons with multiple needs in school settings, only to have them remain isolated in after-school environments for a better part of the day. The instructional procedures that were discussed previously in this chapter (e.g., careful assessment of client needs and preferences, appropriate skill selection, use of behavioral procedures and adaptations during instruction) should be interwoven into the leisure/recreation support system network. Only when these practices are implemented carefully and systemwide in home, school, and community settings (Schleien & Meyer, 1988; Schleien & Ray, 1988; Wetherald & Peters, 1986) will it be possible for persons with severe multiple disabilities to experience meaningful, exciting, and successful lives through expanded leisure and social repertoires and mainstreamed experiences.

APPLICATION OF THE TR PROCESS*

Many innovative and effective practices to teach age-appropriate leisure skills to persons with severe multiple disabilities have been developed by therapeutic recreation specialists and special educators over the past 10 years (Nietupski, Hamre-Nietupski, & Ayres, 1984; Schleien & Yermakoff, 1983). Few studies, however, have included individuals with severe multiple disabilities using an ecological perspective (e.g., programs involving

*A research study is presented here rather than the traditional case study that is used in other chapters. This research investigation was conducted by the author of this chapter with assistance from Jenny Cameron, John Rynders, and Carla Slick.

family members and care providers in the selection of activities, incorporating programs into community activity). This is unfortunate because an ecological perspective considers skill development within the complete range of environments in which an individual functions (Certo, Schleien, & Hunter, 1983). An ecological inventory enables teachers, therapists, and care providers to develop functional, age-appropriate leisure skills with instructional content. This approach, coupled with longitudinal planning, could increase opportunities for individuals with severe multiple disabilities to participate actively in normalized leisure activities in integrated community settings.

The purpose of this program was to teach three chronologically age-appropriate leisure skills to two students with severe multiple disabilities in their special education classroom, and to provide supplemental training to the students' families in their homes. Additionally, an attempt was made to facilitate social interactions and appropriate and cooperative play behaviors within the context of an integrated leisure skill program that included nonhandicapped peers who were trained as companions. Probes in neighborhood community recreation centers and at the participants' homes were conducted by parents to facilitate generalization and maintenance of the targeted leisure skills.

Methods

Setting and Participants. Meadowlake School was a K–6 elementary school with five of the classrooms devoted to special education. The school's special education students, ages 4 to 11 years, had disabilities ranging from mild mental retardation to severe mental retardation with multiple disabilities. Participants were two children with severe multiple disabilities and two same-age peers without disabilities.

Amy, a 5-year-old girl whose diagnosis was congenital cytomegalic virus inclusion (CMV) disease with microephaly, was nonambulatory with very limited use of her left side. Amy used a wheelchair and could also roll on the floor for mobility purposes. Her score of 118 on the Bayley Scale of Infant Development (a ratio IQ score of 32) placed her in the severe to profound range of mental retardation. She showed high rates of inappropriate crying during activity transitions, particularly when events did not go her way (e.g., termination of free play to being instruction on activities of daily living). Crying rarely occurred during highly motivating activities or when she received one-on-one attention by her teacher or parent. She communicated using informal methods (i.e., pointing, touching, moving hands).

Bobby, an 8-year-old boy whose diagnosis was a hypotonic form of cerebral palsy, crawled or scooted for mobility and was beginning to walk with assistance. He functioned in the severe to profound range of retardation, which was determined through criterion-referenced behavioral observations (a standardized test score was not available for him). Bobby recognized people he had met and communicated with simple gestures (i.e., pointing with finger, hand flailing). At the time this study was conducted, Amy and Bobby were not participating in any age-appropriate leisure activities. The nondisabled companions were selected from a second-grade class from the same school.

Program.   The goals of the program were to increase positive social interactions between students with severe multiple disabilities and their peers who were not disabled, and to allow students to acquire the skills needed to participate in age-appropriate recreational activities in their homes and community recreation centers.

Three games, including Toss Across; Flash, The Electronic Arcade Game; and Simon, were selected for leisure skill instruction. The rationale for the selection of these games included the following concerns: (a) age appropriate—played by nondisabled peers of the same chronological age; (b) functional—can be played in homes, schools, parks, and other environments; (c) social—encouraged social interaction by allowing two or more players to participate in the activity simultaneously; (d) motor—required motor skills that were written into the students' Individual Education Plans (IEPs) (e.g., use of the upper extremities for grasping and releasing, gross motor movements of throwing, tossing, and reaching); (e) reactive—responded to players' manipulations with sensory reinforcement (e.g., visual and auditory stimulation); and (f) family "friendly"—family members expressed interest in their children's participating in the selected activities.

Leisure Skills Instruction.   The leisure skills instructors received training in the use of instructional techniques and contingent reinforcement strategies and provided each dyad with instruction during a one-hour time period, two days per week. The companions participated in leisure skills instruction alongside their peers with severe multiple disabilities during only one of these sessions each week.

Each leisure skill was task analyzed, and instruction was provided using an assistance hierarchy (i.e., least-to-most intrusive) or error correction procedure as follows: The task was presented with the initial cue (i.e., "Let's play Toss Across."). A correct response was rewarded with behavior-specific positive feedback (BSPF). An error response or no response within five seconds was followed by a verbal cue from the instructor (e.g., "Amy, pick up the bean bag."). If a correct response occurred, it was rewarded with BSPF. An error response or no response within five seconds was followed by the instructor's repeating the verbal cue and modeling the correct response (i.e., picking up the bean bag). If the modeling did not evoke the correct response, the instructor repeated the verbal cue while physically guiding the learner through the activity and providing BSPF.

Home Training. The children with severe multiple disabilities received additional training on the leisure skills by their parents, at home, once each week to facilitate generalization to the natural environment and skill maintenance. Initially, parents were familiarized with the three games (i.e., Toss Across; Flash, The Electronic Arcade Game; and Simon). During the first home session, the instructors demonstrated the use of the task analysis and the error correction procedure, and also trained the parents in the use of BSPF. For the remaining five home sessions, parents provided instruction to their children with the instructors present but not interactive.

Generalization. One generalization probe on all three leisure activities was conducted at a neighborhood recreation center for each participant. To accomplish this, the instructors met the parents and participants at the recreation center. The nondisabled companions attended the session and participated in all activities. At these sessions, a parent was instructed to give a general verbal cue to the participants, and a maintenance probe was conducted. The participants' behaviors were observed and recorded by the instructors.

Results

Leisure Skills Acquisition. Figures 9.2 and 9.3 illustrate students' performances across the three leisure skills throughout the baseline and instructional phases of the program. Students' independent leisure behavior and leisure performance following physical prompts are presented in the figures.

Individual graphs reveal low and stable baseline performances on each leisure skill, with the exception of Amy's performance on Flash, The Electronic Arcade Game, which shows a slight increase in performance. In the baseline session immediately preceding the intervention phase of the program, Bobby demonstrated independent performance in 2(10%) of the task-analytic steps of Toss Across, 2(7%) of the steps of Flash, the Electronic Arcade Game, and 0(0%) of the steps of Simon. His overall mean baseline performances on the three leisure skills were 17%, 9%, and 0%, respectively. Amy performed independently in 4(20%) of the task-analytic steps of Toss Across, 5(18.5%) of the steps of Flash, the Electronic Arcade Game, and 0(0%) of the steps of Simon during the final baseline session. Her overall mean baseline performances on the same three leisure skills were 15%, 14%, and 0%, respectively.

During nonreinforced baseline probes, generalization from one leisure setting to another was apparent but minimal (i.e., school, to home, to recreation center). The ability to transfer training to other environments only slightly was especially noticeable when the leisure skills were introduced into the community center.

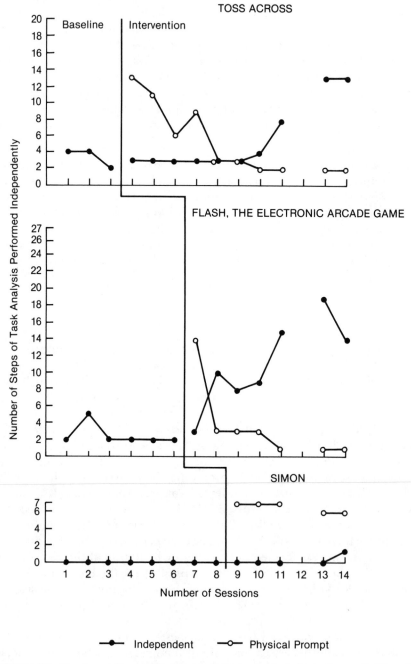

BOBBY

TOSS ACROSS

FLASH, THE ELECTRONIC ARCADE GAME

SIMON

Number of Steps of Task Analysis Performed Independently

Number of Sessions

●——● Independent   ○——○ Physical Prompt

FIGURE 9.2 Number of Steps of Task Analyses Performed Independently or with Prompt by Bobby Across Three Leisure Skills

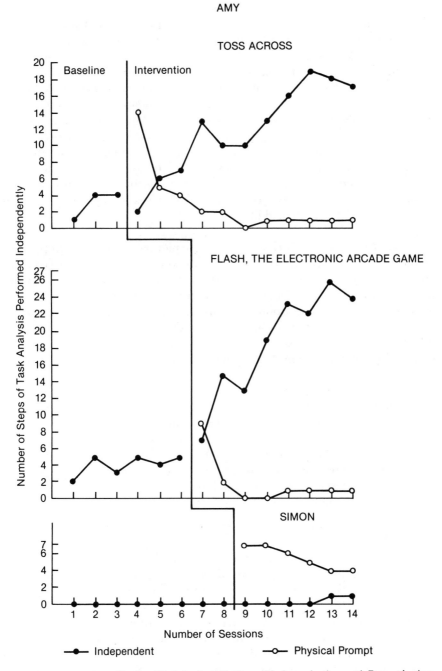

FIGURE 9.3 Number of Steps of Task Analyses Performed Independently or with Prompt by Amy Across Three Leisure Skills

Bobby returned to baseline levels of performance following the introduction of a leisure skill to a new environment except for Flash the Electronic Arcade Game, where he improved slightly. Amy's rate of independent leisure skill performance also decreased in the new environments, with the exception of Flash, The Electronic Arcade Game, but not to baseline levels of performance. Both learners demonstrated increases in their levels of independent performance following instruction on the activities in the new leisure environments. Both Bobby and Amy displayed minimal improvement in the third leisure skill, Simon, possibly due to the fact that the students received only five to six instructional sessions on how to play Simon in school because of the extended baseline and the termination of the school year. Moreover, it is possible that Simon was a more complex task relative to the other activities, necessitating more sophisticated motor and cognitive skills.

Social Interactions.   Prior to the implementation of the companions training program, Bobby received at least one social initiation from his companion, on the average, during 20% of the recording intervals. He did not respond to any of his companion's initiations. Following the companions training program, Bobby's companion initiated at least one social interaction on the average of 67% of the intervals observed, with a range of 40–90%, on a daily basis. During intervention, Bobby responded to his companion's initiations on the average of 26% of the intervals, with a range of 0–60%.

During baseline probes conducted prior to the implementation of the companions training program, Amy received at least one social interaction from her companion, on the average, during 30% of the intervals. She responded to her companion's initiations 67% of the time. Following companions training, Amy's companion initiated social interactions toward her during an average of 80% of the intervals, with a daily range of 55–100%. Amy responded to the initiated social interactions on the average of 76% of the time, with a daily range of 50–100%.

Discussion

Both children with severe multiple disabilities gained enough skill to participate "independently" in two of the three targeted leisure skills. The use of task analysis and other behavioral procedures, including BSPE, contingent reinforcement for positive social interactions, and parent/home training within an integrated leisure setting, were effective in developing their play repertoires and, to some extent, their social skills.

The participants' minimal abilities to generalize the newly acquired leisure skills to the home and community recreation center support the findings of existing generalization research that has identified lack of transfer of training to nontrained environments as a problem (Crawford,

1986; Horner, Albin, & Ralph, 1986; Horner, Williams, & Knobbe, 1985; Stokes & Baer, 1977). Only after systematic instruction was provided by parents in the home setting (which Stokes and Baer refer to as "Train Sufficient Exemplars") did the learners with severe multiple disabilities in the present study perform in the leisure activities at acceptable rates (i.e., 75% proficiency). In fact, following every training session at home on Toss Across and Flash, The Electronic Arcade Game, Bobby and Amy improved their leisure skill performance in school. These data support Horner, Williams, and Knobbe's (1985) findings concerning the "opportunity to perform," implying that newly acquired skills will be maintained in natural performance settings only if there are additional opportunities to practice the skills following acquisition. Thus, the willingness of parents and other care providers to follow through on school training programs appears to be critical. The care provider/leisure skill instructor partnership is vital to the maintenance of leisure activity repertoires in persons with severe multiple disabilities.

The findings involving social interaction and appropriate play support the integration of children with severe multiple disabilities and non-disabled same-age peers. Both participants in the present study demonstrated improvements in these behaviors from baseline to intervention. A fairly steady increase in the receiving of social interactions by the participants with disabilities from their companions and their subsequent responding to these initiations was found. These increases in social contacts may have been because of several factors, including increased level of mastery of the targeted leisure skills, BSPF provided for their socializing appropriately, companions training, increases in cooperative play exhibited by the children with severe multiple disabilities, and familiarity between participants.

TRENDS AND ISSUES

The current trends in the provision of therapeutic recreation services for persons with severe multiple disabilities reflect a growing sophistication in both philosophy and approach. Chief among these trends is the provision of specific leisure skill training in home, school, and community environments on an individualized basis. Related to this programming approach is the use of increasingly sophisticated behavioral engineering strategies and training techniques (e.g., task analysis, shaping and chaining, cue hierarchy and prompting systems) to facilitate leisure skill acquisition. Additionally, the use of the recreational experience to help facilitate collateral skill development (particularly in the areas of communication and language skills) signals a new interdisciplinary era of cooperation and services for these clients.

Along with these trends, however, remain several issues that pose significant challenges to therapeutic recreation program development. Clearly, a coordinated interdisciplinary effort is needed to resolve the use of multiple definitions in identifying and describing these clients. The current conceptual hodgepodge of definitions (some based on type of service received and some on functional characteristics of the person) is too unwieldy and confusing to be useful in planning interdisciplinary interventions and in networking services across agencies. Community resource issues are also a consideration. Therapeutic recreation specialists must particularly deal with the substantial gap that exists between what is available in community recreation programs and the real needs of persons with severe multiple disabilities. Finally, within therapeutic recreation there remain real leisure skill training issues. Chief among these problem areas is the development of effective generalization strategies for transfer of leisure skills acquired in training settings to natural community settings. Perhaps the most conceptually and programmatically challenging, however, will be how to train for and then accommodate the concept of personal preference or choice in the leisure experiences of these clients. The dilemma faced in identifying and/or honoring personal preference in leisure versus allowing nonfunctional and age-inappropriate activities to occur presents both technical and philosophical challenges that will not be resolved easily.

SUMMARY

Serving persons with severe multiple disabilities is a complex, intense, and often extensive task. Providing leisure experiences where these individuals are active and participating members is a challenge directly related to the therapeutic recreation specialist's ability to provide leisure knowledge to the participant, prepare "user-friendly" environments, and establish integrated leisure opportunities.

To be an active participant capable of choosing age-appropriate leisure activities, persons with severe multiple disabilities must be provided with a knowledge base that enables them to establish leisure repertoires. Systematic behavioral techniques must be implemented to facilitate independent leisure behavior that includes skills that are both functional and age appropriate. These skills should also promote participation in lifelong leisure activities, and of most importance, generalization to the larger community of citizens.

An individual with severe multiple disabilities—knowledgeable and capable of making his or her own leisure choices—must have access to environments that encourage participation. To establish such user-friendly environments requires preparation of their physical and human components. This preparation requires the creation or modification of sites with access to all citizens. Materials designed to assist with the adaptation of activities must be created and field-tested. Therapeutic recreation specialists must be provided with usable curricular materials designed specifically for this population. Leaders prepared to service persons with severe multiple disabilities must be educated to the needs and characteristics of this population. These needs include participation in already existing programs and interaction with nondisabled peers. Nondisabled peers, too, should be educated so that they can appreciate and understand the nature of a person's disability and eliminate the barriers that ignorance often creates.

When the person with a severe multiple disability is capable of making personal leisure choices and is provided with environments in which to exercise personal choice, an effective integration process can commence. Through integrated community programs, the individual can exercise his or her basic human right for meaningful participation in leisure/recreation activities. It is then that we all can begin to realize the goals of the recreation experience, including socialization, friendship, play, and fun.

READING COMPREHENSION QUESTIONS

1. Briefly explain the definition problem in regard to individuals with severe multiple disabilities.

2. Describe the idea of skill deficit as it pertains to persons with severe multiple disabilities. Why is this an important issue to the therapeutic recreation specialist?

3. Describe why choice making and self-initiation skills are important components of an individual's leisure repertoire to both individuals with and without disabilities. Why are these skills of critical concern in programming for persons with severe multiple disabilities?

4. Identify at least five goals of a therapeutic recreation program for persons with severe multiple disabilities.

5. Why is a needs assessment important, and what types of information should be solicited during the assessment?

6. What are the factors that should be considered when a therapeutic recreation specialist selects skills to be taught to a person with a severe multiple disability?

7. Describe the concept of task analysis.

8. What are the collateral skills (i.e., leisure-related support skills) necessary for playing a typical board game?

9. Why is networking a vital component to the maintenance and generalization of leisure skills for the individual with a severe multiple disability?

10. Identify and describe what are, in your opinion, the three most important issues facing the therapeutic recreation specialist in regard to programming for persons with severe multiple disabilities.

SUGGESTED LEARNING ACTIVITIES

1. As the therapeutic recreation specialist for a child who is severely mentally retarded and severely visually impaired, generate a list of possible ways to modify materials and environments to promote independent leisure participation.

2. As a therapeutic recreation specialist, you want to integrate a child with autism and severe behavioral problems into a community recreation program. You arrange a meeting with the center director. The director listens carefully to your suggestion but finally rejects your idea, arguing that the center's programs are not designed to serve children with autism. The director suggests that you take your idea to a recreation center designed specifically for this population. Outline and justify the steps you would take to gain access to this program for this child.

3. Select a board game and develop a task analysis that could be used for a leisure skills program with an individual who is severely multiply disabled.

4. In a group, role-play the people involved and types of situations that should transpire in assuring the generalization and maintenance of horseshoes as a leisure activity for an adult with cerebral palsy and moderate metal retardation.

5. A major manufacturer of toys and games contacts you as a therapeutic recreation specialist for ideas on developing play materials designed specifically for individuals with severe multiple disabilities. Give reasons for supporting or not supporting this company's endeavor. Write a letter to the company stating your position and rationale.

REFERENCES

ADKINS, J., & MATSON, L. (1980). Teaching institutionalized mentally retarded adults socially appropriate leisure skills. *Mental Retardation, 18*, 249–252.

ALAJAJIAN, L. (1981). Jogging program for deaf-blind students improves condition and reduces self-stimulation. *News . . . About Deaf-Blind Student, Programmed Services in New England, 6*(1), 3–4.

BAMBARA, L., SPIEGEL-MCGILL, P., SHORES, R., & FOX, J. (1984). A comparison of reactive and non-reactive toys on severely handicapped children's manipulative play. *Journal of the Association for Persons with Severe Handicaps, 9*(2), 142–149.

BANKS, R., & AVENO, A. (1986). Adapted miniature golf: A community leisure program for students with severe physical disabilities. *Journal of the Association for Persons with Severe Handicaps, 11*(3), 209–215.

BARRETT, S. (1987). Trends and issues in developing community living programs for young adults who are deaf-blind and profoundly handicapped. In A. Covert & H. Fredericks (Eds.), *Transition for persons with deaf-blindness and other profound handicaps: State of the art* (pp. 39–49). Monmouth, OR: Teaching Research.

BATES, P., & RENZAGLIA, A. (1982). Language instruction with a profoundly retarded adolescent: The use of a table game in the acquisition of verbal labeling skills. *Education and Treatment of Children 5*(1), 13–22.

BAUMGART, D., BROWN, L., PUMPIAN, I., NISBET, J., FORD, A., SWEET, M., MESSINA, R., & SCHROEDER, J. (1982). Principle of partial participation and individualized adaptations in educational programs for severely handicapped students. *Journal of the Association for the Severely Handicapped, 7*, 17–27.

BELLAMY, T. (1985, June). Severe disability in adulthood. *The Association for Persons with Severe Handicaps Newsletter, 3*(6):1–6.

BELMORE, K., & BROWN, L. (1976). A job skill inventory strategy for use in a public school vocational training program for severely handicapped potential workers. In L. Brown, N. Certo, K. Belmore, & T. Crowner (Eds.), *Papers and programs related to public school services for secondary age severely handicapped students* (Vol. 6, Pt. 1). Madison, WI: Madison Metro School District. Haring, N., & Bricker, D. (Eds.)(1977). *Teaching the severely handicapped* (Vol. 3, rev. ed.). Columbus, OH: Special Press.

BIRENBAUM, A., & RE, M. (1979). Resettling mentally retarded adults in the community—almost four years later. *American Journal of Mental Deficiency, 83*, 323–329.

BROWN, L., BRANSTON, M., HAMRE-NIETUPSKI, S., PUMPIAN, I., CERTO, N., & GRUENEWALD, L. (1979). A strategy for developing chronological age-appropriate and functional curricular content for severely handicapped adolescents and young adults. *Journal of Special Education, 13*(1), 81–90.

CERTO, N., SCHLEIEN, S., & HUNTER, D. (1983). An ecological assessment inventory to facilitate community recreation participation by severely disabled individuals. *Therapeutic Recreation Journal, 17*(3), 29–38.

CHESELDINE, S., & JEFFREE, D. (1981). Mentally handicapped adolescents: Their use of leisure. *Journal of Mental Deficiency Research, 25*, 49–59.

COVERT, A. (1987). Summary, conclusions, recommendations and implications of the conference: Purpose and format. In A. Covert & H. Fredericks (Eds.), *Transition for persons with deaf-blindness and other profound handicaps: State of the art* (pp. 147–157). Monmouth, OR: Teaching Research.

CRAWFORD, M. (1986). Development and generalization of lifetime leisure skills for multi-handicapped participants. *Therapeutic Recreation Journal, 20*(4), 48–60.

CRAWFORD, M., GRIFFIN, N., & MENDELL R. (1978). The assessment process in recreation with severely and profoundly retarded populations. *Practical Pointers, 2*(1), 1–9.

DATTILO, J., & BARNETT, L. (1985). Therapeutic recreation for individuals with severe handicaps: An analysis of the relationship between choice and pleasure. *Therapeutic Recreation Journal, 19*(3), 79–91.

DATTILO, J., & MIRENDA, P. (1987). An application of a leisure preference assessment protocol for persons with severe handicaps. *Journal of the Association for Persons with Severe Handicaps, 12*, 306–311.

DATTILO, J., & RUSCH, F. (1985). Effects of choice on leisure participation for persons with severe handicaps. *Journal of the Association for Persons with Severe Handicaps, 10*, 194–199.

DAY, H. (1987). Comparison of two prompting procedures to facilitate skill acquisition among severely mentally retarded adolescents. *American Journal of Mental Deficiency, 91* 366–372.

Dixon, J. (1981). *Adapting activities for therapeutic recreation services: Concepts and applications.* San Diego: Campanile.

Fardig, D. (1986). Informal assessment for the severely mentally handicapped: Section 2 [Special issue]. *Pointer, 30*(2), 47–49.

Flavell, J. (1973). Reduction of stereotypies by reinforcement of toy play. *Mental Retardation, 11*(4), 21–23.

Ford, A., Brown, L., Pumpian, I., Baumgart, D., Nisbet, J., Schroeder, J. & Loomis, R. (1984). Strategies for developing individualized recreation and leisure programs for severely handicapped students. In N. Certo, N. Haring, & R. York (Eds.), *Public school integration of severely handicapped students: Rational issues and progressive alternatives* (pp. 245–275). Baltimore: Paul H. Brookes.

Fredericks, H. (1987). Those with profound handicaps: Who are they? How can they be served? In A. Covert & H. Fredericks (Eds.), *Transition for persons with deaf-blindness and other profound handicaps: State of the art* (pp. 3–9). Monmouth, OR: Teaching Research.

Fredericks, H., & Baldwin, V. (1987). Individuals with sensory impairments. In L. Goetz, D. Guess, & K. Stremel-Campbell (Eds.), *Innovative program design for individuals with dual sensory impairments* (pp. 3–12). Baltimore: Paul H. Brookes.

Garner, J., & Campbell, P. (1987). Technology for persons with severe disabilities: Practical and ethical considerations. *The Journal of Special Education, 21*(3), 122–132.

Goetz, L. (1987). Recreation and leisure: Practices in educational programs which hold promise for adult service models. In A. Covert & H. Fredericks (Eds.), *Transition for persons with deaf-blindness and other profound handicaps: State of the art* (pp. 119–130). Monmouth, OR: Teaching Research.

Gollay, E. (1981). Some conceptual and methodological issues in studying community adjustment of deinstitutionalized retarded people. In R. Bruininks, C. Meyers, B. Sigford, & K. Lakin (Eds.), *Deinstitutionalization and community adjustment of mentally retarded people* (pp. 89–106). Washington, DC: American Association on Mental Deficiency.

Hauber, F., Bruininks, R., Hill, B., Lakin, K., Scheerenberger, R., & White, C. (1984). National census of residential facilities: A 1982 profile of facilities and residents. *American Journal of Mental Deficiency, 89*, 236–245.

Hill, B., Lakin, K., & Bruininks, R. (1984). Trends in residential services for people who are mentally retarded: 1972–1982. *Journal of the Association for Persons with Severe Handicaps, 9*, 243–250.

Hill, J., Wehman, P., & Horst, G. (1982). Toward generalization of appropriate leisure and social behavior in severely handicapped youth: Pinball machine use. *Journal of the Association for the Severely Handicapped, 6*(4), 38–44.

Horner, R., Albin, R., & Ralph, G. (1986). Generalization with precision: The role of negative teaching examples in the instruction of generalized grocery item selection. *Journal of the Association for Persons with Severe Handicaps, 11*, 300–308.

Horner, R., Williams, J. & Knobbe, C. (1985). The effect of "opportunity to perform" on the maintenance of skills learned by high school students with severe handicaps. *Journal of the Association for Persons with Severe Handicaps, 10*, 172–175.

Horst, G., Wehman, P., Hill, J., & Bailey, C. (1980). Developing chronologically age-appropriate leisure skills in severely multihandicapped adolescents: Three case studies. In P. Wehman & J. Hill (Eds.), *Instructional programming for severely handicapped youth: A community integration approach* (pp. 84–100). Richmond, VA: School of Education, Virginia Commonwealth University.

HUGHES, K. (1981). Adapting audio/video games for handicapped learners: Part 2. *Teaching Exceptional Children, 14,* 127–129.

INTAGLIATA, J., WILLER, B., & WICKS, G. (1981). Factors related to the quality of community adjustment in family care homes. In R. Bruininks, C. Meyers, B. Sigford, & K. Lakin (Eds.), *Deinstitutionalized and community adjustment of mentally retarded people* (pp. 217–230). Washington, DC: American Association on Mental Deficiency.

JAMES, S., & EGEL, A. (1986). A direct prompting strategy for increasing reciprocal interactions between handicapped and nonhandicapped siblings. *Journal of Applied Behavior Analysis, 19* 173–186.

KIBLER, C. (1986). Board games for multihandicapped players. *Perspective for Teachers of the Hearing Impaired, 4*(4), 21–23.

LAGOMARCINO, A., REID, D., IVANCIC, M., & FAW, G. (1984). Leisure-dance instruction for severely and profoundly retarded persons: Teaching an intermediate community-living skill. *Journal of Applied Behavior Analysis, 17,* 71–84.

MATTHEWS, P. (1980). Why the mentally retarded do not participate in certain types of recreational activities. *Therapeutic Recreation Journal, 14*(1), 44–50.

McDONNELL, J. (1987). The effects of time delay and increasing prompt hierarchy strategies on the acquisition of purchasing skills by students with severe handicaps. *Journal of the Association for Persons with Severe Handicaps, 12,* 227–236.

MEEHAN, D., MINEO, B., & LYON, S. (1985). Use of systematic prompting and prompt withdrawal to establish and maintain switch activation in a severely handicapped student. *Journal of Special Education Technology, 7*(1), 5–11.

NIETUPSKI, J., HAMRE-NIETUPSKI, S., & AYRES, B. (1984). Review of task analytic leisure skill training efforts: Practitioner implications and future research needs. *Journal of the Association for Persons with Severe Handicaps, 9,* 88–97.

ORELOVE, F., & SOBSEY, D. (1987). *Educating children with multiple disabilities: A transdisciplinary approach.* Baltimore: Paul H. Brookes.

POWERS, J., & BALL, T. (1983). Video games to augment leisure programming in a state hospital residence for developmentally disabled clients. *Journal of Special Education Technology, 6*(1), 48–57.

PUTNAM, J., WERDER, J., & SCHLEIEN, S. (1985). Leisure and recreation services for handicapped persons. In K. Lakin & R. Bruininks (Eds.), *Strategies for achieving community integration of developmentally disabled citizens* (pp. 253–274). Baltimore: Paul H. Brookes.

RAINFORTH, B., & YORK, J. (1987.) Integrating related services in community instruction. *Journal of the Association for Persons with Severe Handicaps, 12,* 190–198.

RAY, M., SCHLEIEN, S., LARSON, A., RUTTEN, T., & SLICK, C. (1986). Integrating persons with disabilities into community leisure environments. *Journal of Expanding Horizons in Therapeutic Recreation, 1*(1), 49–55.

ROGOW, S. (1976). Play and reality: Essentials of educational planning for blind retarded children. *Education and Training of the Mentally Retarded, 11,* 314–317.

ROGOW, S. (1981). Developing play skills and communicative competence in multiply handicapped young people. *Visual Impairment and Blindness, 5,* 197–202.

RYNDERS, J., JOHNSON, R., JOHNSON, D., & SCHMIDT, B. (1980). Producing positive integration among Down's syndrome and nonhandicapped teenagers through cooperative goal structuring. *American Journal of Mental Deficiency, 85,* 268–273.

SALZBERG, C., & LANGFORD, C. (1981). Community integration of mentally retarded adults through leisure activity. *Mental Retardation, 19*(3), 127–131.

SANDLER. A., & McCLAIN, S. (1987). Sensory reinforcement: Effects of response-contingent vestibular stimulation on multiply handicapped children. *American Journal of Mental Deficiency, 91*, 373–378.

SCHLEIEN, S., ASH, T., KIERNAN, J., & WEHMAN, P. (1981). Developing independent cooking skills in a profoundly retarded woman. *Journal of the Association for the Severely Handicapped, 6*(2), 23–29.

SCHLEIEN, S., CERTO, N., & MUCCINO, A. (1984). Acquisition of leisure skills by a severely handicapped adolescent: A data based leisure skill instructional program. *Education and Training of the Mentally Retarded, 19*, 297–305.

SCHLEIEN, S., KIERNAN, J., & WEHMAN, P. (1981). Evaluation of an age-appropriate leisure skills program for moderately retarded adults. *Education and Training of the Mentally Retarded, 16*, 13–19.

SCHLEIEN, S., & LARSON, A. (1986). Adult leisure education for the independent use of a community recreation center. *Journal of the Association for Persons with Severe Handicaps, 11*(1), 39–44.

SCHLEIEN, S., & MEYER, L. (1988). Community-based recreation programs for persons with severe developmental disabilities. In M. Powers (Ed.), *Expanding systems of service delivery for persons with developmental disabilities* (pp. 93–112). Baltimore: Paul H. Brookes.

SCHLEIEN, S., & RAY, M. (1988). *Community recreation and persons with disabilities: Strategies for integration.* Baltimore: Paul H. Brookes.

SCHLEIEN, S., & WEHMAN, P. (1986). Severely handicapped children: Social skills development through leisure skills programming. In G. Cartledge & J. Milburn (Eds.), *Teaching social skills to children: Innovative approaches* (2nd ed., pp. 219–245). Elmsford, NY: Pergamon Press.

SCHLEIEN, S., WEHMAN, P., & KIERNAN, J. (1981). Teaching leisure skills to severely handicapped adults: An age-appropriate darts game. *Journal of Applied Behavior Analysis, 14*, 513–519.

SCHLEIEN, S., & WERDER, J. (1985). Perceived responsibilities of special recreation services in Minnesota. *Therapeutic Recreation Journal, 19*(3), 51–62.

SCHLEIEN, S., & YERMAKOFF, N. (1983). Data-based research in therapeutic recreation: State of the art. *Therapeutic Recreation Journal, 17*(4), 17–26.

SEDLAK, R., DOYLE, M., & SCHLOSS, P. (1982). Video games; A training and generalization demonstration with severely retarded adolescents. *Education and Training of the Mentally Retarded, 17*, 332–336.

SELIGMAN, M. (1975). *Helplessness: On depression, development, and death.* San Francisco: W. H. Freeman.

SHERRILL, C. (1986). *Adapted physical education and recreation: A multidisciplinary approach* (3rd ed.). Dubuque, IA: William C. Brown.

SINGH, N., & MILLICHAMP, C. (1987). Independent and social play among profoundly mentally retarded adults: Training, maintenance, generalization, and long-term follow-up. *Journal of Applied Behavior Analysis, 20*, 23–34.

SOBSEY, D., & REICHLE, J. (1986). *Components of reinforcement for attention signal switch activation.* Manuscript submitted for publication.

STOKES, T., & BAER, D. (1977). An implicit technology of generalization. *Journal of Applied Behavior Analysis, 10* 349–367.

STOREY, K., BATES, P., & HANSON, H. (1984). Acquisition and generalization of coffee purchase skills by adults with severe disabilities. *Journal of the Association for Persons with Severe Handicaps, 9*(3), 178–185.

VANDERCOOK, T. (1987). *Generalized performance of community leisure skills with peers.* Unpublished manuscript, University of Minnesota, Minneapolis.

VERHOVEN, P., SCHLEIEN, S., & BENDER, M. (1982). *Leisure education and the handicapped individual: An ecological perspective.* Washington, DC: Institute for Career and Leisure Development.

VOELTZ, L., & WUERCH, B. (1981). Monitoring multiple behavioral effects of leisure activities training upon severely handicapped adolescents. In L. Voeltz, J. Apffel, & B. Wuerch (Eds.), *Leisure activities training for severely handicapped students: Instructional and evaluational strategies.* Honolulu: University of Hawaii, Department of Special Education.

VOELTZ, L., WUERCH, B., & WILCOX, B. (1982). Leisure and recreation: Preparation for independence, integration, and self-fulfillment. In B. Wilcox & G. Bellamy (Eds.), *Design of high school programs for severely handicapped students* (pp. 175–209). Baltimore: Paul H. Brookes.

WEHMAN, P. (1977). *Helping the mentally retarded acquire play skills: A behavioral approach.* Springfield, IL: Charles C. Thomas.

WEHMAN P. (1979). *Recreation programming for developmentally disabled persons.* Austin, TX: PRO-ED.

WEHMAN, P., & SCHLEIEN, S. (1979). *Leisure skills curriculum for developmentally disabled persons: Virginia model.* Richmond, VA: School of Education, Virginia Commonwealth University.

WEHMAN, P., & SCHLEIEN, S. (1980). Assessment and selection of leisure skills for severely handicapped individuals. *Education and Training of the Mentally Retarded, 15* 50–57.

WEHMAN, P., & SCHLEIEN, S. (1981). *Leisure programs for handicapped persons: Adaptations, techniques, and curriculum.* Austin, TX: PRO-ED.

WEHMAN, P., SCHLEIEN, S., & KIERNAN, J. (1980). Age-appropriate recreation programs for severely handicapped youth and adults. *Journal of the Association for the Severely Handicapped, 5* 395–407.

WEST, P. (1981). *Vestiges of a cage: Social barriers to participation in outdoor recreation by the mentally and physically handicapped,* (Monograph No. 1). Ann Arbor: University of Michigan, Natural Resources Sociology Research Lab.

WETHERALD, L., & PETERS, J. (1986). *Mainstreaming: A total perspective.* Silver Spring, MD: Montgomery County Department of Recreation, Therapeutics Section.

WUERCH, B., & VOELTZ, L. (1982). *Longitudinal leisure skills for severely handicapped learners: The Ho'onanea curriculum component.* Baltimore: Paul H. Brookes.

10

Convulsive Disorders

MARK R. JAMES

OBJECTIVES

- State a concise definition of the term *seizure*.
- Understand the classification of seizures.
- Understand the relationship between seizures, convulsive disorders, and epilepsy.
- Recognize the side effects from anticonvulsant medications.
- Realize that most individuals with epilepsy are able to stabilize their seizures with medications and lifestyle adaptations.
- Recognize the key areas where therapeutic recreation services are appropriate.
- Understand the possible activity limitations for clients with epilepsy.

DEFINITION OF CONVULSIVE DISORDERS/EPILEPSY

The term *convulsion*, or *seizure*, refers to an involuntary spasm or contraction of muscles resulting from chemical imbalances in the body. The causes of these chemical imbalances may come from a variety of sources, such as insufficient amounts of sugar or calcium in the blood, toxic poisoning, and disease or injury to the brain or central nervous system (Bleck, 1987).

The diagnostic category of epilepsy refers to a heterogeneous group of syndromes unified by their tendency to produce repeated convulsions, or seizures. Epileptic convulsions result from temporary chemical imbalances in the brain (as opposed to other chemical imbalances) that cause a rapid discharge of intercellular electrical activity. Epilepsy itself is not a disease, but is a symptom of disturbed brain functioning. Although epilepsy represents the largest subgroup of convulsive disorders, it should be noted that not all clients who have convulsions are epileptic.

Prevalence estimates for epilepsy range from 0.5–1.5% of the general population (Hauser, 1978; Juul-Jensen & Foldspang, 1983), or between 1.2 and 3.6 million individuals in the United States. In addition to epilepsy, there are over 100 other neurological syndromes that may cause convulsions (Anderson, Hauser, & Rich, 1986).

CLASSIFICATION OF SEIZURE DISORDERS

Ten factors have been identified to be involved in most of the known etiologies of seizure disorders (Bleck, 1987). Seven are clearly implicated in epilepsy, or repeated seizure syndromes, whereas three are related to episodic, or single seizure, occurrences. Table 10.1 displays these ten factors.

For epilepsy, or repeated seizure syndromes, the seven most prominent causes are (1) genetic influences, (2) birth trauma, (3) various central nervous system infections, (4) head injuries, (5) brain tumors, (6) cerebrovascular diseases or strokes, and (7) immunological disorders. Episodic, or single seizure, occurrences are caused by (1) drug/alcohol withdrawal, (2) acute drug intoxication, and (3) metabolic disorders.

It is important for therapeutic recreation specialists to be able to recognize and describe the various seizure types. This knowledge is necessary for proper documentation of seizures that occur during clinical sessions, and to give feedback to the appropriate medical personnel who work with the client who had the seizure. Although accurate clinical observations are vital to diagnosis, they do not always give a clear indication of the specific disorder; a variety of seizure types may be observed for individual disorders.

Table 10.1
Etiological Factors of Seizure Disorders

A. Epilepsy
   1. Genetic influences
   2. Birth trauma
   3. Central nervous system infections
   4. Head trauma
   5. Tumors
   6. Cerebrovascular diseases or strokes
   7. Immunological disorders

B. Single Seizures
   1. Drug/alcohol withdrawal
   2. Acute drug intoxication
   3. Metabolic disorders

SOURCE: Bleck (1987).

The current classification of seizure types has evolved historically from the distinction between "grand mal" and "petit mal" seizures—labels that are now used less frequently. Two basic divisions of seizures are present: (1) partial seizures, and (2) generalized seizures. Table 10.2 presents an outline of the current seizure types recognized by the Commission on Classification and Terminology of the International League Against Epilepsy (1981).

Partial seizures are those that begin in one specific body site and may or may not involve the loss of consciousness. If consciousness is not impaired, the term *simple partial* is used. If consciousness is impaired, the seizure is referred to as *complex partial*. A complex partial seizure is the most common type in adults with epilepsy. Some partial seizures begin in one body site and progress to a more global type known as a *generalized seizure.*

Generalized seizures do not start in one isolated body site, but rather involve several sites or entire body areas such as the trunk or the extremities. Generalized absence seizures are typified by an abrupt interruption of awareness and behavior, without any loss of muscle tone. It is frequently noted that clients with these seizures display slight eye blinking, mouth twitching, and hand movements. These seizures generally last 5–30 seconds. The five other subgroups of generalized seizures are differentiated by the display of various tonic and clonic movements (tension and relaxation of the muscles).

Most seizures last 1–5 minutes, stopping spontaneously. Infrequently, seizures will continue, and the client will be considered to be in a state of

---

Table 10.2
Classification of Seizure Types

A. Partial Seizures (begin in one specific body site)
    1. Simple partial seizures (consciousness is not impaired)
    2. Complex partial seizures (consciousness is impaired)
    3. Partial seizure evolving into a generalized seizure

B. Generalized Seizures (not confined to one body site)
    1. Absence seizures
    2. Myoclonic seizures
    3. Clonic seizures
    4. Tonic seizures
    5. Tonic-clonic seizures
    6. Atonic seizures

C. Status Epilepticus (continuous seizures)

SOURCE: From Proposal for Revised Clinical and Electroencephalographic Classification of Epileptic Seizures, *Epilepsia, 22,* (1981) pp. 489–501. Reprinted by permission of Commission on Classification and Terminology of the International League Against Epilepsy (1981).

"status epilepticus." This is a very serious condition, and prompt medical attention is needed to prevent residual brain damage or possible death. Recent evidence suggests that permanent neuronal damage can occur after about 20 minutes of status epilepticus (Bleck, 1983).

Dual Diagnosis: Seizure Disorders and Other Pervasive Conditions

In addition to the direct consequences of suffering from a seizure disorder, individuals with epilepsy are commonly considered to be at high risk for other psychological/psychiatric problems (Fenton, 1981). These dual-diagnosed clients present difficulties to their interdisciplinary treatment teams in respect to establishing treatment priorities.

Psychopathology as related to epilepsy generally refers to psychosis, aggression, sexual dysfunction, affective disorders, significant personality and behavioral changes, and other problems. Research into the correlations between epilepsy and psychopathology notes three specific etiological influences: (1) the seizures themselves, (2) social and environmental stressors, and (3) side effects from anticonvulsive medications (Whitman & Hermann, 1986). It is generally felt that either singly or in combination, these three influences foster the greater incidence of psychopathology in clients with epilepsy.

It is not uncommon for a therapeutic recreation specialist who works in a long-term residential treatment center to encounter clients who have mental retardation and epilepsy, or cerebral palsy and epilepsy. In some cases, there may be a single underlying disorder (e.g., Lennox-Gastaut syndrome, tuberous sclerosis) or two separate conditions. Many metabolic disorders that induce seizures respond poorly to medication and thus over time will result in residual brain damage. These cases are rare in comparison with the entire population of individuals with convulsive disorders, but they are commonly seen in certain long-term treatment settings.

DESCRIPTION OF LIMITATIONS

Two key areas present long-term difficulties and challenges to clients with epilepsy: (1) chronic side effects from anticonvulsant medications and (2) life-style modifications. Not surprisingly, how clients handle these two areas significantly affects the stabilization of their seizures. With careful, ongoing monitoring, most individuals achieve satisfactory freedom from seizures.

Clients who have recurrent epileptic seizures should be treated with anticonvulsant medications. There are a variety of appropriate drugs that can be used individually or in combination (Fincham, 1986). Although general guidelines are available for determining which drug works best for specific types of seizures, working out an effective anticonvulsant treatment

Table 10.3
Anticonvulsant Medications

TRADE NAME	GENERIC NAME	SEIZURE TYPE
Dilantin	Phenytoin	Simple partial Complex partial Partial with secondary generalization Generalized
Luminal	Phenobarbital	Simple partial
Mysoline	Primidone	Complex partial Partial with secondary generalization Generalized
Tegretol	Carbamazepine	Simple partial Complex partial Partial with secondary generalization Generalized
Clonopin	Clonazepam	Absence Myoclonic
Zarontin	Ethosuximide	Absence
Depakene	Valproic Acid	Partial with secondary generalization Generalized Absence Myoclonic

SOURCE: Bleck (1987); Fincham (1986).

regimen is a complex task. Table 10.3 outlines some of the common medications and the typical seizure types for which they may be the drug of first choice. It should be emphasized that these are guidelines only.

Clients must understand that anticonvulsant medications do not cure or correct epilepsy, but rather offer a method of prevention of future seizures. The effectiveness of these medications depends upon the maintenance of a stable level of the drug in the client's bloodstream at all times; hence the need for ongoing monitoring. All anticonvulsant medications have the potential to cause a variety of side effects. Therapeutic recreation specialists need to be aware of these in order to conduct valid assessments and outline appropriate treatment strategies. Refer to Table 10.4 for some of the more common side effects.

Several factors have been identified that are thought to aggravate or spontaneously induce seizures (Bleck, 1987; Sherrill, 1976). Each of these is somehow related to a chemical change in the client's bloodstream. Because each of these factors is partially under the control of the client, they often can be monitored and stabilized by life-style modifications. These factors are the following:

1. *Sleep deprivation.* It is commonly believed that rapid changes in sleep habits will hinder the stabilization of seizures.

Table 10.4
Possible Anticonvulsant Medication Side Effects

Sedation
Slowed mental processing
Skin rash
Uncoordinated muscle movements
  (ataxia)
Anemia
Slurred speech
Drowsiness
Fatigue
Vitamin deficiencies
Blurred vision or nystagmus
Depression
Dizziness
Nausea
Vomiting
Unsteady gait
Gastric irritability
Headache
Tremors
Emotional irritability
Water retention
Cardiac arrhythmias
Psychosis
Hair loss
Weight gain

SOURCE: Fincham (1986).

2. *Changes in alkalinity in the blood.* It is preferable for seizure-prone individuals to maintain a slightly acidic diet, usually accomplished by adhering to a ketogenic diet. Foods that are suggested include high-fat milk, butter, eggs, and meat.

3. *Changes in sodium in the blood.* For example, at specific times in the menstrual cycle, women tend to retain sodium, which reduces their seizure threshold.

4. *Excessive drinking of alcoholic beverages.* This does not refer to seizures induced by alcohol withdrawal, but the tendency for individuals' natural seizure thresholds to be reduced by drinking too much alcohol.

Life-style modifications also refer to a variety of activities that are contraindicated for seizure-prone individuals. Contraindicated activities are those that would present a health threat to the client with epilepsy and other participants if a seizure were to occur during the activity. Activities in this category would include scuba diving, sky diving, hang gliding, rock climbing, and unsupervised swimming activities.

Some physicians take a more conservative stance and restrict involvement in sports that may result in head injuries. Examples of these activities include boxing, tackle football, ice hockey, soccer, gymnastics, rugby, lacrosse, and wrestling. Yet other physicians advocate a more liberal position that allows clients to participate in most activities as long as a nonseizure-prone partner is present. These latter physicians still recommend careful consideration for activities where the partner would be unable to offer immediate help, such as scuba diving and hang gliding.

Individuals with epilepsy need to be seizure free for a period of time prior to obtaining a driver's license. This time period is different from state to state. In respect to all potentially restricted activities, it is important to remember that when the seizures are well controlled, those individuals are no different than anybody else (Sherrill, 1976); they need the opportunity to experience risks and challenges just as their peers do.

First aid precautions that the therapeutic recreation specialist should be aware of when a client has a seizure during a session are discussed by Austin (1982). The clinician should not be concerned with trying to stop the seizure, but rather with ensuring the client's safety during the seizure. Objects should be removed from the immediate area, the client should be assisted to lie on the floor if possible, the client's head should be cushioned and turned to one side, and medical assistance should be called for. Additionally, the clinician should remain alert in observing the duration and observable nature of the seizure; this will assist the medical staff and enable accurate documentation of the client's condition.

PURPOSE OF THERAPEUTIC RECREATION

Therapeutic recreation specialists who work with clients with convulsive disorders typically are focusing on either a secondary diagnosis (e.g., mental retardation, mental illness, physical handicaps), psychopathology associated with epilepsy (e.g., learned helplessness, anger, depression), or specific needs related to life-style modifications that would benefit from leisure counseling. Table 10.5 outlines these areas.

Table 10.5
Therapeutic Recreation Intervention Areas for Clients with Epilepsy

A. Secondary diagnoses (e.g., mental retardation, mental illness, physical handicaps)

B. Concomitant psychopathology (e.g., depression, anger, learned helplessness)

C. Life-style adaptations (e.g., restricted leisure activities)

In focusing on a second diagnosis, the clinician needs to remain aware of certain activity limitations, medication side effects, and appropriate procedures for handling seizures that may occur during sessions. The therapist should then follow appropriate strategies outlined for the specific second diagnosis. The latter two areas of concern (psychopathology and life-style modifications) are more directly related to clients' seizures, and thus can be viewed as specific intervention domains of therapeutic recreation services for convulsive disorders.

As noted earlier, clients with epilepsy are at risk for other psychologi cal or psychiatric conditions. Therapeutic recreation specialists should take an active role in addressing some of the psychosocial needs of this population. Three topics will be discussed to highlight this area: (1) stress reduction, (2) leisure life-style, and (3) locus of control.

Mittan and Locke (1982) noted that most individuals with epilepsy live with pervasive fears about having seizures, with approximately 70% believing that they might die during their next seizure. In some instances these fears may be realistic, emphasizing the need for a comprehensive assessment. These individuals should be assessed for their knowledge and use of stress reduction and relaxation skills to counteract the effects of chronic stress. Therapeutic recreation has a documented research base for promoting healthy, effective stress reduction activities, and thus can take a leadership role in providing therapeutic intervention in this area.

Considerable evidence supports the theory that clients with epilepsy are stigmatized by the disorder, even when the seizures are well controlled (Arangio, 1980; Betts, 1982). This stigmatization is both real and perceived, indicating that both society and the clients need to overcome their stereotypes about seizures. In reaction to perceiving this stigmatization, clients commonly reflect affective disorders such as anxiety and depression. By strengthening clients' leisure skill repertoire and developing a rewarding leisure life-style, therapeutic recreation services can assist individuals to remain active participants in social activities, dispelling some of the disorder's stigmatization.

Clients with epilepsy have been shown to reflect more external locus of control scores than nonepileptic individuals (DeVellis et al., 1980). This indicates that these clients do not believe they have the ability to control their lives. This is a realistic consequence of having a chronic health problem, but is psychologically debilitating when the feeling of uncontrollability becomes generalized to other aspects of individuals' lives. Locus of control and perceived control in respect to leisure activities have been discussed by other authors (Iso-Ahola, 1980; Ellis & Witt, 1984), and a comprehensive assessment battery has been developed for use by therapeutic recreation specialists (Ellis & Witt, 1986).

The various adaptations that relate to clients' leisure life-styles are appropriate topics for therapeutic recreation. Although certain physical activities may be contraindicated (or need modifications), it should be remembered that clients with epilepsy still need a well-rounded leisure life-style. This would include social recreational activities, individual and team sports, and solitary hobbies and interests. It should not be assumed that all clients with epilepsy need leisure counseling, but for some individuals these services are appropriate.

By conducting a comprehensive leisure assessment, the clinician can develop recommendations based on clients' strengths. In this manner, clients can focus on the vast activities allowed, rather than dwelling on the few activity limitations.

COMMON SERVICE SETTINGS

Therapeutic recreation specialists will encounter clients with convulsive disorders in all service delivery areas. This is because epilepsy is spread throughout the general population and will be noted randomly in any clinical setting. The majority of clients with convulsive disorders that are in need of therapeutic recreation services will reside in long-term residential treatment centers. These clients include those who are developmentally delayed, have a primary psychiatric diagnosis, or have a variety of multi-handicaps in addition to their convulsive disorder.

Clients who are not dual diagnosed will usually be able to stabilize their seizures with medications and therefore will live at home. These individuals may be referred for therapeutic recreation services to assist with concomitant psychopathology or life-style adaptations. Common service settings for these clients would include community mental health centers, outpatient clinics in general hospitals, university or medical center clinics, or private practices.

Therapists who work in drug and alcohol detoxification units will witness seizures with chronic alcoholics on a regular basis. These seizures are episodic (unless the client also has a convulsive disorder) and are one of the possible features of the alcohol withdrawal syndrome. In these cases immediate medical attention is the standard protocol, and therapeutic recreation services would resume only after the client has passed through this stage of detoxification.

CURRENT BEST PRACTICES AND PROCEDURES

In discussing appropriate services, special attention will be directed toward individuals with concomitant psychopathology or difficulty with life-style adaptations. Readers are referred to other chapters in this text for practices and procedures related to secondary diagnoses such as mental retardation and mental illness.

Assessment

Four global areas should be considered when assessing clients with convulsive disorders: (1) stress reduction and relaxation training, (2) locus of control, (3) social skills, and (4) leisure life-style. Each of these areas can provide useful information to document the need for therapeutic recreation services. The four topics noted here, as well as suggestions of the origins of psychopathology peculiar to individuals with convulsive disorders, are derived from common practice. Additional areas will become evident on an individual basis.

A wide variety of standardized assessment tools are available for locus of control (Rohsenow & O'Leary, 1978) and leisure life-style concerns (Howe, 1984). Checklists, questionnaires, surveys, and therapist observations are more commonly used for identifying stress reduction skills and social skills (e.g., communication, cooperation, and leadership skills).

Few assessment formats have originated specifically for individuals with convulsive disorders, so the clinician will need to be familiar with contraindicated activities when conducting assessments. In most cases no adaptations will be necessary, but the therapist should review clients' medical records and speak with appropriate medical staff prior to beginning an assessment.

Planning

Following the completion of a comprehensive interdisciplinary assessment, the therapy needs must be prioritized and corresponding goals and objectives identified. For most clients the seizures themselves will be stabilized and monitored by the medical staff. Other needs will then be prioritized in consideration of their relationship to each client. Life-style adaptations that are necessary to help stabilize the occurrence of seizures will be given a high priority. An example of this would be the establishment of a healthy balance between proper diet and exercise. If either of these two areas are severely neglected, it may be more difficult to maintain the proper anticonvulsant medication level in a client's bloodstream.

Relaxation training sessions and physical activities to reduce stress can be presented through core therapy sessions (developing prerequisite skills) or counseling sessions (assisting the client to utilize fully the skills already present). Experiential group cooperation activities are useful both for promoting an internal locus of control and for developing appropriate social skills. The topic of leisure counseling encompasses a broad spectrum of services that basically seek to assist the individual in developing a rewarding leisure life-style.

Implementation

The general interaction style of the therapist will vary widely in consideration of the clients' needs. Individuals with severe mental retardation and sporadically controlled seizures needing to develop communication skills will probably do better with a more structured therapy setting than with an adult executive who is avoiding all physical activities out of fear of having a seizure.

All clinical strategies should be continuously monitored to ensure their relevance to the clients' identified needs. The therapist should always remain aware of certain activity limitations, medication side effects, and appropriate procedures for handling seizures if they do occur. Specifically, the therapeutic recreation specialist should watch for signs of extreme fatigue during and after physical activities, excessive breathing, skipping meals, as well as other idiosyncrasies identified on an individual basis.

Evaluation

In those instances where standardized assessments are used (e.g., locus of control), a post-therapy assessment is appropriate. Check sheets and questionnaires should also be monitored to ensure that the progress stated in the goals and objectives was achieved. One question that is important for this particular clinical population is whether the actual activities exacerbated the clients' conditions. This would have been addressed immediately by the therapist, but it should be highlighted in the clients' evaluation summaries and medical records.

APPLICATION OF THE TR PROCESS

CASE STUDY

Edward is a 34-year-old, single, college-educated client who was referred for outpatient counseling for depression. Edward works as an accounts receivable clerk at an industrial manufacturing company. Edward's epilepsy was initially diagnosed at age 7 and has been stabilized since that time, with the last seizure occurring at age 23 and the one previous to that at age 17. In conjunction with helping a co-worker who had a seizure at work, Edward disclosed to his employer that he also has epilepsy. This occurred six years ago, and Edward attributes this to his being overlooked for job promotions since that time. Feelings of depression, helplessness, and extreme frustration led Edward's physician to recommend outpatient counseling.

Assessment

Edward's physician referred him to a local community mental health center that provided outpatient counseling services. Following an initial screening interview, Edward was advised to attend an outpatient leisure counseling group that met twice weekly. The group used a 12-week program format, which was conducted by a certified therapeutic recreation specialist. As part of the therapeutic recreation assessment, Edward completed a nonstandardized leisure interest survey, a questionnaire that identified his current leisure life-style—the Perceived Freedom in Leisure–Short Form (PFL-SF) (Ellis & Witt, 1986)—and the Adult Nowicki-Strickland Internal-External Locus of Control Scale (ANSIE) (Nowicki & Duke, 1974).

The results of the questionnaires indicated that Edward has a diverse, well-rounded repertoire of leisure skills and interests, but had stopped participating in social activities over the past several years. The PFL-SF noted that Edward felt that he was not able to choose his leisure activities freely, that social and environmental constraints dictated his choices. The ANSIE identified that Edward had a global belief that he did not control his actions. The ANSIE reinforced the results from the PFL-SF.

Planning

Based on the results of the therapeutic recreation assessment battery, Edward's physician's comments, the initial screening information, and Edward's own observations, Edward contracted to attend the 12-week outpatient leisure counseling group. Edward and the therapeutic recreation specialist also considered referrals to a clinical psychologist for individual counseling, and classes in biofeedback training (services offered at the same agency). It was decided that these referrals might be appropriate following the 12-week leisure counseling sessions.

Implementation

The 12-week leisure counseling protocol consisted of a structured education/lecture group on each Tuesday. These groups identified specific interests, skills, and strategies that the individual clients could use immediately. On Fridays individual clients presented specific problem areas for discussion and feedback. It was the responsibility of the clients to follow up on the suggestions made in groups, relating their experiences in the following session. Clients who had difficulty being self-motivated were seen individually by the therapeutic recreation specialist to provide more structure. Specific topics that were presented during the Tuesday sessions included the following: the relationship between leisure and work; time management; matching interests with available options; identifying local and regional resources; solitary versus social recreation; self-responsibility; and others. The Friday sessions were more open-ended, typically following up on how individuals were able to generalize the suggestions discussed on Tuesdays into their leisure life-style.

The therapeutic recreation specialist served as the group leader and resource person, offering considerable options and suggestions for the clients to select. It was of prime importance that each client take control of his or her leisure activities, a concept that was repeatedly emphasized throughout the sessions. As long as the group stayed focused and progressed in a productive manner, the clinician retained the role of a resource person during the Friday sessions.

Evaluation

Edward attended all 24 sessions during the 12-week program without demonstrating the need for individual sessions. Edward actively participated in each group and seemed to begin using the suggestions and feedback roughly around the fifth week. During the course of the program, Edward was confronted with his repeated rationalizations and excuses for making positive changes in his life. Edward appeared to accept this positive criticism, albeit reluctantly.

Post-therapy evaluations included the PFL-SF, the ANSIE, and a questionnaire covering the main points of the 12 Tuesday lectures. Edward reflected a more internal locus of control score, was taking more responsibility for his leisure activities, and understood the key concepts of the lectures. Edward noted that he was less depressed and preoccupied about his employment situation, and in fact had spoken to his supervisor about a possible promotion. Edward did not receive the promotion, but received a minor pay raise and seemed satisfied with his supervisor's comments. Apparently, Edward was not only taking a more self-responsible, assertive role in his leisure life-style, but had successfully generalized this concept to other aspects of his life. At a follow-up contact made three months later, Edward reported no recurrence of his symptoms of depression. Edward had continued to make progress by attending a local biofeedback seminar sponsored by the local community library, and he began a moderate exercise regimen twice weekly with several co-workers.

TRENDS AND ISSUES

The stigma associated with epilepsy is undoubtedly the greatest issue with which persons with epilepsy must deal. As discussed earlier in the chapter, even those individuals whose seizures are well controlled face stigma. Both persons with epilepsy and society in general need to overcome stereotypes held about seizure disorders. A related issue is the lack of understanding on the part of some helping professionals regarding life-style modifications for persons who have seizures. Although common sense dictates prudence in the selection of recreational activities, excessive limitations are often imposed on individuals with epilepsy. Fortunately, there is a growing trend toward awareness on the part of both lay persons and helping professionals that most individuals with epilepsy can achieve freedom from seizures by taking anticonvulsant medication, permitting them to have few life-style restrictions.

SUMMARY

Convulsions are caused by abnormal amounts of electrical discharge between cells in the brain. As a result of this, the body sites that are controlled by those brain cells will display spasms or muscle contractions. Epilepsy refers to a group of syndromes that produce recurrent seizures. Although between 1.2 and 3.6 million individuals in the United States have epilepsy, most are able to stabilize their seizures through medications and life-style modifications alone.

Therapeutic recreation services are typically sought for assistance with a secondary diagnosis, concomitant psychopathology, or specific life-style modifications. Certain activity limitations may be recommended on an individual basis because of the individual's seizure history and the nature of the activity. Other activity precautions can be instituted to allow individuals with epilepsy to participate in most activities.

READING COMPREHENSION QUESTIONS

1. What is a convulsion? A seizure? Epilepsy?
2. What are the ten factors that are believed to cause most convulsive disorders?
3. What are the differences between the two global seizure classifications?
4. What should a therapeutic recreation specialist do if a client has a seizure during a session?
5. What are the three areas for which therapeutic recreation specialists usually receive referrals?
6. Are medications usually given to individuals with epilepsy? What are some of the possible side effects?
7. Should clients with epilepsy be allowed to scuba dive? Play volleyball? Tackle football?
8. When would leisure counseling be a recommended approach for clients with epilepsy?

SUGGESTED LEARNING ACTIVITIES

1. Prepare a 3- to 5-page paper that summarizes the history of seizure classification up to the current recommendations of the International League Against Epilepsy.
2. In class, organize two debate teams. One team will take the stance that individuals with epilepsy should not participate in high-risk activities; the other team will advocate for their inclusion.

3. In a small discussion group, identify some of the psychosocial difficulties that individuals with epilepsy may develop. Discuss how therapeutic recreation services may impact on these needs.

4. Prepare a 2- to 4-page paper that discusses one of the three key areas of therapeutic recreation services for this population.

5. Research the local regulations that individuals with epilepsy must satisfy before obtaining a driver's license.

6. Prepare a 3- to 5-page paper that speculates how your life-style would need to be adapted if you had epilepsy.

REFERENCES

ANDERSON, V. E., HAUSER, W. A., & RICH, S. S. (1986). Genetic heterogeneity in the epilepsies. *Advances in Neurology, 44,* 59–75.

ARANGIO, A. (1980). The social worker and epilepsy: A description of assessment and treatment variables. In B. P. Hermann (Ed.), *A multidisciplinary handbook of epilepsy.* Springfield, IL: Charles C. Thomas.

AUSTIN, D. R. (1982). *Therapeutic recreation processes and techniques.* New York: John Wiley & Sons.

BETTS, T. A. (1982). Psychiatry and epilepsy. In J. Laidlaw & A. Richens (Eds.), *A textbook of epilepsy* (2nd ed.). Edinburgh: Churchill-Livingstone.

BLECK, T. P. (1983). Therapy for status epilepticus. *Clinical Neuropharmacology, 6,* 255–269.

BLECK, T. P. (1987). Epilepsy. *Disease-a-Month, 33,* 601–679.

Commission on Classification and Terminology of the International League Against Epilepsy. (1981). Proposal for revised clinical and electroencephalographic classification of epileptic seizures. *Epilepsia, 22,* 489–501.

DEVELLIS, R. G., DEVELLIS, B. M., WALLSTON, B. S., & WALLSTON, K. A. (1980). Epilepsy and learned helplessness. *Basic and Applied Social Psychology, 1,* 241–253.

ELLIS, G. D., & WITT, P. A. (1984). The measurement of perceived freedom in leisure. *Journal of Leisure Research, 16,* 110–123.

ELLIS, G. D., & WITT, P. A. (1986). The Leisure Diagnostic Battery: Past, present, and future. *Therapeutic Recreation Journal, 20*(4), 31–47.

FENTON, G. W. (1981). Personality and behavioral disorders in adults with epilepsy. In E. H. Reynolds & M. R. Trimble (Eds.), *Epilepsy and psychiatry.* Edinburgh: Churchill-Livingstone.

FINCHAM, R. W. (1986). Epilepsy in adolescents and adults. In C. Cann (Ed.), *Conn's current therapy.* Philadelphia: W. B. Saunders.

HAUSER, W. A. (1978). Epidemiology of epilepsy. In B. S. Schoenberg (Ed.), *Advances in neurology: Neurological epidemiology.* New York: Raven Press.

HOWE, C. E. (1984). Leisure assessment instrumentation in therapeutic recreation. *Therapeutic Recreation Journal, 18*(2), 14–24.

ISO-AHOLA, S. E. (1980). *The social psychology of leisure and recreation.* Dubuque, IA: William C. Brown.

JUUL-JENSEN, P., & FOLDSPANG, A. (1983). Natural history of epileptic seizures. *Epilepsia, 24,* 297–312.

MITTAN, R., & LOCKE, G. E. (1982, January/February). Fear of seizures: Epilepsy's forgotten problem. *Urban Health,* pp. 40–41.

NOWICKI, S., & DUKE, M. P. (1974). A locus of control scale for college as well as noncollege adults. *Journal of Personality Assessment, 38*, 136–137.

ROHSENOW, D. J., O'LEARY, M. R. (1978). Locus of control research on alcoholic populations: A review. I. Development, scales, and treatment. *International Journal of the Addictions, 13*(1), 55–78.

SHERRILL, C. (1976). *Adapted physical education and recreation.* Dubuque, IA: William C. Brown.

WHITMAN, S., & HERMANN, B. P. (Eds.). (1986). *Psychopathology in epilepsy: Social dimensions.* New York: Oxford University Press.

11

Neurological and Neuromuscular Disorders

KATHLEEN M. CORNWALL
AND BRENDA WINN-ORR

OBJECTIVES

- Develop an understanding of the terms *neurological* and *neuromuscular*.
- Describe and differentiate between the clinical characteristics of cerebral palsy, muscular dystrophy, multiple sclerosis, spina bifida, and spinal injury.
- Determine the role and purpose of therapeutic recreation services for individuals having neurological/ neuromuscular disorders.
- Describe the common service settings for these populations.
- Understand the current philosophy and current best practices for these types of disorders.
- Acknowledge current issues and trends.

DEFINITION OF NEUROLOGICAL AND NEUROMUSCULAR DISORDERS

Neurological and neuromuscular disorders are bonded by their involvement with impairment of the central nervous system. The range of abilities affected by these disorders varies from a slight difference from the norm in posture or movement, to complete paralysis or quadriplegia. The effects, which may be manifested early in life, gradually cause degeneration of all voluntary and involuntary function, leading to death. In neurological and neuromuscular disorders, the central nervous system is impaired by malformation, degeneration, or both. When progression occurs, it may be gradual, taking years to cause degeneration, or rapid, with early death often the result. In this chapter, characteristics pertinent to common neurological and neuromuscular disorders as well as abilities and contraindications are discussed.

CLASSIFICATION OF DISORDERS AND DESCRIPTION OF LIMITATIONS

Muscular Dystrophy

Muscular dystrophy is described by the national Muscular Dystrophy Association (MDA) as "the general designation for a group of chronic, hereditary diseases characterized by the progressive degeneration and weakness of voluntary muscle." The MDA now recognizes over 40 different neuromuscular diseases that are similar to muscular dystrophy in etiology and disabling effects. These forms of degeneration are the most common group of muscular disorders. It is infrequent but possible to encounter other muscular disorders; but general treatment will be similar in the development of leisure skills.

Classifications of Muscular Dystrophy.   Three common forms of muscular dystrophy are classified by age of onset and affected muscle groups. *Childhood* muscular dystrophy (also known as pseudohypertrophic, or Duchenne's, muscular dystrophy) is the most common type of muscular disease and displays the most rapid progression. Childhood muscular dystrophy is a hereditary disease, transmitted and carried by females but most often manifested in male offspring. The onset occurs during early childhood, usually before age 6. The pelvic musculature is affected first, weakening gait and usually causing some loss of independence by age 10. Progression involves general weakening, loss of voluntary muscle control, and eventual death around age 20 due to secondary involvement (i.e., respiratory infection or cardiac failure). *Lime girdle* dystrophy is identifiable by several general symptoms and by the eventual severity of progression. Paralysis of the pelvic musculature and the shoulder area is typical. The disease usually progresses to complete loss of voluntary movement in these areas and may be a direct or indirect cause of death during middle to later adulthood. A third less common type of dystrophy is called *Facioscapulohumeral*. This type affects persons during puberty. At the onset of disease, a relaxation and loss of control of facial muscles occurs. Progression from the facial area will eventually involve the shoulder girdle and upper arm muscles. The course is usually slow, and disability can remain mild to moderate (O'Leary, 1987).

Description of Limitations.   The patient having muscular dystrophy should generally be included in as many daily activities as possible, should practice good weight control, and should remain moderately active with a regular fitness routine. It is particularly important to encourage comfortably high activity levels prior to and after orthopedic devices are in place. The patient may be feeling a serious loss of independence and needs to realize that she or he is still able to maintain personal fitness and an active life-style.

Contraindicated activities are those that cause extreme muscle strain, cardiovascular stress, or, at the opposite extreme, long periods of nonactivity. Because eventual death usually occurs from respiratory infection or cardiopulmonary weakness, every effort should be made to maintain healthy tissue in these areas. Personal counseling and group therapy also should be made available to individuals to enhance their desire to pursue leisure behaviors.

Cerebral Palsy

Cerebral palsy is a condition that is characterized by the inability to control muscular and postural movement. It is caused by damage done to, or incomplete development of, the motor control portions of the brain (Berkow & Talbot, 1977). The condition is static and will not degenerate; however, preventive therapies are necessary to treat the individual adequately. The causes are varied and are determined on an individual basis. The most frequent causes are prenatal infection, anoxia before or during birth, fetal cerebral hemorrhage, metabolic disturbance, postnatal accident, central nervous system infection, or any cause that may cut off the supply of oxygen to the brain early in life. Diagnoses often cannot support a single cause or causes.

Classifications of Cerebral Palsy.   Persons who have cerebral palsy are classified by the muscular condition and degree of bodily involvement they display. Muscular conditions displayed can be grouped into five areas. It is possible to see any combination of the following descriptions manifested in one individual (Adams, Daniel & Rullman, 1982).

Spasticity:	Spastic cerebral palsy displays increased muscle tone stiffness (hypertonia) and immediate contraction upon stretching of affected muscle tissue.
Athetosis:	Athetoid cerebral palsy is a show of recurring involuntary, gross motor movement that is aggressive and made with no purpose.
Ataxia:	Ataxic cerebral palsy is more subtle and is recognized by a poor sense of balance in walking and standing that may

range from a slightly awkward appearance to quite irregular movement in normal activity.

Rigidity: Rigidity is usually displayed in combination with other types of cerebral palsy and is often intermittent. It is usually associated with extensive brain damage and mental retardation.

Tremor: A tremor is an involuntary motion with a regular rhythm that can occur spontaneously or be present with only specific attempted movements.

Further classification of cerebral palsy involves describing the number limbs affected:

monoplegia—one limb

paraplegia—both legs

hemiplegia—one side of the body, laterally

triplegia—three extremities (rare)

quadriplegia—all four extremities

The amount of residual control can also be used to describe the degree of neurological impairment:

mild—usually ambulatory; speech is understandable

moderate—locomotive impairment; requires assistive orthoses; speech possibly impaired

severe—whole-body involvement; uses wheelchair; usually no speech

Description of Limitations. Persons having cerebral palsy generally should be encouraged to participate as fully as possible in recreational activity. Children should not be excused from physical education classes. Cerebral palsy damage is nonprogressive, and physical activity can help to maintain existing ability. Activity may, however, be contraindicated by seizure activity, and recommendations or limitations should be stated by the neurologist. As normal as possible organizational sports and games and social play should be encouraged. Adaptations that are practical should be made as needed to ensure success in recreational activity.

Multiple Sclerosis

Multiple sclerosis is a disease that attacks various areas of the central nervous system (the brain and spinal column). Its name derives from the characteristics of the disease. *Multiple* means many or varying, and *sclerosis* means scarring or hardening. This disease occurs without known cause and strikes men and women aged 20–40. The process involves spontaneously appearing lesions in the spinal cord or brain at nerve endings because of a disappearance of the protective nerve coverings.

As the lesions heal, sclerosis, or scarring, occurs that can prevent the transmission of neurological impulses to and from the brain. The result of these impaired or lost transmissions can be muscle spasm, loss of sensation, and loss of voluntary movement of large muscle groups (O'Leary, 1987). The exact location and severity of sclerosis will determine the actual individual impairment. The changes in life-style for persons with multiple sclerosis are often drastic, and there is no cure, but prognosis for practical management of the disease is good.

Classifications of Multiple Sclerosis. Multiple sclerosis is not categorized by symptom or type. The only type of class referred to is that which concerns the number of body parts affected. During later progression, the level of severity can be referred to. Multiple sclerosis does not follow any set pattern of development. It effects are strictly determined by the location of lesions and the severity of scarring. Some patients live nearly normal lives, and others suffer severe attacks that leave them very disabled during early onset.

As lesions occur, patients experience severe symptoms; as lesions heal, relief of some symptoms may occur. These episodes are known as periods of exacerbation and remission, and will occur throughout the progression of the disease. A frequent example of this process is the spontaneous loss of independent ambulation during exacerbation, with a return of that ability during remission. Remission can involve a return to nearly normal ability. But if scarring is severe, little or no improvement may be visible. Periods of exacerbation and remission occur on a very individual basis and follow no pattern of progression, though later in life it is common for individuals to need orthotics or personal assistance, particularly in the areas of daily living skill performance. There is no cure or preventative for multiple sclerosis, but uncomfortable symptoms often respond favorably to drug therapy.

Description of Limitations. The patient having multiple sclerosis will display both physical and emotional fluctuation. Counseling is an important part of treatment, as is drug therapy.

Drugs used to treat multiple sclerosis allow the patient lacking muscle control or having sensory impairments to be more comfortable. The following common drug types are used, and each has side effects:

anti-inflammatory—occasional gastrointestinal distress

muscle relaxants—drowsiness, headache, low blood pressure, and feeling of weakness *corticosteriods*—headache, fluid retention, gastrointestinal distress, and depression

Active therapy should be performed at a comfortable pace, set by the patient. Overactivity can cause double vision, slurred speech, and loss of sensation or muscle control. Because of possible loss of sensation, care must be taken in extreme cold to cover and check the affected body parts periodically. Overheating can exacerbate any of the patient's symptoms; therefore, activity should be performed for shortened time periods. Activity that is social and/or ensures successful participation should be encouraged. It is important for social/psychological adjustment that the patient remains in mainstream settings.

Spina Bifida

Spina bifida is a congenital birth defect of the spinal column and/or cord that occurs early in prenatal development as the central nervous system is forming. The defect, usually located in the lumbar area, is present when the covering of the spinal cord is displaced and forms a sac-like protrusion, causing improper formation of vertebrae and leaving the abnormal formation externally exposed. The effects of this birth defect range from not noticeable effects, to paraplegia, to hydrocephalus and its resulting mental retardation (O'Leary, 1987). Prognosis is good for most births, and even the more severe defects are manageable in an everyday setting.

Classifications of Spina Bifida. Types of spina bifida can be delineated by the amount of neurological abnormality present. The original defect will not worsen after repair (Berkow & Talbot, 1977).

Spina bifida occultats—a slight defect in fusion, detectable only by X-ray. This condition can go unnoticed because the skin and spinal cord are unaffected and treatment is not required.

Meningocele—an evident protrusion from the vertebrae that forms but is filled with only spinal fluid. Treatment will involve immediate closure to prevent infection, that is, meningitis. Voluntary function is rarely impaired.

Myelomeningocele—an evident protrusion found at the lumbar level. It contains actual portions (nerves) of the spinal cord and therefore always produces some degree of neurological impairment and loss of voluntary muscle control. The amount of involvement depends upon the vertebral level of the cord lesion. Generally, lower lesions produce less neurological impairment. A common secondary problem accompanying this type of spina bifida is called hydrocephalus. Hydrocephalus involves abnormal enlargement of the head due to unabsorbed spinal fluid. If not treated immediately by "shunting" fluids from the brain to vascular or abdominal cavities, brain damage will result.

Description of Limitations.   The patient having spina bifida should be encouraged to participate in as many normal leisure skills as possible and to work with his or her abilities toward participation in adapted activities such as wheelchair sports. During participation, patients should become accustomed to periodic checks of the area/limbs suffering from lack of sensation or poor circulation. Severe cold can cause frostbite quite rapidly. Decubitus ulcers may occur where friction from orthoses caused by activity cannot be sensed. If the participants is prone to seizure, body temperature and activity should be monitored.

Spinal Injury

The spinal cord is a complex column contained within the vertebrae that serves to provide reflex actions and to transport impulses to and from the brain. If this cord is injured, impairment of this function occurs. The nature of impairment is determined by the extent and location of the injury.

The spinal cord is not able to regenerate; therefore, impairment from spinal injury is permanent. A complete severance of the cord results in loss of function below the injury, and a partial lesion will result in some loss of sensation, depending upon the level and severity of the injury.

Classification of Spinal Injuries.   The vertebrae are numbered and divided into four categories by location. The cervical vertebrae are in the neck and are numbered 1–8. The thoracle segments are numbered 1–12 and cover the area of the upper chest to the lower back. Below are the lumbar vertebrae, numbered 1–5, and the sacral vertebrae, numbered 1–5. Severance in the cervical area will cause sensory and motor losses from the neck and arm muscles to the entire body. A lesion at the thoracic level will cause loss of the sensation below the chest. Lower lesions will cause a variety of sensation losses, including hip, knee, ankle, foot, bowel, bladder, and reproductive organs.

The abbreviated description of the location of an injury will contain the corresponding first letter of the area (C, T, L, or S) and the number of the vertebrae closest to the injury (1–8, 1–12, 1–5, and 1–5, respectively). Patients having spinal injuries are further categorized by the amount of residual voluntary function and are usually paraplegic (two extremities affected) or quadriplegic (four extremities affected) (Adams, Daniel & Rullman, 1982).

Description of Limitations. The patient having a spinal injury may have many more emotional and mental barriers to overcome than the spina bifida patient, even though many of the symptoms, activities, and contraindications are the same. For some patients, recreational therapy may help immediately, and for others, emotional recovery may take priority and much time. In general, physical recovery/rehabilitation is considered to have reached its maximum six months past the original trauma. There may be small changes after this time, but dramatic improvements will not occur. Leisure pursuit can be prescribed to help in overcoming denial, anger, and fear, and should be used as soon as the patient will accept it. In sports competition, the athlete should be sure that his or her chair and safety equipment comply with regulations in order to avoid injury. Frequent checks of the areas without sensation should be made for the prevention of decubitus ulcers. In colder climates, attention needs to be paid to the same areas to prevent skin damage from cold temperatures. In more severely involved individuals, attention must be paid to respiratory problems in all activities. Any suspicion of urinary tract infection should cease activities, and medical attention must be immediate.

PURPOSE OF THERAPEUTIC RECREATION

The goal in the treatment of persons having neurological and neuromuscular disorders is to facilitate maximum leisure participation with a minimum of adaptations. All appropriate objectives reflect this goal. The therapeutic program should provide optimum independence and develop a sense of choice between leisure experiences. It also should enhance development of a leisure life-style that is as normal as possible for the patient. More specific treatment objectives are the following:

1. To enhance physical growth, using purposeful explanation of basic gross motor movement and an adapted environment that allows for freedom of movement.
2. To enhance personal growth through emphasis on sociorecreational activity.
3. To facilitate participation in lifetime leisure skills and those in which individuals can receive the highest level of achievement, with or without adaptation.
4. To include activities that clients can use to develop community access skills toward at least a semi-independent level of functioning.

Many interventions are incorporated in treatment plans. Discussion of six commonly identified interventions follows.

Aquatics

An aquatics program is the most practiced method of treatment currently available for persons with neurological or neuromuscular impairments. Swimming is generally available throughout the community on a year-round basis. Various types of pool facilities include those located in the community or neighborhood, private clubs, hospitals and rehabilitation centers, and recreation centers. Aquatics programs can accommodate nearly any class of disabling condition because aquatics has many possibilities for adaptation. The general therapeutic effects of a regular program include the following:

1. Freedom from orthoses, braces, crutches, body jackets, arm splints, and wheelchairs.
2. Increased circulation through greater movement allowed by buoyancy.
3. Relaxation of spastic muscle groups.
4. Feeling of accomplishment and independence.
5. Increase in or maintenance of strength and endurance.
6. Greater equality to nonhandicapped peers.

Basic swim skills, balance and coordination exercises, body awareness games, games that teach rules of play, hand-eye exercises, cardiovascular and relaxation techniques also provide for general skill improvement.

Horseback Riding

Therapeutic horseback riding arenas have been located in the United States for nearly 20 years. They originated in England, where riding is a very popular sport. The popularity of horseback riding as an accepted therapy is growing rapidly (Adams, Daniel & Rullman, 1982). Goals for the therapist and rider include mastery of a sport, control of a moving animal, stimulation of good balance and postural responses, stretching of muscles, and development of outdoors/animal appreciation activities. Adapted programs are available at many centers across the country. Some of the common equipment adaptations used are the following:

Adapted rein—A wooden handle is added to enhance grip and overall control. Hand-hold loops also can be added for more severe hand involvement.

Safety belts and vests—These supports allow side-walkers to control the rider's balance more effectively and less obtrusively.

Adapted stirrups—The outside face of the stirrup can be made of breakaway material to ensure a release in the event of a fall.

Devonshire boot—This stirrup is shaped like a large boot toe piece and is used for the rider having shortened heel cords or weak ankles.

Arts and Crafts

A therapeutic arts and crafts program incorporates the use of art to develop skills and increase the individual's leisure repertoire. Compensation and adaptation allow for personal success and fine motor movement. Projects that incorporate motor skills can be adapted and motivate the patient to be mobile. Projects such as working on murals encourage socialization, cause interaction, and improve self-esteem. Active art projects such as body tracing or dancing barefoot in finger paint can motivate younger patients to be mobile. Art activities that are movement oriented allow individual success and incorporate useful art skills. Such activities include clay modeling, abstract painting to music, chalk drawing on large surfaces, and creating cardboard likenesses of everyday items made from tactilely-stimulating materials. Common (and easy) adaptations of tools include the following:

1. Foam rubber on grip areas of utensils
2. Velcro strips to strap utensils to arms, hands, even heads
3. Shaving brushes for painting
4. Used roll-on deodorant bottles filled with paint, as paint rollers
5. Blackboard chalk holders (used by teachers)

Occupational therapy departments also have other useful materials adaptations (Rodriguez, 1984).

Skiing

Skiing for disabled persons was formally introduced to this country on a sizable scale when disabled war veterans became vocal in expressing their need and desire to ski. The first adaptations were made for this group consisting of amputees and paraplegics. Teaching adapted ski techniques requires a full assessment of needs. The individual must be intrinsically motivated to learn to ski. The actual teaching of skiing must adhere as closely as possible to the currently accepted American Teaching System to promote the individual's full potential for fulfillment. Skiing can be a big boost to self-esteem and can create feelings of independence. The exercise is strength and endurance building. Most programs employ at least one therapeutic recreation specialist, equipment specialists, and paid and volunteer instructors, and seek the consult of occupational therapists, physical therapists, and physicians. Standard adapted equipment includes the following:

Mono ski and sit ski—devices allowing skiers to ski from a sitting position

Outrigger—forearm crutch with a ski tip and braking system mounted on a rocker base

Ski bra—metal clamps attaching to ski tips connected by an eyelet, used to stabilize the position of the ski tips

Lifts and cants—wedges of various materials up to one inch in size used to fit in under boots or under binding to accommodate postural abnormalities

Walker—short skis, flat mounted to a walker, with the skier using ski bras to stabilize his or her skis with walker skis. Used mostly for the younger skier who may still be using a walker rather than crutches (O'Leary, 1987)

Social Play and Independent Activity

Social games and the development of independent activity compose a sizable portion of therapeutic recreation programs. These types of interaction are often the most feasible and most important in the daily life of the patient having a neurological or neuromuscular disorder. Knowledge of social game play provides a common bond with the mainstream and often, with or without adaptation, allows the disabled player to participate throughout the progression of the disease. In cases where disease onset occurs after birth or in early adulthood, social interaction through social game play can help offset feelings of helplessness and isolation. Special consideration for emotional status and personal interest must be made. The assessment of leisure skills will provide very important baseline information for the therapeutic recreation specialist and other therapists as well. Simple adaptations such as card holders can be made for card play. Playing games using partners will work for some games. In teaching this type of skill, the therapeutic recreation specialist must recognize four important considerations:

1. The client must have reasonable access to the activity.
2. The activity should be common enough to allow frequent social interaction.
3. The participant should participate on an active enough level to feel success.
4. The games learned should easily generalize to a number of settings.

Wheelchair Sports

Formal introduction of wheelchair sports occurred during the early 1950s, and again the first players were paralyzed war veterans. During the

later 1950s, with the onset of polio, many postpolio victims became participants as well. Sports commonly engaged in today are basketball, swim
competition, weight lifting, and marathons. Therapeutic goals for these
activities are related to the establishment of an as normal as possible leisure
life-style (Adams, Daniel & Rullman, 1982). Wheelchair sports have all of
the same benefits for the disabled and nondisabled player. The therapeutic
recreation specialist assumes an administrative role in these types of activities, because they are commonly team or programmatically oriented. The
TR specialist becomes the facilitator by offering and publicizing the programs, creating the practice sessions, and organizing competitive play.

COMMON SERVICE SETTINGS

Therapeutic recreation services are available in a wide variety of settings.
The most common service settings are hospitals, institutions, nursing
homes, small group residential placements, community-based programs,
and private consultative services.

Hospitals

The therapeutic recreation specialist working in a hospital setting will
encounter a number of types of service needs. The short-term patient may
require simple diversional activity while recovering from an operation or
relapse. The patient who has been admitted for physical rehabilitation will
require an interdisciplinary program designed for reentry into the community. A third type of patient is the individual suffering severe symptoms of
later stages of a progressive disease. A program of activity for such an
individual will usually be passive and implemented on a one-to-one basis,
but often will include close family members, either as coparticipants or as
cofacilitators.

Institution

Institutional settings, such as state or county long-term care hospitals,
usually provide care for impaired individuals who are there due to parental
or guardian placement. Some may have no other resource for care. Facility
populations generally are more adult than pediatric.

All institutions supported by public funding will have a recreation
therapist on staff as part of an interdisciplinary team. Each patient is
assessed individually, and personal goals are set. However, because of staff-
to-patient ratio, activity is usually structured for group participation, which
may be a frequent obstacle and can be very dehumanizing to participants.
Treatment in general, for the institutional population, is geared to basic
leisure skill acquisition and socialization. Each individual program will be

oriented to community reentry, even in the most severe instances, to keep as normal a process as possible.

Nursing Home

Private nursing homes, though generally housing an aging population, provide care for persons needing complete 24-hour per day care. Their population will be limited to adults.

Persons having severe impairments during the later stages of progressive diseases such as muscular dystrophy or multiple sclerosis lose voluntary muscle control and display secondary symptoms such as nystagmus (rapid horizontal eye movements), fibrillations and/or fasciculations (errant gross and fine motor firing). Thus they require the level of care afforded by a nursing home. Because such individuals do not fall into the category of traditional nursing home patient, they often have large blocks of idle time. Despite the loss of muscular control, such persons often retain high levels of cognitive ability. Therapy will usually involve passive activity and one-to-one sessions in which special care is taken to provide intellectual stimulation. During the severe stages of disease or severe involvement, the patient suffers from feelings of helplessness and depression. Recreation therapy can alleviate such feelings. When possible, group participation and social interaction should be encouraged, alternating with one-to-one activity.

Residential Care Settings

Residential care can be provided by state or local government, private agencies, or a combination of both. It is likely that the clientele will be adults whose conditions are severe. Residential care facilities are located in a variety of locations within the community. Each facility will usually house three to six individuals and be staffed 24 hours a day by qualified staff. Funding sources for residential care include private insurance, community schools, and government funds. Each resident has a specifically designed program for daily living and, if under age 21, an individual education plan. Prescribed recreation and leisure skill development can occur in either situation. Therapeutic recreation specialists can be school employees, agency employees, or private consultants. The role of the TR specialist can be consultative or direct service related; also, he or she can provide resources and/or leisure education for the residential staff.

Private Care Settings

Private care settings are probably the most personalized and beneficial to the patient. Some individuals have the personal funding to pay for this service, and some insurance plans will allow for this type of cost. The therapeutic recreation specialist is usually hired as a private consultant whose duties include personal program development, direct services provision, and transportation. Ideally, the therapist will provide independent participation opportunities. Although this setting is the most beneficial to patient and therapist, it is by far the least frequently encountered.

Community

The recreation therapist in community-based programs will most often be a provider of direct service. Community-adaptive recreation programs usually provide a variety of leisure opportunities for individuals having mild to moderate disabilities. Programs may offer some group transportation. Classes are usually held on a medium to large group basis. It is common to find students and other community-oriented persons as volunteer staff in such programs.

The recreation therapist in community-based programming may be responsible for program development, instruction, hiring and directing part-time staff and students, arranging transportation, program publicity, and serving as an advocate and agency liaison. The size and scope of community-based therapeutic recreation programs will vary greatly according to the size of the community, the general program acceptance, and the size of the population served. Recently, many wheelchair sports programs have been initiated by public park and recreation systems and various civic organizations.

CURRENT BEST PRACTICES AND PROCEDURES

Assessment

To plan effectively for and direct purposeful prescriptive therapeutic recreation services for individual clients, a thorough assessment of the individual's leisure life-style must be completed. The specific assessment instrument utilized will vary from setting to setting. Relevant points to consider when choosing an assessment tool are (1) the specific needs of the population being served, (2) the programming goals and objectives of the agency, and (3) any accrediting association expectations.

After determining what is needed from an assessment for a specific setting, the practitioner should review current published assessment instruments and contact other similar agencies to compare assessment formats. In many settings, one instrument or assessment tool may not offer sufficient comprehensive information. Several forms of assessment may be combined, such as interest surveys, leisure assessment instruments, interviews, and observations. Once designed or adapted, the assessment format should be reviewed and field-tested for reliability and validity.

A comprehensive assessment format used in programs designed for individuals having neuromuscular or neurological disorders may include the following areas of concentration questions or focus points (Peterson & Gunn, 1984; Fait & Shrivers, 1985; Kraus, 1978):

1. *Clinical findings*—physicians' reports, adjunctive therapy assessment, treatment team recommendations, intake interview notes, patient records (including gross and fine motor assessments), diagnosis, prognosis, and contraindicated activities.

2. *Cognitive domain*—current cognitive functioning level (including reading, writing, and comprehensive abilities), Individual Education Plans (IEPs—special education schools) or Individual Habilitation Plans (IHPs—residential centers).

3. *Affective domain*—psychological testing reports, self-esteem inventories, personality profiles, patient's account of emotional well-being, body image, and patient's reaction to the effects of disease or disorder, observations of the patient's abilities to express effect and emotions.

4. *Social domain*—social skills and interpersonal awareness questionnaires, family and/or social circles, patient's self-report of family relations, assertiveness, social fears, current social activity involvement—group, individual, segregated, or mainstreamed.

5. *Perception of leisure*—current and past leisure activities and interests, attitude toward leisure, perceived barriers toward participation, knowledge of available recreational service funding, transportation, and personal goals for future leisure life-style.

Assessment information is generally summarized in a narrative format and includes all pertinent information, completed instruments, and observational reports. Assessment implementation varies from service setting to service setting. Hospitals often require that the assessment be initiated within 24–48 hours of admission; residential centers may have 7 days, whereas community settings complete assessments prior to or during program participation.

Planning

Once completed, the comprehensive assessment serves as the basis for developing an individual's treatment plan. The treatment plan should also include specific long- and short-term goals and objectives, prescribed leisure activities, interdisciplinary treatment team recommendations, and client input. The goals are generally long-term and should address the need of deficient areas pinpointed in the assessment. Objectives are short-term and should be specific, observable, and measurable statements designed to address the overall goal.

An example case follows: Patient A is nearing completion of hospital rehabilitation following a spinal cord injury that has left him paralyzed from the hip down, requiring utilization of a wheelchair.

- *Designated need area*: Patient lacks knowledge of available leisure services in the community.
- *Goal*: Patient needs to develop knowledge of available adapted community recreational resources.
- *Objective*: Patient will attend biweekly community resourcing session for four weeks, completing a personalized leisure resource guide by the end of the sessions.

Activity prescriptions are often included within specific goals and objectives, yet additional activities related to overall treatment goals that are deemed beneficial to the client are also included within the treatment plan.

Treatment plans should include activities from the three domains of therapeutic recreation services: (1) therapy (activities designed to ameliorate specific need areas); (2) leisure education and counseling; (3) leisure participation (Peterson & Gunn, 1984). A client's specific need areas may require more of one type of activity, and those needs will vary as treatment progresses and goals are met. For example, an individual in a hospital setting suffering from the later stages of a degenerative disease will require more therapeutic/rehabilitative activities than an individual with a mild form of cerebral palsy in a mainstreamed community recreation program. The mainstreamed individual would be in need of participation activities designed to facilitate an independent leisure life-style.

On a scheduled basis, treatment plans should be reviewed, revised, and updated. The specific schedule will vary based on this setting. Charting or logging progress, or lack of progress, toward specific goals is often accomplished on a daily, weekly, or monthly basis. Overall treatment plans are reviewed by the practitioner, therapeutic recreation department, and/or treatment team.

Discharge summary and transition planning are the final phases of treatment planning. Ideally, preparation of discharge should be encompassed within the initial treatment plan through long-range goals. Transition planning is often prepared in consultation with the client prior to discharge. It involves the following:

1. *Projective planning*—determining activities the client is interested in and capable of pursuing within his or her placement.
2. *Leisure education*—educating the client with regard to the recreational resources available within the community and how to utilize them.
3. *Resources*—locating resources available to the client, such as transportation options, equipment sources, and funding availability.

Implementation

In establishing a therapeutic recreation program for individuals who have neurological and neuromuscular conditions, several points should be considered (Fait & Shrivers, 1985; Peterson & Gunn, 1984):

1. Agency or service setting goals and objectives
2. Therapeutic recreation department goals and objectives
3. Purpose of programs
4. Client needs and interests
5. Staff skills
6. Facilities and equipment available

Agency Goals.   The philosophy of service and program objectives set by the agency should serve as the basis for programmatic philosophy formation. Accrediting association guidelines also serve as a basis for establishing programming structure.

Department Goals.   The therapeutic recreation department establishes a philosophy of service, purpose, and goals, and objectives from which specific programs are developed. The programs are designed to fulfill stated objectives and provide services in the three domains of recreational therapy (therapy, leisure education, and recreation participation).

Purpose of Programs.   The program offered within a therapeutic recreation program should have stated intention, directive, and/or programming outlines. Only in this way can programming be purposeful. These are prepared prior to program implementation and should be reviewed and updated as needed throughout programming.

Client Interests and Needs.   The initial client assessment form offers the baseline of information needed to match participant interests and needs with agency programming goals and abilities. If participants interests and needs are not taken into account, the success and relevancy of the program would be in question.

Staffing.   A great deal of program planning revolves around the competency, skills, and composition of available staff. Practitioners and students interested in working with this population should have a thorough knowledge and understanding of neuromuscular and neurological disorders. Course work in anatomy, physiology, kinesiology, and medical terminology are highly recommended. Strong skills in psychology, social work, and counseling are also helpful. Staff need to be aware of and competent in transfer and transportation techniques for persons using wheelchairs.

Familiarity with the variety of orthopedic apparatus and adaptive equipment is essential, as is knowledge of leisure skill adaptation. If staff skills are not adequate for programming needs, additional training is in order.

Facilities.   Facilities and available equipment are important factors to consider in planning and implementing programs. Many facilities or agencies lack the necessary facilities and equipment to provide the programming most beneficial to their population. By networking with another agency's fund raising and by innovative programming, many departments are able to expand programming possibilities. Many agencies will allow other agencies or groups to use their facilities during off-program hours for minimal fees or in exchange for other facility usage. It is important to cultivate a working relationship with agency development office personnel. By making them aware of departmental needs and your "wish list," the practitioner augments the potential for receiving needed equipment and supplies.

In reviewing all these factors and others pertinent to a specific setting, a planned and purposeful program that meets the needs of the population being served can be developed.

The actual programs designed will vary from setting to setting, based on the above factors. For example, the therapeutic recreation department of a large rehabilitative hospital may offer a variety of activities. A representative daily schedule follows:

10:00–10:45	One-on-one diversional bedside activities for bedridden postoperative patients, such as board games, cards, and/or small craft projects.
11:00–11:50	Therapeutic swim for patients requiring range-of-motion exercise prescribed by a physician.
1:00–1:50	Crafts class in the craft room with a variety of small craft projects that can be completed in a short period of time (1–3 session) are available for the participants. Adaptive equipment is also available.
2:00–3:30	Learning to use a sport wheelchair in the gym for patients in the leisure education phase of rehabilitation.
3:45–4:45	Fundamentals of wheelchair basketball for patients nearing discharge and the special recreation phase of treatment.
4:00–4:50	Community resource class for patients prior to discharge to learn about resources available to them within their community; for example, wheelchair-accessible recreational centers, social groups, local

branches of the Muscular Dystrophy Association and the United Cerebral Palsy Association.

6:00–8:00   Movie on grounds (diversional programming component).

6:00–8:00   Out-trip to local mall or community event; leisure education in the community.

The special recreation department of a local park district's programming day may look like this:

10:00–10:50   Preschool nonambulatory swim and water exercise at local hospital's therapeutic pool.

11:00–11:50   Preschool play session integrated program for disabled and nondisabled participants involving age-appropriate games, crafts, and recreational activities.

1:00–2:30   Older adults nonambulatory swim at elderly housing project pool.

3:00–5:00   After-school recreational group for disabled and nondisabled population involving a variety of arts and crafts, music, sports, and out-trips.

6:00–6:50   Wheelchair sports skill session: Monday and Wednesday—basketball; Tuesday—tennis; Thursday—bowling.

7:00–8:30   Cooking class at area high school where participants learn the basics of cooking and the use of adaptive appliances when necessary.

These two examples demonstrate what a typical program serving those with neurological and neuromuscular conditions might look like.

Evaluation

An important factor in any therapeutic recreation program is the evaluation process. The evaluation process involves the review and assessment of the effectiveness of programs, departments, staff, clients, and facilities in relation to preestablished goals and objectives. Evaluation should occur on a periodic basis and should address both qualitative (quality of service rendered) and quantitative (numbers served, efficiency of staff and schedule) information. The format on an evaluation process will vary with agency settings. Hospitals will often require formalized evaluations monitored by the quality assurance and utilization review committees. Community settings are often self-monitored in that the department and participants often evaluate their own program and progress.

Evaluation Criteria.   Treatment plans, client progress notes, updates, charting, and observational reports often serve as the basis for periodic client evaluations. They are reviewed, and progress is assessed in relation to both patient and program goals. Pertinent questions to be approached in the client evaluation process include the following:

- Are goals and objectives of individualized treatment plans being addressed and met in a timely manner?
- Are treatment plans, assessments, progress notes, and updates completed by practitioners in a thorough manner? Appropriately? In a timely fashion?
- Are goals and objectives developed that relate directly to the need areas assessed?

Program outlines, client program evaluations, summaries, and updates completed weekly or monthly that include attendance records, programmatic summaries, and recommendations are useful tools in the program evaluation process. Pertinent questions to respond to during the program evaluation process include the following:

- Are your programs meeting the needs derived from the patient assessment?
- Are your programs fulfilling the interests delineated by your clientele through interest surveys?
- Are your programs fulfilling departmental goals and objectives?

In reviewing these aspects of programming and other information pertinent to a specific setting (e.g., quality assurance criteria, agency goals and objectives), a comprehensive evaluation process can be established and implemented.

APPLICATION OF THE TR PROCESS

CASE STUDY

The patient, Joe, is a preadolescent male who was diagnosed with Duchenne's muscular dystrophy at age 5. Symptoms at the onset of the disease were pelvic girdle weakness and loss of previously attained gross motor skills. The patient currently uses full leg bracing and forearm crutches, as well as a motorized "scooter" for ambulation. The patient lives in his natural home and has two parents and two older male siblings. He has been referred for assessment and prescription of a recreation program for home and neighborhood.

Assessment

After participation in a complete assessment procedure, the following will be considered. The patient is interested in active participation and is quite capable of swimming or wheelchair play. He is cognitively and emotionally sound and continues to score average or above average grades in school. Because of his normal cognitive ability, this patient is maintaining good social contact in and after school. Joe's siblings are able and willing to help when needed. Overall, his family is stable and very supportive.

Planning

In planning a leisure program for Joe, the overall content will encourage the use of existing skills, promote a positive self-image, and develop a more passive leisure repertoire. To achieve this three-fold goal, a program incorporating swimming, popular table games, and arts and crafts will be implemented.

Specific objectives in swimming will emphasize gross motor movement and competition within a handicapped league. Swimming will provide a relaxing outlet throughout the progression of the disease. Table games should be taught in order to promote social interaction and to keep a common bond with peers and siblings even when participation becomes limited. Arts and crafts will provide the same, as well as a release of creative energy, and will adapt easily later. All of the prescribed activities will be first implemented in the clinical setting. To fulfill the family's needs, the therapist will then assist in the generalization to community participation. As specific goals are met or need revision, outpatient visits will be made.

Implementation

Implementation of this program requires an ongoing review and record of the family, patient, and therapist's goals. The family or patient will be asked to document performance records and report to the therapist regularly. Because of the change in muscular status over time, it is very important to document performance to ensure that appropriate adaptations will occur so that continued participation and success is possible. In implementing Joe's swimming program, the therapist should see that skill development is provided in a clinical or otherwise controlled setting. Family teaching can then occur, and the therapist will assist the family in finding community programs, means of transportation, and means of funding on occasion. Specific skill objectives will be reviewed with each swim session (i.e., spring, summer, fall, etc.) participated in. Swim sessions consist of a series of lessons offered three to four times each year.

Clinical techniques for teaching table games mandate that the games played be current, age appropriate, and socially oriented. It is important that games are available in the patient's home and community (i.e., recreation centers or other children's homes). Possible examples are darts, card games, and video game play, with specific objectives for play predetermined.

Tactile and creative stimulation is the general goal for using arts and crafts, and attention again will be paid to community generalization. In determining objectives, the participant's specific needs are considered. Good examples of art skills to be learned through participation are ceramic sculpture (not premade greenware), use of airbrush, and graphic design. Patients may make planters, sculptures, T-shirts, posters, and murals with these skills. Individual or small group participation is required.

Evaluation

Evaluation must occur on an ongoing basis, and referral back to the initial assessment is essential for the individual to record his progress, in spite of his degenerating condition. The patient will be able to see objectives being met, and the therapist can head off potential failures before they happen. During a progressive disorder such as muscular dystrophy, adaptations in participation will occur. For example, swimming will become less competitive and focused more on achieving relaxation as a benefit. Passive leisure will begin to require adaptive devices and physical assistance. Participation may become so limited that alternative leisure choices will be made and new goals and objectives designed. Ongoing evaluation will provide the surest means of keeping a program structured for this individual's needs and is the best way to ensure continued participation and success.

TRENDS AND ISSUES

During recent years, community integration of persons having neurological and neuromuscular disorders has caused a heightened awareness of the need for better accommodations and disease treatments. Different agencies and associations sponsor large public fund-raising efforts to provide service for affected groups. However, such events also help make the public aware of the needs of persons having disabilities. Treatment is moving towards an outpatient and "at home" style as long as is possible and practical in view of the degree of patient disability. The introduction, several years ago, of small group homes has drastically reduced the operation of large care facilities and institutions.

Drug therapy for progressive disease has not provided any curative measures, but large strides have been made in the manufacture of drugs that slow the progression of disease and make patients more comfortable and able to participate in daily life. The growth of genetics counseling programs is also helping people understand and prevent chromosomally transmitted disorders of this type.

Through all of the above, prognosis for patients and their families has been greatly improved. The use of leisure education and therapeutic intervention to develop and maintain a leisure repertoire will continue to play a role in the habilitation and rehabilitation of persons having disabilities. The shift to small group and in-home settings will provide more personal and effective programs.

SUMMARY

This chapter presented an overview of neuromuscular and neurological disorders and the variety of settings in which the therapeutic recreation specialist can become a service provider. The range of ability level is great within this category of disorders, but the goal of maximal independent leisure function remains constant. The treatment varies with each individual case. Current practices have been discussed, yet it remains the responsibility of each therapist to ensure that practice standards are maintained. Assessment and evaluation have been discussed, and the need for and use of frequent documentation of progress has been stressed. A good understanding of neuromuscular and neurological disorders and the practice of the most current treatment will contribute to a more healthy life-style for those affected both directly and indirectly by these serious and debilitating conditions.

READING COMPREHENSION QUESTIONS

1. What are early symptoms of Duchenne's muscular dystrophy? Why are leisure education and physical activity important at around age 10?

2. In prescribing activity for patients having progressive muscular diseases, what are three general goals or concerns the therapist must consider?

3. Describe briefly the contents of a comprehensive assessment.

4. In designing a program of leisure participation for a patient having a recent spinal injury, discuss the importance of the generalization of skills and outpatient or follow-up visits with the recreation therapist.

5. What are the possible therapeutic goals of a regular aquatics program for a person having a neuromuscular or neurological disorder?

6. What is the importance of ongoing and frequent leisure skill evaluation of a person having multiple sclerosis?

SUGGESTED LEARNING ACTIVITIES

1. Visit your community/area adapted sports league. Many leagues have mixed competition so that persons who do not use wheelchairs can participate with wheelchair athletes. Enter a tournament such as a stand-up/sit-down tennis match.

2. Visit and compare service settings of hospital, institutional, private home, and residential (small group home, etc.) facilities in your community. Compare the various roles the therapeutic recreation specialist can assume.

3. Talk with representatives from specific organizations or agencies in your area to learn more about services that are available for persons with neurological and neuromuscular disorders. These include the Muscular Dystrophy Association, the Multiple Sclerosis Association, the Spina Bifida Association, and disabled veterans groups.

4. To learn more about the variation of orthopedic appliances available (their use and care) and appropriate lift and transfer techniques, contact physical therapists, orthopedic professionals, or the Muscular Dystrophy Association requesting information and a demonstration of these devices.

REFERENCES

ADAMS, R. C., DANIEL, A. N. & RULLMEN, L. (1982). *Games, sports, and exercises for the physically handicapped.* Philadelphia: Lea & Febiger.

BERKOW, R., & TALBOT, J. H. (1977). *The Merck manual.* Rahway, NJ: Merck Sharp & Dohme Research Laboratories.

FAIT, H. F., & SHRIVERS, J. S. (1985). *Special recreational services: Therapeutic and adapted.* Philadelphia: Lea & Febiger.

KRAUS, R. (1978). *Therapeutic recreation service: Principles and practices.* Philadelphia: W. B. Saunders.

O'LEARY, H. (1987). *Bold tracks skiing for the disabled.* Evergreen, CO: Cordillera Press.

PETERSON, C., & GUNN, S. (1984). *Therapeutic recreation program design: Principles and procedures* (2nd ed.). Englewood Cliffs, NJ: Prentice-Hall.

RODRIGUEZ, S. (1984). *The special artist's handbook: Art activities for handicapped students.* Englewood Cliffs, NJ: Prentice-Hall.

STOLOV, W. C., & CLOWERS, M. R., (1982). *Handbook of severe disability.* Washington, DC: U.S. Department of Education Rehabilitation Services Administration.

12

Cognitive Impairments

MIRIAM LEAHEY

OBJECTIVES

- Distinguish between the effects of damage to the left and right sides of the brain.
- Identify a minimum of three specific cognitive impairments.
- List three different recreation activities that could be used to strengthen attending skills.
- Describe the three major types of recreation programming planned for the cognitively impaired: therapeutic, leisure experience, and leisure education.
- Discuss the impact of cognitive impairment on social and affective functioning.

DEFINITION OF COGNITIVE IMPAIRMENT

The term *cognitive impairment* refers to a particular kind of disability that involves the loss, either partial or complete, of the following skills: perception, attention, memory, judgment, thinking (especially abstract thinking), decision making, language (both speaking and comprehension), nonverbal communication, problem solving, rote learning, and generalization of learning. Designating these skills as "lost" implies that the disabled person once possessed them, and indeed the focus of this chapter is on those adults who have previously enjoyed the full cognitive functioning that they have lost.

Such loss can come from many sources: depression, infectious disease, improper medication, excessive use of alcohol or drugs, brain tumor, even vitamin deficiency. This chapter will limit its discussion to cognitive impairments resulting from *head injuries* and *cardiovascular accidents* (strokes). Its object is not so much to provide detailed differential diagnoses of cognitive impairments, as to familiarize the reader with behavioral and attitudinal patterns recurring among patients with impaired mentation.

Data from the U.S. Department of Health and Human Services indicate that some 5 million Americans suffer from head trauma and cardiovascular accidents combined (Vital and Health Statistics, 1986). Thanks to improvements in medical technology and more effective rehabilitative procedures, over half of these accident victims will survive (Freese, 1979). In the comprehensive effort to rehabilitate stroke and head trauma clients, recreation plays a very important role (Rosenthal & Kolpan, 1986).

Among the 2,263,000 Americans reported suffering from the effects of head trauma in 1981, males outnumbered females almost two to one, many of them very young adults (Vital and Health Statistics, Nov. 1986). Stroke victims, by comparison, are apt to be older, with mean age 57 reported for the 2,715,000 Americans suffering the effects of cardiovascular disease in 1981 (Vital and Health Statistics, Dec. 1986).

Both head trauma, resulting from exterior accident, and stroke, resulting from internal accident, may result in a variety of limitations—physical, emotional, behavioral, social, as well as cognitive deficits.

CLASSIFICATION OF STROKES AND HEAD TRAUMA

Stroke and head trauma cases may be classified in a number of ways. The severity of the affliction is sometimes gauged by the number of days of post-trauma amnesia (pta). The extent and area of brain damage are very difficult to assess. Perhaps of greater interest to the therapeutic recreation professional is the level of cognitive functioning. The following eight-stage scale is one of the several classifications developed to define cognitive deficit (Ensley, MacLean, & Lewark, 1984).

Stage 1   Coma.

Stage 2   Generalized response, limited and inconsistent, often to pain only.

Stage 3   Localized and purposeful response.

Stage 4   Confused, agitated, heightened state of activity, aggressive, poor ADL (Activities for Daily Living). *This is the stage at which patients enter rehabilitation.*

Stage 5   Confused, inappropriate response, agitated, appears alert but does not respond to commands, highly distractable.

Stage 6   Confused, appropriate response, directive behavior—with cuing as needed. In this stage, old skills and ADL can be relearned. Memory is improving.

Stage 7   Automatic response, appropriate but rather robotlike, minimal confusion, shallow recall. Insight is poor—needs structuring.

Stage 8   Purposeful appropriate response, alert, no supervision needed, can drive, independent ADL, capable of abstract reasoning.

In addition to the above stages, injuries to specific areas of the brain result in different disabilities. Left-brain injury causes right-side hemiplegia, with impaired right-side movement and loss of the right visual field. Speech and language deficits are characteristics of damage to the left side of the brain. Some of the common language disorders are the following:

- *Expressive aphasia* (of thought, speech, writing): the patient knows what he or she wants to say but cannot say it. Patient cannot name objects, has a tendency to repetition, and may resort to gestures to express ideas.
- *Receptive aphasia*: a patient cannot make sense of words spoken or read, and has difficulty concentrating and/or following simple directions.
- *Global aphasia*: both expressive and receptive aphasia are present, and almost all language functioning is lost.

Right-brain injury is accompanied by difficulty in spatial and perceptual tasks. There is marked difficulty in judging size, proportion, and form. Behaviors tend to be quick and impulsive, with poor judgment (for example, in matters of safety). With this group there is apt to be excessive talking and a notably shortened attention span, which precipitates a lack of interest and motivation.

DESCRIPTION OF LIMITATIONS

In addition to the limitations directly imposed by the extent and severity of the accident, psychological distress can be an even more limiting factor. Especially when the victim is a young adult or a breadwinner, the shock of moving from full vigor to a greatly restricted life-style can be overwhelming. Both strokes and head trauma require radical adjustment. The response that any individual makes reflects not only the severity of the precipitating disorders, but also inherent personality patterns, emotional conflicts present at the time of the accident, the environmental situation, and interpersonal relations.

Interpersonal relations are particularly affected when the impact of the accident is felt in identity. When physical prowess or attractiveness is central to identity, not only will the injured person suffer a crisis of identity, but there will also be a resulting confusion in relation to others (MacNeil & Pringnitz, 1982). A further impact on interpersonal relations comes when the accident necessitates radical role shifts; for instance, when the wage earner in a family becomes dependent on others to take over tasks associated with that role.

In addition to the physical limitations of the accident, the recognition of cognitive impairment may evoke a response of shame, depression, or fear. Such a response will shape the client's whole outlook on life, particularly his or her desire to participate in leisure activities. Cognitive impairments, on the other hand, are not equated with loss of affective functioning. Recreation is in many respects the treatment of choice for tapping the immense affective resources of the client with diminished cognitive capacity.

Cognitive limits require clarification. Both stroke and head trauma patients experience problems with attention. The attention span may be drastically shortened, or the focus of attention may be vague. With shifting of attention often comes impulsiveness of behavior, a limitation of particular significance in determining and pursuing goals.

Diminished capacity to focus the attention may contribute to or simply accompany memory problems. Although some patients find their short-term memory affected, with others it is the long-term memory that is affected, and in still other cases rote memory is diminished. Some are skillful at compensating for their memory losses; for others, the resulting insecurity is a major limitation to social interaction and to structuring and organizing behavior. Perhaps more than any other limitation, memory loss creates an enormous dependency on others. Professionals who have a strong need to nurture or to control need to be aware of this dependency in order not to contribute to it.

A further cognitive limitation in some clients is the weakening of the ability to think in the abstract, with a resulting preference for the concrete. This limitation is important for recreation program planning, because failure to recognize it may result in programs that exceed client capacity in subtle ways.

Rigidity of thought process is a further characteristic of those with cognitive impairment. In its effect, this is almost the opposite of the flitting of attention. With rigid thinking comes perseveration, the inability to let go of a syllable.

A general slowing of the mental processes may also serve to limit client abilities. Even more, it may limit others' perceptions of those abilities. It is important for the therapeutic recreation professional to recognize that not all client limitations arise from the client. Some of them come from the institutional environment and some, even, from the therapist.

Indeed, whatever the extent of cognitive limitations in these clients, the limitations are not nearly so global and unceasing as staff and family sometimes imagine. Although such limits are real, they are not total and unremitting. This is of vital importance, particularly for dealing with clients whose potential for cognitive rehabilitation is perceived as minimal. The very severely impaired will have times when they are able to focus their attention and even make decisions.

PURPOSE OF THERAPEUTIC RECREATION

As with any other special population, the purposes of therapeutic recreation with the cognitively impaired may be broadly divided as follows: (1) *therapeutic/clinical*, in which the therapeutic outcome is paramount; (2) *leisure/recreational*, in which quality of life and personal experience are paramount; and (3) *educational*, in which the development of leisure awareness, skills, and resources is paramount. It is frequently found in rehabilitation settings that of these three the first is seen as primary.

For clients with cognitive impairments, the therapeutic outcome centers around the acquiring or reacquiring of specific physical, affective, cognitive, or social skills. Because of the radical changes in life-style necessitated by the accident responsible for the cognitive loss, vocational goals are seen as very important in the treatment program. For clients whose cognitive impairment is concurrent with physical disabilities, the therapeutic outcome sought may be the maximizing of physical gains. In fact, Long, Govier, and Cole (1984), in their discussion of brain trauma, note that recovery from these injuries is largely viewed as a physical/medical problem in the United States.

In the same way, where the client's affective response to the loss presents the greatest obstacle to functioning, it must be the central focus of therapeutic intervention. Therapeutic recreation purposes in the affective domain may seek to reduce excessive/inappropriate affect or may attempt to facilitate release through expression. Affective goals will depend on the nature and extent of affective disorder, which will reflect personality and coping styles, support systems, and role reversals.

Cognitive retraining as an explicit purpose of therapeutic recreation has been the scope of much recent investigation (Fazio & Fralish, 1988). Indeed, recreation, because it can be more familiar and less threatening than many other interventions, may be a most effective vehicle for cognitive retraining. The word *retraining* implies a potential for restoration of functioning, but such restoration does not come about automatically. Cognitive training requires all the effort, patience, and commitment of physical training. Successful cognitive retraining also requires precise assessment of specific cognitive deficits. More than anything else, perhaps, it requires full collaboration between client and professional. Through this collaboration, skill can be strengthened in such a way as to touch many areas of a client's life. A recreational activity can be chosen to build a particular cognitive skill, such as attention. Strengthening attending skills will result in a reduction of impulsive behaviors, irritability, and frustration arising from the inability to focus attention. Reducing these unpleasant emotional responses will allow the client to participate in social situations with greater confidence. In this way, the circle of gain can expand so that therapeutic outcome is extended to many dimensions of the client's life.

If, at the same time, the chosen recreational activity is one that brings joy and delight and a sense of fun and freedom, then not only is the client's life enriched in the way in which everyone expects to be enriched through leisure, but for people with cognitive impairments, the leisure experience offers the added benefit of relief from the stress and demands of rehabilitation. Moreover, not only is the leisure experience refreshing, freeing, and even healing—in the holistic sense of that word—but for clients whose life-style has been abruptly shattered, it provides a continuity with life before the accident. Recapturing the enjoyment of former leisure pursuits is a way of rejoining one's own past. For these clients, that means rejoining a life that in many other ways is lost to them.

Therapeutic recreation purposes with stroke and head trauma patients look beyond the rehabilitation setting to the transitional phase of treatment and join the purpose of all interventions—to prepare clients for community living. Social skills, adjustment to the disability, confidence, and a host of other facets of reintegration are all part of the therapeutic recreation professional's concern for the client (Hackel, Berger, & Putz, 1986). A very special part of that concern is the developing of leisure awareness, leisure skills, and a leisure resource file for each client and his or her family (Heckathorn, 1979). The leisure education program is vital to cognitively impaired clients. It can mean the difference between successful community reintegration and a sense of loneliness and boredom that leads to further regression. Research indicates that leisure education is especially important for those clients who will not be able to return to work (Oddy & Humphrey, 1980). The emphasis on leisure education in the treatment of head trauma and stroke patients can lead to the adoption of an educational model for their care. In some facilities, leisure education is a collaborative effort of the education and leisure service programs (Heckathorn, 1979).

COMMON SERVICE SETTINGS

The accidents that result in head trauma or stroke are very different. One is internal and may not be noticed when it occurs; the other is external and is usually accompanied by violence. Because both result in brain damage, the injured person is brought to an acute care hospital for emergency treatment. After emergency measures are completed, intensive care and surveillance follow. There is then a period in a rehabilitation unit until discharge to a transitional living facility or the patient's home (Green & Eismont, 1984).

Each of the four treatment phases takes place in a different service setting. During the emergency treatment and intensive care, of course, patients are too seriously ill for recreation. In the rehabilitation and transitional phases of treatment, however, recreation has a very important contribution to make to a client's recovery, well-being, and future quality of life.

Within these two settings, therapeutic recreation specialists are an integral part of the rehabilitation team, working together with physiatrists, psychologists, nurses, social workers, speech therapists, occupational therapists, physical therapists, and neurologists. Because the patient's injury affects her or his whole life, she or he must be treated as a whole person. The team approach is considered the most effective way to provide holistic treatment (Adamovich, Henderson, & Auerbach, 1985).

The therapeutic recreation specialist, working within the team, is concerned not only with appropriate leisure functioning, but also with recreation activities to promote general treatment goals; for instance, strengthening social skills, cognitive skills, and other skills needed to live and work in the community.

At interdisciplinary team meetings, priorities are determined for intervention with stroke and head trauma patients. In many rehabilitation centers, a separate team is assigned to each disability; for example, there may be a stroke team, a head trauma team, a spinal cord injury team (Bolger, 1982). The teams become familiar with precise patterns within their area of specialization. The TR specialist, for instance, learns to see activity analysis in reference to the specific needs of stroke patients or of head trauma patients. Such team sharing can be very enriching for the professional as well as the client, but it can be very time consuming. In addition, it requires close communication among team members and a capacity to move beyond the traditional interpretation of professional roles (Howe-Murphy & Charboneau, 1987). A danger with the team approach is that the professionals may become so caught up in their own interaction that they leave out the most important member of the team—the patient.

In some rehabilitation and transitional settings, the educational model predominates. Particularly for young adult accident victims, vocational training is seen as a top priority, for the goal is to enable them to rejoin society as productive, self-sustaining members of the work force. The schedule in such settings resembles a school or work situation, with a highly structured series of classes or training sessions. Units with this type of focus may relegate recreation programs to the evening or weekend hours. Such an approach is not inappropriate for the patients, because even though seemingly displaced by work and school, leisure remains a central factor in the overall treatment program (Barthe, Chandron, & Fichter, 1985).

CURRENT BEST PRACTICES AND PROCEDURES

The dramatic increase in head injury and stroke survivors has necessitated the expansion of services to clients suffering from these injuries. Postacute rehabilitation services in particular are now more carefully differentiated to reflect levels of client need (Zahara & Cuvo, 1984).

Assessment

Assessment of cognitively impaired clients requires a review of all residual deficits from the injury, including cognitive, behavioral, physical, and emotional disabilities. With the concurrence of the treatment team, treatment goals will be determined by the deficit that presents the most serious obstacle to the client. When the client is not able to make this prioritization, family members may be able to act on his or her behalf. An important focus of the assessment process is on the capacity to return to previous roles. As with any other special population, assessment procedures with the cognitively impaired rely on observation, interviews with client, family, and staff, and review of the case history, including medical charts. Because these patients cannot always speak for themselves, careful observation is central to their assessment. In working with cognitive loss, it is important not to label clients as incompetent. Because their response is slow, their attention flits, and they find it hard to focus, it is easy to perceive stroke and head trauma patients as incapable of thinking or deciding. The staff's inner labeling can be a confirmation of the patients' own dark fears, so special care must be taken to believe in their potential.

Planning

Following upon assessment and triaging among residual deficits with the client, program planning in therapeutic recreation takes with this population the same course as with any other group, except that activities will be planned with special emphasis on preparing the client for reintegration into the community. Cognitive retraining is a special part of preparing for life at home—cognitive retraining for the full life, which includes social and leisure dimensions in addition to the work role.

Leisure activities for the development of cognitive and social skills begin very simply. Games of strategy and chance are appropriate for guiding clients from step to step in the process of organizing information, making decisions, planning a course of action. For those with very low tolerance for interference or competition, the first steps may have to be made in the company of the therapist alone or with a single partner. Wood (1983) describes the use of the board game Yahtzee, which makes no social demands but does call for selecting a strategy in order to win points. She compares this game with the more demanding Pit, played with hand signals and no verbal interaction, thus requiring eye contact and other nonverbal forms of communication. In this activity, attention must be focused on one's companions (competitors) in addition to one's own personal strategy.

Computer games are especially appropriate for clients who are cognitively impaired. These games can be adjusted to reflect individual skill levels and can be played alone, with one partner, or in a group. A number of them have been designed to meet the needs of this special population. Resistance to distraction can also be built into the computer game as a further training in attending. For the TR specialist who is interested in becoming an entrepreneur, developing special software for the cognitively impaired client would probably yield double gains.

Writing is especially valuable as an activity for stroke and head trauma patients. The physical act itself is beneficial, but even more important is the opportunity to get in touch with one's thinking through seeing it in writing. Educators for some time have recognized the importance of writing for learning—not just for learning to write, but for tracking one's process of thinking (Fulwiler, 1987; Parker & Goodkin, 1987; Gere, 1985). Keeping personal logs, free writing (very informal) or focused free writing (informal but directed), double-entry notebooks in which actions and reflections are recorded in separate columns, imaginary dialogues with favorite authors or heroes—all these are writing activities that will enable the clients to develop their powers of expression and at the same time will help them analyze their thinking process. If the client chooses to share these with the therapist, such sharing is received with utmost respect. The writings are in no way intended to be diagnostic indicators or the subject for team discussions. They are very private and personal. Their main value and strength lie in their not being judged. Clients who feel strong enough to share their writing in a group may wish to collaborate in creating a poem, essay, or story. For example, at the Kennedy Center in Edison, New Jersey, patients are asked to uncover the details of a story after having been given a brief vignette. All questions that will help solve the dilemma are posed in the story. Creative recreation professionals will see in this example a source of much rich programming.

The creative arts too can be used as a source for writing. Listening to music, contemplating a piece of fine art, watching a dance or a play, in addition to being enjoyable experiences can serve to provoke reflection; and the reflection can be written up, either for an increased sense of control of one's thoughts, for self-knowledge, or for sharing with the therapist, a friend, or even a group—all at the discretion of the client.

Implementation

The therapeutic recreation specialist learns from working with clients who are cognitively impaired that even apparently simple recreation activities require the capacity to organize information, to make decisions, and to engage in complex cognitive planning that is taken for granted in normal life. When these skills are lost, they require careful rebuilding. The most successful rebuilding takes place when all the agents are working together; this means that the client must have an integral part in planning the program. Because upon discharge clients will plan their own programs, it is necessary that they begin to address this task within the rehabilitation setting. Wood (1983) describes how clients at her rehabilitation center take turns planning outings. In a group, they analyze the possibilities and make decisions about the trip. At an early level of participation in this exercise, the decision might be as simple as choosing a movie from a list of those available. At a more progressive level of decision making, clients might volunteer to work with staff in such tasks as making reservations. Groups may brainstorm for ideas about special outings or may join the staff in researching information needed for the trips. At an even more sophisticated level, the groups might work through to a compromise on decisions.

As clients work though problems and difficulties, the process moves from being staff responsible to being client responsible. All of this, although part of a normal recreation program, involves the clients at a much more responsible level of participation than in the ordinary TR program, and constantly presses the client to greater levels of self-determination. Even if clients make mistakes (and they will!), they learn to correct the mistakes and prepare for a future when there will be no staff around to solve their problems.

Evaluation

The therapeutic recreation specialist constantly observes, analyzes, and records patient progress. With this population, precise documentation of functional change is imperative, for the whole team needs to be aware of gains or regressions, and these may make themselves manifest in the recreation hour as in any other. Checklists may be prepared so as to chart progress more efficiently, and good TR professionals are very creative at drawing up new forms to make the paperwork less tedious. With this population, paperwork is not just a drudgery; it is as vital a part of the therapeutic recreation professional's intervention as the tracking of an airplane that has met with an accident. Those on the ground (the professionals) do not know exactly where the airplane is and must depend on any available indicators to help track it. So it is with cognitively impaired clients. They are not able to say where they are, so very precise observation is necessary if they are to be guided to safety. For the same reason, self-report is extremely important with this group.

The whole team is depending on the precise progress notes of all team members. As the time for discharge draws near, the patient is carefully evaluated for reentry into the community. Here the evaluation of leisure awareness, leisure skills, and a leisure resource file is crucial. Trips to the community are part of the development of leisure resources. Evaluation of the family support group and of the capacity to return to the world of work is also part of the predischarge evaluation. A study by Weddel, Oddy, and Jenkins (1980) found that two years after discharge from rehabilitation, head trauma patients who were not working had fewer leisure activities and were more bored and more dependent on their families than were the workers who had been discharged at the same time.

Among the goals for leisure education programs among head-injured adults in rehabilitation, the following were reported by Fazio and Fralish (1988) as rated the most important by clients: development of social skills, decreasing isolation and withdrawal, community integration, and independent leisure involvement. To the extent that these goals are met, a therapeutic recreation program with the cognitively impaired might be evaluated as successful.

APPLICATION OF THE TR PROCESS

The following case is presented with a view to applying the four stages in the therapeutic recreation process to a client suffering from brain trauma.

CASE STUDY

George is a 24-year-old white male who sustained multiple injuries, including head injuries, in an automobile accident. The left side of his brain was injured, with resulting right-side limited mobility and expressive aphasia. George has a wife, aged 20, and a 2-year-old daughter. Prior to his accident, he was employed as a shoe salesman in a retail store. He is frantic about his wife and child, for whom he is sole means of support. His anxiety is exacerbated by his inability to express himself. Physical therapy and speech therapy are his main interests. Because he has never worked at any other job but selling shoes, his one goal is to recover in order to return to that work.

Assessment

Before meeting George, the TR professional will have reviewed his medical records, discussed his case with other professionals on the team, and interviewed his wife. An important fact is gathered in this process, namely, that George is left-handed, so the right hemiplegia is not as disruptive to his functioning as it would be if he were right-handed. He is able to write, although he cannot speak. Although George has a number of cognitive disorders—difficulty concentrating, paying attention, and communicating—the deficit that presents the most serious obstacle to his functioning is affective. This is readily apparent at the initial assessment interview. His anxiety escalates as he attempts to explain to the TR specialist that he is not interested in recreation. He sputters and stammers in his attempt to speak, and finally bursts into tears. The TR specialist sits with him in silence for a few moments; then, in a brief, empathetic (not pitying) response, lets him know that she will return and that together they will work on his goal of returning to his home and work.

As in most cases, the first interview with George occurs when the client is at a very low point. He has just been discharged from acute care but is still unaccustomed to the radical life change brought about by the accident, and to the full reality of his limitations. A major task in this first interview is to establish a relationship of mutual trust and respect, to deal honestly with the client, and to communicate a willingness to collaborate with him in the pursuit of his goals. Even though little seems to be accomplished in the initial interview with George, the assessment process has begun. It will continue, but sufficient information has been gathered to start the program planning.

Planning

Together with the interdisciplinary team, the TR specialist focuses on the need to reduce anxiety as the immediate treatment goal for George. Beyond that, TR goals are to strengthen attending skills through participation in adapted bowling (George's wife has indicated that prior to the accident he had been enthusiastic about bowling). A long-term goal is to help George identify activities that he might enjoy when he returns to the community, and help him find community settings where he might participate in the selected activities.

Appropriate behavioral objectives that George will achieve by the time he is discharged might be stated as follows:

- He will daily undertake to write about his feelings in a personal journal.
- He will engage in the bowling activity at least once weekly.
- He will identify a minimum of three activities in which he would like to participate in the community.
- He will make at least three trips to the community to visit recreation facilities near his home.

Implementation

From the outset, it is important that the therapeutic recreation specialist recognize her own feelings about George's impairments, and also about George's reactions to them. In this case, George was an innocent victim of an automobile accident, but it often happens that head trauma patients have been responsible for the accident in which they (and perhaps others) were injured. It is important for the therapist to examine his or her own feelings about the whole situation in order to come to the client with that "total positive regard" that Carl Rogers considers to be necessary for therapeutic relationships (1970).

Following upon the first visit, the therapist can invite George to attend a movie or other entertainment, either with his wife or in the company of the therapist. If George can write down his feelings, he can get some sense of control over them. This is especially necessary for those who cannot speak. Perhaps he will choose to share his journal with his wife or with the therapist. When he gets more emotional control, he may choose to share his writings in a discussion group.

If possible, one of the patients who belongs to the bowling group could escort George for his first bowling session, preferably a patient who had been as impaired as George has, but who shows improvement. In his wife's company, George can be escorted to a few community recreation facilities in order to choose among them. The choice will reflect activities offered, accessibility, and ambience, along with other preferences George may have.

Because George will be in the rehabilitation unit about six weeks, he has time to pursue these objectives at the same time that he works to regain his speech and full ambulation. He might be allowed a home pass two weeks prior to discharge in order to help him adjust to his living situation, including his leisure arrangements.

Evaluation

The TR professional keeps accurate and detailed notes of George's progress. Because he is highly motivated to get better, each gain spurs him on to new aspirations. It is important to keep these aspirations realistic and not to let him try to do everything at once, or he will set himself up for disappointment. If bowling, at which he once excelled, proves to be a source of dismay because he cannot reproduce his former high level of achievement, then another activity may be chosen. Perhaps learning a new activity would be better if he is competing with his former performance.

Essentially, the evaluation asks if the goals set at the beginning of the TR process have been met. In responding to this question, concrete examples are provided as evidence. In the ideal situation, a follow-up program would be drawn up in which George could return to the rehabilitation facility once a month for leisure counseling with the therapist. Where this is not possible, the TR specialist might ask George if she could call him from time to time to see how he is progressing. Providing some follow-up contact at the time of closure signals to the client that the therapist indeed does care, that the trust that has been build is genuine and is founded on a professional relationship, not just a professional obligation.

TRENDS AND ISSUES

Improvements in medical technology have recently brought higher levels of sophistication to the rehabilitation of stroke and head trauma patients. New interventions are costly, however, and recent attempts to contain medical costs have sharply limited the length of stay in rehabilitation facilities. In New York, for instance, new legislation will allow 37 days of rehabilitation to stroke patients and 47 days to head trauma patients. This will mean, of course, that some patients will be discharged too quickly. The newest legislation gives the patient 24 hours to refuse to accept discharge plans, in which case their appeal will be heard by an independent professional review board (N.Y.S. Hospital Code 405-25). Therapeutic recreation professionals will be drawn into this process, principally by being asked to document precisely the evaluation of their interventions. It means more paperwork and also a more stringent environment in which to pursue rehabilitation goals. The very thing necessary to avoid with head trauma and stroke patients is a sense of hurry, yet this will be necessitated under the new regulation. It will mean a higher degree of stress for the treatment team.

Increasingly important in rehabilitation are such ethical issues as: the right to refuse treatment, the right to be informed precisely of the procedures and objectives of treatment, the right to surrogate decision makers for those who are incompetent—such considerations add to the time and costs of service. They are very important parts of service delivery, but they place additional burdens of responsibility on the TR professional.

SUMMARY

Cognitive impairment may be attributed to a number of causes. This chapter focused on two of them—head trauma and cardiovascular accident (stroke). Both result in brain damage that may impair not only cognitive but also physical functioning. Further disorders—social, affective, or behavioral—may be caused by the accident victim's reaction to radical changes in his or her life-style.

The therapeutic recreation professional plays a vital role in the rehabilitation of brain-damaged persons. As part of a treatment team, she or he shares the primary goal of restoring the client to the highest possible level of functioning.

Three different types of recreation programming are planned for the cognitively impaired: (1) a clinical program, in which activities are chosen to rebuild cognitive skills; (2) a leisure experience program, in which joy and freedom afford a welcome relief from the stress of rehabilitation; and

(3) a leisure education program, which prepares clients for a full, rich life in the community.

Working with cognitively impaired persons is highly rewarding for those professionals who can believe in the potential of this client group, despite setbacks, and who can work patiently with them in the challenge of rebuilding their lives.

READING COMPREHENSION QUESTIONS

1. In what ways may the impact of the stroke or head trauma affect the patient's sense of identity?

2. What are four phases of treatment for head trauma and stroke patients?

3. Why are precise progress notes of special importance for working with the cognitively impaired?

4. In addition to cognitive impairment, what other losses may accompany stroke or head trauma?

5. Describe the changes in the head trauma patient as she or he moves through the eight stages of cognitive impairment.

SUGGESTED LEARNING ACTIVITIES

1. Visit a nearby rehabilitation facility and observe a therapeutic recreation activity designed for cognitive retraining.

2. Survey community recreational resources within a one-mile radius of your home or school.

3. Role-play the following dialogue with a classmate. One person plays a TR specialist; the other plays a client in a rehabilitation setting who is suffering damage to the right side of the brain from a motor accident. The client explains to the therapist how it feels suddenly to be unable to ambulate or move one's left arm. The therapist responds.

4. Interview a therapeutic recreation director in a rehabilitation setting. Ask about length-of-stay restrictions in his or her facility and about the impact of such restrictions on service delivery.

5. Interview three cognitively impaired clients in a rehabilitation setting. Ask them what they see as most important in a therapeutic recreation program.

6. Describe the ethical implications of labeling clients "cognitively impaired."

REFERENCES

ADAMOVICH, B., HENDERSON, J., & AUERBACH, S. (1985). *Cognitive rehabilitation of closed head injured patients: A dynamic approach.* San Diego: College-Hill Press.

BARTHE, B., CHANDRON, J., & FICHTER, B. (1985). Evaluation of working capacity: An approach to occupational orientation in persons with head injuries. *Readaptation Revue, 14*, 23–34.

BOLGER, J. P. (1982). Cognitive retraining: A developmental approach. *Clinical Neuropsychology, 4*(2), 66–70.

ENSLEY, G., MACLEAN, J., & LEWARK, N. (1984). The rehabilitation care approach to cognitive retraining. *Cognitive Rehabilitation, 2*(March-April), 8–11.

FAZIO, S., FRALISH, K. (1988). A survey of leisure and recreation offered by agencies serving traumatic head injured adults. *Therapeutic Recreation Journal, 22*(1), 46–54.

FREESE, A. (1979). *Stroke: New approaches to prevention and treatment.* New York: Public Affairs Committee.

FULWILER, T. (Ed). (1987). *The journal book.* Upper Montclair, NJ: Boynton.

GERE, A. R. (Ed). (1985). *Roots in the sawdust: Writing to learn across the disciplines.* Urbana, IL: National Council of Teachers of English.

GREEN, B. A., & EISMONT, F. J. (1984). Acute spinal cord injury: A systems approach. *Central Nervous Systems Trauma, 1*(2), 173–195.

HACKEL, J. M., BERGER, A., & PUTZ, G. (1986). How much reintegration can be achieved in patients after severe head and brain trauma? *Anaesthetist, 35*(3), Number 171–176.

HECKATHORN, J. (1979). Leisure education as part of the team approach to the rehabilitation of the stroke patient. In D. SZYMANSKI & G. HITZHUSEN (Eds.), *Expanding horizons in therapeutic recreation* (Vol. 6). Columbia, MO: Department of Recreation and Park Administration.

HOWE-MURPHY, R., & CHARBONEAU, B. G. (1987). *Therapeutic recreation: An ecological perspective.* Englewood Cliffs, NJ: Prentice-Hall.

LONG, C., GOVIER, W., & COLE, J. (1984). A model of recovery for the total rehabilitation of individuals with head trauma. *Journal of Rehabilitation, 50*(1), 39–45.

MACNEIL, R. D., & PRINGNITZ, T. D. (1982). The role of therapeutic recreation in stroke rehabilitation. *Therapeutic Recreation Journal, 16*(4), Number 26–34.

ODDY, M., & HUMPHREY, M. (1980). Social recovery during the year following severe head injury. *Journal of Neurology, Neurosurgery and Psychiatry, 43*, 798–802.

PARKER, R., & GOODKIN, V. (1987). *The consequences of writing: Enhancing learning in the disciplines.* Upper Montclair, NJ: Boynton.

ROGERS, C. (1970). *Carl Rogers on encounter groups.* New York: Harper & Row.

ROSENTHAL, M., & KOLPAN, K. (1986). Head injury rehabilitation: Psychological issues and roles for the rehabilitation psychologist. *Rehabilitation Psychology, 31*(1), Number 37–46.

U.S. DEPARTMENT OF HEALTH AND HUMAN SERVICES. (1986, November & December). *Vital and health statistics: Types of injuries and impairments due to injuries.* Data from the National Health Survey Series 10 N. 159.

WEDDELL, R., ODDY, M. & JENKINS, D. (1980). Social adjustment after rehabilitation: A two-year follow-up of patients with severe Head Injury. *Psychiatric Medicine, 10*, Number 257–263.

WOOD, J. (1983). Therapeutic recreation in cognitive rehabilitation. *Therapeutic rehabilitation: Dynamic alternatives* (pp. 124–134). Mid-East Therapeutic Symposium Proceedings.

ZAHARA, D., & CUVO, A. (1984). Behavior applications to the rehabilitation of traumatically head injured persons. *Clinical Psychology, 4*, Number 477–491.

13

Geriatric Practice

MICHAEL L. TEAGUE
AND BARBARA A. HAWKINS

OBJECTIVES

- Identify the classification of mental disorders for the elderly by emotional, functional, and developmental categories.
- Discuss the purpose of rehabilitation of the elderly as a unique process.
- Discuss the role of therapeutic recreation in psychosocial rehabilitation of the elderly.
- Critique reality orientation, stimulation programs, behavior therapy, and psychotherapy as psychosocial treatment models for the elderly.
- Identify the most common types of programs and settings in which the elderly population may receive therapeutic recreation services.
- Identify appropriate assessment, planning, implementation, and evaluation information for elderly clients.
- Describe the best practices in program implementation and evaluation.

DEFINITION OF AGING

Aging involves a myriad of aging processes that consist of lifelong changes that begin shortly after birth. The dictionary definition of aging is simply "becoming old" or "becoming aged." However, three views of aging—biological (senescence), sociological (eldering), and psychological (geronting)—are commonly recognized.

Biological aging is defined as the individual's present position with respect to potential life span. Measurement of biological aging encompasses the assessment of functional capacities of life organ systems. Social aging refers to roles and norms with respect to other societal members. Measurement of social aging is the assessment of the dynamic process or eldering, that is, the individual's course of life through the social institutions of which one is a member. Psychological aging refers to the behavioral capacities of individuals to adapt to changing environmental demands. Thus, psychological aging addresses the adaptive capacities of memory, learning, intelligence, skills, feelings, motivations, and emotions for exercising behavioral control of self-regulation.

CLASSIFICATION OF MENTAL IMPAIRMENTS

Older adults with mental impairments constitute a small but significant subgroup of the aged population. Approximately 10% of the elderly are estimated to have mental problems severe enough to warrant professional attention (Butler & Lewis, 1983). Classification of these impairments can be divided into three categories: (1) emotional problems, (2) mental disorders, and (3) developmental disabilities.

Emotional Problems

Adaptation implies a continual interaction between the person and his or her environment, each making demands on the other. Positive adaptation may be viewed as the person's ability to meet biological, social, and psychological needs satisfactorily in light of changing environmental conditions. Negative adaptation is the person's failure to meet basic needs, or the ability of the person to meet these needs only at the cost of suffering, pain, and/or disorder. Thus, negative adaptation to the changes—both social and personal—that characterize later life may lead to emotional problems (e.g., grief, loneliness, guilt, depression, anxiety, sense of impotence, helplessness, rage).

Although adaptation is a necessary process common to individuals of all ages, some sources of adaptive changes are more common in later life. Figure 13.1 identifies three major sources of change in later life and potential issues related to each source. The reader will note that there are some sources of adaptive change that are unique to the elderly; for example, retirement, age segregation, grandparenthood. Pfeiffer (1977) has suggested that most age-specific adaptation issues are variations of three adaptive problems: (1) adaptation to loss, (2) identity review, and (3) remaining active. Adaptation to loss (e.g., loss of spouse, loss of work relations) is one's ability to replace some of those losses with new relationships and roles, or learn to make do with less. Identity review is an

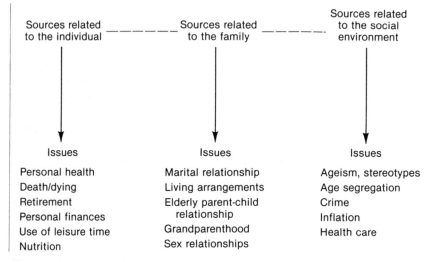

FIGURE 13.1   Common Sources of Major Adaptive Change in Later Life. SOURCE: From D. M. Rosenthal & N. Colangelo, "Counseling the Elderly: Individual, Family, and Social Perspectives," in M. L. Teague, R. D. MacNeil, & G. Hitzhusen (Eds.), *Perspectives on Leisure and Aging in a Changing Society* (Columbia, MO: Department of Recreation & Park Administration, 1982). Reprinted by permission of the University of Missouri Board of Curators.

evaluative backward glance at one's life in which the person weighs such elements as accomplishments versus failures and satisfactions versus disappointments. Failure to delineate a self-identity that is reasonably positive is likely to result in emotional problems. Remaining active implies that a positive correlation exists between participation in satisfying activities and the maintenance of healthy physical, social, and psychological functioning (MacNeil & Teague, 1987).

The salient issue is not that old age carries with it unique adaptive changes. Instead, the critical issue is the extent to which older adults are capable of adapting to the challenges of later life. A principal by-product of negative adaptation to environmental challenges is stress. Coping with stressful events requires the mentally healthy individual to assess the situation, choose a way to respond, act upon the choice, and evaluate the success or failure of the chosen action. However, a stressor perceived as too overwhelming to be handled by the usual coping mechanisms may lead even the mentally healthy adult to resort to alternative damaging strategies. Substance abuse and suicide, a well-documented response of the inability of many older adults to cope with insurmountable stress, are among such strategies. For example, Butler and Lewis (1983) reported that older adults account for approximately 25% of reported suicides, despite representing only 11% of the population. Depression and failing health are the most common reasons cited for suicide in later life (Wantz & Gay, 1981).

Mental Disorders

The mental disorders of aging consist of two kinds: (1) functional disorders, for which the origins appear to be emotional rather than physical, and (2) organic disorders, which have a physical cause.

Functional disorders are generally diagnosed as being either neurotic or psychotic. A neurosis is a condition characterized by anxiety associated with unconscious emotional turmoil. Psychosis includes conditions marked by varying degrees of personality disintegration and difficulty in testing and correctly evaluating external reality.

Depression, whether psychotic or neurotic, is the most common functional disorder associated with old age. Symptoms of depression, such as withdrawal into solitude, apathy, inertia, and quiet self-deprecation, are linked far more frequently with older adults than with any other age-group (Butler & Lewis, 1983).

In most cases, functional disorders in later life are carried over from the earlier stages of life. Once functional disorders are diagnosed, the resulting conditions are not necessarily progressive or irreversible. In many cases they can be treated and their symptoms dissipated through psychosocial intervention and medication (MacNeil & Teague, 1987).

Organic brain disorders impair the cognitive ability to function at a "normal" level. Butler and Lewis (1983) identified five mental signs characteristic of organic brain disorders: (1) impairment of memory, (2) impairment of intellect, (3) impairment of judgment, (4) impairment of orientation, and (5) ability and shallowness of effect.

Two distinctive types of organic brain syndrome are usually distinguished. Acute Brain Syndrome (ABS) is characterized by a decrease in level of awareness, which may fluctuate from mild confusion all the way to stupor. The victim of ABS frequently experiences disorientation, restlessness, and uncooperativeness, and also may display visual hallucinations or delusions of persecution. Head trauma, infection, diabetes, congestive heart failure, drugs, alcohol, and toxic substances are but a few of the many factors contributing to ABS. It should be noted that ABS is known as "reversible brain syndrome" because its manifestations have been consistently alleviated by removal of the causative agent.

Chronic Brain Syndrome (CBS), unlike ABS, which occurs in individuals of all ages, most often occurs in old age. Behavior associated with CBS includes deterioration of intellectual processes, memory loss, and emotional instability. CBS is characterized by a physiological degeneration of the brain that is usually visible upon autopsy. Physical changes associated with CBS include hardening and thickening of blood vessels in the brain, loss and damage of tissue and nerve cells in the brain and spinal cord, and the appearance of senile plaques. CBS is considered irreversible.

CBS is commonly divided into three subcategories: (1) senile dementia, (2) psychosis associated with cerebral arteriosclerosis, and (3) presenile dementia. It is difficult to differentiate clinically between these three sub-categories because their behavioral symptoms are similar. Thus, distinctions are usually based on the speed by which the symptoms appear. Senile dementia is noted by a gradual decline in brain function, whereas cerebral arteriosclerotic psychosis is marked by an uneven and erratic downward progression. Little is known about the causes of senile dementia. However, arteriosclerotic (narrowing and closing the vessel) psychosis is usually attributed to vascular damage in the brain due to arteriosclerosis and atherosclerosis (hardening of the vessel wall). Either of these conditions restricts blood flow to the brain. Consequently, the lack of oxygen and nutrient delivery to the brain results in brain cell and tissue death.

Presenile dementia includes a group of brain disorders that clinically mimic senile dementia in older people; however, they occur earlier in life, that is, in the 45–50 age-group (Butler & Lewis, 1983). The two predominant features of presenile dementia are intellectual deterioration and personality disintegration. Alzheimer's disease is one form of presenile dementia that has received special attention. This disease is a progressive disorder marked by memory loss (most notably recent memory), restlessness, reduced attention span, and, eventually, the loss of orientation and ability to care for oneself. Death usually occurs 2–10 years after onset.

Pick's disease, very similar to Alzheimer's, is the second presenile dementia to receive special attention. Onset of Pick's disease is usually in the fourth decade of life, but onset also may occur after age 65. Lack of initiative characterizes Pick's disease, as opposed to the overactivity seen in Alzheimer's. Behavioral symptoms include early selective impairment of mental functioning, with memory usually intact except for recent material. At a later stage, localized symptoms such as aphasia, aphrasia, and aprexia appear, and eventually the person sinks into a vegetative existence before death. The prognosis is irreversible, with death occurring 2–15 years after onset.

Developmental Disabilities

Definitions of aging developmentally disabled adults have been generally based upon clinical assumptions rather than empirical data. Janicki and colleagues (1985) note that most of these definitions imply that the beginning of aging for developmentally disabled persons occurs around the mid to late 40s or early to mid 50s, depending on the nature of the disability. In other words, most definitions associate entry into an aging status with chronological age. Janicki and colleagues argue, however, that three other factors in addition to chronological age should be used to classify a developmentally disabled person as aging. They are "(a) greater physical disability and lessening of physical reserve attributable to chronological age (rather than trauma or illness); (b) diminishing levels of functional skills, particularly in areas of self-care, personal hygiene and toileting; and (c) for less mentally impaired individuals, the self-perception of aging and desire to seek age-appropriate or normative roles and activities" (p. 291).

MEDICAL LIMITATIONS

Antidepressant (e.g., Tofraneil, Elavil, Norpramin) and antianxiety agents (e.g., barbiturates, Valium, Mellaril) are common drugs used for the treatment of depression. Drug therapy for functional and organic brain disorders focuses on compounds that attempt to improve brain function (e.g., Hydersine, Papaverini) and substances that facilitate increased oxygen to brain cells (e.g., hypoerboric oxygen). Mentally impaired older adults also are likely to be suffering from physical illness. Thus there is an exhaustive list of potential drugs that the elderly may take; for example, beta-adrenergic blocking agents, diuretics, calcium-channel blockers, tranquilizers. Many of these drugs will have an impact on the elderly client's functioning.

A discussion of pharmacodynamic changes associated with aging and the impact of individual drugs on physical activity (e.g., individuals with diabetes must carefully balance physical activity intensity and duration because of insulin injections that may lead to insulin shock) are beyond the scope of this chapter. The reader is encouraged to consult Piscopo (1985) for a thorough discussion of drug implications for physical activity programs. It should be noted, however, that the elderly are particularly sensitive to central nervous system depressant drugs because of changes in brain tissue caused by aging. Thus, it is imperative that the therapeutic recreation professional have a working knowledge of how drugs work and their effects on body function in order to avoid an interaction between a drug and the intended recreation program.

PURPOSE OF THERAPEUTIC RECREATION

The purpose of rehabilitation, "to restore an individual to his/her former functional and environmental status, or alternatively, to maintain or maximize remaining function, needs to be at the heart of all care provided to the aged to help them live as full a life as possible" (Jette, 1986, p. 2). Thus functional independence, not disease eradication, has become the principal goal of care for the aged. However, it is very important to note that rehabilitation of the elderly is quite different from rehabilitation of the young. The impact a disability has on an individual's life is not only a function of the nature of the disability. The stage of life in which it occurs, the number of alterations in life-style that it demands, the way it is perceived by the individual, and how the individual and significant others respond influence the elderly as well.

The nature of a psychosocial view of geriatric rehabilitation has to do with the issues of the mind and the relationship of the elderly individual with society. These issues are imperative because therapists interact with (treat) whole persons whose minds (psycho) and relationships with society (social) are intensely relevant to the quality of life of the elderly (Davis, 1986). The elderly are marked already by fewer resources and a decrease in status, roles, and authority. Elderly persons who add an afflicted disability need timely and effective psychosocial intervention to regain their maximum independence or to maintain their present independence. The following four approaches to treatment are reviewed: (1) reality orientation, (2) stimulation programs, (3) behavior therapy, and (4) psychotherapy. The review includes a discussion of their purpose, methods, and effectiveness.

Reality Orientation

Reality orientation uses environmental and interpersonal cues in daily classes with staff reinforcement on a 24-hour basis to present information on person, place, and time to patients. Relatively simple and easily learned, this technique enables staff to have specific things to say and do and thus relieves the staff from needing to decide on information used for interacting with patients. Recreation therapists and nursing assistants are often charged with leading reality orientation classes. Although principally developed for use with elderly "senile" clients, classes generally include all patients who exhibit confusion or disorientation, regardless of age or symptom etiology (Gugel & Eisdorfer, 1986).

The premise of reality orientation is that orientation has become impaired due to disease, loss of motivation, or brain deterioration. Practice and feedback can be used to reorient the patient. Unfortunately, empirical data on the effectiveness of reality orientation is equivocal at best. The lack of objective evaluation and methodological flaws in reality orientation studies have contributed to the equivocal results. However, systematic evidence does indicate that gains attained through reality orientation do not generalize to patients' other behaviors (Citrin & Dixon, 1977). Because of this lack of empirical support, the popularity of reality orientation as a psychosocial intervention has been seriously questioned. As Brody concludes: "Perhaps it speaks to the hunger of caregivers for treatment methodology" (Brody, 1981, p. 320).

Stimulation Programs

Stimulation programs employ a highly structured group approach directed at improving overall functioning or such aspects of functioning as environmental awareness, physical movement, perceptual integration, attention span, daily living skills, and level of interaction with the environment. Regressed elderly patients who exhibit varying degrees of lethargic, apathetic, and withdrawal behaviors are the targets of stimulation programs. Many patients in these programs are noncommunicative and display limited environmental awareness (Gugel & Eisdorfer, 1986).

Each program session consists of a variety of components that include activities that emphasize bodily response, perceptual integration, cognitive stimulation, and function. Concrete activities with specific stimuli for each program aspect are the foundation of stimulation programs. Familiar activities that promote security and a sense of mastery are used, with at least one novel activity in each program component to stimulate and promote higher-level functioning. Stimulation programs require a highly skilled group leader who has the professional ability properly to engage elderly regressed patients. Recreation therapists and occupational therapists are generally charged with such leadership responsibility.

Weiner, Brok, and Snadowsky (1978) have reported success in using stimulation programs with regressed elderly patients. However, most studies on stimulation intervention have been subjective evaluations. Despite the lack of strong empirical evidence, stimulation programs are promising for improving the function of regressed elderly persons in areas of environmental awareness and overall responsiveness, and for increasing sociability and appropriate behavior. But it is not clear whether the effects of stimulation programs can be generalized to other settings or whether such effects are sustained after program termination (Gugel & Eisdorfer, 1986).

Behavior Therapy

Behavior therapy is used to change nonfunctional behavior to functional behavior. Focus areas for change include self-care, verbal behavior, walking behavior, food consumption, incontinence, purposeful activities, appropriate behavior, and sociability (Krasner, 1971). Positive reinforcement is the specific technique employed in behavior therapy programs; for example, praise, refreshments, prizes, special privileges, tokens. This intervention technique requires a thorough understanding of the basic steps of behavioral therapy. They include analysis of the nonfunctional behavior, definition of the specific behavior to be treated, and establishment of a baseline frequency of the behavior. Once behavior has been established, therapy requires formulation of concrete goals, identification and training of staff who will provide the treatment, an outline of specific treatment procedures, and accurate documentation (Gugel & Eisdorfer, 1986).

Empirical evidence does suggest that behavior therapy is an effective intervention technique for altering specific behaviors in elderly patients. Particular success has been reported in the areas of sociability, self-care, and purposeful activity. Changing cognitive and emotional functioning levels have generally not been successfully attained through this psychosocial technique. Moreover, behavior therapy success tends to become extinct when the program is terminated. Despite evidence supporting the value of behavior therapy, few clinicians use this technique.

Psychotherapy

Psychotherapy uses two types of therapy: supportive psychotherapy and insight-oriented therapy. The primary goal of supportive psychotherapy is to strengthen existing defenses and to restore the elderly person to an adaptive equilibrium. Specific techniques used for achieving this purpose include information giving, suggestions, advice, reassurance, encouragement, emotional support, and active intervention on the patient's behalf. The principal goals of insight-oriented therapy are to break down distortions, remove or alter pathologic defenses, resolve conflicts, and develop more appropriate and effective behavior. Techniques used to attain these goals include reflection, questioning, clarification, identification and labeling of feelings, examination of past behavior and general patterns of reaction, reality testing, interpretation of reality, and examination of transferences. Both individual and group psychotherapy sessions may be used; however, group psychotherapy remains the preferred option. The group leader is usually a psychiatrist, psychologist, or social worker.

The empirical literature does suggest that psychotherapy is an effective intervention technique for improving overall behavior, cognitive functioning, sociability, self-concept, discharge rates, and a decrease in depression. Interestingly, few elderly persons were considered appropriate candidates for psychotherapy intervention in the distant past. Many believed the process of psychotherapy too intensive and costly to be of benefit to the elderly. However, the past three decades have been marked with increased attention by clinicians for using psychotherapy techniques with both community-based elderly and the institutionalized elderly (Gugel & Eisdorfer, 1986).

COMMON SERVICE SETTINGS

Therapeutic recreation services for the elderly have traditionally been more fully developed and entrenched in long-term care settings such as nursing homes. However, an increasing share of public funds is now beginning to be directed toward community settings. This shift in public funding demands that therapeutic recreation professionals be creative in adapting programs to fit the diverse needs of the elderly in both institutional and community settings.

Institutional Facilities

Institutional facilities vary in the level of services and intensity of care provided. For example, services range from medically oriented life support to support in activities of daily living (personal care and grooming, personal business, and keeping one's personal environment clean and neat). Three types of institutional facilities are discussed in this section: (1) skilled nursing facilities, (2) intermediate care facilities, and (3) congregate care facilities.

Skilled Nursing Facilities (SNF) focus directly on health care. They typically offer a wide range of medical services; for example, physician and nursing, dietary, laboratory and diagnostic, pharmaceutical, social, and rehabilitation (Teaff, 1985) services based on the treatment of illness and the disease of the elderly client. Therapeutic recreation programs, in turn, focus principally on treatment goals. In SNF settings, much of what takes place under the auspices of recreation programming is actually diversionary activity directed toward keeping the client occupied.

Intermediate Care Facilities (ICF) differ from SNFs due to resident needs that include both social and rehabilitation services. Because many long-term care facilities are certified as both SNFs and ICFs, current trends in federal regulation standards are incorporating a single set of standards for both SNFs and ICFs. The proposed uniform regulations, however, do not include specialized standards for ICFs for the mentally retarded.

The implosion effect (aging of the aged) in demographic trends and the continued maturity of the developmentally disabled population will have dramatic implications for both SNFs and ICFs. Particular implications focus on the attempt to meet the needs of the mentally retarded. Sirrocco (1987) noted that 8,276 nursing homes have mentally retarded residents. Moreover, Henney (1983) reported that 27% of mentally retarded/developmentally disabled residents in nursing homes were over age 65. Thus, therapeutic recreation professionals working in SNFs and ICFs will need training in gerontology and developmental disabilities to better meet client needs.

Congregate Care Facilities (CCF) include board and care, personal domiciliary care homes, and homes for the elderly. Regimented schedules and less personal aspects are the foremost attributes of these institutions. These facilities are usually loosely regulated by state codes. Because of relaxed state codes, therapeutic recreation services may or may not be included in CCF. If residential therapeutic recreation services are not provided, residents are directed to such organizations as Retired Senior Volunteer Program (RSVP), the In-Home Senior Companion Program, and public park and recreation programs.

Relocation to a long-term care facility at an older stage of life can be traumatic, especially as related to the loss of friendship with the outside world and lack of daily routine control. Staff attitudes toward the elderly client can also compound the impact of living in institutional settings. Therapeutic recreation services, therefore, can help offset the "closed" environmental characteristics of institutions by emphasizing friendships, social relationships, reminiscence, creativity, community outings, and health maintenance.

Community Settings

Community-based programs and services are increasing rapidly all across the nation. Senior centers, adult day care, in-home services, retirement communities, senior volunteer programs, and senior educational programs are a small sampling of such programs. Senior centers, adult day care, and in-home services are discussed in this section.

Senior Centers provide a place for older adults to come together for socialization, leisure activity, and other services. The growth of popularity in senior centers was enhanced by the 1965 Older Americans Act. A national survey completed by the National Institute of Senior Centers in 1974 indicated that most of the senior centers were located in urban and suburban programs. Today, however, it is not uncommon to find an increasing number of senior centers and programs in small rural areas.

Some senior centers are highly organized, with full-time and part-time staffing and a well-developed program of activities. Other centers are loosely organized, managed by a small professional staff and/or volunteers, and primarily focused on community involvement by seniors. In either case, the primary concept behind senior centers is to promote senior citizen involvement in the community.

Typical services found in senior centers include leisure services, education, information, counseling and referral, health programs, employment assistance, financial aid and counseling, legal aid, nutrition, transportation services, in-home services, and day care (Teaff, 1985). Centers deliver these services either by providing center-based programs and outreach services, or by making the needed linkages with community service agencies.

Adult Day Care programs are also developing rapidly in communities. Adult day care is a general term. Behren (1986), however, provides a more specific definition:

> [An adult day care program is] a community-based group program designed to meet the needs of functionally impaired adults through an individual plan of care. It is a structured, comprehensive program that provides a variety of health, social and related support services in a protective setting during any part of the day but less than 24-hour care. (p. iii)

The term *adult day health care* is used when the program focus becomes medically oriented; the term *adult day care* is used when the program focus is essentially social.

Adult day care centers are a relatively new community-based resource for older adults who have a level of impairment that necessitates supervision and care. In a national survey of such centers (Behren, 1986), more than half the respondents cited four service priorities: (1) alternatives to premature or inappropriate institutionalization, (2) maximizing functional capacity, (3) respite for care givers, and (4) psychosocial supportive services.

The range of services commonly provided in adult day care programs, either by contract or by direct care staff, include medical and health-related care (e.g., podiatry, dentistry); social services; physical, occupational, speech, recreational, art, music, and reality therapy; dietary counseling and meals; transportation; and personal grooming and care (Behren, 1986). Typical funding sources for adult day care are Medicaid, participant fees, Social Services Block Grant, Title III of the Older Americans Act, local government funds, and donations and fund raisers. Services are provided by full-time and part-time administrative and professional staff, and a significant contribution is made by volunteers (Behren, 1986).

In-Home Services offer a home-based, professional care alternative to older adults in need of additional health, social, and/or support services; for example, homemaker, handyman. Many refer to these services as "home health care." However, the term *in-home services* is preferred because it suggests the inclusion of services broader than a medical focus. Services provided in the home are especially popular with older adults because they enable the elderly to remain in their own home or community. Thus, premature placement of older adults in institutional facilities may be avoided. Such services provide assistance with daily living activities (e.g., grooming, self-care), social services (e.g., companionship, reality orientation), and health care, but not at the intensity level familiar in institutional facilities. Fees and charges, Medicare, Medicaid, Title XX of the Social Security Act, and Title III of the Older Americans Act are used to support in-home services (Teaff, 1985).

Some states are expanding the in-home services option as an important resource for infirmed, impaired, and disabled elderly individuals. For example, in 1986 the Indiana General Assembly passed a state law expanding the in-home services programs for elderly and disabled persons. In 1979, Oregon implemented a major in-home services program that resulted in the prevention of thousands of new nursing home placements and the movement back to the community of about 5% of its nursing home residents (Severns, 1986). As the in-home services program continues to develop and upgrade eligible services, therapeutic recreation may be one of the core therapies included.

CURRENT BEST PRACTICES AND PROCEDURES

The understanding of late adulthood is a very complex task that requires one to appreciate the image of later maturity as a function of both past and present status. One must view the life course as a series of changes marked by the "succession of age-related roles prescribed by the culture, by the biological and cognitive development of the individual, and by the particular historical events . . . that define the context in which the individual lives" (McCrae & Costa, 1984, p. 298). Therapeutic recreation practices and procedures are grounded in this life review process and include four principal phases: assessment, planning, implementation, and evaluation.

Assessment

Standardized instruments and procedures for assessing the leisure skills and interests specific to the elderly have not been fully developed or validated. There are, however, acceptable applications that may provide useful information for guiding therapeutic recreation interventions. These applications for a psychosocial assessment of the older adult should minimally include the following:

- A mental status examination to assess major cognitive and emotional difficulties and help define the proper psychological treatment, based upon standard methods and procedures.
- A social and vocational history focusing on previous roles, marriages, and sexual history, sources of life satisfaction, achievements, and values.
- A personality assessment focused on the individual's self-perception, character, method of dealing with crises in the past, interpersonal relations, responses to stress, and nature of previous losses.
- The person's own perception of the rehabilitation process and motivation for improvement.
- An assessment of the current family situation, including relations with family members, sources of support, quality of housing, and the presence of other sick or disabled persons.
- An assessment of the home environment through a visit to determine architectural barriers, nature of neighborhood, how the person functions at home (as opposed to functioning in a hospital), and community resources.
- In interview of the patient's family (if agreeable with the patient) to determine their view of the patient, concerns, and resources. (Kemp, 1985, p. 659)

Psychosocial or behavioral aging can be assessed by building a social history of the patterns of behavior and life-style for the individual client. Interviews with individual clients, as well as family members or other care givers, can be useful in constructing the social history. A social history also can be helpful in understanding psychosocial aspects of later maturity, such as changes in personality, role, and activity, social and health attitudes, self-concept, and socioeconomic status (Davis, 1986). Understanding and documenting major life events that may influence adjustment (e.g., loss of a loved one, illness) and/or needs for socialization (e.g., recent relocation to a new residence) will be important to understanding the life course and the need for therapeutic intervention.

Leisure skills and interests, both past and present, will be the key information in the assessment record. Leisure interest surveys can be used or developed to gather information regarding the older client's past behavior patterns as well as current activities and interests (Herrera, 1983; McKechnie, 1975). Using a variety of approaches, information should be sought regarding the older person's repertoire of activities, preferences, interests, and expectations, as well as capacity for independence (such as activities of daily living, use of public transportation, capacity for self-protection, and the like). Howe (1984) noted that leisure assessment instrumentation can be organized by those measuring leisure attitudes, leisure states, leisure behavior, leisure satisfaction, and leisure interests. For a more complete listing of instruments in these categories, consult Howe (1984, p. 17).

For clients with verbal skills and higher cognitive functioning, interviews and pencil/paper surveys are useful approaches (Davis, 1986). For lower functioning individuals, constructing leisure behavior patterns from client records and observations may be the applied data collection technique. Few assessment instruments exist for application with older developmentally disabled clients. However, Joswiak (1975), Herrera (1983), and Cousins and Brown (1979) provide sample assessment instruments to use with these clients.

Planning

The objectives for psychosocial intervention include (1) assessment of the client's cognitive, affective, and functional status; (2) resolving the crisis of disability, depression, and grieving; (3) helping clients maintain independence; (4) promoting self-esteem; (5) improving family relations; and (6) identifying suspected organic ailments that may impair optimal functioning (Kemp, 1985). Therapeutic recreation professionals play a key role in meeting these objectives through a variety of programs and services. Programs briefly discussed here include physical fitness, reality orientation, reminiscence, nutrition, and activities of daily living.

Physical Fitness is a program area that has received considerable attention in recent years. The intent of physical fitness programs includes cardiovascular endurance, flexibility, strength and endurance, body composition, balance, and motor coordination. Psychological benefits from exercise have also been derived for stress relief and anxiety reduction. For a complete review of fitness programs for older adults, consult Teague (1987) and Piscopo (1985).

Reality Orientation Therapy, as discussed earlier, assists the older adult in maintaining an awareness of time, place, person, and things of interest. During later maturity, it is not uncommon for the individual to become confused regarding where or who he or she is, and who is his or her care giver or peer. Sometimes confusion or disorientation is associated with a major change, such as loss of a loved one, change in residence, illness, or disease (e.g., organic brain syndrome). A number of treatment modalities can be used in reality orientation intervention. These modalities include attitude therapy, remotivation, memory therapy, reinforcement therapy, self-image therapy, resocialization, and sensory training (Herrera, 1983). The use of a reality orientation group on a regular basis (one to three times per week) is one approach for the "ongoing process of supplying information, correcting disoriented [sic] information, and reinforcing behaviors that approximate or reflect meaningful interactions with the individual's environment" (Herrera, 1983, p. 24).

Reminiscence draws attention to the importance of and use of life review both as a recreation experience and as a strategy for identifying potential recreation activities for the client. This technique is important not only for emotional development in the later years but as a device for bridging the gap between the young and the old through recapitulation of past and present significant events. Recapitulation can be very important for emotional and social adjustment (e.g., reduced feelings of isolation) and for reducing cognitive dissonance about who we are, particularly for those elderly persons who are newly institutionalized and are experiencing an excerbated sense of loss of control. Thus, reminiscence can be viewed as both a recreative tool and as a process for reexperiencing past leisure activities and interests. Consult Clements (1982) for an excellent presentation on how reminiscence can be used with older adults.

Nutritional Programming extends beyond meeting nutritional health needs by including opportunities for social interaction. For many older adults, meals may be one of the very few opportunities for experiencing interpersonal relationships beyond immediate family members. Meal sites, as well as homebound meal programs, are excellent vehicles for the expression of cultural heritage (e.g., holidays and other celebrations), for developing and maintaining social relationships, and for enhancing general health. The reader can consult Teague (1987) for a review of nutrition as a health promotion and social adjustment program for older adults.

Activities for Daily Living (ADL) serve two principal purposes: (1) development or maintenance of self-help skills (e.g., eating, dressing, personal grooming, financial management, shopping, personal safety), and (2) development of and participation in recreational activities. The ADL program is a major area for promoting involvement, productivity, social interaction, the expression of personal interests and skills, and reinforcing fine motor and communication skills. ADL programs are also an excellent way of promoting an older person's sense of belonging to the larger community.

Other types of common programs for older adults include senior creative arts programs, volunteer activities, educational programming (pre-retirement, adult education), travel and touring, horticulture, and outdoor recreation. Each of these programs provides opportunities for therapeutic intervention and diversion. Consult Teaff (1985) and MacNeil and Teague (1987) for an excellent review of these programs.

Implementation

Typically, older adults want to be treated with dignity. Developing programs that enhance dignity requires the structuring of program autonomy, independence, and meaningful involvement. Obviously, leadership skills employed by the therapeutic recreation professional are essential for implementing programs that meet these criteria. Jones (1987) provides the following leadership considerations that apply especially for working with older adults. Staff should do the following:

- Demonstrate respect for mature adults.
- Cultivate understanding and empathy through the demonstration of interest and genuine concern for the individual.
- Show enthusiasm by projecting excitement and/or enjoyment of being with the older client.
- Be flexible and adaptable by developing and expanding activities as situations occur, thus cultivating spontaneity.
- Recognize planning and creativity as important cornerstones to successful programs and services. (pp. 4–8)

Other considerations in program implementation should include environmental design and modification to accommodate physical changes commonly associated with aging. Older adults benefit from environments that support easy access to rest rooms, have flexible climate control, do not pose undue obstacles to movement around the facility, and support diminished vision and hearing with appropriate lighting and acoustical design features. MacNeil and Teague's (1987) discussion of developing "open" environments may be especially helpful in designing appropriate program settings.

Evaluation

The aim of rehabilitation, "to restore [the elderly client] to his/her former functional and environmental status, or alternatively, to maintain or maximize remaining function" (Jette, 1986, p. 2), lies at the heart of the evaluation process. As cited earlier in this chapter, the goal of rehabilitation is functional independence, not disease eradication. Thus, health professionals need to evaluate their programs in reference to impairments, functional disabilities, and handicapped conditions. Kiresuk, Lund, and Schultz's (1981) quality assurance model and Austin's (1982) stepwise program evaluation model are valuable evaluation tools. However, the rehabilitation therapist may improve these evaluation models by incorporating them within the functional assessment/evaluation process described in Figure 13.2.

The salient point of Figure 13.2 is that the processes of assessment, planning, implementation, and evaluation are interconnected. However, the bottom line is the impact that program interventions have on functional disabilities that are represented by basic living skills (walking, performing bed-to-bed chair transfer, dressing) and instrumental living skills (climbing stairs, preparing meals, washing dishes, shopping, taking medication). Pertinent instruments used in the assessment of basic and instrumental living skills include the Functional Status Index (Harris et al., 1986), Functional Independence Measure (Granger et al., 1986) and the Older Americans Resource Service Multidimensional Functional Assessment Questionnaire (Fillenbaum, 1985).

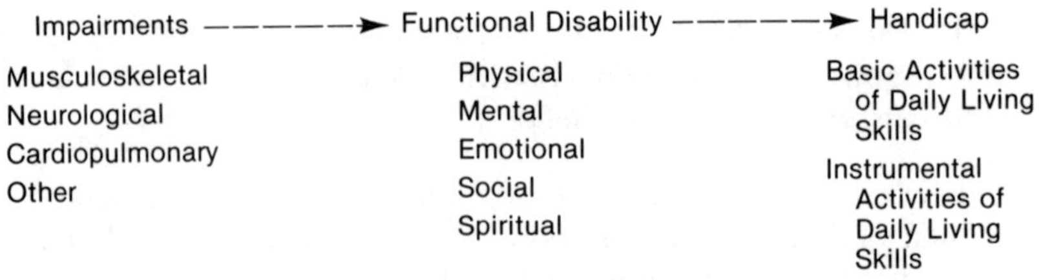

Impairments ----> Functional Disability ----> Handicap

Impairments	Functional Disability	Handicap
Musculoskeletal	Physical	Basic Activities of Daily Living Skills
Neurological	Mental	
Cardiopulmonary	Emotional	Instrumental Activities of Daily Living Skills
Other	Social	
	Spiritual	

FIGURE 13.2   A conceptual framework for functional assessment

APPLICATION OF THE TR PROCESS

The elderly segment of the general population is a unique group in terms of the general needs associated with this life stage. It also is a diverse group in that there is broad variety among older citizens in terms of individual experience, interests, and needs. The following case example provides a unique and diverse view of an older man with mental retardation who lives in a group home for older adults.

CASE STUDY

Joe is a 61-year-old man with Down's syndrome. Joe recently moved into the group home because of the failing health of his then-living father (since deceased) and mother. His surviving aged mother lives in a nearby rural community of under 10,000 people, where Joe also lived prior to his move to the group home. Joe has a younger sister who lives out of state with her husband and two children.

Assessment

History: Joe spent most of his adult life working in a sheltered work activity center in a nearby community. During his mid to late fifties, Joe showed changes in his behavior that were characterized as withdrawn and uncooperative. He was easily distracted from his work. This situation regressed until he was unmotivated to participate in his work activities. His mother requested that he be moved out of vocational activities and be given greater opportunities to explore other day activities that focused on his recreational interests. Because Joe has had fairly good health except for occasional arthritis inflammations, he was successfully transitioned out of the workshop and into adult day activities that focused on maintaining his physical and social involvement. Before moving to the group home in a larger community, Joe was being prepared to enter a senior day activity program.

Present Behaviors: Joe is interested in bowling, swimming, watching game shows, cooking (which he did a lot of with his mother), talking about his family, taking long rides in the car, eating, and mealtimes. Many of these pursuits are activities that he has done with his parents and their friends for most of his life. He did belong to a bowling team from the work activity center where he was previously employed.

Joe frequently has periods of withdrawal and depression, and needs to be careful about his diet and weight. Joe has needs for assistance with his adjustment to the group home. He also needs help dealing with the loss of his father and the separation from his mother. Building upon his strengths, it is possible to use many reinforcers to get Joe to talk about his feelings and become involved in home activities.

Planning

Because Joe is easy to draw out, his individual habilitation plan is based upon maintaining his repertoire of skills and involvements, in addition to expanding opportunities for developing new interests and friendships through accessing community-based senior programs.

Long-Term Goal: To minimize periods of loneliness, withdrawal, and depression.

Short-Term Goals: (1) To assist Joe in developing ways to cope with feelings. (2) To develop new opportunities for Joe to participate in his favorite leisure activities.

Objectives: Joe will be given opportunities to prepare meals and lead mealtime socialization in order to (1) build his relationships with housemates, (2) reinforce his interests in cooking, (3) learn about diet and nutrition, (4) help him deal with troublesome feelings, and (5) maintain connection with his past through reminiscence. Joe will prepare at least two meals per week for the next three months, and assist with the preparation of other meals.

Joe also will be taken to the local senior citizen center at least twice per week for the next four weeks to visit its programs and enroll in at least one program.

Joe will call his mother two to three times per week and visit with her at least once in every two weeks.

Content: Joe will discuss and plan meals, talk about his family and his interests, and increase his awareness of recreation activities available in his new community, specifically at the senior center. Joe will maintain contact with his mother and other family members.

Process: Senior center staff will (1) encourage Joe to attend the programs, provide background understanding of Joe and his abilities and needs, and identify a peer model at the senior center for Joe; (2) assess Joe for identifying additional leisure interests; (3) hold sessions with Joe to develop reminiscence skills; and (4) make provisions using the transportation program for the elderly to visit Joe's mother.

At this stage of programming, the therapeutic recreation specialist will be implementing both an individual plan with the client as well as developing the capacity of both the home environment and the community environment to accept Joe.

Implementation

The client will participate in the home routine, with a special emphasis on the use of meals as a social and daily skills building program. New leisure activities will be sought as the client gains access to the community senior program. Anecdotal and frequency records will be maintained for the client's moods and behaviors.

Evaluation

The Individual Habilitation Plan (IHP) for the client will serve as the documentation of client goals and objectives, as well as progress in meeting them. Periodic review of progress notes and changes/additions to the client IHP provide evaluative feedback to the primary care givers and therapeutic recreation professional. Other significant persons should be consulted for their review of the client's progress and program design. (In Joe's case, staff and other participants at the community-based senior program could be consulted for information useful in the evaluation of his program and progress.) Comprehensive review of the IHP on an annual basis should also include a conference with Joe, his mother, and other family members.

TRENDS AND ISSUES

It is the contention of the authors that the practice of psychosocial rehabilitation has much to offer the disabled elderly for attaining more normal and useful lives. The graying of the American population and the concurrent increase in chronic illness and disease will require a more equitable distribution of psychosocial rehabilitation services for the elderly. The trend will not be the invention of new systems of care for the elderly, but a more effective and efficient use of the health systems we presently have. Inherent within this trend is the rehabilitation focus for treating functional deficits of the elderly in order to promote greater independence.

Functional areas of concern include mobility, sensory abilities, communication, emotional stability, hand dexterity, activities of daily living, and health maintenance. These areas are not the usual domain of traditional medical and nursing practice. Thus, allied health professions will continue to develop to meet these functional needs. Medical and allied health professionals can be expected to be organized into an interdisciplinary rehabilitation team, because the elderly are likely to have multiple chronic conditions, periodic acute medical problems, and psychosocial complications (e.g., less family support, less societal visibility). Members of the interdisciplinary teams will include physicians, psychiatrists, nurses, physical therapists, social workers, occupational therapists, speech therapists, nutritionists, and recreation therapists.

SUMMARY

Professionals who work to rehabilitate the elderly often experience frustration. The frustration rarely stems from not knowing how to treat psychosocial or physical disabilities alone. Rather, the professional is challenged by the multiple, concurrent problems of the elderly, each influencing the others and affecting the quality of the clients' lives. For example, when arthritis leads to severe depression, confusion, and despair, the therapist is tempted to treat only the physical symptoms associated with the disease rather than such potential concurrent factors as death of a spouse or a financial crisis.

The underlying theme throughout the authors' discussion of psychosocial rehabilitation programs for the elderly is that recreation therapists interact with more than just bodies. Charm and fascination of work with the elderly are a by-product of their unique personalities. As Davis (1986) states: "They are (for the most part) interesting people who have led long lives characterized by day-to-day decisions that have brought them unique characters" (p. vi). Thus, the nature of the psychosocial views of rehabilitation has to do with the issues of the mind and the relationships of the individual with society. The more the recreation therapist knows about psychosocial aspects of rehabilitation, the better prepared he or she is to effect meaningful change.

READING COMPREHENSION QUESTIONS

1. Debate this statement: "Therapeutic recreation programs are primarily diversionary rather than treatment interventions used in psychosocial rehabilitation of the elderly."

2. Adaptation is a process common to all ages of life, but some sources of adaptation appear to be unique in older life. List the adaptive changes you view as unique, and compare this list with your classmates.

3. Your authors stated that rehabilitation of the elderly is quite different from rehabilitation of the young. Do you agree with this statement? Why or why not?

4. Assume that you are interviewing for a job as a recreation therapist in a geriatric rehabilitation facility. One of the interviewers asks that you explain the role that therapeutic recreation can play in reality orientation, stimulation, behavior therapy, and psychotherapy programs. What is your response?

5. Compare and contrast the following three types of institutional facilities: (1) skilled nursing facilities, (2) intermediate care facilities, and (3) congregate care facilities.

6. Compare and contrast the following three types of community settings: (1) senior centers, (2) adult day care, and (3) in-home services.

SUGGESTED LEARNING ACTIVITIES

1. Assume that you have been invited to teach a unit on cognitive disorders associated with aging to a group of college students. Provide a list

of exam questions you could use to test the student's knowledge of the following:

    a. Chronic Brain Syndrome

    b. Acute Brain Syndrome

    c. Senile dementia

    d. Presenile dementia

    2. Arrange an interview with staff and volunteers at a state institution. Ask the staff and volunteers about the major rewards, problems, and frustrations they experience when working with elderly clients.

    3. Survey your local senior centers to determine the types of services and programs they provide to meet the biological, sociological, psychological, and spiritual needs of senior residents.

    4. Inventory the long-term care facilities in your community. Determine the number of facilities and the types of services rendered, costs, patient characteristics, and so on.

    5. Make a list of a number of elderly individuals who you think are living proof that mental abilities can remain strong throughout life. Compare your list with other classmates. What principal characteristics do these elderly individuals have that contribute to their mental strength in later life?

    6. Assume that you are asked to give an in-service workshop to a nursing home's nonrecreation personnel. Your assigned topic is "The Role of Therapeutic Recreation in Psychosocial Rehabilitation of Institutionalized Elderly." Outline the major ideas you would stress in your presentation. Compare your ideas with those of your classmates.

REFERENCES

AUSTIN, D. R. (1982). *Therapeutic recreation processes and techniques.* New York: John Wiley & Sons.

BEHREN, R. V. (1986). *Adult day care in America: Summary of a national survey.* Washington, DC: The National Council on the Aging and National Institute on Adult Daycare.

BRODY, E. M. (1981). The formal support network: Congregate treatment settings for residents with senescent brain dysfunction. In N. E. MILLER & G. D. COHEN (Eds.), *Clinical aspects of Alzheimer's disease and senile dementia aging* (Vol. 15, pp. 301–333). New York: Raven Press.

BUTLER, R. N., & LEWIS, M. I. (1983). *Aging and mental health.* New York: Mosby.

CITRIN, R. S., & DIXON, D. N. (1977). Reality orientation: A milieu therapy used in an institution for the aged. *Gerontologist, 17,* 39–43.

CLEMENTS, W. M. (1982). Therapeutic functions of recreation in reminiscence with aging persons. In M. L. TEAGUE, R. D. MACNEIL, & G. HITZHUSEN (Eds.), *Perspectives on leisure and aging in a changing society* (pp. 339–351). Columbia, MO: Department of Recreation and Park Administration.

COUSINS, B., & BROWN, E. (1979). *Recreation therapy assessment.* Jacksonville, FL: Amelia Island ICFMR.

DAVIS, C. M. (1986). Introduction. *Topics in Geriatric Rehabilitation, 1*(2), vi–ix.

FILLENBAUM, G. G. (1985). Screening the elderly. *Journal of the American Geriatrics Society, 33*(10), 698–706.

GRANGER, C. L., HAMILTON, A. A., KEITH, R. A., ZIELEZNY, K., & SHERWIN, F. S. (1986). Advance in functional assessment for rehabilitation. *Topics in Geriatric Rehabilitation, 1*(3), 59–74.

GUGEL, R. N., & EISDORFER, S. E. (1986). Psychosocial interventions. *Topics in Geriatric Rehabilitation, 1*(2), 27–34.

HARRIS, B. A., JETTE, A. M., CAMPION, E. W., & CLEARY, P. D. (1986). Validity of self-report measures of functional disability. *Topics in Geriatric Rehabilitation, 1*(3), 31–42.

HENNEY, R. L. (1983). *Persons who are developmentally disabled in nursing homes in the state of Indiana.* Valparaiso, IN: Institute for Comprehensive Planning.

HERRERA, P. M. (1983). *Innovative programming for the aging and aged mentally retarded/developmentally disabled adult.* Akron, OH: Exploration Series Press.

HOWE, C. Z. (1984). Leisure assessment instrumentation in therapeutic recreation. *Therapeutic Recreation Journal, 13*(2), 14–24.

JANICKI, M. P., OTIS, J. P., PUCCIO, P. S., RETTIG, J. H., & JACOBSON, J. W. (1985). Service needs among older developmentally disabled persons. In M. P. JANICKI & H. M. WISNIEWSKI (Eds.), *Aging and developmental disabilities* (pp. 289–304). Baltimore, MD: Paul H. Brookes.

JETTE, A. M. (1986, April). Functional disability and rehabilitation of the aged. *Topics in Geriatric Rehabilitation, 1*(3), 1–8.

JONES, L. (1987). *Activities for the older mentally retarded/developmentally disabled.* Akron, OH: Exploration Series Press.

JOSWIAK, K. F. (1975). *Leisure counseling program materials for the developmentally disabled.* Washington, DC: Hawkins & Associates.

KEMP, B. (1985). Rehabilitation and the older adult. In J. E. BIRREN & K. W. SCHAIE (Eds.), *Handbook of the psychology of aging* (pp. 647–663). New York: Van Nostrand Reinhold.

KIRESUK, T. J., LUND, S. H., & SCHULTZ, S. K. (1981). Service delivery and evaluation from the consumer's point of view. *New Directions for Program Evaluation: Assessing and Interpreting Outcomes, 9,* 57–70.

KRASNER, L. (1971). Behavior therapy. *American Review of Psychology, 22,* 483–532.

MACNEIL, R. D., & TEAGUE, M. L. (1987). *Aging and leisure: Vitality in later life.* Englewood Cliffs, NJ: Prentice-Hall.

MCCRAE, R. R., & COSTA, P. T. (1984). Aging, the life course, and models of personality. In N. W. SHOCK, R. C. GREULICH, R. ANDRES, D. ARENBERG, P. T. COSTA, JR., E. G. LAKATTA, & J. D. TOBIN, *Normal human aging: The Baltimore longitudinal study of aging* (DHHS-NIH Publication No. 84-2450, pp. 292–303). Washington, DC: U.S. Government Printing Office. (Reprinted from *Review of Human Development,* 1982. New York: John Wiley & Sons.)

MCKECHNIE, G. E. (1975). *Manual for the leisure activities blank (LAB).* Palo Alto, CA: Consulting Psychology Press.

PFEIFFER, E. (1977). Psychopathology and social pathology. In J. E. BIRREN & K. W. SCHAIE (Eds.), *Handbook of the psychology of aging* (pp. 640–671). New York: Van Nostrand Reinhold.

PISCOPO, J. (1985). *Physical activity and aging.* New York: John Wiley & Sons.

SEVERNS, S. R. (1986). *Answers to commonly asked questions about the home care campaign.* Unpublished manuscript.

SIRROCCO, A. (1987). The 1986 inventory of long-term care places: An overview of facilities for the mentally retarded. *Advance data from vital and health statistics* (No. 143). (National Center for Health Statistics, DHHS Publication No. PHS 87-1250). Washington, DC: U.S. Government Printing Office.

TEAFF, J. D. (1985). *Leisure services with the elderly.* St. Louis, MO: Times Mirror/ Mosby.

TEAGUE, M. L. (1987). *Health promotion: Achieving high-level wellness in the later years.* Indianapolis, IN: Benchmark Press.

WANTZ, M. S., & GAY, J. E. (1981). *The aging process: A health perspective.* Cambridge, MA: Winthrop Publishers.

WEINER, M. B., BROK, A. J., SNADOWSKY, A. M. (1978). *Working with the aged: Practical approaches in the institution and community.* Englewood Cliffs, NJ: Prentice-Hall.

14

Pediatric Play

JERRY G. DICKASON
AND ANDREW CHASANOFF

OBJECTIVES

- Understand the purpose of therapeutic recreation in a pediatric setting.
- Distinguish between pediatric play and therapeutic recreation.
- Understand the hazards of pediatric classification systems.
- Identify appropriate recreation intervention techniques.
- Comprehend the application of the therapeutic recreation process.
- Review current trends and issues in recreation services for exceptional children.

DEFINITION OF PEDIATRIC PLAY

Children play. Play manifests a child's developmental process. All play theories have one thing in common: people engage in play because it contains that undefinable experience—fun. When a child's play is hampered, all other aspects of the child's life are adversely affected.

Pediatric play is a structured program, in a health care setting for children, that encourages normal patterns of play behavior and minimizes disability and psychological trauma. The play program is designed to encourage cognitive, psychosocial, and sensormotor skills so that children

Note: The authors wish to thank Donna Provenzano, CTRS, Children's Special Hospital, for her professional contributions to this chapter.

can meet their personal leisure needs and adapt to the demands of their environment. The program is conducted by qualified personnel and encourages the participation of all staff, volunteers, and family members.

CLASSIFICATION OF CONDITIONS

Former Secretary of the U.S. Office of Health Education, and Welfare (HEW) Elliott L. Richardson called for a systematic review of the classification and labeling techniques used in the treatment of children. In response to his call and the existing national concern, 10 federal agencies joined together to sponsor the Project on the Classification of Exceptional Children. The project was to increase public understanding of problems associated with the classification and labeling of children who are handicapped, disadvantaged, or delinquent. An objective of the project also was to improve the professional practice of educators, psychologists, physicians, lawyers, social workers, and others responsible for the well-being of exceptional children.

On completion, the project would provide a rationale for public policy. It would identify practical suggestions for legislation and for administrative regulations and guidelines bearing on classification and its consequences. The two-volume *Issues in the Classification of Children: A Source Book on Categories, Labels and Their Consequences* (Hobbs, 1976) describes the results of the project's research on the current practice and thinking regarding the classification of exceptional children.

The project found that classification systems generally fall under three different theoretical perspectives: (1) as a science (biologically based); (2) as psychometric procedures (that measure mental states); and (3) as sociological/social control consequences (environmentally induced factors). The project also concluded that all three of these perspectives and their subsystems are inadequate in relation to what current understandings permit. It established that classification systems cause serious problems because of the following:

- Lack of sophistication in taxomony.
- Presence of strong-running professional biases.
- Preoccupation with dominant symptoms, to the neglect of important determinants of behavior.
- Transposition of adult-appropriate schemes to children.
- Use of classification to legitimize social control of the individual.

Consequently, to classify children's (infant to age 12) and adolescents' (ages 13–20) performances sensitively and accurately as possible, personnel must address three fundamental conditions:

1. The child's current status (health/medical picture).
2. The genesis of the child's condition (etiology) in relation to a social/medical history of the developmental stages, family experiences, and other factors.
3. The implications of intervention, in regard to choice of treatment, method, and prognosis, with possible and/or desirable integration among all these factors.

DESCRIPTION OF LIMITATIONS

It is clear that personnel working with exceptional children must maintain an open position in regard to a child's ability for anything. Children are not accustomed to functioning with preconceived behavior limitations. Their world of play allows them to transcend limitations to achieve a level of satisfaction. Thus, they naturally function in the realm of abilities, not disabilities. Child development is sequential only within each individual, and the progression of developmental stages takes the form of adjustments to changes in the child's physical, emotional, and cognitive experiences. Some changes enhance abilities; and some evoke limits. Children's adjustments to these changes (very often through play) show that they are making sense of, or rather assigning some sort of order to, their experiences. Thus, the adults in a child's life should not arbitrarily assign limits but rather try to understand the self-imposed limits, if any, that are in place.

Personnel must be aware of the effect of drug medications. Children and adolescents are much more unpredictable in regard to reaction time and length of effect. Certain settings, by their nature of treatment, imply limitations, particularly in play programs. For example, in psychiatric programs, sharp implements (scissors and knives) must be used under strict supervision. Isolation orders can severely limit play activity and require a great deal of ingenuity.

PURPOSE OF THERAPEUTIC RECREATION

The purpose of therapeutic recreation, regardless of age or of setting, is to use recreation/play/leisure activity as a treatment modality for some predetermined health/medical problem. The aim or overall goal of therapeutic recreation is to enable individuals to function in any leisure pursuit of their choice at the maximum of their potential. Proper therapeutic recreation programming will move each client along a planned path of steadily decreasing therapist involvement. The therapist encourages the client to become increasingly inner directed or intrinsically motivated.

Pediatric play programs vary according to setting. Not all pediatric play is therapeutic, nor is all therapeutic recreation play. *Pediatric play* is exactly what it says—children with health/medical conditions, requiring intervention services, voluntarily at play. *Therapeutic recreation* is a predetermined plan of recreation/play/leisure activities designed for an individual or a group in response to a specific diagnostic condition.

Whether it is pediatric play or therapeutic recreation, the commonality is usually so strong that the therapeutic recreation department offers both of these services. To illustrate the duality of this purpose, note the six objectives for the Therapeutic Recreation Department of Children's Special Hospital of Mountainside, New Jersey. The first three objectives are designed to allow for both pediatric play and therapeutic recreation. The last three objectives are not treatment goals; rather they are designed to advocate play opportunities for disabled children as well as promote therapeutic recreation as a service.

1. Provide recreational opportunities to best maintain existing abilities and facilitate interests of the patient in as meaningful and purposeful a manner as possible.
2. Introduce leisure activities to promote independence, allow self-direction, and encourage development of self-discipline in the adjustment to irreducible and progressive disability.
3. Heighten patient awareness of the recreational opportunities available through organized private and community programs and commercial leisure services.
4. Enhance the overall effectiveness of the rehabilitation process by sharing information, training, and skills with each team member so that the patient may derive maximum benefit from therapy.
5. Heighten community awareness of the role of the recreation therapist and therapeutic recreation in a rehabilitative children's hospital.
6. Offer a comprehensive training experience for therapeutic recreation students, aiding them in their clinical preparation to best serve patients in a therapeutic activities program. Exposure to program planning and team-oriented treatment is emphasized.

COMMON SERVICE SETTINGS

Children play everywhere; play is not confined to or dependent upon a location. Children can play alone or with others, with or without toys or any props. Pediatric play refers to play that goes on in those settings that offer health/medical care to children.

Pediatric care services usually fall into three categories, based on length of stay: long-term (over 30 days), short-term or acute (less than 30 days), and day care (one day only). Long-term and acute services are residential by their very nature of services in order to provide a continuity of care in treating the diagnosis. Examples of long-term and acute care settings are developmental centers for the mentally retarded and multiply handicapped, physical rehabilitation centers for the physically disabled, juvenile delinquency residences for the socially maladjusted, psychiatric centers for the emotionally and mentally ill, cancer hospitals and hospices for the terminally ill, residences for the blind or the deaf, and general hospitals for the unexpected accidents and illnesses. Many of these settings offer day care services as well as local recreation and parks departments, human service agencies, and disability-specific agencies.

CURRENT BEST PRACTICES AND PROCEDURES

Therapeutic recreation is a four-phase cyclical process. First, the therapist assesses the client's needs. Second, the therapist and others plan goals and objectives to address the assessed needs. Implementing programs in response to those goals and objectives is the third phase. This is followed by applying a systematic evaluation procedure that allows the therapist to determine the effectiveness of the implemented program.

Assessment

Assessments are inventories of the client's current state. Evaluations are estimates about behavior judged against a standard behavior for consideration of change. Testing is a quantitative measurement of the client's ability.

The application of assessments, evaluations, and tests will vary according to the setting in which they appear. For example, in a physical rehabilitation setting, the recreation therapist might assess a client's cognitive function. The therapist would then evaluate the client's potential for increasing memory, orientation, direction following, and scanning. Next the therapist would test to see if cognitive awareness has increased.

Most settings have their own established procedures for doing assessments, evaluations, and testing. The information received is generally recorded on predetermined forms, which are referred to as instruments or tools for collecting the information. Most therapeutic recreation instruments are patterned after well-known instruments such as the Gesell Chart on Childhood Development, Erik Erikson's Stages of Development, and the Adaptive Behavior Scale of the American Association on Mental Deficiency.

The following instruments are available specifically to assess performance abilities for therapeutic recreation purposes:

"I Can" (Wessel, 1977)

Leisure Diagnostic Battery (LDB) (Witt, 1982)

Play Observation Scale (POS) (Rubin, 1986)

Recreation Behavior Inventory (RBI) (Berryman & Lefebvre, 1981)

Structured Observation of Academic and Play Settings (SOAPS) (Roberts, Millich, & Looney, 1985)

Planning

Therapeutic recreation is one of many services that exist for the sole purpose of the betterment of the child. Most setting encourage all service programs to meet jointly and prepare, in an interdisciplinary effort, the best program possible for each child.

In an educational setting, this program is referred to as an Individual Education Plan (IEP). In a clinical setting, the program is often called an Individual Treatment Plan (ITP) or an Individual Program Plan (IPP).

Regardless of setting, all plans are formulated to meet the individual needs of each child. They address the needs of the whole child through their interdisciplinary design. Plans are goal oriented to achieve specific behaviors. They are implemented through sequential procedures and are continually evaluated to determine the future direction of improvement.

Implementation

A full array of program ideas and activities are possible tools for implementation. Such ideas and activities should express the general interest of the child. The activities should be specific and within the capacity of the individual or group to provide opportunity for immediate satisfaction and evident progress. An activity should be a stimulation for further related activity. However, for treatment purposes it is important to remember that activities are only tools to achieve therapeutic recreational goals.

For example, puppetry as an activity provides an opportunity to indulge in fantasy and unadulterated play. As a therapeutic tool, puppetry allows the child to express feelings directly through another character. And through such expression, a child can relay concerns about confinement, abandonment, body image, and medical uncertainties. At the same time, verbalizing through the other character allows the child to control the concerns by promoting the transfer of thoughts to his or her own situation (Linn, Beardslee, & Patenaude, 1986).

To accomplish therapeutic ends through activities, the therapist must do the following:

- Plan actions for each patient based on listening, analyzing, and acting in accordance wit the evaluated data.
- Increase his or her knowledge through observations of the patient and discussions with other therapists.
- Use all existing facilities to enrich the program.
- Teach and lead activities in order that the patient learn skills as well as have fun.
- Help the patient lead activities and gain his or her own skills in sharing learned activities.
- Use other specialists to add breadth and variety to the program.
- Plan for future actions, using foresight and hindsight facilitated by recording and evaluating past meetings and experiences.

Evaluation

Keeping in mind that evaluations are estimates about behavior judged against a standard behavior, the therapist first must identify the expected standard of behavior. The therapist then can determine how far the behavior deviates from the standard.

The therapist's judgment of this deviation is the evaluation, which can be recorded in several different ways. The common recording methods are progress notes, evaluation instruments, and team meeting summaries. Progress notes, the therapist's written comments on the progress and/or performance of the client, are kept in the patient's chart. They are to be recorded after each therapy session. Evaluation instruments provide a list of predetermined standards against which the therapist rates the patient's present level of performance. The same instrument is used periodically to document change in the patient's performance. Team meeting summaries are recorded summary statements declaring the patient's current performance. These summary statements result from interdisciplinary staff discussions of the patient's performance.

Each evaluation is a benchmark for determining further action and becomes the new starting point for treatment of the patient. Thus the cycle is complete and initiates its own beginning.

APPLICATION OF THE TR PROCESS

In order to better understand the therapeutic application of recreation, the client, Joey, is presented to illustrate the TR process. Information regarding Joey's case is given in each of the four phases.

CASE STUDY

Joey is a 12-year-old boy who was involved in a motor vehicle accident and sustained a spinal cord injury. He was transferred to Children's Special Hospital for rehabilitative services. Shortly after his admission, he was referred by the attending physician for therapeutic recreation.

Assessment

The therapist gathered information in the following categories before the initial contact with Joey:

1. *Specific etiology of the impairment.* Joey has a spinal cord lesion at the T-12 level. T-12 is the thoracic vertebra just above the first lumbar vertebra. (A traumatic disruption of the spinal cord is often associated with extensive musculoskeletal involvement; such trauma may cause varying degrees of paraplegia and quadriplegia.)

2. *Functional limitations.* Joey is a nonambulatory paraplegic. He must use a wheelchair and back brace, and perform self-catheterization every four hours.

3. *Family social history.* Joey is the third child of five children, with two brothers older (ages 14 and 16) and two sisters younger (ages 7 and 11). His father is an electrician, and his mother is a schoolteacher (second grade). The family is very active in their church and community affairs. (Additional information is most often available through the social service department's intake report, which is placed in the patient's medical chart.)

4. *School standing/school report.* Joey is in the seventh grade. He is an average (B−, C+) student and plays first string on the soccer team.

After collecting the above information, the recreation therapist makes contact with Joey and conducts an initial assessment within 10 days of the admission date. During this initial contact the therapist carrys out the following tasks:

1. Develops rapport by informally introducing self to Joey and his family before asking any questions. This is followed by explaining the purpose and functions of the TR department—the role of the recreation therapist(s) as well as the various programs, activities, and their location. To put Joey at ease, the therapist can ask Joey general information questions, such as age, school, siblings, interests.

2. Determines Joey's past recreation and leisure experiences and current leisure/prevocational interests. This is accomplished by first having informal conversations with him regarding his interests, hobbies, and music or sports activities. Are there any strong

interests or dislikes? Family members often provide unsolicited descriptions of the patient's interests. The therapist then conducts a leisure interest survey, reviews social service assessment, and gathers information form other team members to augment the informal discussions.

3. Assesses Joey's behaviors. What are his gross motor and fine motor abilities? What is his cognitive ability? What are his sensory abilities?

4. Records assessment of Joey's interests, abilities, behavior characteristics, orientation, affect, and self-image. The therapist must observe Joey's relationships with other patients and staff. Is he friendly, withdrawn, manipulative, cooperative? What is his emotional state? Does he laugh or smile? Is he depressed, immature, shy, impatient? What are Joey's conversation patterns? Can he initiate conversation, or does he respond only when spoken to? Does he need help in staying on the topic? Does he need frequent cuing to recollect words? Is he able to express wants and needs? During discussions about recreation interests and the leisure interest survey, the therapist should document whenever Joey shows interest in recreation activities.

5. Assesses Joey's gross and fine motor skills. Do the lower extremities (LE) function? What is the body's posture? Is there balance and coordinated movement? Do the upper extremities (UE) function (i.e., dominant hand, grasp/release of objects, tremors, manipulation of objects, writing skills, left UE and/or right UE weakness/paralysis, use of nondominant UE as gross motor assistance during activities)? Are there coordinated movement and bilateral skills (i.e., use of both arms, cross midline)?

6. Assesses Joey's cognitive skills. What is Joey's level of orientation? For example, is he oriented to person, place, and time? Is he aware of the environment and those around him? What is Joey's memory ability? Does he display past (before the injury), recent (within a month), or immediate (within two hours) memory? The therapist must observe Joey's attention span, comprehension of auditory and visual information, problem-solving skills, ability to organize and present sequential information, and level of safety awareness.

Planning

When planning therapeutic recreation goals and objectives, the therapist must take into account the overall goals of the rehabilitative team and the data collected from the initial assessment.

Joey's overall rehabilitative goals are to acquire independent mobility, develop upper extremity strength, and have command of his activities of daily living.

The therapist now reviews the observations noted from initial contact during the first 10 days of hospitalization. Joey in general demonstrates a positive affect. He easily engages in conversation with staff, openly expresses his opinions, is friendly and outgoing, initiates interactions with roommates, and has become familiar with other staff in the hospital in a short amount of time.

He appears to function at age-appropriate levels. He displays good attention span as well as carryover, following-through, and organization and strategy formulation abilities.

He is able to talk sensibly about his life before the accident and demonstrates memory for past, present, and immediate events, He talks about his participation in school sports and is oriented to person, place, and time. He seems extremely close to his father and appears to have a good relationship with both parents. He is beginning to show an awareness of the implications of his impairment.

Before determining the therapeutic recreation goals and objectives, the therapist should consider the following factors:

- At what age did the accident occur?
- What were the factors relevant to the patient's life at that time, such as family relationships, network of friends, and social events?
- What were the previous interest and level of participation?
- What is the psychological impact of the transition from being ambulatory to nonambulatory?
- How easy is it for the patient to communicate with staff and peers?
- What are the possible cognitive deficits?
- How involved will the family be in the rehabilitative process?

After considering all of the above information, the recreation therapist can determine both short- and long-term TR goals. In Joey's case the goals are the following:

Short-Term Goals

1. Improve upper extremity strength.
2. Improve wheelchair mobility.
3. Increase peer interaction/socialization.
4. Increase involvement in various recreation groups such as adaptive cooking, teen group, evening programs.
5. Increase awareness of wheelchair sports.
6. Increase awareness of the opportunities for trips and travel.

Long-Term Goals:

1. Initiate voluntary participation in out-trips.
2. Participate in wheelchair sports in the community.
3. Participate in commercial travel programs.

Within one month from his initial involvement in therapeutic recreation, the previously set goals for Joey are reviewed and new treatment plans are formulated which involve the following participation requirements:

1. Participate in a minimum of three gross motor activities a week to strengthen UE to adjust to wheelchair mobility.
2. Interact with peers in a small group setting 3 times a week for 30 minutes each.
3. Participate in one evening out-trip.
4. Be introduced to a racing chair used in wheelchair sports.

Implementation

During this phase of the treatment process, the therapist works toward addressing the emotional, physical, and social needs of the patient. Initial sessions help the patient become familiar with the therapists, staff, and hospital setting. This contributes to establishing a rapport of concern and trust with the patient. The recreation therapist needs to be creative in planning, adapting, and carrying out activities that are challenging to the patient and that encourage him to achieve his potential.

In Joey's case, the recreation therapist first schedules him for individual recreation, one-half hour daily. During these session, the therapist introduces him to gross motor activities (wheelchair basketball and hand soccer) and cognitive games. On a one-to-one basis, Joey is able to express feelings and talk about his injury and the impact it is having on his life. Such sessions prepare Joey for the transition from individual to small group activity. The small group environment of patients about the same age and cognitive ability enables Joey to generalize his condition and realize that others are similarly handicapped. This allows Joey to socialize with his peers in a relaxed atmosphere and share experiences with them.

Throughout both individual and group sessions, the therapist gradually introduces Joey to wheelchair sports that allow him to remain physically active and provide health opportunities to compete against himself as well as others. Simultaneously, Joey participates in several community trips to local and regional softball games, movie theaters, and concert auditoriums. During trips to nonstructured settings, the therapist observes

Joey's ability to negotiate physical barriers such as curbs and rough terrain, and social barriers such as having people stare or make an issue of his condition. From these observations, the therapist is able to "coach" Joey on some technical maneuverability skills and make him feel comfortable with his own responses to the environment. Consequently, Joey begins to feel comfortable enough to reestablish contacts with his community and to establish new contacts, especially among wheelchair sports enthusiasts.

Evaluation

During this final phase, the therapist compares observations of the patient from the time of admission until the patient's discharge. The therapist's evaluation report should include statements about the following:

1. Affect, behavior, social skills.
2. Physical, mental, and social level at the time of discharge.
3. Recreation skill levels at time of discharge.
4. Gains made in recreational therapy.
5. Areas that still need improvement.
6. Suggestions for future involvement in recreational/leisure activities.

On the basis of such information, the therapist determines the effectiveness of the activities/programs selected for the patient's treatment as they relate to the preestablished goals and objectives.

In regard to Joey's case, the recreational therapist continues to assess his behavior and performance weekly. Directly following his treatment sessions, the therapist notes observations for future documentation in monthly progress reports.

Throughout his hospitalization, Joey was included in a variety of recreational therapy programs. Joey's behavior remained fairly consistent over the four months that he was seen. He was a friendly, cooperative, and outgoing participant in most programs. He most often displayed a positive affect, had a good sense of humor, and interacted well with both peers and staff.

During both individual and group sessions, Joey was introduced to a variety of higher-level cognitive games, which he was able to play independently. At the time of discharge, he was able to select appropriate activities for these sessions as well as teach them to peers and staff.

In terms of his gross motor abilities, Joey was able to participate actively in such sports as wheelchair basketball. He learned to maneuver his wheelchair fairly accurately and was able to negotiate rough/smooth terrain, such as grass and pavement. During one hospital leave to his home,

Joey participated in a practice basketball game with a local adult wheelchair team.

Through the various trips, Joey became aware of several barriers/ obstacles that he would have to consider in his own community/ environment before going out with family and friends. While participating on such trips, Joey displayed appropriate social skills and good safety judgment.

At the time of discharge, the staff recommended that Joey pursue his interest in active sports through a wheelchair sports program and/or established wheelchair basketball team. Through a series of leisure counseling sessions, the recreation therapist provided him and his family with the necessary resources in their community that would promote his involvement in wheelchair sports in his area.

In summation, therapeutic interventions led to the accomplishment of the short-term rehabilitation goals. At the time of discharge, Joey's coordination and strength were greatly improved through his participation in gross motor activities, such as wheelchair basketball and hand soccer. He was able to maneuver his wheelchair independently over various types of terrain. Participation in active games and trips strengthened his wheelchair mobility. The involvement in such trips with small groups also increased his spontaneity in initiating interactions with peers. Teen group and adaptive cooking activities had increased his involvement in various groups. At the time of discharge, Joey had successfully made the transition to group sessions. He no longer required individual treatment to manage his feelings about his disability.

TRENDS AND ISSUES

The hospitalization of children has declined considerably over the past several years. This decrease is caused by several factors: an increase in the number of physicians with knowledge about health care who treat a problem before it becomes serious; and expansion of community health care services that focus specifically on children's services; and the lowered birthrate.

Because the pediatric inpatient occupancy rates are declining nationally, hospitals feel a need for new programs to generate income. Such programs use existing pediatric facilities and staff resources without adding to the hospital budget. An exemplary new program is a children's sick room, where parents can bring sick children on a day-to-day basis. This concept meets several community needs.

Most schools and day care programs do not provide medical attention or even the supervision of medical treatment. There are a growing number of families where both parents have careers, and such health care is necessary so that parents are not required to use sick days or vacation days. Also, there are a growing number of working single parents who need such services to maintain their children's health as well as the family's source of income (Harrison, 1987).

Sickness usually restricts play behavior, but boredom remains. Quiet play activities and caring attention are needed to enhance the recuperating process. For such reasons, the pediatric home care programs are an emerging trend for children who have special needs of a longer duration but do not require constant specialized services. Play and recreation opportunities are extremely important to these children during convalescence.

Child Life is a newly organized discipline within pediatric settings. Child Life programs "strive to promote optimum development of children, adolescents and families, to maintain normal living patterns and to minimize psychological trauma. As integral members of the health care team in both ambulatory care and in-patient settings, Child Life staff provides opportunities for gaining a sense of mastery, for play, for learning, for self-expression, for family involvement and for peer interaction" (Child Life Position Statement, 1983).

The goals of Child Life programs are the following:

• To minimize stress and anxiety for the child and adolescent.
• To provide essential life experiences.
• To provide opportunities to retain self-esteem and appropriate independence.
• To educate persons interested in becoming Child Life specialists.

In Radlett, England, the Save the Children Fund cosponsored Playtrac, a unique mobile play resources center that travels from setting to setting, including community homes and institutions. Playtrac's aim is to give advice on creative play and support to workers and relatives of mentally handicapped people. Playtrac also offers training to staff on play methods and helps them be aware of the role of play (Landford, 1987).

Pediatric programs are beginning to conduct parent orientation programs that encourage parents to be an active part of their child's treatment program. Some settings offer planning sessions with parents to establish individual guidelines as to how the parents can participate in the care of their child. In such settings the recreation staff invite family members to participate with their children in on-site and off-ground programs (Koch-Critchfield, 1987).

Technological advances in alternate breathing procedures, mechanical ventilation, and specialized respiratory equipment have evolved into the subspecialty of neonatology. Consequently, there is an ever-growing number of survivors who are dependent on these life support devices and sophisticated care. It was noted during the 1982 Surgeon General's Workshop on Children with Handicaps and Their Families that this new technol-

ogy has created the ventilator-dependent patient (VDP), and that ventilator-dependent children particularly need additional technology as well as
staff-family training and communication to relieve the state of dependency. Posch and Edwards (1988) point out that in New Jersey's Children's
Specialized Hospital "an increasing number of admission inquiries regarding ventilator-dependent children has [*sic*] been received, prompting the
hospital administration to explore the feasibility of and need for a special
program." A program was initiated. The therapeutic recreation staff's
assessment of the needs of these children determined that play and developmental activities would be conducted bedside. They would be performed
on an individual basis until the patient was able to participate physically,
emotionally, and technologically with others.

SUMMARY

This chapter provides an overview of pediatric play services in a variety of
settings that specialize in health/medical care for children. Pediatric play is
a structured program in a health care setting for children that encourages
normal patterns of play behavior and minimizes disability and psychological trauma.

Pediatric diagnostic classification systems generally fall into three
different theoretical perspectives: (1) as a biologically based science, (2) as
psychometric procedures that measure mental states, and (3) as sociolog-
ical/social control consequences (environmentally induced factors). Regardless of the classification system, all systems must address (1) the child's
current health/medical status, (2) the genesis of the child's condition (etiology) in relation to a social/medical history of the developmental stages,
family experiences, and other factors, and (3) the implication of intervention in regard to choice of treatment, method, and prognosis, with possible
and/or desirable integration among all these factors.

Pediatric play programs vary according to setting. Not all pediatric play is therapeutic recreation, nor is all therapeutic recreation play. In
spite of the increase of specialized medical services for children, the hospitalization of children has declined considerably over the past several
years.

READING COMPREHENSION QUESTIONS

1. Why are classification systems inadequate?
2. Cite some examples of how a classification becomes a labeling
device.
3. What is the difference between pediatric play and therapeutic
recreation?

4. How do therapeutic recreation objectives vary depending upon the setting?

5. Identify the difference between assessment, evaluation, and testing.

6. What is an IEP and ITP? What do they have in common?

SUGGESTED LEARNING ACTIVITIES

1. Visit two different pediatric play programs.

2. Discuss with the recreation therapists, in each setting, the focus of recreation for their program.

3. Compare the two settings and justify their different approaches to providing recreation services.

4. After visiting a pediatric setting, discuss with your classmates the classification system used in that setting.

5. Identify the therapeutic recreation objectives that are unique for a particular setting.

6. Review the assessment, evaluation, and/or testing instruments of a pediatric play program. What kind of questions are asked? What is done with the information received?

REFERENCES

BERRYMAN, D. L., & LEFEBVRE, C. B. (1981). *Recreation behavior inventory*. Denton, TX: Leisure Learning Systems.

CHILD LIFE POSITION STATEMENT. (1983). Association for the Care of Children's Health, 3615 Wisconsin Avenue, Washington, DC 20016.

HARRISON, L. (1987). Establishing and evaluating a children's sick room program. *American Journal of Maternal Child Nursing, 12*(3), 204–206.

HOBBS, N. (Ed.). (1976). *Issues in the classification of children: A source book on categories, labels and their consequences* (2 vol.). San Francisco: Jossey-Bass.

KOCH-CRITCHFIELD, M. (1987). When a child needs his parents most: Caring for a dying child. *RN, 50*(7), 7–8.

LANDFORD, R. (1987). Time to play. *Nursing Times, 83*(7), 40–41.

LINN, S. BEARDLSEE, W., & PATENAUDE, A. (1986). Puppet therapy with pediatric bone marrow transplant patients. *Journal of Pediatric Psychology, 11*(1), 37–46.

POSCH, C. M., & EDWARDS, P. A. (1988). The ventilator-dependent child: Challenge and opportunity, *Rehabilitation Nursing, 13*(1), 15–18.

ROBERTS, M. A., MILICH, R., & LOONEY, J. (1985). *Structured observation of academic and play settings (SOAPS): Manual*. (Available from Mary Ann Roberts, Ph.D., Hospital School, University of Iowa, Iowa City, IA 52242.)

RUBIN, K. H. (1986). Play, peer interactions, and social development. In A. Gottfried & C. C. Brown (Eds.), *Play interactions* (pp. 163–174). Lexington, MA: Lexington Books.

WESSEL, J. (1977). *Planning individualized education programs in special education: With examples from "I can" physical education*. Northbrook, IL: Hubbard.

WITT, P. A. (1982). *The leisure diagnostic battery user's guide*. Denton, TX: Division of Recreation and Leisure Studies, North Texas Sate University, 1982.

15

Cardiac Rehabilitation

FRANCIS A. McGUIRE
AND LODENE GOODWIN

OBJECTIVES

- Know types of cardiac conditions.
- Comprehend the phases of cardiac rehabilitation programs.
- Appreciate the role of therapeutic recreation in cardiac rehabilitation.
- Demonstrate a knowledge of the settings where cardiac rehabilitation takes place.

DEFINITION OF CARDIAC DISEASES

According to Ford (1986), mortality from cardiovascular disease (CVD) has changed to the point where more people are living longer with CVD than ever before. Monteiro (1979) estimates that 85% of the individuals experiencing an acute myocardial infarction (heart attack) will survive and return to previous activity. This will increase the likelihood that therapeutic recreation professionals will work with clients with cardiac conditions. In some cases this may occur in cardiac rehabilitation programs. In other cases this may occur in other settings, because cardiac diseases are pervasive in our society.

Ford (1986) provided the following facts about CVD:

- CVD is the leading cause of death in the United states.
- Approximately 42 million Americans suffer from CVD, more than any other disorder.
- More deaths result from CVD than from cancer and accidents combined.

- The most common types of CVD are hypertensive heart disease (37 million patients), coronary heart disease (4.5 million), rheumatic heart disease (2 million), and cerebrovascular accident (stroke) (1.8 million).

CLASSIFICATION OF CARDIAC DISEASES

According to Montoye and colleagues (1988), cardiovascular disease is "a term for any of the many diseases that can negatively affect the health of the heart and/or blood vessels" (p. 220). The largest categories of cardiovascular diseases are heart attacks and strokes. Because strokes are discussed in Chapter 12, this chapter will focus on heart attacks and other cardiac conditions.

Most heart diseases are actually vascular diseases that constrict or block normal flow of blood either in or out of the heart. Other diseases, such as rheumatic fever, syphilis, and infections, also cause heart damage.

Congenital heart disease results from some defect in the development of the heart before birth. The heart begins to develop toward the end of the first month of fetal life and looks like an adult heart toward the end of the second fetal month. Congenital heart disease is a condition originating from failure of the necessary twisting, joining, and division of two primitive arteries to take place in proper sequence, as the heart is forming its four chambers, valves, and arteries. Congenital defects of the heart and residuals from rheumatic fever are the two most common causes of heart disease, and in both areas cardiac surgery has had remarkable results (DeBakey & Gotto, 1977).

In hypertensive heart disease, the heart is forced to pump harder because of the constriction of the arteries caused by increased blood pressure. This disease strikes all ages and both sexes, although blacks are more commonly affected than whites.

Heart failure is described as the failure of the heart to pump sufficient blood to maintain normal circulation. It can result from high blood pressure, heart attack, birth defects, or rheumatic heart disease. Congestive heart failure occurs when heart failure results in congestion in the body's tissues. Fluid gathers in the legs, lungs, and abdomen. Rheumatic heart disease results from damage done to the heart as a result of rheumatic fever. The heart valves are typically damaged in rheumatic heart disease (American Heart Association, 1980).

Coronary heart disease results from the narrowing of coronary arteries and a resulting decrease in blood supply to the heart. Coronary heart disease is also called ischemic heart disease and coronary artery disease (American Heart Association, 1980).

Arteriosclerosis, the most common form of heart disease, is actually a group of diseases that are characterized by a thickening and loss of elasticity of the artery walls. Atherosclerosis is a type of arteriosclerosis in which deposits of a fatty substance, called plaque, makes the inner layer of the artery wall thick and irregular (American Heart Association, 1980).

Any abnormality of the heart rate or rhythm is called cardiac arrhythmia. An arrythmia may decrease the amount of blood the heart pumps each minute, which in turn decreases blood supply to the body's organs.

Cardiac arrest, or cessation of the heartbeat, results in a drop in blood pressure and curtailment of circulation of the blood (American Heart Association, 1980).

A myocardial infarction is the death or damaging of an area of the heart muscle as a result of an interruption in the blood reaching that area (American Heart Association, 1980).

PURPOSE OF THERAPEUTIC RECREATION

A greater number of people survive open heart surgery and myocardial infarctions today than 20 years ago. Indications are that even greater numbers will survive in the future as a result of better medical care, advanced technology, and emphasis on prevention. Increasing emphasis is being placed on postinfarction care and postoperative care of patients. Rehabilitation is designed to assist the patient in achieving the greatest physical, social, and economic usefulness possible.

Generally, the physical aspects of recovery are less trying on the cardiac patient than are emotional and social recovery. The individual who has experienced a cardiac event faces emotional adaptation during recovery. The patient responds psychologically to a loss and may experience functional problems such as fatigue, shortness of breath, sleeplessness, loss of appetite, nervousness, and impotence. These functional problems are symptomatic of the grieving process. Denial may be one strategy used by some; others may be very knowledgeable of their illness, thus attaining a feeling of greater control. Prescribed exercise of a physical nature may also produce a feeling of control when the pain decreases and the heart develops greater efficiency (Gentry & Williams, 1975).

Individuals who do not develop effective coping strategies experience a higher mortality rate due to prolonged physiological stress. Psychological intervention should be accomplished to assist the cardiac patient in developing more effective and appropriate coping skills.

Although the role of exercise in the cardiac rehabilitation process has been well established, leisure's role is less clearly identified. Hoeft (1982) stated that there are few references made concerning the enhancement of cardiac patients' leisure attitudes, interests, satisfaction, and leisure self-concept. She indicated, however, that there is limited evidence that a lack of leisure satisfaction correlates with stress in postmyocardial patients.

Activities that assist patients in reducing stress and others factors (such as obesity, smoking, lack of exercise, and poor nutrition) related to heart attacks are a necessary component of the rehabilitation process. Efforts designed to assist patients in developing life-style changes that reduce the likelihood of further cardiac problems are often included in patient education programs (Hayes & Antozzi, 1982).

According to Cornett and Watson (1984), a cardiac rehabilitation program has three goals: (1) assisting the patient in returning to work and previous activities, (2) educating the patient about heart disease, its management and prevention, and (3) maintaining psychological and social well-being. The therapeutic recreation specialist can be instrumental in meeting all these goals. Programs such as stress reduction, use of leisure activities to incorporate more physical activity gradually into the patient's life, and life-style education aimed at identifying and removing risk factors such as poor nutrition, smoking, and lack of physical activity.

Rehabilitation begins almost immediately upon hospitalization and must extend beyond this period of recovery. Cornett and Watson (1984) report that cardiac patients who receive expert care during the acute phase of their illness but are discharged with no further treatment often require readmission to the hospital. Therefore, rehabilitation is a lifelong process focusing on disability adaptation, health maintenance, and illness prevention (Cornett and Watson, 1984). The four-phase rehabilitation program that has received wide acceptance is designed to accomplish those goals.

The focus during the rehabilitation process shifts as the patient progresses. Phase I is an inpatient program lasting approximately 7–14 days. Phase II is an outpatient program lasting approximately 2–3 months. Phase III is a supervised community-based program lasting 6–12 months, and Phase IV is an unsupervised or maintenance program that is indefinite (Wilson, Edgett, & Porter, 1986).

The primary foci during cardiac rehabilitation are exercises to return the patient to as high a level of physical functioning possible and education to reduce the likelihood of a further cardiac event. The relative importance of these two purposes shift as the patient passes through the four phases, but they are present at all times.

COMMON SERVICE SETTINGS

There are primarily four settings where cardiac rehabilitation services occur: hospital inpatient, hospital outpatient, the community, and the home. Rehabilitation begins almost immediately upon admission to the hospital and continues through discharge. While in the hospital, rehabilitation moves from the patient's room to a cardiac rehabilitation facility within the hospital. After discharge from the hospital, patients continue rehabilitation through regular outpatient programs at the rehabilitation center as well as at home. Upon completion of the rehabilitation program at the hospital, patients typically continue to participate in community-based programs in facilities such as YMCAs.

According to Wenger (1986), rehabilitation of cardiac patients should be designed to limit the impact of the illness while seeking to maintain and restore an optimum level of functioning in all areas of behavior. This process begins during the first days of hospitalization (Phase I). Initial rehabilitation efforts, done within those first days, are aimed at early ambulation and education. Helping the patient develop a positive attitude is also part of this early inpatient rehabilitation. Early ambulation programs are appropriate for individuals with uncomplicated myocardial infarction. Physical activities during this initial rehabilitation phase are limited to activities that are low in intensity. These include activities such as eating, simple self-care, simple passive and active arm and leg movements, and sitting in a chair. These occur while the patient is still in the intensive care or coronary care unit.

Upon leaving this unit, the focus is on increasing cardiovascular functioning to a level sufficient for personal care and independent living upon discharge from the hospital. Typical activities include simple leg and arm movement, and simple calisthenics and walking.

The outpatient phase (Phase II) of the rehabilitation program has several objectives (Fardy, 1986). These include a restoration of physical functioning, restoration of confidence, reduction of anxiety and depression, enhancement of life-style habits, development of a commitment to physical activity, and management of myocardial arrhythmias (p. 424). A program of exercise and education is followed to meet these objectives.

Fardy suggests that Phase II exercise programs focus on rhythmic movements of large muscle groups. These would include upper as well as lower extremities. Anaerobic activities, heavy resistance activities, and isometric exercises are contraindicated during this phase of rehabilitation. Patient education during this times should focus (Fardy, 1986) on providing information that will provide physical and emotional support during rehabilitation.

Miller and colleagues (1986) state that many individuals can enter community-based rehabilitation programs sooner than ever before after their heart attack. As a result, Phase II rehabilitation may not be necessary for all individuals. In that case, the patient would enter a community program. This has traditionally been considered Phase III in the rehabilitation process.

The community program focuses on the development of healthy lifestyle approaches. Patients are provided education on risk factors, and they achieve improved functional capacity during this phase (Miller et al., 1986). This period, ranging form 6–12 months, is a time when the patient works to replace destructive habits with constructive ones. Locations available for community-based cardiac rehabilitation programs include university medical schools; community colleges and public schools; YMCAs, YWCAs, and community centers; hospital exercise programs; and independent cardiac rehabilitation facilities. Heart clubs, often sponsored by the heart association, are primary community support organizations for heart disease patients.

The program of the Cardiac Rehabilitation Center of the Greenville, South Carolina, Hospital System is reflective of the phases in the rehabilitation process as well as the settings where that rehabilitation takes place (Greenville Hospital Systems, undated). The rehabilitation program focuses on exercise and behavior change.

The Greenville Hospital cardiac rehabilitation program is designed to improve the cardiovascular functioning and physical fitness of the following:

- Patients with acute myocardial infarction.
- Patients who have had coronary artery bypass graft or other cardiac surgery.
- Patients who have coronary heart disease or are considered to be at high risk of developing it.

Phase I of the rehabilitation process begins at the patient's bedside. It will occur in the patient's room or on the nursing floor. Once a patient has progressed sufficiently, Phase I rehabilitation shifts to an inpatient exercise center within the hospital. Equipment such as stationary bicycles, treadmills, and stairs are used in the rehabilitation program.

Phase II participants are those discharged from the hospital. They visit the cardiac rehabilitation center in the hospital 3 times a week for a period of 4–12 weeks. The same equipment used during Phase I is used during this phase. In addition, Phase II patients are given a home exercise program to follow. Phase II clients are composed of Phase I graduates as well as other individuals with documented heart disease.

Phase III and Phase IV patients participate in a medically supervised program at the YMCA. In addition, they continue a home exercise program.

CURRENT BEST PRACTICES AND PROCEDURES

Assessment

Assessment of cardiac patients is designed to gather data in two main areas: medical and life-style. The medical information is primarily used to develop an appropriate exercise regimen for the patient. The life-style assessment is done to identify risk factors, such as poor nutrition or inactive leisure, that will become the focus of a behavioral modification program.

Although the recreation therapist must be aware of the medical assessment and any activity contraindications resulting from it, he or she will be more directly involved in the life-style assessment unless he or she is trained in exercise physiology.

Comoss and colleagues (1979) define assessment with cardiac clients as "the collection and analysis of information about the patient's health status." The precise nature of the assessment process they describe varies across the four phases of the rehabilitation process. During Phase I, data related to early educational needs of the patient, as well as physiological factors such as heart rate and blood pressure, are crucial. The focus during Phase II shifts to assessing activity readiness as well as determining the educational needs of the client in areas such as stress reduction, nutrition, smoking, medical procedures, or activity management.

Assessment during Phase III focuses on gathering subjective information related to demographics, cardiac history, general health, and a psychosocial history dealing with patient life-style. In addition, exercise testing is done to measure work capacity.

Phase IV assessment revolves around a nursing history, cardiovascular examination, and an exercise stress test. Part of the nursing history assessment is designed to identify factors, such as chronic congestive heart failure, that limit exercise participation. In addition, signs, such as angina, to be aware of during exercise will be identified during the Phase IV assessment. Information also is needed about medications and their side effects.

Cornett and Watson (1984) specifically identify areas to be included in an activity assessment. These include a description of daily and weekly activities, frequency and type of exercise, living arrangements, sexual activity, and sleep patterns. They also acknowledge that all aspects of the rehabilitation process, including assessments, be carried out by a team of professionals.

The therapeutic recreation specialist will be most heavily involved in assessing the patient's social history. According to Wilson, Fardy, and Froelicher (1981), the social history will include information related to occupational physical activity; job satisfaction; family and work responsibilities; leisure time physical activity; family medical and socioeconomic history; smoking, drinking, and eating habits; sexual activity; and geographic history (p. 235).

Planning

A basic term TR specialists should understand prior to planning programs for cardiac rehabilitation clients is *Metabolic Units* (MET). One MET is the equivalent of the energy the body consumes when it is at rest. METs provide a way of evaluating activities to determine their energy costs (Cohn, Duke, & Madrid, 1979).

As patients move through the four phases of cardiac rehabilitation, they are capable of increasing the METs at which they can function. Cornett and Watson (1984) indicate that activities in the 1–2 MET range are appropriate as the Phase I program begins; they call this the "acute" phase. Activities in this range include reading, watching television, playing card, and sewing. In Phase II, the "convalescent" phase, patients progress to activities requiring 3–4 Mets. This includes activities such as gardening, bowling, horseshoes, and slow bicycling.

The TR specialist should work with the exercise physiologist or physician who has developed an exercise prescription for the patient, in order to incorporate recreation activities into that prescription. Consultation will also help the therapist identify the maximum physical load to place on clients.

In addition to planning activities that provide appropriate levels of activity, TR specialists also must participate in educational activities that will result in permanent life-style changes. This includes planning programs aimed at stress reduction, use of leisure in productive ways, and appropriate levels of leisure involvement within the patient's level of physical fitness.

Limitations

The primary limitations on cardiac rehabilitation patients are in the areas of physical activity. The use of the MET requirement of activities is useful in identifying upper levels of exertion. In addition, individuals working with cardiac patients must be aware of danger signals that indicate excessive exercise. According to Cornett and Watson (1984), an activity is excessive if it results in a variety of symptoms, including diaphoresis, pallor, cyanosis, nausea, and dyspnea. A significant increase in blood pressure and increases in heart rate also indicate excessive activity. Concerns after exercise include insomnia, excessive excitement, exhilaration, weakness, fatigue, muscular cramping, skeletal muscular pain, gastrointestinal disturbances, nausea, and vomiting (Wilson, Fardy, & Froelicher, 1981, p. 371).

A variety of drugs are used in cardiac programs (Cornett & Watson, 1984; Ewy & Bressler, 1982; Ford, 1986; Lowenthal & Stein, 1986), and a variety of classification systems are used. Any individual working in a cardiac rehabilitation program should learn the name of prescribed medications and their purposes. Any activity contraindications linked to a specific drug must be followed.

The American Heart Association (1980) has identified several drugs used by cardiac patients. Among these are digitalis, which increases the strength of the heart's contractions; diuretics, which increase the output of salt and water from the body; vasodilators to relax blood vessels; beta-blocking agents, which reduce heart rate and the strength of contractions;

anticoagulants to prevent clotting; drugs to inhibit the abnormal conduction of impulses in the heart; and drugs to lower cholesterol.

Wilson and colleagues (1981) provide specific activity guidelines based on medication being used by patients. For example, they suggest that beta-blocking agents reduce the heart rate, and as a result, the maximal heart rate clients should reach is reduced to 100–125 beats per minute. Nitrates, including nitroglycerin, can result in headaches or fainting. Any recreational therapist working with cardiac clients must have an in-depth understanding of medications and their effects.

APPLICATION OF THE TR PROCESS

CASE STUDY

Fred is a 40-year-old male who has been admitted to the hospital after experiencing a myocardial infarction. He is married, has two children aged 10 and 12. He owns his own clothing store.

Assessment

The assessment will vary as Fred moves through the phases of rehabilitation. Assessment for Fred involves examination of his current health status and risk factors. It also includes a life-style inventory and history. According to Comoss and colleagues (1979), Phase I assessment will include a description of the illness that brought the patient to the coronary care unit and his past and family medical history. It will include an assessment of physiological stability, including measurements such as heart rate, blood pressure, and cardiovascular examination findings. In addition, it is necessary to assess his educational needs relative to understanding the heart problem and how to manage it during this early stage.

Phase II assessment includes gathering data on the patient's physical state, his psychological state, and his educational needs related to both life-style and the cardiac condition. In addition, the patient's physical readiness to participate in activities must be determined. This would be a time to assess leisure interests and relate preferred activities to recommended MET levels.

Phase III assessment includes an examination of previous hospital records, family history, exercise test results, and medications. Psychosocial assessments, including activity preferences and involvement, also must be completed.

Prior to the initiation of Phase IV, a cardiovascular examination should be completed and reviewed to ensure patient safety during activity involvement. An exercise stress test should be done to determine exercise capacity. Also, assessments should be completed to determine education needs in areas such as stress management and activity selection.

It is likely the transition from the hospital-based program in Phase I and II to the community-based Phase III will result in a change in personnel. In that case, the TR specialist working with the client in the hospital will need to communicate assessment information with the therapist taking over during Phase III.

Planning

The assessment indicated that Fred was extremely work oriented, which resulted in a great deal of stress in his life. In addition, he participated in few noncompetitive leisure activities.

After gathering information from Fred, the therapist involved in his Phase II rehabilitation identified the following actions:

- Assist Fred in identifying ways to increase his activity level as his physical functioning improves.
- Assist Fred in developing an activity agenda that he will use as he moves through the rehabilitation process. The activities will be selected within the appropriate MET levels at each point in rehabilitation.
- Help Fred identify life-style changes, especially stress reduction strategies, that will reduce the risk of further cardiac problems. Specifically, assist Fred in developing stress reduction strategies.
- Provide Fred with the motivation to participate actively in the Phase I rehabilitation and continue with Phase II upon discharge.
- Help Fred explore current leisure preferences and develop a plan for incorporating leisure into postdischarge life.

Implementation

The recreation therapist will use a variety of approaches to reach the objectives outlined for Fred. Because several of the changes in his life will involve the entire family, they should be involved in his therapy. Specifically, Fred should become involved in a leisure counseling program to identify leisure activities appropriate to a more active life-style. Once those activities have been identified, methods of adapting them to reduce their cardiac requirements must be identified. The MET requirements of a variety of leisure activities must be determined, and their role in Fred's exercise program should be established. Fred should be placed in a stress reduction class with other cardiac rehabilitation clients.

Evaluation

Prior to release from the hospital and completion of the Phase I program, a discharge summary will be completed for Fred. Evaluation will include a predischarge exercise test to determine if this is the case. Evaluation of psychosocial and educational outcomes, including knowledge of heart disease and risk factors related to heart disease, should be conducted at this time. Knowledge of pulse taking, prescribed medications, and exercise requirements should also be evaluated at this time.

TRENDS AND ISSUES

A major issue for therapeutic recreation specialists is their absence from treatment teams associated with cardiac patients (Hayes & Antozzi, 1982). There are few settings where they are included. In fact, in researching materials for this chapter, little mention was made of therapeutic recreation specialists in any of the general literature. The role of a variety of professionals, including physical educators, exercise physiologists, occupational therapists, and physical therapists, was discussed. However, the field of therapeutic recreation was conspicuous by its absence. Clearly, therapeutic recreation specialists need to educate physicians responsible for cardiac rehabilitation programs. In addition, this outreach effort must be accompanied by increased competency in the area of exercise physiology if TR specialists are to establish themselves as contributing therapists with this population.

Increased public awareness of risk factors associated with cardiovascular diseases, as well as the use of drugs to prevent heart disease, will reduce the number of individuals suffering heart disease. This may result in an increased focus on prevention programs, similar to Phase IV, designed to bring about lifetime cardiac fitness. Improved medical care and technology may also result in increased life expectancy in those individuals who experience a cardiac problem. Therefore, it is likely that, whereas the number of individuals with cardiac conditions will decrease, the number of individuals who survive cardiac disease and participate in rehabilitation programs will increase.

SUMMARY

This chapter has examined cardiac conditions and the role of the therapeutic recreation specialist in the rehabilitation process. Cardiac rehabilitation programs are long-term efforts that progress from the coronary care unit in the hospital to at-home rehabilitation that lasts for life. During the rehabilitation process, the focus is on physiology as well as life-style. Patients must learn to deal with the cardiac event as well as develop strategies that optimize recovery and reduce the likelihood of further problems. These efforts revolve around exercise and behavior modification.

Many cardiac rehabilitation programs occur in four phases that begin with hospitalization and continue to community-based programs. Throughout the process, the TR specialist must assist the client in developing alternative life-style patterns that will contribute to cardiac wellness.

If recreation therapists want to become part of the growing field of cardiac rehabilitation, they will need a background that includes study in exercise physiology. Other skills that will be useful in a cardiac rehabilitation program include leisure counseling, activity analysis and adaptation, and stress reduction techniques.

READING COMPREHENSION QUESTIONS

1. Define cardiovascular disease and identify a least five types.
2. What are the four phases of cardiac rehabilitation?
3. List the two major purposes of cardiac rehabilitation programs.
4. What risk factors increase the likelihood of a heart attack? What roles can the therapeutic recreation specialist have in reducing these risk factors?
5. What are METs, and how do they relate to the selection of recreation activities for patients in cardiac rehabilitation?
6. Explain the relationship of therapeutic recreation specialists to other members of the treatment team in cardiac rehabilitation programs.
7. Identify the major categories of drugs used by cardiac patients. What are some activity contraindications of each?

SUGGESTED LEARNING ACTIVITIES

1. Develop a list of all the recreation activities you do in a typical 24-hour period. Use a MET table to determine the MET level of each.
2. Visit a cardiac rehabilitation program. Discuss the role of therapeutic recreation in cardiac programs with the physician in charge.
3. Discuss why therapeutic recreation specialists have not traditionally been included on treatment teams for cardiac patients. How might the profession change this state of affairs?
4. Take a stress test, and discuss the role of such a test in the cardiac rehabilitation process.
5. Examine your life-style, and identify risk factors that may increase the likelihood of your having a heart attack. What can you do to reduce these risk factors? How might you help clients reduce risk factors in their lives?

REFERENCES

AMERICAN HEART ASSOCIATION. (1980). *The American Heart Association heartbook.* New York: E. P. Dutton.

COHN, K., DUKE, D., & MADRID, J. (1979). *Coming back: A guide to recovering from heart attack and living confidently with coronary disease.* Reading, MA: Addison-Wesley.

COMOSS, P., MC CALL, E., SMITH, A., & SWAILS, S. H. (1979). *Cardiac rehabilitation: A comprehensive nursing approach.* Philadelphia: J. B. Lippincott.

CORNETT, S. & WATSON, J. E. (1984). *Cardiac rehabilitation: An interdisciplinary team approach.* New York: John Wiley & Sons.

DEBAKEY, M., & GOTTO, A. (1977). *The living heart.* New York: David MacKay.

EWY, G. A., & BRESSLER, R. (Eds.). (1982). *Cardiovascular drugs and the management of heart disease.* New York: Raven Press.

FARDY, P. S. (1986). Cardiac rehabilitation for the outpatient: A hospital-based program. In M. Pollock, D. Schmidt, & D. Mason (Eds.), *Heart disease and rehabilitation* (2nd ed.). New York: John Wiley & Sons.

FORD, R. D. (Ed.). (1986). *Cardiovascular care handbook.* Springhouse, PA: Springhouse Corporation.

GENTRY, W. D., & WILLIAMS, R. B. (Eds.). (1975). *Psychological aspects of myocardial infarction and coronary care.* St. Louis, C. V. Mosby.

GREENVILLE HOSPITAL SYSTEM. (n.d.). *Cardiac rehabilitation center.* Greenville, SC: Greenville Hospital System.

HAYES, G. A., & ANTOZZI, R. K. (1982). Philosophical basis for therapeutic recreation and leisure lifestyle adjustment in cardiac rehabilitation. In L. L. Neal & C. R. Edginton (Eds.), *Exetra perspectives: Concepts in therapeutic recreation.* Eugene, OR: Center for Leisure Studies.

HOEFT, T. M. (1982). Leisure counseling: A component of cardiac rehabilitation and heart disease intervention programs. In L. L. Neal & C. R. Edginton (Eds.), *Exetra perspectives: Concepts in therapeutic recreation.* Eugene, OR: Center for Leisure Studies.

LOWENTHAL, D. T. & STEIN, D. T., (1986). Drug effects: Exercise testing and training. In M. Pollock, D. Schmidt, & D. Mason (Eds.), *Heart disease and rehabilitation* (2nd ed.). New York: John Wiley & Sons.

MILLER, H. S., RIBISL, P. M., ADAMS, G. E., BOONE, W. T. & MORLEY, D. (1986). Community programs of cardiac rehabilitation. In M. Pollock, D. Schmidt, & D. Mason (Eds.), *Heart disease and rehabilitation* (2nd ed.). New York: John Wiley & Sons.

MONTEIRO, L. A. (1979). *Cardiac patient rehabilitation: Social aspects of recovery.* New York: Springer Publishing.

MONTOYE, H. J., CHRISTIAN, J. L., NAGLE, F. J., & LEVIN, S. M. (1988). *Living fit.* Menlo Park, CA: Benjamin/Cummings Publishing.

WENGER, N. (1986). Rehabilitation of the patient with acute myocardial infarction during hospitalization: Early ambulation and patient education. In M. Pollock, D. Schmidt, & D. Mason (Eds.), *Heart disease and rehabilitation* (2nd ed.). New York: John Wiley & Sons.

WILSON, P. K., EDGETT, J. W., & PORTER, G. H. (1986). Rehabilitation of the cardiac patient: Program organization. In M. Pollock, D. Schmidt, & D. Mason (Eds.), *Heart disease and rehabilitation* (2nd ed.). New York: John Wiley & Sons.

WILSON, P. K., FARDY, P. S., & FROELICHER, V. F. (1981). *Cardiac rehabilitation, adult fitness, and exercise testing.* Philadelphia: Lea & Febiger.

16

Burns

ANN JAMES

OBJECTIVES

- Understand the nature of burn injuries and the role of therapeutic recreation in burn care.
- Identify the purposes to which therapeutic recreation services are directed and the process by which they are implemented.
- Learn therapeutic recreation interventions used in pain control.

NATURE OF BURN INJURIES

Over 300,000 Americans are hospitalized each year for treatment of burns. More than 70,000 patients receive specialized, intensive treatment involving from 6 weeks to 2 years of hospitalization. Many of these patients must wage fierce battles for their lives. Survival, once assured, is followed by weeks or months of painful recovery. Although the pain eventually abates, pronounced disfigurement and mobility impairments may remain for years while the patient undergoes periodic reconstructive procedures. Burn care is among the most expensive of medical treatments. Because most burns are incurred outside of the workplace, where they are not covered by some types of insurance, patients may be faced with financial as well as social, psychological, and physical trauma (Gaynor, 1978).

Severe burns assault a person's life. If defeated there, they continue to assault the individual's capacity to endure pain, to regain function, to maintain self-esteem, to prevail socially—to live fully. Each step of the way, recreation therapists, as members of the burn team, ally with patients to help them achieve recovery. During acute stages of the trauma, the recreation therapist supports the patient's efforts to survive and to cope with pain. Throughout recovery, the therapeutic recreation specialist selects activities that will maintain mobility of burned limbs. Finally, the therapeutic recreation specialist works to support a positive self-concept, to mobilize social coping mechanisms, and to develop living skills to enable patients to reintegrate successfully into the community.

CLASSIFICATION OF BURN INJURIES

Burn injuries may result from a wide variety of causes. Flame, scalding, chemicals, electricity, sunburn, and frostbite are all capable of destroying the skin and underlying tissue. Burns are classified by the severity of the injuries as measured by the extent and depth of the burns.

Extent of Burn

The extent of the burn is indicated by the percentage of body surface area (BSA) that is damaged. A rough estimate of the affected body surface may be made by using the "rule of nines." The upper extremities are each calculated as 9% of the body's surface. The head and neck area constitute 9%. The front and back of the trunk are each 18%, and the lower extremities count as 18% each (O'Shaughnessy, 1981).

Depth of Burn

Burns to the epidermis, which consists of the outer layer of dead skin cells and the underlying new skin cells, are designated as *superficial* burns (formerly, as first degree burns). Superficial burns result in redness, edema, and pain, but usually do not require hospitalization.

Supporting the skin is a layer of connective tissue called the dermis. The dermis cushions the skin and is deeper in areas that withstand frequent pressure, such as the palms of the hands and the soles of the feet. Contained within the dermis are a variety of structures known as appendages. These include capillaries, sweat glands, hair follicles, sebaceous glands, and nerve endings. The appendages are composed of epithelial cells that are capable of generating new skin cells if the epidermis has been destroyed. Burns that invade the dermis to varying levels are referred to as *partial thickness burns* (second degree). This classification may be further subdivided for treatment purposes as *superficial partial thickness burns* and *deep partial thickness burns.* The former designation would indicate damage of the connective tissue, and the latter would indicate that damage has penetrated into the capillaries, nerve endings, and other appendages. Partial thickness burns can result in pain, infection, and loss of body fluid. Large areas may require skin grafting.

Burns that totally destroy the dermis and all its appendages (third degree) and sometimes underlying muscle and other tissues (fourth degree) are called *full thickness burns*. Even when involving small areas, full thickness burns are serious injuries that require hospitalization (O'Shaughnessy, 1981).

Much of the patient's treatment will be determined by the seriousness of the injury as described by this classification system. A partial thickness burn over 20% of the body is considered a life-threatening injury (Mannon, 1985).

DESCRIPTION OF LIMITATIONS

There are several limitations imposed by thermal injuries that the recreation therapist must accommodate when working with burn patients. These factors are dynamic and change with the status of the patient's condition.

Decreased Stamina

The skin provides a seal that keeps our body fluids where they belong, nurturing our bodies. If this seal is extensively breached, widespread evaporation and escape of vital fluids and energy result. One of the first procedures administered to the newly burned patient is the replacement of the fluids and calories that the patient is so rapidly losing. Although intravenous and enteral fluid and nutrient supplies may be established to supplement or, if necessary, to replace oral ingestion, it may be a difficult battle to match the enormous energy needs (Wachtel, Kahn, & Frank, 1983). The efforts of the physical therapist will be enlisted early in the treatment process to maintain mobility of burned limbs and to inhibit the development of contractures that could deform limbs and constrict movement. If energy loss is great, the physical therapist will direct the patient through the minimum activity required to achieve these objectives. All the patient's energy may be directed to survival, eating, and the movement needed to maintain mobility and support functioning. The recreation therapist must monitor the patient's changing energy status and adjust interventions accordingly.

Infection Control

Infection is the most frequent cause of death from burns (Hartford, 1981). The burn wound, composed of dead organic material, is a favorable medium for bacterial growth. Attempts are made to reduce the contaminating potential of all those who come in contact with the patient. Some hospitals use laminar flow isolation units that surround the patient's bed with walls of transparent plastic. Sterilized air is vented into these enclosed environments. Patients within these units can communicate with recreation therapists and view activity materials through the transparent barriers.

Procedures to protect patients from contamination vary among burn units, and procedures on one unit may vary for different patients. When attending patients in isolation, recreation therapists are required to don hair covers, masks, and gowns, and to wash hands before and after working with each patient. Game equipment and activity materials also harbor bacteria and are subject to restriction. Only materials that can first be decontaminated may be brought into the presence of isolated patients. Once contaminated by an infected patient, materials that cannot be effectively sterilized cannot be reused. Magazines and paperback books are provided to patients unused, sometimes with covers removed, and are destroyed when patients are finished with them. Disposable game boards can be made by photocopying. Playing pieces can be autoclaved or disposable pieces fashioned for limited use. Infection control procedures will vary according to the susceptibility of patients to infection. The recreation therapist must ascertain the procedures in force for the unit and for each patient thereon and plan accordingly.

PURPOSE OF THERAPEUTIC RECREATION

During the acute phase of treatment, recreation therapy is directed chiefly at helping the patient cope with pain and maintain the will to prevail. As the patient recovers, recreation therapy will be increasingly enlisted to maintain mobility of burned limbs and to prepare the patient mentally and physically for return to the community.

Helping the Patient Cope with Pain

Any areas of the patient that are burned to less than full thickness will be sources of pain. Because nerve endings are destroyed in full-thickness burns, little pain is perceived in these areas until nerves reemerge during the healing process.

The patient must daily undergo many procedures that will exacerbate pain. Surface tissue that does not thrive or that is destroyed by infection must be removed. This material, called eschar, is removed by debridement procedures. One method of removal uses a hydrotherapy area commonly referred to as the tank room. The affected limb or the entire patient, if necessary, is immersed in a Hubbard tank filled with a saline-water solution. The gentle action of the water loosens and frees the eschar from the thriving tissue. Eschar that does not drift free from the patient is removed by the hydrotherapy team. Some patients must undergo this process daily until eschar formation has ceased. Dressing changes, exercises, eating, and other procedures may all bring increased pain to the patient. Difficulty in sleeping may further reduce the patient's tolerance to prolonged discomfort.

Although drugs are given for pain in all burn treatment facilities, the types and regimens vary among burn centers and physicians. At some centers, physicians avoid prescribing narcotics. Physicians at other centers, citing studies indicating that narcotics when used in treatment seldom incur addiction, use them among their standard arsenals of pharmacological agents to combat pain. Regardless of the type of drug used, medication can not eliminate all the pain induced by extensive partial thickness burns nor by the procedures that exacerbate that pain (Bernstein, 1983).

Neural pathways that transmit pain from the skin merge with other nerves as they wend their ways to the spinal cord and the brain. As these pathways combine, impulses from one source can interfere with impulses from another. Thus, sometimes alternate stimuli can block or dull the perception of pain (Perry, Heindrich, & Ramos, 1981).

A primary intervention of recreation therapy is the provision of these diversional stimuli. Recreation activities, guided visualizations, meditation exercises, and hypnotic suggestion may be enlisted to counter pain. Because the recreation therapist cannot attend each patient during each painful experience, it is important to teach the patient as many of these techniques as possible and appropriate. Thus armed, the patient can actively oppose his or her pain rather than helplessly submit to it.

Controlling Stimulation Levels

Burn patients may experience a chaotic sensory existence, from periods of overstimulation to periods of understimulation. The treatment day may sometimes appear as an endless round of excruciating experiences, from morning tanking and dressing changes to afternoon exercises. It may seem to the patients that someone is cajoling them to eat, move, or endure another painful procedure every minute of the treatment day. After most of the burn team has left the unit, however, the scene may change dramatically. Now, for patients in isolation, there may be precious little and no one to distract them from the single remaining stimulus, pain. It is not uncommon for burn patients to experience hallucinations, paranoid feelings, or other reactions to extreme states of stimuli. Sleep deprivation and certain medications may contribute to the formation of these reactions (Hayward, 1983).

The recreation therapist must assess the stimuli that confront the patient throughout the 24-hour day and the patient's responses to them. During peak episodes, the patient may benefit from a stimulus-reducing technique such as meditation. During lonely and boring times, the selective heightening of stimuli via music, art, or other activities may be the more therapeutic intervention.

Encouraging the Patient to Eat

Due to fluid loss and increased energy demands, the extensively burned patient is in danger of starving to death. Although the patient will be provided a high calorie diet and encouraged to eat more often than usual, loss of appetite or pain incurred by eating oppose efforts to increase consumption. Anything that the recreation therapist can do to help the patient consume the level of calories needed each day will contribute to the survival and recovery of the patient. Because Americans frequently indulge in refreshments while participating in leisure activities, it is appropriate to provide snacks with many recreation activities. Sometimes this association will motivate the patient to eat, particularly if favorite foods can be integrated with recreation events. The recreation therapist needs to coordinate these efforts with the unit dietician (Cozart, 1983).

Marshaling Hope for Recovery

The pain, physical limitations, and disfigurement associated with a patient's condition may be so compelling that it is difficult for the patient to envision a better future. The patient must be frequently reassured that pain will subside, function will improve, and appearance will become more acceptable. The recreation therapist may secure the help of recovered burn victims to demonstrate that lives are effectively resumed after burn trauma. The National Burn Victim Foundation, composed of former burn patients, has volunteers prepared to offer support and to share coping strategies with patients (Gaynor, 1978). Although hope can justifiably be offered that appearance will be improved, the recreation therapist should not give the patient the impression that premorbid appearance can be perfectly restored (Constable, 1983).

Maintaining Interest in the Outside World

The intrinsic stimulus of pain continually draws the patient's attention inward. This focus is reinforced by the activities of the burn team, which also revolve around the patient. Lengthy hospitalization and confinement to isolation serve to distance the patient from life beyond the institution. All these forces conspire to shrink the patient's world to a very small sphere. The recreation therapist can counter these forces with activities that involve current events, premorbid leisure interests, and references to life beyond the burn unit. When the patient is removed from isolation, using volunteers to assist with program delivery will widen the patient's contacts and reawaken interest in the community.

Providing Means for Self-Expression

The role of patient comes with limited opportunities. Members of the burn team are invested with power by virtue of their expertise. Patients may see their options as being either to cooperate with or to resist the team's ministrations. Cooperation will be rewarded with pain, but resistance will forestall recovery. To add to this dilemma, patients may feel compelled to express their gratitude for procedures they do not enjoy. Everyone does things to patients and for patients, but patients are never asked to do things for others. Patients must live in environments that are not of their design and that reflect little of their personalities. Few opportunities remain to enact roles as mothers, bankers, students, or competent persons. Most patients hate the existence but are hesitant to vent their anger on their caretakers. Some don't hesitate (Mannon, 1985). Recreation therapy can provide activities with safe outlets to vent frustrations, acknowledge pain, and express fears. Finger paints or other media can enable patients to smear out their feelings in living color. Recreation activities also present opportunities to make decisions, manipulate the environment, experience success, and express personalities in a myriad of ways not usually afforded by the patient role.

Maintaining Mobility

As the patient's energy reserves increase, the recreation therapist can increasingly involve the patient in physically active experiences, particularly in activities that encourage movement of burned limbs through full ranges of motion. The patient will be involved in an exercise regimen directed by the physical therapist. Recreation activities can augment the exercise program by giving purpose to movement, which enhances motivation, and by providing diversion from the pain that movement provokes. The recreation therapist should consult with the physical therapist regarding exercise regimens for each patient.

Mobilizing Social Coping Skills

Disfigurement from burn injuries may remain with the patient for several years until reconstructive surgery can be completed. Surgeons can reconstruct destroyed noses, chins, ears, and eyebrows, and render acceptable appearances. The patient who expects complete restoration to premorbid appearance, however, is likely to be disappointed (Constable, 1983).

While new skin growth is maturing, patients may wear specially fabricated and individually fitted dressings to cover burned areas. If an arm is burned, a sleeve of this elastic material is constructed for the patient. If the face is burned, a pressure garment resembling a ski mask is fashioned. Pressure dressings are worn 24 hours a day, except during bathing, until scar maturation. This could be from 6 months to 2 years, depending upon the age of the patient. Pressure dressings are worn to inhibit hypertrophic scarring—the knotty, irregular formation of excess scar tissue (Artz, Moncrief, & Pruitt, 1979).

Upon discharge from the hospital, the patient will return to the community wearing pressure garments. Although the garments may conceal deformities, the dressings, of themselves, present atypical appearances. Maturing skin growth itches and may blister. Recurring pain is experienced from burned areas as changes in temperature and barometric pressure occur; this recurring pain is similar to pain fluctuations associated with arthritis. The patient may still have limitations in movement that make some work and leisure activities difficult or impossible.

It becomes obvious to burn patients that fate has dealt them a rough hand and that life is fraught with obstacles and limitations. Obscured by the trauma is the reality that patients remain in control of many options regarding their destiny. Throughout rehabilitation, the recreation therapist should illuminate the alternatives from which patients select courses of action. Patients choose to submit passively to their injuries or to participate actively in their recovery. Patients choose to become preoccupied with their appearance, over which they have little control, or they choose to invest that energy in areas in which they can demonstrate competence. They focus on limitations or on possibilities; they center wholly on themselves or are mindful of others; they withdraw from social contact or dare to reestablish relationships. It is necessary to vent frustrations, own pain, and acknowledge loss. It is also necessary to reassert control and get on with life.

The recreation therapist prepares the patient for reentry into the community by arranging a continuum of increasingly challenging experiences throughout the patient's hospitalization. The continuum of social experiences begins with the patient's interactions with the burn team. Veteran burn therapists rapidly adjust to disfigurement and establish contact with the person beyond the wounds. The novice recreation therapist will soon find that as activities allow the patient to reveal his or her personality, it becomes easier to see past disfigurement and relate to the person. It is gratifying to the patient that his or her appearance does not adversely affect relationships with the burn team, but the experience does not appreciably bolster his or her confidence because staff are not perceived as representative of the "real" world. As infection control measures permit, the recreation therapist can insert selected volunteers into the program. This small cadre of volunteers, who become the patient's first encounters with strangers, should be carefully screened for emotional maturity and systematically prepared for their assignments.

If time and circumstances allow, it is important to extend the social continuum further. Surrounding the patient with only accepting volunteers who are accustomed to the altered appearance of burn victims will not give the patient an entirely realistic experience nor help develop ways of coping with the full range of reactions that can be expected from the public. When danger of infection is past, the patient can be involved in activities with patients from other units and with groups from the community. The presence of former burn victims who are socially competent may provide role models at these occasions. Shopping trips, activities at parks and community centers, and other excursions can be used to round out the patient's exposure to a variety of social encounters. Throughout this continuum, meetings with patient support groups, feedback from patients and staff, and role-playing opportunities can assist the patient in developing coping behaviors that can be drawn upon as he or she reestablishes contacts with family, friends, co-workers, and the public.

With the patient's prior approval, the recreation therapist may contact individuals in the community who can facilitate the client's reintegration. Consultations with personnel in the municipal recreation department may be used to ascertain leisure resources and to inform staff of client interests, skills, limitations, and activity needs. The recreation therapist may visit a child's school, let classmates examine pressure garments, ask questions, and discuss appropriate ways of interacting with their soon-to-be-returning classmate.

Special Considerations with Children

Children's interpretations of pain may be distorted by limited experience. Children are accustomed to having parents relieve them from discomfort and protect them from pain. They may conclude from unrelenting pain of burn injuries that parents have abandoned them or that they are being punished (Bernstein, 1983). These or other misinterpretations may be revealed in children's play. The recreation therapist is attentive to verbal and nonverbal expressions of fears and is prepared to offer correct information. Play situations may be developed to reflect more realistic scenarios of events. Preoperative play activities may be designed to check children's understanding of debridement, splinting, and grafting procedures (Cozart, 1983).

Support of the Burn Team

As you have gathered by now, life on the burn unit is intense. Members of the burn team are there because of the expertise and skill they can apply toward the patient's treatment and recovery. Although members may be accepted by the team in varying degrees, the team is usually a cohesive unit. Both personal and professional bonds are formed among team members (Hayward, 1983).

The recreation therapist can serve an important maintenance role among this group by arranging and participating in social activities. Such efforts demonstrate that the recreation therapist's concerns are not confined to the interests of the discipline but extend to other members of the team and to the unit as a whole.

A paradox shared by members of the burn team is that the immediate result of the activities rendered to help the patient is increased pain. This consequence is in direct opposition to the motives that drew them into helping professions. The recreation therapist can provide some relief to this situation by extending a standing invitation to staff, periodically reissued, to join in therapeutic recreation activities with patients. Interaction among staff and patients during cognitive and social activities allows staff to cement bonds with patients in non–pain-inducing circumstances and allows patients to reveal aspects of their personalities seldom disclosed in the helpee role. Staff participation will also expand the recreation opportunities that can be provided to patients in isolation.

COMMON SERVICE SETTINGS

Persons with burn injuries are usually treated in burn centers or in burn units of hospitals. A burn center is a facility at which staff serve only burn patients. A burn unit is a segment of a hospital that draws upon physicians and other staff at the hospital who have expertise and skills in treating burn injuries. When bed occupancy on a burn unit is low, the skills of the staff can be used elsewhere in the hospital. For this reason, burn units can often be operated more economically than burn centers (Gaynor, 1978).

Because of the highly specialized nature of burn treatment, the geographic areas from which burn centers receive patients may be quite extensive. Patients may be transported hundreds of miles for hospitalization, which can limit contact with family and friends. Estrangement from personal and occupational responsibilities can add to the patient's worries and sense of loss.

CURRENT BEST PRACTICES AND PROCEDURES

The standard therapeutic recreation process that includes assessment, planning, implementation, and evaluation is applicable when working with patients with burn injuries.

Assessment

Emergency care will have been provided prior to the recreation therapist's contact with the patient. This may include the administration of fluids and nutrients, catheterization, and debridement. Care will be directed to any conditions that warrant it, such as shock, other injuries, or complications. Medications may be given for pain and other conditions as indicated. The patient is placed in isolation and may remain there for several weeks.

After admission, the medical records will reflect important data on the patient's physical condition, some demographic information, and perhaps a statement regarding the patient's degree of alertness, orientation, and emotional state. If the recreation therapist will be seeing the patient prior to a treatment team meeting, the therapist may consult the admitting physician or the patient's primary nurse for further information. If possible, the cause of the injury should be ascertained. Sometimes patients involved in unavoidable accidents or in accidents caused by others are more voluble in their expressions of pain than are patients who feel responsible for their injuries (Artz, Moncrief, & Pruitt, 1979). Depending on the condition of the patient, the recreation therapist may make several contacts before completing the leisure history. Leisure inventories may be used to assess premorbid leisure patterns, and family members may be consulted for much of the leisure assessment.

As more team members become increasingly involved with the patient, assessment data will expand. The dietician will assess caloric and nutrient requirements and subsequently plan diets. The physical therapist will see the patient on the first or second day, assist in positioning the patient, and establish an exercise regimen. The occupational therapist may be enlisted to design and fabricate splints to aid in mobility or prevent contractures. The medical social worker will prepare a social history of the patient and assist with family and personal problems. Information may also become available from the psychologist or psychiatrist and from the chaplain. Nursing personnel will manage the unit and be the constant monitors and providers of patient care. Some units will assign each patient a primary nurse who will have major responsibility in following the patient throughout his or her hospitalization (Mannon, 1985).

If the need arises, the recreation therapist may consult individually with any of the burn team professionals, or more routinely, exchange information via medical charts and treatment team meetings or rounds. The recreation therapist will serve as a major source of information on psychosocial functioning, physical performance during recreation activities, and, as the patient recovers, community reintegration.

Planning

Common interventions used for pain control are relaxation techniques, guided imagery, meditation, and hypnosis. Pain induces tension that exacerbates pain and continues the cycle. Modified relaxation techniques that induce relaxation through alternate contraction and release of muscle groups may be effective in reducing muscle tension for some patients (Charlesworth & Nathan, 1984). If contractions exacerbate pain, this technique should be restricted to muscle groups in noninjured areas. This technique is contraindicated for extensively burned or debilitated patients.

Guided imagery, sometimes called guided fantasy or visualization, is easily adapted to accommodate patient and environmental constraints.

Using selected, descriptive phrases, the therapist guides the patient on a mental journey to pleasant and relaxing environs. Guided imagery is the formation of mental stimuli to divert the patient from the stimulus of pain. The setting and experience to be envisioned can be determined by the patient or selected from options suggested by the therapist. Presenting selected details perceived by several senses will encourage the formation of compelling images. For example, suggesting the smell of newly mowed grass, the touch of a butterfly alighting on the hand, or the sound of a bird calling across the meadow helps the client to form images more concretely. When giving cues, it is important to allow long moments of silence between suggestions to enable images to form fully. Some patients are responsive to suggestions that a burned area "feels cool," particularly if the image of a snowy landscape has been fully developed. For other patients, the mention of a burned limb merely draws their attention back to pain stimuli and destroys the image. The therapist might avoid references to burned areas for the first few sessions until the patient develops facility in forming intense images and maintaining focus on them.

Meditation is the focusing of your entire concentration on a single stimulus. The more successful you are in maintaining your concentration on that single object, sound, or sensation, the more successful you will be in blocking out other stimuli. The object of focus should be simple and unwavering. Changes in the object will interrupt your concentration. The monotonous drone of a ventilation system, a mark on the ceiling, or the repetition of a word can serve as a point of focus. Breathing is often used as an object of concentration because you can control its rhythm.

Try this meditation exercise. Sit or lie with your spine straight. As you inhale slowly and evenly, focus your attention on the sensation created by the air entering your nostrils at the edge of your nose. Don't follow the path of the air as it continues into your body; maintain your focus on the flow of air past the entry to your nose. Focus on the same point as you exhale. As you become conscious of a thought that has entered your mind, bring your focus back to the object. Don't try to block thoughts or awareness of other stimuli; simply return to the object when you realize that your concentration has wandered. Try this for 10 minutes.

Meditation is a skill, and, as with other skills, performance gets better with practice. Better, in this case, means that the meditator becomes less distracted by other stimuli. Meditation is often used as a relaxation technique because of its effectiveness in quieting the mind. With burn patients, meditation serves additionally to block or dull the perception of pain.

Hypnotic suggestion is another technique that is often taught to patients experiencing pain. Hypnosis is not a competency imparted by standard academic curricula, but it can be acquired from specialized training. Recreation therapists interested in working in pain control should consider adding this skill to their repertoires of intervention resources.

Art, music, and other activities that provide visual, auditory, intellectual, or social stimulation also offer diversion from pain. Many of these activities serve additional purposes, allowing patients to vent emotions and affect their environments. While patients are in isolation, environmental constraints must be accommodated. When staff are not available to join activities, participation is confined to the recreation therapist and the patient. Sometimes the therapist can relay information among isolation patients, introducing them to one another, sharing information on leisure interests, and establishing participation *in absentia*. Chess games can be played between patients in different rooms with staff conveying moves to opponents on their regular visits. Friendly competition and comradery can be developed through football pools (prizes are awarded to patients who predict the most winners; no money is exchanged) and other contests. These activities among invisible fellow-travelers stimulate awareness and interest among patients who will probably meet when released from isolation.

As patients near the end of the acute phase of the injury, strength and energy can return rapidly, and participation in activities with greater mobility requirements can be expanded. Activities that provide exercise for general conditioning as well as range of motion (ROM) activities are indicated. The recreation therapist seeks the specific activity to produce the desired result. Shuffleboard, for example, encourages extension of the elbow. Fussball requires rotation of the wrists. When aquatic activities are permitted, the breast stroke mandates abduction and adduction of upper and lower limbs.

Implementation

When a severely injured and disfigured patient, coping with a long and sometimes lonely hospitalization, meets an accepting and caring therapist, the relationship can become characterized by dependent attachment. The patient needs to be reassured that he or she is liked because he or she is likable and not because of any transcendent powers of the therapist. Enabling the patient to experience success and demonstrate competence will also help to dispel feelings of worthlessness. As soon as the patient's injuries are not vulnerable to infection, the therapist should broaden the patient's contacts to loosen attachment to the therapist.

The recreation therapist must remember that the treatment objective of range of motion activities is to stimulate movement through the range prescribed. The outcome of the game is secondary. To avoid pain, the patient may try to complete the activity with as little movement of the affected limbs as possible. The therapist must focus on how the patient performs the activity, not on the result of the game. Reinforcement is given for executing the prescribed motion, whether or not the motion scores a hit. Like other members of the burn team, the recreation therapist's actions must be dictated by the patient's needs and not by the therapist's needs for immediate approval and love.

Patients aren't the only people who need to develop healthy coping mechanisms. Recreation therapists have days when it seems that all their patients are angry with them. That may be one reason why strong relationships are often formed among burn team members. All recreation therapists need to develop sources other than their patients for meeting their psychosocial needs. This is particularly true when working with burn patients.

When implementing social programs with burn patients, it is important to arrange opportunities for patients to process their experiences. Through discussions with the recreation therapist and support groups composed of other patients and recovered burn victims, patients can vent their fears, acknowledge their social successes, and explore difficult situations (Hanson, 1983).

Evaluation

Frequent evaluations are made to measure patient progress, to assess the effectiveness of interventions, and to plan subsequent treatment. Behavioral objectives established at the outset of planning facilitate evaluation of outcomes. Most evaluation is done by observation of the patient's social, emotional, or physical functioning in designated circumstances. Few standardized tests are used in evaluation with this population.

APPLICATION OF THE TR PROCESS

The following extracts from a case study are used to illustrate the therapeutic recreation process as it might be applied to a specific patient.

CASE STUDY

Staff have been alerted that a "fifty percenter" is being airlifted to the burn center from Oil City, where he was injured in an industrial explosion. At this time, it is known only that the victim is a young male.

Assessment

The processes of admission to the center and administration of emergency care will generate some demographic information and considerable data on the patient's physical status. Information will be added to this base throughout the patient's stay and will change as the patient undergoes further procedures and his condition changes. The following data will be collected by the recreation therapist and periodically reassessed:

General:
1. Name
2. Age
3. Location in the center
4. Primary care givers

Physical Status:
1. BSA, depth, and location of burns
2. Complications or other injuries (vascular problems, respiratory involvement, amputations)
3. Major disfigurements
4. Infection status
5. Medications
6. Exercise regimen, mobility restrictions, and splints applied
7. Caloric requirements, supplementary feeding, dietary restrictions, favorite foods
8. Procedures pending
9. Vision (temporary edema, cataracts, etc.)
10. Ability to speak
11. Sleep problems

Psychosocial Status:
1. Alertness and orientation
2. Response to pain
3. General emotional state
4. Reporting of hallucinations or perceptions of persecution
5. Social functioning
6. Self-concept
7. Motivation, participation in treatment
8. Expression of anger, fear, etc.

Social History:
1. Family status
2. Community resources
3. Occupational status
4. Educational status
5. Socioeconomic status

Leisure History:
1. Skills
2. Interests
3. Attitudes
4. Resources
5. Barriers

Planning

John is a 20-year-old white single male welder admitted June 15. He sustained partial and full thickness burns to 50% of his body, including anterior portions of head, neck, chest, and upper legs, and to almost all of hands, arms, and axillae. John expresses determination to return to his active life-style with no limiting sequelae. He has cooperated with all burn team members and participated fully in all aspects of the program. He is scheduled for entire wound closure via autografting of all full thickness burn areas tomorrow. After several weeks of painful exercises and debridement, John expresses eagerness for the next stage of treatment, optimism regarding the grafting procedure, and expectations of imminent release from isolation. Exercise of burned areas will cease for approximately a week after grafting.

This case citation reflects the dynamic nature of burn care. Patient status and subsequent planning can change dramatically throughout rehabilitation. At this juncture, the recreation therapist notes that the patient's desire for recovery of function has motivated his active participation throughout painful procedures and that he is expecting the rewards of his efforts. The recreation therapist anticipates that postsurgical changes in routine and temporary cessation of the exercise program may erode feelings of control. Fewer visits by the physical and occupational therapists will reduce social and physical stimulation during this period.

GOAL: John will adapt to grafting procedure, including subsequent pain and reduction of motor and social activity, and will sustain optimism regarding eventual recovery.

Objectives:

1. John will express his understanding of the temporal nature of the change in treatment and concomitant restrictions.
2. John will affirm outlets for expression of feelings and energy.
3. John will acknowledge increased access to cognitive and sensory activities compensatory to reduction in motor and social activities.

Procedures:

1. Increase bedside therapeutic recreation sessions to two per day.
2. Increase quiz activities, particularly those related to television programming and leisure activities that patient enjoys.
3. Integrate music, sound and voice identification quizzes, and visual recall activities. Add odor identification quizzes if released from isolation.
4. Leave activity materials with family and staff to use with John as opportunities permit.

Implementation

John has become increasingly sullen and withdrawn since Dr. Jones informed him that he could go home at the end of the week.

It is not unusual for news of imminent discharge to result in depression. When extending reassurance to the patient, it is important that the recreation therapist not paint an unrealistically rosy picture of the future.

John's disfigurement will present social and possibly occupational barriers. Helping the patient to recount the resources that brought him this far in his recovery will help to instill confidence that he can cope with the obstacles that lie ahead. Facilitating interaction with former burn victims can be particularly helpful at this time.

Evaluation

After each contact with John, the therapist reflects on the interaction, giving particular attention to behaviors that relate to treatment objectives. The therapist describes the observations as accurately as possible, using terminology that communicates a consistent image to all burn team members. Interpretations of John's feelings and motives are avoided in favor of citations of comments and illustrations of behaviors. Generalizations such as "John has increased his socialization behaviors" are avoided in favor of the more descriptive "John attends activities in the recreation lounge, is responsive to conversation initiated by community volunteers, but approaches only patients and staff."

TRENDS AND ISSUES

Burn treatment is constantly evolving as new procedures and medications modify or replace antecedents. Moreover, practices that are standard procedures at one center may be disavowed at another. As in other areas of health care, the issue of cost-containment versus quality of care is being debated in burn treatment. Investigations are currently directed to ascertain if the smaller burn units can provide care more economically while not reducing the treatment outcomes achieved at burn centers. The trend toward decreased lengths of stay in hospitals requires recreation therapists to intensify community reintegration programs and to increase communication with community resources.

SUMMARY

Severe burns traumatize an individual socially and psychologically as well as physically. Therapeutic recreation services constitute a major portion of the treatment efforts to help the patient achieve the highest possible level of psychosocial functioning. In addition, therapeutic recreation offers unique resources to complement burn team efforts to effect a physical recovery. Therapeutic recreation is an integral service in any burn treatment program that attempts to treat the whole person.

READING COMPREHENSION QUESTIONS

1. What does the abbreviation BSA represent?
2. If a patient has burns extending over both arms, what is the approximate percentage of BSA involved?
3. What distinguishes a partial thickness burn from a full thickness burn?
4. Why is less pain experienced with full thickness burns than with partial thickness burns?
5. If the epithelium has been destroyed, how does the body regenerate skin?
6. Identify three daily procedures administered during the acute stage of treatment that may exacerbate pain.
7. Why would therapists, who are dependent upon receiving immediate gratification from patients, have difficulty in helping burn patients recover?
8. Identify three interventions that the recreation therapist can use to help clients cope with pain.
9. What assessment information could the recreation therapist obtain from the dietician?
10. What constraints do infection control measures place on the program?
11. Define: eschar, premorbid, contracture, and debridement.
12. What is the purpose of pressure garments?
13. What are the purposes of splints?
14. What is meant by a continuum of services?
15. How does therapeutic recreation contribute to the efforts of the burn team?

SUGGESTED LEARNING ACTIVITIES

1. Script a guided fantasy for a patient with painful burns to the legs. Tape-record your presentation.
2. Contact the Jobst Institute, Inc., Toledo, OH 43601, for a sample of pressure dressing material.
3. Contact the burn center nearest you to obtain the name of a local representative of the National Burn Victim Foundation. Ask the member for an interview, or invite the representative to participate in a class discussion regarding experiences that contribute to or impede recovery.
4. Patients in isolation become adept at identifying people whose faces are partially hidden behind surgical masks. Prepare a flash card quiz of famous eyes by collecting pictures of political leaders, prominent athletes, and noted entertainers. Cut a strip containing the area between the

nose and the hairline from each picture. Attach each strip to card stock and write the famous person's name on the back. Sometimes flash cards must be viewed at a distance by patients in isolation, so pictures must be large. When used at a burn center, pictures of staff can be integrated among the eyes of the famous faces. Try the activity on your classmates.

5. Identify activities that require the following:
   a. flexion of fingers (burned fingers are splinted to return to extended positions)
   b. extension and flexion of wrist
   c. extension and flexion of knee
   d. abduction of upper limbs
6. Determine the pronunciation of debridement.

REFERENCES

ARTZ, C. P., MONCRIEF, J. A., & PRUITT, B. A. (1979). *Burns: A team approach.* Philadelphia: W. B. Saunders.

BERNSTEIN, N. R. (1983). Psychological perspectives on pain intervention. In N. R. Bernstein & M. C. Robson (Eds.), *Comprehensive approaches to the burned person* (pp. 141–146). New York: Medical Examination Publishing.

CHARLESWORTH, E. A., & NATHAN, R. G. (1984). *Stress management.* New York: Atheneum.

CONSTABLE, J. D. (1983). Limitations of aesthetic reconstruction. In N. R. Bernstein & M. C. Robson (Eds.), *Comprehensive approaches to the burned person* (pp. 285–290). New York: Medical Examination Publishing.

COZART, E. S. (1983). Pediatric recreation therapy service. In N. R. Bernstein & M. C. Robson (Eds.), *Comprehensive approaches to the burned person* (pp. 199–216). New York: Medical Examination Publishing.

GAYNOR, H. J. (1978). Burn injuries. In R. M. Goldenson, J. R. Dunhan, & C. S. Dunhan (Eds.), *Disability and rehabilitation handbook* (pp. 296–300). New York: McGraw-Hill.

HANSON, N. N. (1983). Practice and planning in physical therapy. In N. R. Bernstein & M. C. Robson (Eds.), *Comprehensive approaches to the burned person* (pp. 174–198). New York: Medical Examination Publishing.

HARTFORD, C. E. (1981). Environmental control. In M. M. Wagner (Ed.), *Care of the burn-injured patient: Multidisciplinary involvement* (pp. 217–225). Littleton, MA: PSG Publishing.

HAYWARD, G. (1983). The challenge of burn nursing. In N. R. Bernstein & M. C. Robson (Eds.), *Comprehensive approaches to the burned person* (pp. 78–88). New York: Medical Examination Publishing.

MANNON, J. M. (1985). *Caring for the burned: Life and death in a hospital burn center.* Springfield, IL: Charles C. Thomas.

O'SHAUGHNESSY, E. J. (1981). Burns. In W. C. Stolov & M. R. Clowers (Eds.), *Handbook of severe disability* (pp. 409–418). Washington, DC: Department of Rehabilitation Medicine, University of Washington.

PERRY, S., HEINDRICH, G., & RAMOS, E. (1981). Assessment of pain by burn patients. *Journal of Burn Care Rehabilitation, 2*, 322–326.

WACHTEL, T. L., KAHN, V., & FRANK, H. A. (Eds.). (1983). *Current topics in burn care.* Rockville, MD: Aspen Systems Corporation.

17

Corrections

STEPHEN C. ANDERSON

OBJECTIVES

- Describe the prevalence of people incarcerated in the United States.
- Describe the classification of major types of law offenders.
- Describe the different types of correctional facilities.
- Describe the history of corrections in the United States.
- Describe the purpose of therapeutic recreation in corrections.
- Describe the therapeutic recreation process as it applies to corrections.
- Describe the trends and issues in corrections that pertain to therapeutic recreation.

INTRODUCTION TO CORRECTIONS

During the 1970s, the criminal justice system in general and prisons in particular were a major issue facing our society. The rioting at Attica Prison in 1971, Kansas State Prison in 1973, Washington State Penitentiary in 1979, and the New Mexico State Prison in 1980 brought the media and politics to the forefront of the issue. From the Walnut Street Jail of 1790 to the uprisings in the 1970s, little attention was paid to corrections in the United States. Law offenders were sent to prison to be locked up and forgotten while being punished for the crimes they committed. Today, more than a decade later, the situation has returned to the out-of-sight out-of-mind thinking prior to the 1970s. With the exception of a small number of publications, there has not been much mentioned about prison problems or reform. *Time* (1982) and *Newsweek* (1986) both had cover stories on prisons. One of the components of prison reform is recreation and therapeutic recreation. A review of the literature on this discipline finds that the topic has not been addressed thoroughly since Fogel (1974), Hormachea (1972), and McCall (1981) did special issues featuring recreation and corrections.

In spite of concentrated efforts during the 1970s, the problem of prison reform has not been solved, nor should it be forgotten. The total population of state and federal prisons increased by an average of more than 16,000 per year between 1977 and 1981. In 1981 alone, the net annual gain (37,309 inmates) was nearly 90% of the total gain from 1977–1980 (*Report to the Nation, n.d.*). Overpopulation in prisons has become a crisis alone.

According to the American Correctional Association (1987), as of June 30, 1987, there were 502,906 adults in our nation's 559 prisons. Of those in prison, 475,934 were male and 26,972 female. There were 93,476 housed in maximum security, 64,001 in close custody, 190,878 in medium security, 131,823 in minimum security, and 22,728 in other types of security. Of the total number of inmates in institutions, 206,637 were white, 226,601 were black, 53,233 were Hispanic, and 16,435 were classified as "other." In a report from the Legal Defense Fund (1988), as of March 16, 1988, of the 502,906 adult prison inmates, there were 2,000 men and 21 women on death row. In addition to those persons in institutions, there were another 15,124 in work release, 9,550 in furlough/supervised release, 16,048 committed but pending in county jails, 4,463 in state operated or contracted community homes, and 17,569 in other types of programs. In total, there were approximately 565,660 adults under correctional authority. This does not include the number of juvenile offenders who were incarcerated, which accounted for approximately 24,696 in secure institutions and another 19,700 in nonsecure detention facilities such as group homes. There were another 33 juveniles on death row.

Therapeutic recreation services usually are not provided in our nation's 3,493 local jails (156 were built before the year 1875); however, the jail population should be addressed in order to gain a complete picture of incarceration in the United States. The South, which operates about half the jails in the nation, houses about 43% of the national inmate population. At midyear 1986, local jails held an estimated 274,444 persons, 7% more than a year earlier. During the year ending June 30, 1986, there were 16.6 million jail admissions and releases. Males constituted 92% and females 8% of all jail inmates. Whites comprised 58% of the jail inmates, blacks made up 41%, and other races equaled 1%. Unconvicted inmates (those on trial or awaiting arraignment or trial) were 53% of the jail population, whereas convicted inmates (those awaiting or serving a sentence or returned to jail for violating probation or parole) were 47% of the jail population. One in every 648 adult residents of the United States was in jail on June 30, 1986. Fewer than 1% of the inmates of the nation's jails in 1986 were juveniles. Most juveniles in correctional custody (about 83,000 in 1985) were housed in juvenile facilities (U.S. Department of Justice, 1986). According to the president's Commission on Law Enforcement and the Administration of Justice, commonly called the "Crime Commission," approximately 1.3 million persons were being held within the correctional system on any given day (Hormachea & Hormachea, 1977).

As pointed out in the other chapters, therapeutic recreation services are provided to many special populations. Some of those groups can be found in general prison populations. Based on the *Diagnostic and Statistical Manual of Mental Disorders* (DMS-III), Collins and Schloenger (1983) found that 70% of the inmates have qualified at some time for a DMS-III diagnosis of mentally disordered. Bentz and Noel (1983) placed 32% in the psychiatric-disorder category and found that an additional 43% of the inmates showed mild to moderate symptoms. A jail study conducted by Guy and colleagues (1985) concluded that 66% of the inmates admitted had a psychiatric disturbance. According to Mobley (1986), an average 1–2% of the nation's prison population are schizophrenic, 5–8% have serious depression problems, and 1–2% exhibit mania or mixed manic-depressive disorders. Additionally, approximately 1–5% of the population are at the level of mild mental retardation. In fact, of the 100 executions between January 1977 and June 1988, six inmates executed were mentally retarded (IQ below 70). (In January 1986, Terry Roach was strapped into South Carolina's electric chair. He was mentally retarded, with an IQ of 70. Although he was 25 when executed, he was only 17 when he participated in the murder of two other teens.) Roughly 10–50% of the inmate population experience anxiety disorders, specific fears or phobias, less serious depression disorders, stress, or psychologically related medical disorders. Antisocial personality types are likely to be found in 30–50% of the overall inmate population; chemical dependency in 65–75%, and sexual deviation (specifically rape and child molestation) in 8–16%.

CLASSIFICATION OF OFFENDERS

Classification systems have had different purposes. Some aid in determining treatment. Some have less application and seek out causes or explanations for criminal behavior that may bear on correctional treatment ultimately but are not framed in these terms directly. Several efforts have been made to work toward a common basis for groupings. There seems to be considerable agreement about the validity of the following major types of offender as a preliminary classification (Winslow, 1977).

The *prosocial offender* is usually viewed as "normal" and identifies with legitimate values and rejects the norms of delinquent subcultures. His or her offenses usually grow out of extraordinary pressures. The offender is most frequently convicted of crimes of violence, such as homicide or assault, or naively executed property offenses, such as forgery. Those who exhibit neurotic symptoms need treatment aimed at resolving the anxiety and conflicts exhibited. These offenders need greater insight into the reasons for their delinquent behavior and need to learn how to manage conflicts and anxieties more effectively. Thus, individual and group counseling, psychotherapy, and family services are most frequently recommended. A major concern is to get the prosocial offender out of the correctional cycle before he or she is harmed by contact with other offenders.

The *antisocial offender* identifies with a delinquent subculture or exhibits a generally delinquent orientation by rejecting conventional norms and values. The offender does not see himself or herself as delinquent or criminal but rather as a victim of an unreasonable and hostile world. His or her history often includes patterns of family helplessness, indifference, or inability to meet needs of children, truancy in school, and inadequate performance in most social spheres. The antisocial offender should be provided an environment with clear, consistent social demands but one in which concern for his or her welfare and interests is regularly communicated to him or her. Methods of group treatment are recommended in order to increase the offender's social insight and skill. The offender's value system must be changed. The attempt to get him or her to identify with a strong and adequate adult role model is an important part of most treatment programs. Treatment also aims at enlarging the cultural horizon of the antisocial offender, redefining his or her contacts with peers, and broadening and revising his or her self-conception.

The *pseudosocial manipulator* is described as not having adopted conventional standards, as being guilt free, self-satisfied, power oriented, nontrusting, emotionally insulated, and cynical. Personal histories reveal distrustful and angry families in which members are involved in competitive and mutually exploitative patterns of interaction. Some authorities recommend long-term psychotherapy. Others encourage the offender to redirect his or her manipulative skills in a socially acceptable manner.

The *asocial offender* is one who acts out his or her primitive impulses, is extremely hostile, insecure, and negativistic, and demands immediate gratification. This type of offender has an incapacity to identify with others and an inability to relate to a therapist or to the social world around him or her. Most experts recommend a simple social setting offering support, patience, and acceptance of the offender, with only minimal demands on his or her extremely limited skills and adaptability. Before pressures toward conformity can be exerted, the asocial offender needs to learn that human interaction is always a two-way process. Methods need to be used that reduce the offender's fear of rejection.

Although a standardized classification for all correctional purposes remains elusive, the value of classifications formed for specific management and treatment seems much clearer. Methods of classification are still in almost all cases far too cumbersome for routine administration.

PURPOSE OF THERAPEUTIC RECREATION

Punishment versus rehabilitation has always been a controversial issue regarding corrections. Saney (1986) points out that the rationale of punishment has changed several times under the influence of different theories. For a long time, people's concern in punishment was revenge, killing, or inflicting pain on a person who had committed murder or caused injury to someone. As early as 1870, the American Prison Association adopted the concept of rehabilitation. The idea emerged that the criminal justice system can and should rehabilitate and reeducate the offender. Proponents of rehabilitation argued that people are not responsible for what is actually conditioned by more primary forces, such as family and other social institutions, over which they cannot exert any effective control. The concept of punishment is thus unfounded and should be discarded. Instead of looking to past responsibility and guilt, our concern should be directed toward the future; and in place of punishment, we should use more humane and effective methods that are better suited to the protection of society.

The unfortunate fact is that even under the best of conditions, the methods and the approach used to rehabilitate past offenders have been basically ineffective. For one thing, to assume that the causes of criminal behavior are essentially personal is to miss the mark. Each person learns his or her behavior in the larger context of social life and under conditions created and maintained by society. Thus, unless social conditions and the structure and value system of the several groups in which the offender has been raised and to which he or she will most probably return after his or her term are improved, the past offender, even if completely rehabilitated, will as a rule revert to criminal activity when faced with strong outside stimuli.

Contrary to rehabilitation is the concept of punishment. One argument in support of punishment is that it aids in deterring future crime. The objective of deterrence has two aspects. In specific deterrence we are concerned with the future behavior of a particular offender. The idea is that somehow by subjecting the offender to punishment or other measures, we discourage that person from engaging in any criminal activity in the future. General deterrence refers to the fact that the public will feel assured that the criminal justice system works and that it is unlikely that any offender can avoid the consequence of his or her criminal act. The idea is that by setting the example of the convicted offender, we can convincingly discourage others from engaging in criminal activity. One of the oldest sentiments and concepts associated with punishment is revenge. When a person does something wrong, "he or she should pay for it"; he or she should be punished.

In recent decades, the concept that has predominated in the field of penology is rehabilitation. If offenders are really victims of social forces and circumstances over which they have no control, it is only fair that while they are being punished for their offenses, we should also try to modify their behavior, to equip them with some knowledge and skill that may be profitably put to use after leaving prison. In rehabilitation, we are no longer concerned about the past of the offenders; our interest lies in their future. We want to reeducate them, to cure them of their former socio-psychological maladjustments. For this purpose, the concept of guilt or responsibility is irrelevant in the same way it would be irrelevant to the treatment of a physical illness. Also, as in the case of any other treatment, the concept of time is irrelevant to our objective. We have to spend as much or as little time as necessary to "cure" the offender; and this, again, is incompatible with the traditional idea of determinate punishment, which should be proportional to the degree of guilt and social harm caused by a particular crime. Using the rehabilitative model, we would be forced to have indeterminate rather than fixed sentences. In practice, however, most prisons have failed to achieve these desired objectives. It is all but impossible to rehabilitate inmates under present-day prison conditions. Past experiences of failure in the rehabilitative ideal in prisons do not mean that the ideal is unsound. What is needed is a different approach and different practices.

Recreation is recognized by the American Correctional Association as an integral part of the rehabilitation program of offenders. The purpose of therapeutic recreation in corrections is actually twofold. The first purpose is to provide recreation services. Everyone needs a diversion from one's regular routine. We can only imagine how important this purpose is in a correctional facility. The second purpose is that of intervention and rehabilitation. Each inmate should have an individualized rehabilitation plan, and therapeutic recreation should be included in the treatment. Of course, leisure education is an important component of both recreation and therapeutic recreation and should be offered to develop leisure and social skills. As reported by Cipriano (1987), there are several benefits to offering therapeutic recreation. Included in these benefits are (1) decreasing the recidivism rate, (2) improving an individual's self-image, (3) improving physical health and fitness, (4) improving mental health, (5) increasing constructive leisure skills, (6) improving communication and ties with family members, (7) offering outlets for frustration and aggression, (8) developing leadership skills, (9) helpful readjustment upon release into society, and (10) opportunity to develop talents and skills that may be useful vocationally as well as in leisure.

COMMON SERVICE SETTINGS

The colonial situation in the United States was based on English tradition. Jails were established for the purpose of detention. Inmates were awaiting trial, corporal punishment such as flogging, or capital punishment by burning at the stake, hanging, or being broken over a wheel. Minor offenses were punished by degradation, such as standing in the stocks in public. William Penn constructed a new penal code for the Province of Pennsylvania, which reduced capital crimes to only that of homicide. The new code replaced corporal punishment with imprisonment at hard labor. The Walnut Street Jail was constructed in Philadelphia in 1790 as the first facility to be used solely for convicted felons. Treatment initially consisted of solitary confinement. Later, treatment included some work and religious or moral instruction. Soon after the Walnut Street Jail, two penitentiary philosophies were developed. The first was the Auburn system in 1816. This philosophy practiced solitary confinement at night and silent labor as a group during the day. The second philosophy was the Pennsylvania system in 1826, which practiced constant solitary confinement and labor in the cells. Inmates were not allowed to communicate with other inmates and had only limited and monitored communication with family members (Saney, 1986).

The rise of the reformatory system began at Elmira Reformatory in New York in 1876. This new system developed education programs, trade training, grades and marks (points to earn for release), intermediate sentencing, a parole system, and organized athletics as a substitute for labor or industrial programs. This was the early beginning of the rehabilitation philosophy that had its origin in the mid-twentieth century. However, because of limited facilities and funds and overcrowded conditions, rehabilitation was only a philosophy and was not really practiced until later. The American Correctional Association was formed in 1870; it created as its first principle "Reformation, not vindictive suffering, as the purpose of penal treatment of prisoners" (Saney, 1986).

Today, *jails* are operated by local governments. The purpose of jails is to hold persons awaiting trial or those sentenced to confinement for less than one year. Because of the usual short jail terms and lack of funding, therapeutic recreation is ordinarily not found in jails. However, recreation is offered in at least 25% of the nation's jails as diversional activities (*Report to the Nation,* n.d.).

Prisons are operated by state or federal governments to hold persons sentenced under state or federal laws to terms of confinement of more than one year. There are 38 federal prisons and 521 state prisons. Prisons are often classified by the level of security. *Maximum* or close custody prisons are typically surrounded by a double fence or wall (usually 18–25 feet high) with armed guards in observation towers. Such facilities usually have large interior cell blocks for inmate housing areas. About 41% of the maximum security prisons were built before 1925. Approximately 52% of all prison inmates are held under maximum security. *Medium* custody prisons typically have double fences topped with barbed wire to enclose the facility. Housing architecture is quite varied, consisting of outside cell blocks in units of 150 cells or less, dormitories, and cubicles. More than 87% of the medium custody prisons were built after 1925. About 37% of all prison inmates are held under medium security conditions. *Minimum* custody prisons typically do not have armed posts and may or may not have fences to enclose the institution. To a large degree, housing consists of open dormitories. More than 60% of the minimum security prisons were built after 1950. Around 11% of all prison inmates are held under minimum security conditions (*Report to the Nation*, n.d.).

Community-based facilities are operated publicly or privately (under contract) to hold persons for less than 24 hours a day to permit the offender limited opportunities for work, school, or other community contacts (*Report to the Nation*, n.d.).

CURRENT BEST PRACTICES AND PROCEDURES

Most corrections professionals generally agree that the main goal of adult prisons and the rest of the system is rehabilitation of the inmate. The concept of individualized treatment began in 1916 at the Auburn Prison in New York and later in other state prisons and within the federal prison system. Unfortunately, few states have the resources to provide the treatment promised in many statutes. Active treatment consists of a written individualized plan that is based on a diagnosis and goal relative to arrest, reversal, or amelioration of the disease process and aimed at restoring the individual's adaptive capacity to the maximal extent possible. It is comprised of defined services, activities, or programs related to the objectives, and is specific as to the responsibilities for the conduct of such services or activities; specific as to the means to measure the progress or outcomes and clear as to periodic review and revision of the plan.

Assessment

Assessment, usually referred to as classification in corrections, according to the American Correctional Association *Manual of Correctional Standards* (n.d.) is the development and administration of an integrated and realistic program for the individual, with procedures for changing the program when indicated. Five general approaches are recognized: (1) analysis of individual problems through the use of every available diagnostic technique, (2) evolution of a treatment and training program in staff conference, with participation of the inmate, (3) implementation of the recommended program, (4) revision when indicated, (5) relating the institutional program to the planned parole program. Assessment information is assembled through several channels. One of the most important documents is the presentence investigation provided by the courts. Input can also be gathered from the inmate, his family, community agencies, and official records. Other information is gathered by administration of diagnostic examinations such as psychological aptitude and educational tests. Observations by staff members who have contact with the inmate are also valuable. From these sources, a profile of the needs and aspirations of the inmate emerges.

Planning

Common types of services used in corrections is or at least should be the same as with other populations served by therapeutic recreation. It is essential that the therapeutic recreation programs provide a balance between a broad range of leisure activities and physical fitness, with a common thread throughout being a strong leisure education program. The balanced program will reflect recognition that physical fitness, recreation, and leisure education are necessary to the overall mental and physical health of the inmate. Typical therapeutic recreation programs are divided into two major areas—passive and active. According to Cipriano (1987), a more viable division of programs would be in-cell and out-of-cell activities. In-cell activities are those that can be carried out by individuals or several inmates within the cell and "bull pen" area. Usually these activities require little if any supervision. Out-of-cell activities are those that take place in a designated recreation hall, library, gymnasium, or in the yard.

According to a study of inmate recreation participation conducted by Aguilar and Asmussen (1988), the most frequent activity was watching sports on television (72%), followed by being a spectator in the gym (42%) and hanging out in the gym (39%). The authors noted that these are clearly passive activities and are very consistent with previous research on participation patterns. Softball attracted 39% of the respondents, and jogging was identified as a frequent activity for 35% of the inmates. One fourth of the inmates reported never using any of the recreation facilities. However, nearly three fourths of the sample (72%) reported using the facilities at least one hour per day.

Cipriano (1987) states that *innovation* is the key word in planning therapeutic recreation programs. New ideas and programs should be encouraged and not be dismissed without reason. Although security is the key element in any correctional environment, it is essential that the therapeutic recreation specialist does not fall prey to letting the concept overrule all others. Many programs can be implemented comfortably within the security regulations, and yet can be innovative. It is important that the people responsible for the program develop a plan to initiate the program. The plan should contain a review of the objectives of the program, the rationale for providing such services, and an evaluation of the resources available to the facility.

Implementation

According to O'Morrow (1980), we have two conflicting philosophies about inmate treatment. One philosophy—the "custodial prison" in which security is the primary purpose and the idea of treatment is tolerated—reflects the past. The second is the "progressive prison" or treatment type that superimposes on the discipline philosophy programs of classification (assessment), medical care and service, vocational and academic training, religion, counseling, therapeutic recreation, and involvement in the outside world.

We must focus our attention on the progressive prison model. The therapeutic recreation process adheres to the treatment concept, and implementation of those philosophies and objectives is a key to rehabilitation. Leadership in therapeutic recreation programs is necessary to establish order and to assure continuity and program progression. Leadership should come from within the central administration of the institution from persons who understand the role of therapeutic recreation. It should be the duty of such persons to develop an overall program in consultation with other staff members. The therapeutic recreation specialist should carry professional credentials, such as certification, in the field of therapeutic recreation. He or she should be trained in all aspects of recreation (arts and crafts, music, drama, games and sports, social activities, collecting, and literary activities) and particularly in leisure education and leisure counseling. Correctional officers should be used to assist in the implementation of the program. Such is the recommendation of the American Correctional Association, in order to have a more efficient and better-managed program.

Equipment, facilities, supplies, and personnel for therapeutic recreation services should comprise a part of the institutional budget. Such a budget should be carefully planned to meet the needs of the inmates. Adequate physical facilities are a necessary component of a successful therapeutic recreation program. It is essential that planning be coordinated with the institution's administration in order to develop the area allocated to therapeutic recreation (Hormachea & Hormachea, 1977).

Evaluation

One of the most important components of the therapeutic recreation process is the evaluation phase. However, it is perhaps the most overlooked aspect of programming. As Cipriano (1987) stated, through evaluation, information can be developed concerning participation, response, and the overall cost effectiveness of the program. To accomplish the evaluation, the therapist should keep accurate individual progress reports.

Ultimately, the main reason for evaluation is to measure the effectiveness of the therapeutic recreation program. It is important to identify if the inmate's behavior during incarceration is improving and the recidivism rate is lowered. Evaluation is essential to the overall rehabilitation process. Evaluation reports also serve to advise the administration of the effectiveness of the overall therapeutic recreation program. These reports are of special value in planning future program activities and projecting possible participation as well as estimating manpower resources necessary to carry out the function.

APPLICATION OF THE TR PROCESS

Prior to applying the therapeutic recreation process, we need to examine the typical inmate housed in a maximum security prison today. According to Irwin (1980), the escalation of violence and the takeover of the violent cliques and gangs have produced a new prison hero. Actually, the prison-oriented leader has been undergoing changes for decades. The upsurge of rapacious and murderous groups has all but eliminated the ideal inmate and drastically altered his or her identity. Most of all, toughness has pushed out most other attributes, particularly the norms of tolerance, mutual aid, and loyalty to a large number of other regulars. Earlier, toughness was reemphasized as a reaction to the soft, cooperative inmate identity fostered by the rehabilitative ideal. Toughness in the new hero in the violent men's prisons means, first, being able to take care of oneself in the prison world, where people will attack others with little or no provocation. Second, it means having the guts to take from the weak. Today, the respected public prison figure stands ready to kill to protect himself, maintains strong loyalties to some small group of other inmates (invariably of his own race), and will rob and attack or at least tolerate his friends' robbing and attacking other weak independents or their foes. He openly and stubbornly opposes the administration, even if this results in harsh punishment. Finally, he is extremely assertive of his masculine sexuality, even though he may occasionally make use of the prison homosexuals or, less often, enter into a more permanent sexual alliance with a younger inmate ("punk"). Today, inmates who embrace versions of this ideal and live according to it with varying degrees of exactitude dominate the indigenous life of the large violent prisons. They control the contraband distribution systems, prison politics, the public areas of the prison, and many prison activities. To circulate in this world, the inmate must act like a prisoner and, with a few exceptions, have some type of affiliation with a powerful racial clique or gang.

Given this stereotypic illustration of inmates and the prison environment, we are ready to apply the therapeutic recreation process. Keep in mind that each inmate is an individual, as is each prison different, especially when we distinguish between minimum, medium, and maximum security prisons. The following case will be used to illustrate the therapeutic recreation process as it relates to corrections.

CASE STUDY

Vini served two years for burglary. Shortly after release from prison, he returned to the use of narcotics. He had used both marijuana and heroin in moderation since his midteens, but never had a narcotics arrest, nor was there any indication in his record of heavy involvement in narcotics traffic. After becoming addicted, he became involved in drug traffic in order to support his habit. Four months later, he was arrested in possession of nine ounces of heroin. He pled guilty to a charge of possession and was given the maximum term allowed—1–10 years. This, however, was imposed consecutively to the sentence—1–15 years—that he was serving; so in effect, he returned to prison with a sentence of 1–25 years, of which he had served a little more than 2.

Assessment

The therapeutic recreation assessment of Vini will include (1) a leisure interest inventory of what Vini did during his leisure time prior to his first arrest, after he had served his first two years, and what he is currently interested in doing; (2) a review of what leisure activities he engaged in while serving his first sentence and an observation of what Vini is currently involved in during the assessment period.

Different techniques are used to collect assessment information. Some of these are information provided by family members and friends via case workers, police and parole records, reports compiled during his first incarceration, medical and psychological reports, behavioral observations, and, of course, interviews with him regarding his needs and interests. The purpose of the assessment is to identify the social, emotional, mental, and physical needs to gain a holistic profile and assist with the individual's rehabilitation. After reviewing all the assessment data, the therapeutic recreation specialist develops a rehabilitation plan.

Planning

From the assessment we determine that Vini could use therapeutic recreation assistance with the following:

Adjustment to prison life

1. Adjust to the prison environment.
2. Develop appropriate social and physical skills.
3. Identify constructive leisure activities.

Preparation for return to community living

1. Identify community leisure resources.
2. Develop appropriate leisure skills.

Implementation

Prior to the implementation phase, it is important to remember that the entire process has been an interdisciplinary rehabilitation team approach that has focused on Vini as an individual. It is also important to keep in mind that Vini has been invited to participate throughout the process and provide input at each step. Before implementation, Vini is again involved, and the implementation plan is discussed with him. A contract is written, and Vini accepts the terms by signing it.

In the case of Vini, several strategies would be implemented. In order to achieve the goals of adjustment to prison life, both recreation and therapeutic recreation activities would be scheduled. Furthermore, frequent leisure counseling sessions would be planned. These activities would be aimed at (1) allowing Vini an avenue to release frustrations and energy through diversional recreation activities, (2) helping Vini develop appropriate social and physical skills that have carryover value, and (3) intensely discussing Vini's use of free time during incarceration and after he is released.

As Vini approaches possible parole, he should be considered for work release. In preparation for work release, Vini needs to attend numerous leisure education sessions. The purpose of these sessions would be to familiarize Vini with community resources. This could be accomplished through the use of discussion, community information packets, and field trips to the community where he will be returning.

Evaluation

Evaluation is a very important step in the therapeutic recreation process. The results of the evaluation will have direct impact on the inmate's privileges and eventual release.

In general, the evaluation process should be both formative and summative. The formative aspect should be conducted each month by the rehabilitation team assigned to the individual inmate. The inmate should be present, and the personal contract should be reviewed. The team will examine the inmate's strengths and weaknesses during incarceration and possibly make alterations to the contract. If the inmate has not fulfilled the obligations of the contract, the contract will be deemed unsatisfactory. The inmate will need to repeat the contract, thus prolonging his stay in the institution.

The summative evaluation occurs when the inmate has completed the contract, met the objectives, and in essence served his term. This evaluation

is usually conducted by a parole board; however, input from the rehabilitation team (including the therapeutic recreation specialist) is considered. If
the parole board feels the inmate is ready, he is released. In most states, the
individual is assigned to a parole officer who works with the parolee and
continues to evaluate his progress for months after release. The final stage
in evaluation of the individual's progress and, therefore, the effectiveness
of the overall treatment is the examination of recidivism.

TRENDS AND ISSUES

In 1965, Congress enacted the Federal Prisoners Rehabilitation Act. This
act was directed toward those offenders in federal institutions and concerned itself with community-based treatment programs wherein inmates
work at jobs and attend academic or vocational schools in the community.
Furloughs, another provision of the act, allow inmates to make unescorted
trips home for emergency visits, to seek jobs, and for other approved
purposes. Furthermore, academic training is available under the Elementary and Secondary Education Act. In an attempt to combat the crime
problem of youth, Congress passed the Juvenile Delinquency Prevention
and Control Act in 1968. The act was directed at rehabilitating delinquents
and aiding potential troublemakers. In 1974, the Juvenile Justice and
Delinquency Prevention Act was passed. One purpose of the act was the
development of programs designed to divert and prevent youngsters from
entering the juvenile justice system.

A trend developing today is the practice of private businesses operating prisons for profit. In most cases, a company leases a prison from a
governmental agency. However, there are examples where the prison has
been purchased and a few cases where private industry has actually constructed a new prison facility. The advantages appear to be better management and less cost to the taxpayer; more employment opportunity for the
inmates, which in turn has many positive effects; and perhaps industrial
advantages such as lower salaries due to nonunionization. The concept is
still reasonably new, and, therefore, we should not judge its merits. We will
have to wait to examine the results and assess any disadvantages.

The National Correctional Recreation Association was established in
1966 during the annual meeting of the Amateur Athletic Union National
Committee for Sports in Correctional Institutions at the Indiana State
Prison for Adults in Michigan City. Its objectives are to create and maintain
professional standards and to foster national interest in correctional recreation, as well as to promote, through therapeutic recreation, the reorienta-
tion of offenders to society. The association sponsors and encourages
postal prison meets wherein offenders participate in various physical and
social activities through use of the mails.

As a rehabilitative tool, prison confinement has not been successful.

Unfortunately, the contemporary prison system is here to stay. Despite talk about "alternatives to incarceration," the public will accept no substitutes that are more humane than confinement. In 1977, the Netherlands imprisoned 20 law offenders per 100,000 persons; Denmark, 28; Sweden, 32; the United Kingdom, 75; Canada, 95; and the United States, about 255. And all of these countries had crime rates either comparable to or lower than the United States (*Impact*, 1977). Today's prisons are torn by violence, with residents assaulting each other and the officers. Gang warfare is common. For example, in 1973 the murder rate inside San Quentin was 20 times higher than that in the outside world. Our way of dealing with law offenders—incarcerating as many as possible—will only result in overcrowding. Constructing new prisons will not solve the problem of crime in this country. Data on this point show that 80% of all crimes committed are by people who have already been incarcerated. With many opinions leaning toward the view of punishment, there are still some supporters of rehabilitation.

One individual concerned about the move toward punishment is John Irwin, an ex-inmate and currently a professor of sociology at San Francisco State University. Irwin agrees that rehabilitation has not worked, but adds that prisons have not really practiced rehabilitation. He states:

> Prisons punish people. Heaping punishment upon those sent to prison embitters and damages them. We could increase deterrence and reduce the turmoil in prison if we were honest about what we are doing—punishing prisoners. [During the period of rehabilitation, the average sentence increased from 24 months in 1950 to 38 months in 1968.] Prison confinement has failed as a rehabilitation tool. People abruptly returned from a prison's artificial community to the responsibilities of freedom are often unprepared. They have no job, no place to live, and usually no money. Their family may have gone on welfare; they may have been divorced while in prison. Too many ex-inmates, unprepared for the changes they must confront, are soon living outside the law once again, and return to the prison system through the revolving door. (Irwin, 1978)

To predict the future role of corrections is difficult because of the rehabilitation-punishment controversy. If the rehabilitation theory is supported and practiced, therapeutic recreation could play a major role in corrections. On the other hand, what is the first service withdrawn when punishment is practiced? Therapeutic recreation programs will continue to be inadequate and diversional unless we advocate for services and convince others of their merits. We must realize that therapeutic recreation is not a cure-all. It does not solely prevent, control, or cure unacceptable behavior. However, therapeutic recreation does have an important role in the total treatment and rehabilitation process. During the American Psychological Association's 84th Annual Convention in Washington, DC, September

1976, a study conducted on ex-inmates was presented. It was found that the nonrecidivist engaged in more leisure time activities than did the recidivist. These results and others like them need to be pointed out to authorities in the correctional system. Therapeutic recreation specialists need to become involved in these issues. Following are some recommendations on what action is necessary (Anderson, 1979).

Therapeutic Recreation Program

1. The therapeutic recreation budget needs to be increased. Presently, therapeutic recreation receives only 1% of the budget in state and federal prisons.

2. The correctional staff needs to be educated as to the merits of therapeutic recreation.

3. All inmates should be able to participate in all aspects of the therapeutic recreation program.

4. The therapeutic recreation program should be systematically planned with individualized rehabilitation plans in mind.

5. Therapeutic recreation programs should be provided that have variety and flexibility to meet a wide range of needs and interests and have carryover value in the community.

6. Inmates should be involved in the total planning, implementation, and evaluation of the program.

7. The family should be involved. Such practice is usually not the case. At many prisons, the same person may visit only once every 14 days. A 3-year grant at the Dwight Correctional Center in Illinois is federally funded to establish a program that allows incarcerated mothers and their children to spend a night camping together (N. Stumbo, personal communication, May 13, 1988).

8. Community facilities and resources should be used as frequently as possible.

Therapeutic Recreation Personnel

1. Each prison should have a minimum of one professionally trained full-time therapeutic recreation specialist. The specialist should possess at least a bachelor's degree in recreation with a concentration in therapeutic recreation from an accredited college or university and be certified with the National Council for Therapeutic Recreation Certification.

2. Therapeutic recreation personnel should be compensated commensurate with individuals with similar responsibilities within and outside of the prison.

3. Trained correctional officers should be part of the therapeutic recreation program and total rehabilitation process.

4. Select inmates should be trained and used as indigenous leaders.

5. Assistance should be sought from outside consultants and professionals.

Correctional System

1. A therapeutic recreation specialist should be represented on the central correctional agency staff.

2. We should advocate for government spending to be directed at the roots of crime, such as unemployment (40% of all residents are without previous work experience) (Association, 1972), poor housing, poor parenting, poor education, and poor medical attention.

3. We should advocate for sentence reductions to "time served" for all those serving time for crimes that do not cause physical harm to others, where release would be followed by treatment. Wardens testify that no more than 50% of the prisoners in state prisons need to be locked up (Association, 1972). Likewise, according to a 1977 Congressional Budget Office study, only 11% of prisoners in federal prisons are being held for robbery and other violent crimes. The other 89% could be released into alternative programs.

4. We should advocate for reduction of overall length of the original sentences, and include restitution, suspended sentences, third-party custody, and community-service orders in sentencing practices.

Public Education

The last area, and the most difficult, is to educate the public as to the importance of rehabilitation of law offenders. The public does not understand that crime is not an individual problem but a social problem. Society many times is just as guilty as the individual who carried out the crime. Therefore, it is our problem; we must accept part of the blame and support total rehabilitation.

Caryl Chessman provided the following statement just before he was executed on May 2, 1960.

> It seemed to me, just as it usually seems to my kind, that society was simply trying to strip or rip off my shield, that it was willing to do so ruthlessly, that it didn't care about me personally, or the amount of humiliation or degradation it might inflict in the process. I stubbornly balked at being manipulated, regulated, or being compelled to conform blindly through fear or threat or punishment, however severe. Indeed, I came to question the validity of a society that appeared more concerned with imposing its will than in inspiring respect. There seemed to me something grossly wrong with this. "We'll make you be good!" I was told, and I told myself nobody should, would or could *make* me anything. And I proved it. (*Time*, 1982, pp. 42–43)

SUMMARY

Prisons are here to stay. Of course, there are different types of incarceration facilities; however, as long as we have crime, we will have prisons. Most prisons are overcrowded and very expensive. Today, only about 20% of inmates have a one-man, 60-square-foot cell. This is considered bathroom size and is recommended by the American Correctional Association. Prisons are extraordinarily expensive to build and operate. Medium security prisons cost approximately $40,000 per cell, whereas maximum security facilities cost around $80,000 for each cell. It costs about $15,000 to feed and guard an inmate for one year.

Any prison will punish. Some people fear that prisons are now too cushy, so spiffed up that chastisement is nullified. But the "country club prison" does not exist. A plain deprivation of freedom—the average inmate serves two years or so—is quite severe all by itself. Conjugal visits between inmates and spouses are permitted in only nine states. More typical of prison permissiveness is allowing *Playboy* pinups in cells and unlimited seconds on bread in the chow lines (*Time*, 1982).

Although the public's opinion is that we are creating "country clubs," very few prisons enjoy that type of atmosphere. In fact, many prisons do not offer planned and organized therapeutic recreation programs, and the quality of others is very questionable. The picture may appear impressive to the taxpayer regarding leisure activities; however, note that 75% of all jails have no recreation. The essence of prison life is that it is boring—boring by definition and by design.

Prison officials need to reemphasize rehabilitation. Therapeutic recreation holds a place in the rehabilitation process. According to Haun (1965), the anomic prisoner is not excluded from his environment. There is sensory input of significant, although reduced, magnitude. May not the problem here be a lack of certain necessary components of a balanced "diet," with the central nervous system unable to function normally because it receives only "carbohydrate" precepts and no "protein" or "fat" input? Haun continues with the point that research clearly demonstrates the need for sensory input if the central nervous system is to function normally. The normal functioning of the human central nervous system is critically dependent upon the maintenance of sensory input. In origin, the sensory input can be operationally divided among housekeeping, work, and recreation. Housekeeping tends to be affectively neutral. People's normal function is related to the balance between work and recreation. Haun states that the recreation specialist has a vitally significant mission as the guardian of balance. Furthermore, Haun (1965) states that recreation "competently administered and skillfully presented, encourages the timid, disarms the aggressive, motivates the lethargic, calms the restless, and diverts the melancholic" (p. 53). Haun's philosophy can be applied to inmates in prisons just as well. As a necessary part of a prison environment, genuinely attuned to the needs of the inmate, recreation merits our serious attention.

READING COMPREHENSION QUESTIONS

1. What are some of the factors influencing the increase in prison populations?
2. What are the functional characteristics of the major classifications of law offenders?
3. Justify the need for therapeutic recreation in correctional settings.
4. Distinguish between minimum, medium, and maximum security prisons.
5. Why are many corrections authorities abandoning the idea of rehabilitation and reverting again to punishment?
6. Why is the individualized rehabilitation plan appropriate for prison populations?
7. Discuss some of the future directions the criminal justice system might take.

SUGGESTED LEARNING ACTIVITIES

1. Organize a field trip to as many of the following types of correctional facilities as possible:

- local jail
- work release center
- diagnostic and treatment center
- minimum security prison
- medium security prison
- maximum security prison

2. Interview an inmate currently serving time.
3. Develop a case study for an inmate met during one of the field trips.
4. Interview a therapeutic recreation specialist employed in a prison.
5. Survey a correctional facility population regarding their leisure interests.
6. Invite a correctional officer to class to discuss the criminal justice system.
7. View the following films:

- *Attica*
- *Crime and the Criminal*
- *Children in Trouble*

8. Read *Letter from a Condemned Man*, by Ruben Elis Nazario (New Haven: Rencove Publishing, 1980).

9. Debate the concepts of rehabilitation vs. punishment.

10. Write a paper on a current issue facing corrections today.

REFERENCES

AGUILAR, T. E., & ASMUSSEN, K. (1988). *Recreation participation patterns in an adult correctional facility.* Paper presented at the Fifth Annual Therapeutic Recreation Research Colloquium, Illinois State University, Normal, IL.

American Correctional Association. (1987). *Adult inmate population.* College Park, MD.

American Correctional Association. (n.d.). *Manual of Correctional Standards.* College Park, MD.

ANDERSON, S. C. (1979). The role of recreation in corrections. *Profile, 1.*

Association of State Correctional Administrators. (1972). *Uniform correctional policies and procedures.* Columbia, SC.

BENTZ, W. K., & NOEL, R. W. (1983). The incidence of psychiatric disorder among a sample of men entering prison. *Corrective and social psychiatry and journal of behavior technology, methods, and therapy, 29*(1).

CIPRIANO, R. E. (1987). *A prototype recreation program for inmates in correctional institutions.* Middletown, CT: Special Education Resource Center.

COLLINS, J. J., & SCHLOENGER, W. E. (1983). *The prevalence of psychiatric disorder among admissions to prison.* Paper presented at the American Society of Criminology, 35th Annual Meeting, Denver, CO.

FOGEL, D. (Ed.). (1974). Recreation in corrections [Special issue]. *Parks and recreation, 9*(9).

GUY, E., PLATT, J. J., SWERLING, I., & BULLOCK, S. (1985). Mental health status of prisoners in an urban jail. *Criminal justice and behavior, 12*(1).

HAUN, P. (1965). *Recreation: A medical viewpoint.* New York: Teachers College Press.

HORMACHEA, C. (Ed.). (1972). Recreation in corrections [Special issue]. *Therapeutic Recreation Journal, 6*(3).

HORMACHEA, M., & HORMACHEA, C. (1977). Recreation and youthful and adult offenders. In T. A. Stein & H. D. Sessoms (Eds.). *Recreation and special populations* (2nd ed.). Boston: Holbrook Press.

Impact. (1977). Washington, DC. (Available from the American Correctional Association, 4321 Hartwick Road, Suite L208, College Park, MD 20740.)

Inside America's toughest prison. (1986, October 6). *Newsweek.*

IRWIN, J. (1978, September 13). The prison community: A war behind walls. *Bloomington Herald-Telephone,* 32.

IRWIN, J. (1980). *Prisons in turmoil.* Boston: Little, Brown & Company.

Legal Defense Fund. (1988). *Executions in America since 1976.* New York: NAACP Legal Defense and Educational Fund.

McCALL, G. E. (Ed.). (1981, April). Issues in correctional recreation [Special issue]. *Journal of Physical Education and Recreation.*

MOBLEY, M. J. (1986, May). Mental health services for inmates in need. *Corrections Today.*

O'MORROW, G. S. (1980). *Therapeutic recreation: A helping profession* (2nd ed.). Reston, VA: Reston Publishing.

Report to nation on crime and justice. (n.d.). (Available from the American Correctional Association, 4321 Hartwick Road, Suite L208, College Park, MD 20740.)

SANEY, P. (1986). *Crime and culture in America.* Westport, CT: Greenwood Press.
   Time. (1982, September 13). The inmate nation: What are prisons for?
U.S. Department of Justice. (1986). *Jail inmates 1986.* Bureau of Justice Statistics
   Bulletin.
WINSLOW, R. (1977). *Crime in a free society* (3rd ed.). Belmont, CA: Dickenson
   Publishing.

18

Management, Consultation, and Research

JUDITH E. VOELKL

OBJECTIVES

- Describe how the management of a department or facility may influence the professional growth of a therapeutic recreation specialist.
- Explain the difference between general supervision and clinical supervision.
- Define consultation.
- Explain the differences between the four types of consultation.
- Describe the roles that the consultant may take in the consultation process.
- Know the research topics that have been ranked as very important by therapeutic recreation specialists.
- Reduce the research process to a series of steps.
- Know resources that provide therapeutic recreation specialists with information on current research studies.

Throughout this book a great deal of information has been presented on the use of the therapeutic recreation process with individuals who have a variety of disabilities. As a result of these readings or previous experiences, many readers may have identified a specific group of individuals with whom they would like to work. Future course work and practical experiences may be planned to allow the student to gain specialized skills in the provision of services for a particular group of individuals. What many students may not have considered, however, is the avenues an entry-level therapeutic recreation specialist must have for continuing the attainment of new skills and enhancing his or her current level of clinical skills. The continued attainment of high-level skills and the refinement of previously learned skills will aid the therapeutic recreation specialist in providing quality services for clients.

The responsibility that each therapeutic recreation specialist has for improving his or her clinical skills is evident in the National Therapeutic Recreation Society's Code of Ethics. The Code of Ethics states that the therapeutic recreation professional "is committed to the continuous task of learning and self-improvement to increase his/her competency and effectiveness as a professional . . . [and] is guided by the accepted responsibility of encouraging and providing quality services to the client/consumer" (Code of Ethics, 1985). Individuals studying therapeutic recreation may consider what processes inherent in the workplace will continue to support and enhance their professional growth following the completion of their formal education.

The purpose of this chapter is to consider several processes within the workplace and the profession that support the professional growth of therapeutic recreation specialists. In the first section we will reflect upon how management and the supervision process may enhance the further development of clinical skills; in the second section the focus will be on the consultation process; and in the third section the role research plays in enhancing our professional knowledge will be addressed.

MANAGEMENT

Management involves the planning, organizing, staffing, directing, and controlling of human and nonhuman resources (Culkin & Kirsch, 1986; Kraus & Curtis, 1982). In therapeutic recreation management, a manager considers a therapeutic recreation staff member to be a human resource and assigns staff members specific job responsibilities that are in line with departmental and organizational goals. Managers of therapeutic recreation departments oversee not only human resources, such as a therapeutic recreation specialist, but they also deal with nonhuman resources, such as equipment, supplies, and space or work areas available to staff members (Keller, 1985). In this section we will explore how management influences the job responsibilities, availability of resources, professional participation, and supervision that a staff member receives. Furthermore, we will briefly examine how these areas influence a therapeutic recreation specialist's opportunities for professional growth in an agency.

Most entry-level therapeutic recreation specialists report to or are directly responsible to a supervisor who is in a management position. The manager/supervisor may be the director of therapeutic recreation services, the director of activities, or a director or chief of a unit within a hospital or agency. The manager/supervisor is an important person to consider when an entry-level therapeutic recreation specialist is interviewing for a position at an agency. The entry-level therapeutic recreation specialist may ask the following questions to discover the viewpoint of management and how this viewpoint may influence his or her job responsibilities and opportunities for professional growth:

- What are the goals of the manager/supervisor in relation to the department or unit?
- How does the manager/supervisor interpret the supervisee's job description and role within the department/unit/agency?
- How does the manager/supervisor influence the supervisee's access to equipment, supplies, or monies for new items?
- What types of supervision are provided for the staff?
- Does the department or agency support the staff's participation in professional organizations?

The way in which the manager/supervisor interprets an employee's job description and the goals the manager/supervisor has for the department may directly influence a staff member's job responsibilities. For instance, a therapeutic recreation specialist interested in developing a leisure education program within a program for adults with a chemical dependency may not feel professionally challenged or fulfilled while working under a manager who believes that the job responsibility of the staff member is to provide diversional recreation programs. This type of work situation would prevent the therapeutic recreation specialist from further developing his or her skills as a leisure educator. When considering a therapeutic recreation position, an individual needs to "interview" the manager/supervisor carefully by asking questions regarding the purpose of the therapeutic recreation service and the associated job responsibilities.

Another area that may influence a therapeutic recreation specialist's task of providing services is the availability of resources such as equipment, supplies, space for running activities, and monies for the purchase of new equipment and supplies. A therapeutic recreation specialist without the proper location or equipment may need to cancel an activity, for it may be unsafe to implement an activity under those conditions. It is important for a therapeutic recreation specialist considering a potential job to ask the manager/supervisor about the availability and allocation of nonhuman resources.

The types of supervision provided by a department or agency are another area for a potential employee to consider when applying for a professional position. Most therapeutic recreation specialists receive general supervision, which entails a supervisor directing and evaluating employees' work, and informing employees of policies, procedures, standards, or legislation that affect the provision of services (Austin, 1986; Cogan, 1973). In recent years an increased amount of attention has been paid to the provision of clinical supervision for therapeutic recreation specialists (Austin, 1986).

Clinical Supervision

Clinical supervision is a dynamic process in which the supervisor, often a person different from the individual providing general supervision, works with a therapeutic recreation specialist in order to identify his or her strengths and weaknesses in regard to clinical practice. The supervisor possesses extensive experience, skills, and knowledge in the area of therapeutic recreation services. The supervisor and the therapeutic recreation specialist share in the task of identifying clinical skills that the therapeutic recreation specialist would like to improve. The clinical skills that are addressed in the clinical supervision process may include charting, development of individualized treatment plans, or selection and application of a therapeutic approach (e.g., behavioral, client-centered, etc.) for a therapeutic recreation group. As part of the process, the supervisor and the therapeutic recreation specialist decide how they will work together and how to evaluate progress. Throughout the clinical supervision process, the supervisor and supervisee discuss the difficulties of learning new skills and acknowledging areas of weaknesses. Supervisors seek to support and acknowledge a supervisee's progress and feelings about clinical supervision.

Therapeutic recreation specialists participating in clinical supervision may be involved in individual conferences or group meetings. Individual conferences are held on either a weekly or biweekly basis, and the content addresses the identified needs of the supervisee. Group meetings may occur biweekly or monthly, and the content may address preidentified needs of the group or a discussion of specific problems (Austin, 1986).

The benefits of participating in clinical supervision are evident in the fact that it has been found to influence employees' work satisfaction positively (Cherniss & Egnatios, 1977). Furthermore, the positive outcomes of clinical supervision include an improved level of services for clients, which enhances the achievement of organizational goals, and the provision of professional growth for supervisees (Austin, 1986). It appears that the process of clinical supervision will support the therapeutic recreation specialist who is attempting to "increase his/her competency and effectiveness as a professional" as is stated in the Code of Ethics—National Therapeutic Recreation Society (1985, p. 71).

Professional Organizations

Participation in professional organizations is another avenue therapeutic recreation specialists have for enhancing their professional growth.

Several national-level organizations exist (e.g., American Therapeutic Recreation Association, National Therapeutic Recreation Society), and numerous organizations exist on the state level for therapeutic recreation specialists. Professional organizations are instrumental in the dissemination of information regarding new developments and issues in the field. For example, members of professional organizations in therapeutic recreation may receive information regarding how standards, legislation, and research influence professional practice. Many professional organizations sponsor yearly conferences with sessions on such topics as innovative programs, tips for devising effective treatment plans, or practical approaches for working with specific groups of individuals. Information received from professional organizations may directly influence and enhance the therapeutic recreation specialist's delivery of service in the workplace. The entry-level therapeutic recreation specialist considering a position needs to discover how the management of a department and agency views professional involvement. More specifically, therapeutic recreation specialists need to clarify whether management will provide time and possibly the financial support for membership in professional organizations and attendance at professional meetings.

The management of a department, including departmental goals, design of job descriptions, availability of equipment and facilities, the types of supervision offered, and support for participation in professional organizations, all interact to influence the opportunities a staff person has for developing clinical skills. Therefore, these areas directly influence a therapeutic recreation specialist's opportunities for professional growth in the workplace. Therapeutic recreation specialists seeking positions need to consider how the management of a specific department or agency will enhance or hinder their professional growth and development.

CONSULTATION

Consultation involves a process in which a consultant, an individual with specialized skills, works with a consultee. The consultee may be a therapeutic recreation specialist, a therapeutic recreation department, or an agency that includes therapeutic recreation personnel. Consultees usually enter into the consultation process on a voluntary basis. The purpose of consultation is for the consultant to help consultees become more effective and efficient in their work (Kurpius, 1978).

In this section we will explore the conditions under which an entry-level therapeutic recreation specialist may work with a consultant. Furthermore, information on the types of consultation, the consultation process, and several roles that the consultant may use during the process will be presented. We will begin by presenting several case examples in order to exemplify when a consultant may assist a consultee in addressing problems that occur in the workplace.

> Case Example 1: A group home for individuals with emotional disturbances has decided to begin accepting individuals with mental retardation. Most of the staff members have had little experience working with individuals with mental retardation. A consultant with expertise in working with the mentally retarded is hired to help staff provide services to meet the needs of the new clients.
>
> Case Example 2: A new psychiatric facility hired a number of occupational therapists and a number of therapeutic recreation specialists. While developing the program, tension arose between the OTRs and the TRSs regarding the differences between the programs provided by each group. A consultant is hired to help mediate the process of how staff identify the boundaries between the OTRs and the TRSs.
>
> Case Example 3: A 160-bed nursing home was recently reviewed by the state. The therapeutic recreation department was cited for failing to comply with several standards. When talking with the administrator, the director of therapeutic recreation states that her department is doing the best it can with limited resources, and she feels unsure of how to meet all the standards. The administrator suggests that a consultant be hired to help the director evaluate current services and consider alternatives that would ensure the meeting of all standards.
>
> Case Example 4: Plans to open an adult day care center are being discussed by a planning committee representing a number of organizations within a small community. The chairperson of the planning committee states that a specialist in recreation should be hired. However, none of the committee members know anything about therapeutic recreation. They decide to hire a consultant who can aid them (1) in outlining the type of program that a therapeutic recreation specialist could provide and (2) in hiring an entry-level therapeutic recreation specialist.

The case examples exemplify various situations in which a consultee may benefit from a consultant's specialized knowledge and skills. Different types of consultation may be used to address the problems in these various situations. Caplan (1970) outlined four types of consultation: (1) *Client-centered case consultation* involves a consultant helping a consultee plan an effective treatment plan for working with a specific client. (2) *Consultee-centered case consultation* focuses on providing staff with the necessary skills for working with clients for whom they were previously unable to provide services effectively. For instance, it may involve a consultant working with staff regarding common problems or issues in working with a group of clients, as was described in Case Example 1. Two other types of consultation are focused at the agency or management level. (3) *Program-centered administrative consultation* involves program development. Program-centered administrative consultation would be the type of consultation used in Case Examples 2 and 4. (4) *Consultee-centered administrative consultation* assists the consultee in examining problems and issues in administration. Consultee-centered administrative consultation would be the approach taken in Case Example 3.

The Roles of the Consultant

Within each consultation situation, a consultant may take on several roles in order to assist a consultee in addressing the issue or problem at hand. For example, the consultant hired in Case Example 1 may take on the roles of technical specialist and trainer/educator in order to provide staff with the knowledge and skills necessary for successfully working with individuals with mental retardation (Lippitt & Lippitt, 1986). In contrast, the consultant hired in Case Example 2 may serve as a mediator for the two groups and would focus on finding out the facts, reflecting the feelings and beliefs of the consultees, and processing the interactions among staff. Lippitt and Lippitt suggest that the roles used by a consultant may include being an advocate for a specific method or intervention. Other roles include functioning as a problem solver, information specialist, trainer/educator, collaborator or joint problem solver, identifier of alternatives, fact finder, process specialist, or objective observer. Kurpius (1978) indicates that a consultant may also take on the role of a mediator or collaborator in the consultation process.

Another role frequently used by consultants is being a catalyst of change. Thinking back on the case examples, it seems that change would need to occur in order to begin addressing any of the issues. For instance, in Case Example 3, staff may need to alter the manner in which they provide services in order to ensure that they meet state standards. Change is an essential part of most consultation processes. In many instances, however, change is difficult for people. There are times in the consultation process when it is upsetting for a consultee to consider the changes that will occur, and he or she may feel that the changes being suggested are an indication of professional weakness or a form of criticism. One of the skills possessed by consultants is the ability to help people adjust to the process of change. In the consultation process, time is provided for consultees to discuss how they feel about change, including the drawbacks and benefits of the change process. Frequently, the benefits of change are observed in the increased quality of care and the opportunities for personal and professional growth on the part of the consultees.

It appears that the consultant who can address the needs of all the consultees listed in the case examples would need to be a miracle worker! In reality, it may be that four different consultants, each possessing different strengths and specialized knowledge, need to be found for the case examples. The first stage in the consultation process allows a consultee to find the best consultant for a specific job. This occurs during the *entry* stage of the consultation process. The consultee would spend time talking with several different consultants to make sure that the consultant who is chosen has the necessary skills and values, understands how staff feel about change, and exhibits an approach to working with people that would fit in well in the agency (Snow & Corse, 1986). The entry stage allows the consultant and consultee to size each other up! If both parties agree that they could work well together, a contract is drawn up. Most entry-level therapeutic recreation specialists would be involved in meeting potential consultants, even though supervisory level personnel usually draw up the contract.

The Consultation Process

After an agreement is worked out between the consultant and the consultee, they enter the *data gathering and diagnosis* stage. They work together to identify the facts surrounding the problem or issue that has bought them together. They want to discover the reasons for the problem. The consultant will ask questions, observe, ask consultees to keep records surrounding the problem issues, and interview individuals and groups of employees (Snow & Corse, 1986). The results of the data gathering will be presented to all the consultees, and a diagnosis will be made by the consultant and consultees.

After correctly identifying the problem, the consultees and consultant must decide on an *intervention*. An intervention is a plan of action that outlines the changes that will occur, the tasks related to each area of change, and the parties responsible for each task. How actively involved the consultant is in this decision will depend on the role he or she has taken. If a consultant is serving as a mediator or collaborator, he or she will support the consultees in making decisions. However, if the consultant is serving as a provider of specialized information, he or she will take a more active role in identifying the appropriate intervention. When deciding on an intervention, decisions need to be made regarding each individual's role, a time line, and how the intervention will be evaluated (Snow & Corse, 1986).

Evaluation will be an ongoing process that starts with the beginning of the intervention. If the evaluations indicate that the outcome of the intervention is not satisfactory, changes need to be made. In instances where the outcomes are positive, the intervention is seen as working as anticipated.

When positive outcomes are found from an intervention, the consultant and consultees must decide how long the consultant will stay working in the system. Plans for *termination* of the consultant's services need to be made. Plans will include the identification of tasks that need to be attended to by the consultee rather than the consultant. It may also be decided that the consultant will conduct periodic checkup visits with the consultee in order to make sure all is running smoothly.

We have reviewed a great deal of information regarding the types of consultation, roles of a consultant, and the stages of the consultation process. Many entry-level therapeutic recreation specialists may find that they take part in a consultation process. In order to clarify how the various aspects of consultation may be experienced by an entry-level therapeutic recreation specialist, let's take Case Example 2 and work through the process (see Table 18.1).

In the case of the Wasatch Nursing Facility discussed in Table 18.1, Connie, the consultant, spent approximately nine months in the facility. This is an example of a short-term consultation process. Some consultation processes may span several years and are considered long-term consultation.

As we have discussed in this section, consultation is a process that involves a consultant assisting a consultee in making changes. The consultation process allows the consultee to learn new skills and approaches to problem solving that will assist him or her in functioning more competently as a therapeutic recreation specialist.

RESEARCH

Research is defined as a systematic and well-planned process that allows the researcher to examine the relationship between naturally occurring phenomena (Kerlinger, 1973). For example, a research study may be designed to examine the effect of participation in a recreation activity upon individuals' self-esteem. A study designed to examine the influence of various leadership styles on individuals' participation in recreation groups is another example.

The importance of designing research studies in therapeutic recreation to examine the relationship between naturally occurring phenomena has been discussed by numerous leaders in the field (Austin, 1982; Compton, 1984; Iso-Ahola, 1988; Witt, 1988). Entry-level practitioners and students of therapeutic recreation, however, may ask a variety of questions regarding the role of research in therapeutic recreation. For instance, what role would an entry-level therapeutic recreation specialist take in relation to therapeutic recreation research? What are the research questions most frequently asked by therapeutic recreation specialists? How do therapeutic recreation specialists stay informed of research being conducted in the field?

Table 18.1
Consultation Process and Roles: Wasatch Nursing Facility

Sarah—the Director of Therapeutic Recreation
Connie—the Consultant

Current Situation: A 160-bed nursing home, Wasatch Nursing Facility was recently reviewed by the state. The therapeutic recreation department was cited for failing to comply with several standards. While talking with the administrator, Sarah states that her department is doing the best it can with limited resources, and she feels unsure of how to meet all the standards. The administrator suggests that a consultant be hired to help Sarah evaluate current services and consider alternatives that would ensure the meeting of all standards.

Entry Phase: Sarah and Connie will meet to discuss problems with meeting standards. Connie will talk about her approach to working with a consultee. Connie tells Sarah that she considers this type of consultation a *consultee-centered administrative consultation,* and she will act as a *collaborator, identifier of alternatives,* and *catalyst of change.* Following the meeting with Connie, Sarah recommends that the administrator of the nursing home hire Connie as the consultant.

Data Gathering and Diagnosis: Sarah and Connie review the report filed by the state inspector and the job description/responsibilities of each employee in the therapeutic recreation department. Connie interviews the employees and asks them to keep a diary of how they spend their time. Connie and Sarah meet to discuss findings and alternatives. Connie and Sarah meet with the department to discuss findings.

Intervention: The department decides on an intervention that alters each person's job responsibilities to ensure that state standards are met. As part of the intervention, Connie provides an in-service training session on treatment plans and progress notes.

Evaluation: While planning the intervention, the department decides that Connie will conduct monthly reviews on the employees' progress and will meet with them after three months and then after six months. Improvement is noted at the three-month and six-month reviews.

Termination: At the six-month review, it is decided that Sarah will take over monthly reviews. Connie no longer is an official consultant with the nursing home. However, she periodically talks with Sarah to check on how the therapeutic recreation department is getting along. The therapeutic recreation department receives an excellent report during the next state inspection.

The findings from a study by Bullock, McGuire, and Barch (1984) shed some light as to why research is important to therapeutic recreation specialists, the role taken by therapeutic recreation specialists in regard to research, and the research topics that have been identified as being important to therapeutic recreation specialists. Bullock, McGuire, and Barch surveyed members of the National Therapeutic Recreation Society from nine states regarding their use of research reports and ranking of research topics. The findings of the study suggest that therapeutic recreation specialists are interested in research topics that are closely related to practice. Many of the research areas ranked as very important are those that the therapeutic recreation specialist is confronted with on a daily basis. Respondents ranked the following six research topics as the most important:

1. Identifying effective teaching/therapy strategies to use with individuals.
2. Identifying techniques to motivate individuals to participate in activities.
3. Evaluating program effectiveness.
4. Studying the role of recreation in treatment.
5. Determining needs that can be met through leisure.
6. Designing tools to measure leisure abilities of individuals. (Bullock, McGuire, & Barch, 1984; p. 21)

When answering questions about the role of the therapeutic recreation specialist in research, the respondents indicated that the two most important roles were to (1) keep up to date on research in the field and (2) incorporate research findings into their jobs.

Several examples of research that address the needs identified by the respondents in the study by Bullock, McGuire, and Barch are presented in the section that follows.

Evaluating Program Effectiveness. A number of studies have been designed to examine the benefits experienced by clients participating in leisure education groups (e.g., Aguilar, 1987; Backman & Mannell, 1986; Wolpe & Riddick, 1984). Backman and Mannell's study will be used to provide a specific example of a research study designed to evaluate program effectiveness. Their study was conducted with older adults residing in a senior citizens' facility. Each person was assigned to a different group. The groups included (1) a leisure counseling group, (2) a leisure activity group, (3) a leisure counseling and leisure activity group, and (4) a control group consisting of older adults who did not participate in a leisure counseling or leisure activity group. All the older adults participating in the study completed questionnaires on leisure attitudes, work attitudes, activity participation, and satisfaction derived from activity participation. These questionnaires were completed prior to group participation (treatment), during participation in the groups, and following participation in the groups. Individuals participating in the leisure counseling group and those participating in the combined leisure counseling and leisure activity group showed a significant increase in leisure attitudes and satisfaction in activity participation over the course of the program. Only those individuals participating in the combined leisure counseling and leisure activity group showed a significant increase in activity participation. No significant changes in work attitudes were found for any of the four groups. Backman and Mannell suggested that perhaps the combination of increasing activity skills and examining leisure attitudes simultaneously provided the best combination for positively influencing the leisure attitudes and participation of older adults residing in a senior citizen facility.

The variety of studies (Aguilar, 1987; Backman & Mannell, 1986; Wolpe & Riddick, 1984) evaluating the effectiveness of leisure education programs allow therapeutic recreation specialists to examine how the structure of different groups (e.g., leisure counseling versus leisure activities) may positively influencing clients' leisure attitudes and behavior.

Designing tools to measure leisure abilities. Ellis and Witt (1986) designed an assessment tool, the Leisure Diagnostic Battery (LDB), for measuring the leisure abilities of individuals with disabilities. The LDB is based on a continuum which spans from perceived freedom, a central indicator of leisure functioning, to learned helplessness. The results of the LDB may be used along with information on a client's leisure preferences, leisure knowledge, and barriers to leisure, to devise an appropriate treatment plan. Use of the LDB in practice allows for the therapeutic recreation specialist to determine the necessity of treatment and measure the effectiveness of treatment. (Ellis, Witt, & Niles, 1982)*

Program effectiveness and assessment are issues that confront therapeutic recreation specialists on a regular basis. Striving to stay informed of current research allows therapeutic recreation specialists to be aware of innovative and unique approaches to carrying out the therapeutic recreation process. Furthermore, research findings indicate under what conditions therapeutic recreation interventions are effective.

A number of journals are available for therapeutic recreation students and professionals who are interested in keeping themselves informed of the research findings in the field. The *Therapeutic Recreation Journal, Annual in Therapeutic Recreation,* and *Journal of Leisurability* are all publications that include research reports. Therapeutic recreation specialists may also stay informed of current research in the field by attending national and regional conferences where research is presented (e.g., the Leisure Research Symposium, which is part of the National Recreation and Park Association Congress, the American Therapeutic Recreation Association Annual Conference, the Midwest Symposium on Therapeutic Recreation).

Some therapeutic recreation specialists may work in facilities where research is routinely conducted. Other therapeutic recreation specialists may observe researchers periodically entering their facilities to conduct a research study. In order to benefit from the research that may occur in the workplace and to better understand research reports, it helps to recognize that different types of research exist and the various steps in the research process. We will briefly talk about types of research and the steps in the research process.

SOURCE: From C. Bullock, F. McGuire, & E. Barch, Perceived research needs of therapeutic recreators. *Therapeutic Recreation Journal, 18*(3), (1983), 17–24. Reprinted by permission of Therapeutic Recreation Journal.

When listening to people talk about research projects and when examining research, it becomes obvious that many different types of research are conducted. Two types of research that are frequently used are experimental and survey. *Experimental research* involves a researcher manipulating or changing something in the environment, which is considered the independent variable, and measuring its effect on the dependent variable. For instance, Backman and Mannell (1986) examined the relationship between leisure counseling, leisure activity, and leisure counseling/activity (the independent variable) upon older adults' leisure attitudes and behavior (the dependent variables). *Survey research* is another type of research often found in the literature. For example, the study completed by Bullock, McGuire, and Barch (1984) was a survey. They surveyed therapeutic recreation specialists regarding their opinions on the importance of research in therapeutic recreation.

When observing the process of conducting a research study or when involved in assisting with some aspect of a research study, a therapeutic recreation specialist will notice that the researcher follows a number of steps. The research process may be broken down into six steps:

1. The researcher begins by identifying the problem, which often begins by asking questions.
2. The researcher then investigates what is currently known about the research problem. A review of literature is undertaken.
3. At this point the researcher is ready to begin designing the study. The researcher decides what methods to use for collecting data and identifies subjects/clients for inclusion in the study.
4. Data is collected.
5. Data is analyzed.
6. Findings are reported. The researcher will usually report the findings to the agencies involved in the study. Furthermore, findings are reported at professional conferences and in professional journals.

Further study of research methods and processes will assist students and entry-level therapeutic recreation specialists in fully understanding research reports and articles. Many students are able to take classes designed to focus solely on the research process. Being able to understand research reports and staying informed of the research being conducted in the field is one way for therapeutic recreation specialists to broaden their understanding of the effectiveness of the therapeutic recreation process. Research is another avenue therapeutic recreation specialists have for enhancing their knowledge and seeking professional growth.

SUMMARY

Therapeutic recreation professionals are continually committed to gaining new clinical skills and refining previously learned skills. Upon entering the workplace, there are a number of avenues available to therapeutic recreation specialists seeking professional growth. The management of the department or agency in which one works will influence staff members' job descriptions, resources, and supervision. A therapeutic recreation specialist who finds himself or herself in a position with a job description that matches his or her professional interests, indicates adequate resources, and offers general and clinical supervision may be in an optimal environment for professional growth. The consultation process is another arena in which a staff member may have the opportunity to develop further his or her professional skills. Lastly, research in therapeutic recreation is an exciting means by which therapeutic recreation specialists may continually question current practice and broaden their understanding of the effectiveness of the therapeutic recreation process.

READING COMPREHENSION QUESTIONS

1. What is meant by human and nonhuman resources?
2. What types of questions would a job applicant want to ask a manager/supervisor in order to obtain information on opportunities for professional growth?
3. What is the difference between general and clinical supervision?
4. Name several clinical skills that may be evaluated during the clinical supervision process.
5. In what contexts does clinical supervision occur?
6. Outline a situation that calls for a consultant. What type of consultation would you need in this situation?
7. What are the different types of consultation?
8. What types of roles does a consultant use during the consultation process?
9. Why is it important for a consultant to act as a catalyst of change?
10. Describe the stages in the consultation process. How do they differ from one another?
11. Define research.
12. What are the research topics that are ranked as very important by therapeutic recreation specialists?
13. How do therapeutic recreation specialists stay informed of research being conducted in the field?
14. What are two of the roles taken by therapeutic recreation specialists in relation to research?
15. Describe two types of research.
16. Outline the steps in the research process.

SUGGESTED LEARNING ACTIVITIES

1. Invite several therapeutic recreation supervisors to class to discuss opportunities that entry-level therapeutic recreation specialists have for professional growth.

2. Contact the professional organization for therapeutic recreation in your state. Request information on the cost and benefits of membership. Also ask for information on the organization's committees, including the titles and tasks of the committees and how the committees disseminate information to the members.

3. Work on the following problem in a small group. You are a therapeutic recreation specialist working in a rehabilitation facility. Plans for a geriatric wing have been announced. Your department has the opportunity to hire a consultant who is knowledgeable in the area of gerontology to help plan a new program. Discuss the type of consultation, consultant roles, and the process that you would most likely experience in this situation.

4. Interview a therapeutic recreation consultant and determine the types of consultation and roles most frequently used by the consultant.

5. Working with a small group of students, identify one research question for each of the six research topics that were rated highly in the study by Bullock, McGuire, and Barch.

6. Review a research study that has been reported in *Therapeutic Recreation Journal, Journal of Expanding Horizons in Therapeutic Recreation, Journal of Leisurability* or *Annual in Therapeutic Recreation.*

REFERENCES

AGUILAR, T. (1987). Effects of a leisure education program on expressed attitudes of delinquent adolescents. *Therapeutic Recreation Journal, 21*(4), 43–51.

AUSTIN, D. R. (1982) Therapeutic recreation research: An overview. *Abstracts from the 1982 Symposium on Leisure Research.* National Recreation and Park Association.

AUSTIN, D. R. (1986). Clinical supervision in therapeutic recreation. *Journal of Expanding Horizons in Therapeutic Recreation, 1,* 7–13.

BACKMAN, S., & MANNELL, R. (1986). Removing attitudinal barriers to leisure behavior and satisfaction: A field experiment among the institutionalized elderly. *Therapeutic Recreation Journal, 20*(3), 46–53.

BULLOCK, C., McGUIRE, F., & BARCH, E. (1984). Perceived research needs of therapeutic recreators. *Therapeutic Recreation Journal, 18*(3), 17–24.

CAPLAN, G. (1970). *The theory and practice of mental health consultation.* New York: Basic Books.

CHERNISS, C., & EGNATIOS, E. (1977). Styles of clinical supervision in community mental health programs. *Journal of Consulting and Clinical Psychology, 45*(6), 1195–1196.

Code of Ethics—National Therapeutic Recreation Society. (1985). *Therapeutic Recreation Journal, 19*(1), 71–72.

COGAN, M. L. (1973). *Clinical Supervision.* Boston: Houghton Mifflin.

COMPTON, D. (1984). Research priorities in recreation for special populations. *Therapeutic Recreation Journal, 18*(1), 9–17.

CULKIN, D. F., & KIRSCH, S. L. (1986). *Managing human resources in recreation, parks, and leisure services.* New York: Macmillan.

ELLIS, G., & WITT, P. (1986). The Leisure Diagnostic Battery: past, present, and future. *Therapeutic Recreation Journal, 20*(4), 31–47.

ELLIS, G., WITT, P., & NILES, S. (1982). *The Leisure Diagnostic Battery remediation guide.* Denton, TX: North Texas State University.

ISO-AHOLA, S. (1988). Research in therapeutic recreation. *Therapeutic Recreation Journal, 22*(1), 7–13.

KELLER, M. J. (1985). Creating a positive work environment for therapeutic recreation personnel. *Therapeutic Recreation Journal, 19*(1), 36–43.

KERLINGER, F. N. (1973). *Foundations of Behavioral Research.* New York: Holt, Rinehart & Winston.

KRAUS, R. G., & CURTIS, J. E. (1982). *Creative management in recreation and parks.* St. Louis: C. V. Mosby.

KURPIUS, D. (1978). Consultation theory and process: An integrated model. *Personnel and Guidance Journal, 56,* 335–338.

LIPPITT, G., & LIPPITT, R. (1986). *The consulting process in action.* San Diego, CA: University Associates.

SNOW, D. L., & CORSE, S. J. (1986). The process of consultation: Critical issues. In F. V. Mannino, E. J. Trickett, M. F. Shore, M. G. Kidder, & G. Levin (Eds.), *Handbook of mental health consultation* (pp. 393–431). Washington, DC: Department of Health and Human Services.

WITT, P. (1988). Therapeutic recreation research: Past, present, and future. *Therapeutic Recreation Journal, 22*(1), 14–23.

WOLPE, R. A., & RIDDICK, C. (1984). Effects of leisure counseling on adult psychiatric outpatients. *Therapeutic Recreation Journal, 18*(3), 30–37.

19

Trends and Issues

MICHAEL E. CRAWFORD

OBJECTIVES

- Describe the relationship between forces present in American society and community special recreation services.
- Realize the relationship between applied and action research priorities and specific client treatment issues.
- Understand the issues surrounding uniformity of TR university curricula on a national basis.
- Describe the relationship between licensure of personnel and extended preparation of practitioners.
- Understand the issues surrounding multinational organizations for TR.
- Describe the relationship between TR and other national activity therapy groups.
- Realize the issues involved in creating a mechanism whereby a code of ethics can be monitored and enforced.

In Chapter 2, six different characteristics of a profession were presented to organize a discussion of the chronology of therapeutic recreation as it has occurred in this country. In this chapter we will continue to organize the internal trends and issues affecting therapeutic recreation along these six criteria. Additionally, certain economic, social, and political trends in society at large will be alluded to. These larger macro-trends of American society will be discussed briefly as external forces shaping human services philosophy and delivery in general, and professional therapeutic recreation services in particular.

EXTERNAL FORCES SHAPING THERAPEUTIC RECREATION

Issue: Economic Forces

The so-called taxpayer revolution began in California in the late 1970s with the passage of Proposition 13, the now famous tax-lid bill. The impact of Proposition 13, which effectively set limits on the amount of money a legislature could spend, was a reprioritization of public spending (Murphy, 1980, p. 207). Unfortunately for recreation professionals, most taxpayers agreed that fire, police, and sanitation services were more important than recreation centers, parks, and golf courses. As copycat bills of Proposition 13 spread across the country, traditional recreation services suffered greatly in the "budget wars" that followed. Because of this mandated reduction, recreation budgets were reprioritized, and within this process programs for special populations were either substantially reduced, eliminated, or, as was more often the case, never established. The recreation profession thus was placed at a great disadvantage in attempting to respond to the normalization and mainstreaming ethics of the time. Just as legal and social trends were placing emphasis on provision of community services for formerly institutionalized citizens, the recreation profession's ability to respond in kind with greater diversity of programming was severely limited budgetarily. As a result, there are still many communities today (particularly in small town settings—populations of 100,000 or less) where no formal municipal special recreation programs exist or only a few token efforts, such as participation in special olympics or senior centers, are provided as a very unsatisfactory partial solution. One of the most pressing challenges for therapeutic recreation practitioners in the 1990s and beyond will be to reintroduce the service ethic of the TR profession to public recreation services by pushing for increased budgetary and programming resources.

Issue: Social Forces

Many sociologists and social-psychologists have discussed the 1980s as the end of the era of social activism (Raab & Lipset, 1980, p. 138). The 1980s were the decade when the "me" generation came to the forefront. Suddenly, social issues that had been so central to American thought in the 1960s and 1970s—environmental quality, racial desegregation, normalization of institutionalized special populations—took a backseat to more myopic causes. The so-called neo-radical movements of the 1980s—women's rights, gay rights, and the unionization of traditionally professional groups resulting in teacher and nursing strikes—were symptomatic of a society that had become self-concerned. As the "I've got mine, you get yours" approach to life-style became more entrenched, many important social programs and movements that had flourished and gained momentum in the 1970s were cut back (Lasch, 1984). The result today of this backsliding of social concern can be seen in part in the epidemic number of homeless and street people in our country (Szasz, 1988). Similarly, shocking social statistics such as the number of children living below the poverty line (*Newsweek*, 1987), the increasing recidivism in our institutional mental health systems (*Time*, 1987), our overcrowded prisons (Hull, 1987), and the deplorable condition of many of the nation's nursing homes (Teaff, 1985, p. 5) all speak of a society that effectively has turned a deaf ear to the cries for social reform necessary to build the "kinder and gentler society" that President Bush called for in his 1988 campaign. Therapeutic recreation services can and should have an impact in the repair of the social welfare network and the improvement of our human services systems. To do so, however, requires greater assertiveness with our policymakers at the national level as well as effective local educational and political strategies. As we enter the 1990s, one of the greatest "survival" issues for the TR profession will be whether the TR profession is sufficiently mature enough to mount and be effectively viewed as an important social advocate for our populations that are in crisis.

Issue: Political Trends

The majority of the legislative efforts of the 1970s and early 1980s were aimed at prohibiting the exclusion of persons with disabilities from facilities and programs. To this end, a number of laws (the most important of which were reviewed in Chapter 2) were enacted to guarantee equal opportunity. In the main, however, these laws were limited to rights of physical access. Whereas you could not build a building with federal monies that a wheelchair patron could not physically get in and out of, there were no forceful companion programming provisions that insisted or encouraged you to provide anything inside the building. The wave of fiscal conservatism for social programming that flourished during the eight years of the Reagan presidency resulted in shrinking federal dollars for human and social services. The rationale for such cuts was that new social factors—namely, increased volunteerism, corporate giving, and cooperation between advocate associations and recreation and park departments—would take place and in effect take up the fiscal slack. As noted above, however, the "me" generation wasn't particularly interested in such social advocacy, and corporate giving simply either didn't keep pace or was mistargeted. For example, offering public symphony-in-the-park concerts as a one-shot charitable programming event does much for the corporate image of giving but doesn't meet the daily recreation needs of inner-city youth and the problems they face with so much unchallenged discretionary time. Thus, in the 1980s the budget dollars to support the programming need that had been established by the important legislative inroads in the areas of equal access and educational and vocational equality didn't materialize.

As the political agendas for the 1990s are developed, it remains to be seen if the recreation profession can reestablish itself as a key ingredient in master social planning. The Reagan era essentially promoted and to a degree was successful in deprofessionalizing the public image of recreation services (why fund it when you can do it with volunteers and corporate advocacy?). The reprofessionalization of service delivery will depend in large measure on mounting a counter public campaign that will arrest the steady erosion of financing therapeutic recreation in the public sector.

Macro-social, political, and economic issues may well determine ceilings under which therapeutic recreation services can operate in the upcoming years. However, the direction and development of the profession are still in large measure in our own hands. With this in mind, there are a number of internal trends and issues, some positive and some negative, that bear identification and elaboration. Using the six characteristics of a profession previously identified in Chapter 2 as an organizational scheme, some of the more prevalent trends and issues will be briefly discussed.

INTERNAL TRENDS AND ISSUES

Service Motive

In some ways, the most pressing agenda for the TR profession in bringing its service motive forward is a more aggressive posture in ensuring that the limited practice standards that do exist are enforced. Although it is encouraging that NTRS has finally asserted practice guidelines for clinical, residential, and community settings, the compliance aspect of these documents is still purely voluntary. Even so, these standards have undoubtedly affected service in a positive way. Simply having the force of a national association behind you in attempting to convince an administrator or treatment team that a certain approach or resource is essential can go a long way in helping you to achieve that resource. However, most authorities acknowledge that the current standards do represent rather minimal attempts at defining a service mandate (Mobily, 1983). In fact, one of the main agendas for the young ATRA leadership is to attempt to influence and further clinical standards of practice by following a philosophy of closer political affiliation with the allied medical health professions' lobby, as opposed to the traditional NRPA/NTRS parks and recreation power base. Also, a critical issue for ATRA and NTRS will be to what level of success clinical standards of practice may be accelerated in the next few years. The first major publication by ATRA on quality assurance (Riley, 1987) represents one tangible product thus far that begins to put some "teeth" into the ATRA bark.

Although it could be argued that one of the side issues facing clinical standards is that there are too many organizational advocates (NTRS,

NCTRC, and ATRA combined)—thus creating the potential for disagreement and confusion—an equally problematic issue for community practice standards is the lack of organized advocacy from an organizational standpoint. The "special recreation movement" within the TR profession has attempted to raise the visibility of special populations programming within communities by asserting that it is the responsibility more or less of all recreation and park personnel. Although such sentiments are understandably supportive of the overall goals of mainstreaming, they do little in the way of defining specific roles for the TR specialist. Are TR personnel with the special recreation settings to be consultants? Active program leaders? Evaluators? Perhaps more disappointing than the lack of specific practice standards that clearly define the role and mission is the inability of practitioners to move beyond incorporation of the minimal practice guidelines by integrating the research base into the service motive. By way of example, consider the current research base for community programming with the mentally retarded. This particular literature is more advanced and conclusive than any other aspect of our science to date. We have validated that the use of precision teaching techniques, combined with small group instruction conducted in natural environments, will result in increased leisure functioning for even the severely and multihandicapped individual (Crawford, 1986). This process should therefore be our practice standard. Yet, as Schleien and his associates have so clearly articulated, we continue to accept massed, segregated programming within community centers in what has been described as a para-militaristic takeover of the facility (Schleien et al., 1985) as an acceptable and all-too-often dominant form of program delivery. It is simply unacceptable, with the knowledge we have, to continue to allow "yellow bus" programming of special participants to continue to dominate service provision within our communities. It should rapidly become a historical footnote for us. Just as physicians tell their students of the days when they used to give insulin shock therapy to the mentally ill instead of treatment through psychotropic medication, we too should eventually have to whisper about the days when we had to conduct massed segregated programming within communities.

One final side issue related to service motive deals more with the effective stagnation of our service delivery reach. Our inability to respond quickly to rapid societal needs in service settings remains a symptom of our relative youth. Today's example is the AIDS crisis, which has reached epidemic proportions. As more and more of the population at large require medical care in skilled nursing, hospice, and death and dying centers, over the next few decades the question must be raised, How will TR respond? Have we assembled a national task force to study the issue and recommend policy? What place does our therapy have within the treatment cycle for the AIDS patient? Other members of the allied health professions team are scrambling to lobby the public and private sectors for support and funding so they may more effectively respond to the crisis at hand. Unfortunately, TR hasn't even gotten in line yet. We have a prime opportunity to extend, promote, and define clearly our service motive and abilities to the public. Our failure to organize and contribute in a meaningful way will not serve us well as future crises befall society. By contrast, during the polio scare of the 1950s (the last national health scare analogous to the hysteria surrounding the current AIDS crisis), activity therapists among polio wards were very much in demand and very central to hospital adjustment, care, and treatment of polio patients. This may have happened in part because the polio disease was so endemic to children (more than any other age-group), and somehow the public as well as our own professional perception saw the importance of recreation as magnified. By contrast, AIDS (largely a disease of adults who are for the most part members of deviant or "devalued" groups, i.e., drug addicts and homosexuals) has not roused within us a clamor for action. This response displays at best indifference and at worst social bigotry on our part as professionals. Whether or not the national leadership of NTRS or ATRA can organize and respond in this current hour of need may write a great deal of the profession's future history in medical care settings.

Scientific Basis

Our body of knowledge has overall a very uneven base. For some populations and settings (e.g., the mentally retarded) there is a fairly rich and growing research base that may be used to direct programming decisions and create clear practice standards. With other combinations of conditions and settings (e.g., cystic fibrosis patients and acute medical care settings), the number of research articles is almost nonexistent. In fact, it is more often true than not (and particularly for the so-called minority disabilities, e.g., low incidence rates) that the claims of the TR profession for client growth are based in large measure on philosophical models and clinical subjectivity. Programming is often not delivered on an objective activity prescription basis, but more on the old hospital recreation, diversionary events routine. Even in sophisticated settings like rehabilitation hopsitals, the most common theme around which recreational services are organized still is the "monthly calendar," with its emphasis on group diversional programming. Therefore, the remaining issue for the field to deal with is that the "leisure ability model" is in large measure a service philosophy (some say process) that remains unvalidated in many service settings and for many disability groups.

The lack of applied and action research that validates the effectiveness of the TR process as a client change agent in residential, clinical, and community settings remains the number one research priority of the field. Near the top of the list in this regard is the need for specific documentation of the long-term effectiveness of leisure counseling and education interventions and how these techniques might relate to reduced recidivism among institutional populations.

In a related vein, there are service or client-specific side issues that urgently need to be addressed. Perhaps most pressing is the growth of high-technology innovation within the medical rehabilitation field and what the rapid and exciting advancements might mean for increased leisure functioning. New sophisticated orthotic and prosthetic devising needs to be evaluated for recreational applicability. Adaptations like the "Chicago hand" (an adaptation of space age robotics driven by miniature servomechanisms controlled by the amputee's own residual nerve endings at the stump site) now can replace in some cases the old claw utility hook (*Social Issues and Health Care Review*, 1988). Similarly, exteronervous and skeletal systems using the latest in microcomputer technology and aluminum and plastic robotics are making it possible for para- and quadriplegics to ride bikes and walk again (Frank, 1988; *USA Today*, 1988). Experimental work is also occurring with personal radar units and artificial optical systems for the blind (National Federation for the Blind, 1985), as well as increasingly sophisticated interactive computer technology for the multihandicapped (Datillo & Barnett, 1985). Therapeutic recreation professionals should have a role in the development, testing, and refinement of these systems. Our own researchers and social scientists should be in the forefront of setting goals and priorities, and defining development issues for the engineers, biomechanists, and computer scientists to solve. Yet all too often we are in a reactive mode when it comes to such innovation. Positioning ourselves as a profession to move to a proactive versus a reactive status regarding the cutting edge of medical technology should become a high priority for the field as the turn of the century approaches.

Extended Preparation

The current uniformity of national TR educational curricula is a mess (Mobily, 1983). In general, our body of knowledge is still debated and not well organized, and elective course patterns designed to support it are widely divergent across the curricula. Also, even though standards are clearly articulated, the relative importance or weight of such is unclear; thus in one curriculum, leisure counseling skills require an entire course, whereas in another, they require not more than a two-week unit within an advanced tools class. Part of the current confusion over skill is based in part on how to divide the three basic areas of knowledge, skills, and abilities into a fair and representative position within the curricula. Personal competency in all three are needed for effective TR practice: (1) knowledge, that is, the knowing of reality; (2) skills, that is, technical expertise with activities, evaluation instruments, and so forth; and (3) abilities, often referred to as the "art of therapy" (the attitudes, values, and ethics that each practitioner brings to the therapeutic relationship). Probably this last area, personal abilities, is the most under-researched and under-represented area within current curricular approaches in higher education (O'Morrow & Reynolds, 1989, p. 136). Only curriculum models in special education and counseling and guidance have developed effective methods of developing and delivering feedback to students in the area of personal abilities. Therapeutic recreation educators would do well to attempt to emulate these efforts as curriculum enrichment achieves more stature within our educational endeavors.

It seems inevitable that some standardization of the curricula across colleges and universities that is above what is currently in place will become essential to professional survival. Keeping up with our sister therapies, specifically OT and PT, would dictate such a goal. The beginning of national standardization of skills and tools will not take place, however, without considerable exchange and debate among educators. Unfortunately, there are few formal forums for such exchange. The Society for Professional Recreation Educators (SPRE) does produce an annual journal with a focus on pedagogical concerns; however, a more direct organization of TR educational knowledge is probably needed in order for work on such reform across curricula to begin in earnest. Despite the difficulties in achieving standardization, we should not be dissuaded from pursuit of it nor underestimate the importance of it. We commonly accept, in fact insist, that medical surgeons, regardless of what medical school they attended, employ standard diagnostic procedures, standard and accepted surgery procedures, and so forth. Why then is it unreasonable to expect that the delivery of leisure education curricula and the employment of a leisure history inventory—the procedure used to evaluate posthospital leisure functioning—not be standardized at a minimum level across the country? Surely, any profession that considers itself worthy of licensure of its personnel should "have it together" well enough to ensure a more or less standard core education for its work force.

The trend toward licensure of personnel as the central goal of formal higher education brings us to another problem with therapeutic recreation education. The issue is the bachelor's degree as our entry-level degree. Currently, the TR specialist is often the most undercredentialed member of the treatment team. Almost every other discipline requires at least a master's degree in order that a person "qualify" for hire (this is true in social work, psychology, educational therapy), or that they come from a professional school of training with a rigorous and highly specialized curricula (as is the case for occupational and physical therapists). Because of our historical ties to traditional parks and recreation degree programs, TR students inherit requirements for core classes (ranging from 12 to 27 hours nationally) that only indirectly support their training as clinicians. Further, and perhaps less helpful still, is the traditional notion among parks and recreation professionals that the bachelor's degree is sufficient training for entry-level professional responsibilities. Faced with a rapidly expanding knowledge base, increasingly specialized job functions, and a rigid traditional curriculum with little room for negotiation or reform, TR educators simply are not able to fit everything into as few as three courses and a supervised internship. In the next decade of degree development, something will have to give. Either bachelor's degree programs will have to add additional hours as more and more TR courses must be developed to keep up with the knowledge base (forcing TR majors to graduate with more hours than other types of recreation majors), or serious and radical reform of core requirements within recreation and parks for TR majors will have to occur (meaning that the old adage that you are a parks and recreation professional first and a TR major second will have to be reversed in order of importance), or the field must push for expansion to a fifth-year program so that the master's degree becomes the entry-level degree (as have the fields of clinical audiology, speech therapy, psychology, etc.).

Related to the topic of curriculum expansion and reform noted above is the issue of content specialization within curricula. Proponents of the need for clinical specializations basically assert that the TR educational model should emulate the course of development within special education curricula. Thus, students would be expected to take a minimal TR core (in addition, one assumes, to a minimal general parks and recreation core) and then select one or more areas of clinical specialization, a decision driven for the most part by what population and service a student was most interested in. By way of example, then, just as there are special education teachers who have certificates that limit their employment to deaf/blind, or mentally retarded, or learning disabled, there would be TR specialists who would be certified only in clinical areas, such as geriatrics, mental retardation, psychiatric service, and so forth. Conceivably, of course, one could elect as few or as many clinical specializations as desired. The criticisms of this approach are many. Some argue that decisions about how much course work should constitute an area of specialization would at this time be arbitrary (Carter, 1984; Mobily, 1983). Others maintain that we are too young a field in terms of research base to worry about specialization and have too few university programs large enough to support all of the course-work patterns that would be necessary to support such a model. Others argue that such diversity would considerably complicate such personnel issues as certification and licensure; different exams and procedures would be needed for different clinical specializations, for example. However, one should note that the current approach to internship within the field does have the effect of "forcing" specialization upon the student. Despite a more or less generic pattern of TR course work, the student must pick a specific service and clientele to complete his or her training. This requisite of a single experience is much different from our sister therapies of PT and OT, where students do multiple affiliations across a variety of client and service settings. It seems clear that we need to decide where within the curriculum we will diversify. If we want to produce a generic entry-level specialist who can

work across settings, then the current approach to internship works directly against such a goal. If on the other hand we wish to move to specializations within entry-level positions, then inevitably we must begin curricula
expansion and face an equally tough set of decisions regarding degree
alignment and requirements. To do nothing in the face of these two dilem-
mas is to ignore the rapidly approaching obsolescence of the bacheleor's
degree within the allied health field.

Macro-changes in the design and structure of curriculum aside, simply trying to work with upgrading and timely revision of the current
competencies already in place is in and of itself a very unpredictable and
uneven process. The minimal competencies by which curricula are currently evaluated and accredited will need continued assessment and upgrading as the knowledge base of the field continues to grow. By way of
example, 10 years ago concepts such as quality assurance, third-party
reimbursement, and interagency cooperation were simply not considered
or were at the very periphery of the curriculum. Today they are the hottest
topics at national and regional training symposia, yet their place within a
national curriculum is unclear. Formal alliance between traditional education curricula standards and continued education efforts might be an
effective means of prioritizing student needs. If something like 10% of
formal curricula is set aside for revision and reallocation every 3 years, for
example, each college or university program could establish a trends and
issues course that every three years, on the basis of regional and national
practice issues, could be subject to formal expansion or shrinkage. A
national curriculum council might be invoked to provide leadership and
serve as a broker for materials to be shared. Not to plan for curriculum
expansion of basic competencies at a national level assures eventual obsolescence.

Within many TR curricula there are also facilitation skills being
taught that are practiced on an interdisciplinary basis and are increasingly
the subject of bitter debate regarding ownership in practice act disputes
among OTs, PTs, rehabilitation counselors, nurse practitioners, and
CTRSs. Perhaps the best example is stress management techniques. The
traditional Jacobsonian deep-breathing muscle relaxation techniques can
be practiced in some way by all of the above, as well as by psychologists,
nurses, and medical doctors, and are represented in some measure in the
professional preparation of each. Yet some practice acts have narrowly
defined services in such a way as to preclude one professional from delivering something as simple as relaxation techniques because only the "licensed" therapist can do so. Thus, you have a technique developed originally by a physical educator that has now become the sole province of
physical therapy in one state, occupational therapy in another. Or in
another state, the technique can be delivered only by physician prescription
and direction. You can also have a situation where in one midtown hopsital
the psychologists are the only ones to deliver these techniques, and in

another hospital across town only nurse therapists may do so. The educational dilemma facing curricula designers is what to keep in and what to leave out as skills and techniques are territorialized. If we reach a point where a majority of states do not allow TR specialists to conduct relaxation sessions, then we should by default eliminate them from all of our curricula. On the other hand, to do so if only a few states so decide may give away our position to lobby for their preservation for interdisciplinary practice. No national statistics are kept at present related to some of the more intimate details of skills and techniques that are being territorialized that have traditionally been interdisciplinary in nature. A watchdog posture is important over the next few years so that we do not find ourselves in the position of preparing clinicians to deliver techniques that are no longer our province.

Finally, a word regarding standards for internships. There are currently two different sets of internship standards. The certification requirement for NCTRC is 10 continuous weeks for a total of 360 hours. By contrast, NTRS calls for 600 clock hours at 15 weeks. On top of this disparity are varied university requirements, with some schools that operate on quarters using 8-week internships and others that have traditionally required internships of from 10–14 weeks. The confusion and pragmatic complexities this situation has caused within and across universities must be resolved. The University of Missouri provides an interesting case study of this problem. Missouri has required a 12-week internship for all recreation majors for the last 10 years. Yet graduate students argue that 10 weeks to meet certification standards of NCTRC is all they should have to take, particularly because they have already completed a bachelor's degree, and so they are allowed to do so. Thus, the 12-week internship manual is shrunk to 10. At the same time, several undergraduates are excepted by clinical facilities whose directors insist on following the more stringent NTRS standards for 15 weeks. Now the 12-week manual is expanded to 15. Still other undergraduates are excepted by facilities that agree to accept the university 12-week requirement. Therefore, at Missouri during any given semester there may be TR interns receiving 10, 12, and 15 weeks of internship experience. The disparities across facilities and experiences can be remarkable. A related issue is whether or not the current requirement of continuity of experience within a single setting doesn't force specialization of interest. By contrast, OT students do 3 separate clinical internships (known as affiliations) across a variety of client and service settings. If the BA is to remain the entry-level degree for TR specialists, then shouldn't it be a more generic degree (using a multiple internship approach) instead of one providing a student field experience in only a single setting?

Autonomy of Judgment

In some ways, one of the potentially most devisive issues in the field of TR today revolves around the certification versus licensure issue. Simply put, this controversy has served to divide the field into two rival camps, which unfortunately more often than not have pitted academics against practitioners. It is not difficult to understand how this division has occurred; each group is motivated by a different agenda for the profession. The academic camp argues that those professionals urging licensure of the work force are way ahead of the knowledge base of the profession. To make make individual practitioners legally "liable" for their actions or inactions (one aspect of licensure acts) is premature. They argue the subjectivity inherent within activity prescription and leisure counseling techniques currently practiced supports the basic premise of the antilicensure lobby. Those practitioners in the front line counter that the future of the profession is now; and if we wait too long to assert ourselves, we will find our professional "turf" already accounted for by our sister therapies. In support of this position are the licensure laws already on the books in some states in which OTs have successfully won definition of their services to include such things as leisure counseling, development of play skills, and delivery of recreational services. The licensure "wars" for skills directly related to our service delivery model, as well as for the more generic traditionally interdisciplinary skills discussed in the above section related to curriculum, are not minor issues. Additionally, a concurrent movement among hospital administrators to provide resources only to those services that can generate third-party reimbursment (usually limited to "licensed" personnel) makes the crisis more acute.

There are no easy answers to this dilemma. It is difficult to argue against the very compelling political realities of service that prolicensure advocates point to. Increasingly, hospital administrators, when faced with the decision of hiring a TR specialist (whose salary comes out of the fixed bed rate of the facility) or hiring an OTR (whose salary can be paid largely through insurance company reimbursements that can be directly billed for) will hire and support the more independent and income-generating activity therapist. There are instances where entire recreation therapy programs have been eliminated and also where RT and OTR departments have been merged under a single activity therapy department, with RTs being placed under the "supervision" of OTRs so that costs of services could be recouped (Cook, 1987). Yet, on the other hand, to "sell the public" on a service ethic that we cannot fully validate or account for is too similar to the carnival "snake oil salesman" approach (e.g.: "Come to TR; we will fix your self-esteem, increase your leisure repertoire, positively impact your value system.") for many researchers to accept. Currently, with the exception of the two states that have already pushed for licensure, the field has accepted a kind of holding pattern. Many CTRSs continue to lobby against licensure acts of sister therapies in an attempt to postpone or prevent our own interests as well as interdisciplinary skills from being "gobbled up," while at the same time holding off on moving very aggressively or proactively on a TR act. Nebraska serves as an interesting case study of this division. In 1988 a group of practitioners did circulate and attempt to introduce a practice act for TR. A group of university faculty felt obliged on the basis of ethical and scientific grounds to write a formal letter of protest to the president of the state association indicating their lack of support. The result for Nebraska was that the bill was withdrawn for further "study." Interestingly enough, just the year before, a powerful interdisciplinary lobby, including the two different groups of TR professionals, blocked an overly aggressive OT practice act within the state. Whether or not TR can continue successfully to hang on to its identity in the face of current political and fiscal pressures while the knowledge base catches up remains to be seen.

Regardless of the eventual outcome of the national certification versus licensure issue, there are also immediate problems with which we should be concerned. The field now finds itself operating under multiple systems of autonomy of judgment (national certification standards, independent state certification standards in some areas, as well as licensure requirements in two states). Thus, there is also a personal practice issue related to the unevenness in state-to-state standards now in existence. For the first time, TR specialists must consider personal geographic and career mobility restriction (Carter, 1984). Practitioners now face at best impediments in moving from state to state and at worst relocation in a state where they cannot pass the licensure examination and cannot work. Given how rapidly the curriculum in higher education for TR has expanded and how uneven undergraduate preparation is (based on minimal standards), it is remarkable that an examination of licensure could be put in place so early (as it was in Utah and Georgia) and not face a legal test by those not passing it. The alternate argument, of course, would be that current exams are so easy or watered down (so as to by design be all inclusive) that they truly do not meet the intent of licensure, a term that by definition is put forward as a governmental action to "protect" the consumer from poor services. In a related light, if more and more states pass licensure acts, then eventually reciprocity between states has the potential to become even further diluted, and more and more of the work force may find themselves in uncomfortable and untenable positions in negotiating across state boundary moves.

If we consider what has happened to our sister therapy OT as it has developed licensure, we find a further unenviable dilemma. Despite the fact that the national OT leadership produced and distributed a model practice act for OT, in some states this practice act had been considerably expanded and in others considerably compromised, depending upon the nature of the political lobby for or against it. Thus, in some states OTs are allowed to develop play skills and conduct leisure counseling, and actually supervise recreational therapists; in other states they may not. The point is that what an OT may have been trained to do and what he or she is allowed to do may not always match up well, depending upon the specifics of the state's practice act. Conceivably, we could reach this same point in TR.

Thus, in the future a TR specialist may make the decision not to move to take a job in another state, not only out of fear of not being able to pass the state's licensing examination, but also because the restrictions of the practice act are such that the day-to-day responsibilities of being a TR specialist may be considerably different from the those they want to practice. The new responsibilities may either be restricted or expanded from what their current duties are.

Professional Organizations

The reader will recall from Chapter 2 that the early days of TR were dominated by different organizational forces and philosophies that in the main could not relate to one another. One of the two principal majority perspectives was the position of the Hospital Recreation Section of the American Recréation Society (ARS), which essentially held the "recreation for all" perspective (sometimes referred to as the recreation for recreation's sake). These professionals felt that the inherently beneficial aspects of recreation should be available to everyone, especially those confined to institutions as a result of illness or disability. The second and principally rival philosophy held by the National Association of Recreation Therapists (NART) has over time been referred to as the recreation-as-therapy viewpoint, the major premise being that recreation could serve as an intervention, a specific tool of treatment or rehabilitation effective in combatting primary disability (Austin, 1986). The merger of these two groups into a single NTRS membership in 1966 can now be viewed as an uneasy coalition. With the formation of ATRA in 1984, the old NART philosophy, or recreation-as-therapy position, once again separated and a separate organizational advocate emerged. It would be inaccurate to infer that all of the remaining NTRS membership necessarily hold to the recreation-for-all ethic of the old Hospital Recreation Section of ARS (it should be noted that some professionals do hold dual memberships across ATRA and NTRS). However, the key aspects of this position are present in the modern-day definition of the leisure ability model that NTRS has adapted as its national philsophy position. So, although it is true that the old hopsital recreation ethic is alive only in part within NTRS, the creation of ATRA in the main represents a renewal of an old philosophical struggle of recreation versus therapy, and remains a nagging undercurrent within the professionalization priorities of the field. You simply can't develop what you can't define, and the philosophical devisiness of professionals has resulted in an organizational circle game, leaving us in some ways no better off organizationally than we were in the 1950s. Every other aspect of the field's professionalization could be affected by a duality of missions across organizations; issues ranging from curriculum development up to and including the overall political effectiveness of our national lobby effort could be seriously compromised. Some argue that a new organization simply reflects a metamorphosis of thought that will help the profession grow more swiftly. The underlying premise to this more optimistic view is that once the effective growth work is done (work that supposedly could not take place within the NTRS structure), the main body of new ideas and concepts will be reassimilated into a majority position within the field.

Although there may be some logic to the more optimistic view of what dual national organizations may afford in terms of creative growth, there are few precedents for such actions across our sister therapies. Neither occupational nor physical therapists have to be asked the question, So which organization do you belong to and why? If in fact the TR profession cannot come to agreement regarding philosophical mission, then, rather than persisting along the path of separate organizations (What will be next? A new national organization for community recreation and TR?), it would be far more effective to follow the subspecialization model that the American Psychological Association (APA) has perfected. Within the APA there are 12 different branches of subspecialization, each with its own journal, mission, and constituency; yet there is one APA political lobby, one APA unified membership, one APA code of ethics, and so forth. Why isn't it possible for a single national TR organization to offer a clinical branch, a community branch, and so forth? At a time when therapeutic recreation's political effectiveness is most needed to offer resistance to hostile practice acts from other therapies and to lobby proactively for increased federal, state, and local support for services, the very public fractionalization of the membership that having two national organizations provides for sends a very disjointed and potentially problematic message to outside groups.

A related issue to organizational efffectiveness and range is the sitation created by outlier activity therapy groups, the so-called singular-medium therapies such as dance therapy, music therapy, horticulure, and art therapy. Here again we have professionals who use some form of activity medium in a therapuetic sense yet define themelves as separate from TR. They have created their own national organizations, curricula, political lobbies and so forth. Another outlier group, the largest group and in some ways a group that represents the greatest failure of TR to develop a truly encompassing or more global service ethic, is the national Activities Director Association (ADA). In recent years, the ADA national plan has become a near carbon copy of the NCTRC certification plan. Its approach to continuing education, political lobby efforts, and so forth, have all resulted from a careful study of NTRS efforts. Why does the public need two different activity therapy organizations concerned with the delivery of services within nursing homes? As in the scenario above regarding ATRA and NTRS, an umbrella organization representing a powerful combined membership and political lobby, built along the lines of the APA branch model, could bring all of the singular-medium therapies as well as incorporate the service concerns of ADA, NTRS, and ATRA under a single-activity therapy banner. Such a coalition, could it ever be achieved, would represent a significant advancement in the overall professionalization of activity therapy as a public service ethic. The old adage "united we stand, divided we fall" may prove particularly relevant in the years ahead as increasingly high health costs, changing insurance standards, licensure bills, and mandates from federal regulatory bodies continue to assault and demand swift change and accountability across all the activity therapies.

Code of Ethics

This aspect of professionalism is still in its infancy for the TR profession. Although the existence of a code of ethics is at least a start in the right direction until an organizational enforcement branch is put into place, the code of ethics is largely window dressing. The inability to develop enforcement is directly tied to the subjectivity of current practice and the underdeveloped research base under which we are currently operating. Theoretically, if a CTRS is programming against current practice standards you enforce those standards, but how do you translate general standards of practice into specific procedures and practices? For example, if a physician delivered an outdated treatment to a patient (e.g., treating an aggressive psychiatric patient with insulin shock therapy), then the consumer can point to a clear violation of current best practice standards and force revocation of license to practice. What is the parallel example for a CTRS? If a CTRS practices in such a way as to inhibit or prevent the social development or personal development of his or her client (e.g., offering only segregated services to mentally retarded clients instead of normalized ones), then should he or she be found guilty of professional misconduct and face being stripped of certification privileges? These are difficult distinctions to draw, made more difficult by the lack of a definitive research base against which to reference outcomes and practices.

What does the trend from certification of personnel to licensure of personnel mean for a code of ethics and its enforcement? If a CTRS in a state with licensure (meaning a professional is personally culpable for his or her treatment decisions) recommends a suicidal youth for an off-campus outing, and during the course of the outing, the patient suicides, shouldn't this decision to prescribe such an activity be subject to professional review and possible revocation of license to practice? Is the CTRS guilty of poor diagnosis and activity prescription, perhaps forcing a level of social stimulation that was excessive, or is he or she simply guilty of providing poor supervision, in effect using poor judgment while conducting the activity? Certainly, if a physician prescribed a drug that had a lethal or ill effect on a patient, the family would seek recourse; if a fully licensed CTRS prescribes an activity program that results in similar consequences, then shouldn't he or she be as culpable as the physician? If eventually we can agree on a definition, how will we monitor such transgressions? Will we have state or regional or national boards of ethics? Do we need all three with built-in appeals systems, or should each state be responsible for enforcement? If a professional is stripped of certification in one state, should he or she be allowed to practice in others? If not, how will the profession inform service providers nationally of individuals "banned" from the profession?

The first legal tests of our professional code of ethics have not occurred because as a profession we have not developed the report, review, appeal, and enforcement aspects that physicians, psychologists, and social workers all have in place. These licensed professionals lay their careers and personal credibility on the line daily in making clinical decisions about treatment efficacy and effectiveness. If the day comes that our own research base will support similar precision in our practice standards, then the time will come to operationalize fully our code of ethics and to hold our membership personally accountable for their actions or inactions. Until that time, our code of ethics remains a philosophical position that we can say we believe in, and even are committed to, yet are still striving toward.

SUMMARY

In this chapter, external economic, social, and political forces affecting the growth of the TR profession were discussed. Events like the taxpayer revolution, shifting social consciousness, and failed strategies such as corporate giving have all effectively combined to limit the programmatic vitality of TR, primarily because of their effect on budgets and resources. More aggressive promotion of our service ethic within the public sector is needed to reverse these effects.

The six characteristics of a profession reviewed originally in Chapter 2 provided a forum to discuss trends and issues internal to the profession. Among the most prevalent are (1) more clearly defining our practice standards, (2) validating the leisure ability process across clients and settings, (3) improving curriculum uniformity and dealing with issues of providing for clinical specializations and more sophisticated internships, (4) resolving the certification versus licensure dilemma for personnel, (5) dealing with the philosophic complexities of multi-TR and rival activity therapy organizations, and (6) developing enforcement mechanisms for our professional code of ethics.

In some ways, the work ahead, challenging us as it does on so many fronts, at times seems overwhelming. Yet when we consider how far we have come, from such humble and disconnected beginnings, it is easier to accept the burden of the future by taking the long view and being patient enough to measure change across generations and not years. It is possible to see a future where the full professionalization of TR will take place. For now, those of us in the front lines must continue to push ahead where we can and accept what we can't immediately change as the challenge for the next generation.

READING COMPREHENSION QUESTIONS

1. What was the result of the so-called taxpayer revolution for community recreation services?

2. The general backsliding of social concern that occurred during the "me" generation has left what special populations at crisis in this country?

3. What social factors did politicians offer as solutions (in lieu of funding) for recreational programming in the 1980s?

4. If you were to establish a programming standard for community special recreation services for the mentally retarded, what would that standard incorporate?

5. Do you agree with the parallel drawn between the AIDS and polio epidemics, and do you agree with the suggestion as to why TR hasn't been more involved?

6. Can you identify some of the high-technology advancements under research and development that TR may have to interface with at the turn of the century?

7. Do you agree that national standardization of TR curricula is an important issue for the field?

8. Can you articulate the criticisms of why the bachelor's degree in TR is considered obsolete by some as the national entry-level degree?

9. Do you agree that clinical specializations for CTRSs is the model our curricula reform effort should adopt?

10. Which skills are the subject of debate among TR and other interdisciplinary groups regarding practice acts?

11. What do you think about the differences in the TR internship requirements and OT clinical affiliations? Should TR students have to do more than one internship?

12. What activity therapies are classified as single-medium therapies?

13. Do you agree that the APA model of professional specialization makes sense for TR? For the inclusion of other activity therapies as well?

14. Do you favor individual states having separate licensure laws, or is a national certification plan the best way to proceed in developing our demonstration of autonomy of judgement?

15. Can you identify clear violations of conduct that you feel should result in an individual's national certification being rescinded? Should that person ever be allowed back into the profession? Under what conditions?

SUGGESTED LEARNING ACTIVITIES

1. Develop a statement of purpose for a TR program for AIDS patients in the terminal phase of the disease. List a number of program components that would be attached to this statement. What changes in college and university training programs might have to take place in order to prepare clinicians for working with this population?

2. You are a director of a community parks and recreation program and have just been directed by the mayor to develop a therapeutic recreation program for the large number of homeless people in the community. Develop a list of professional contacts and consultants you will use to develop the program's goals and philosophy.

3. Develop a list of clinical skills that a CTRS should acquire for working in mental health settings. Do the same for mental retardation and physical disability settings. Cross-check your three lists to see how many skills overlap and how many are unique to service with specific types of clients. Now write a 1- to 2-page reaction paper in which you articulate your position on what clinical skills should be part of a standardized national curriculum for all CTRSs.

REFERENCES

Austin, D. R. (1986). The helping profession: You do make a difference. In A. James & F. McGuire (Eds.), *Selected papers form the 1985 Southeast Therapeutic Recreation Symposium.* Clemson University Extension Services.

Carter, M. J. (1984). Issues in continuing professional competence of therapeutic recreation. *Therapeutic Recreation Journal, 18*(3), 7–10.

Cook, G. (1987). Personal communication with author. Ms. Cook is former director of therapeutic recreation at St. Josephs Hospital, Omaha, NE.

Crawford, M. E. (1986). Development and generalization of lifetime leisure skills for multi-handicapped participants. *Therapeutic Recreation Journal, 20*(4), 48–60.

Datillo, J., & Barnett, L. A. (1985). Therapeutic recreation for individuals with severe handicaps: An analysis of the relationship between choice and pleasure. *Therapeutic Recreation Journal, 19*(3), 79–91.

Frank, K. (1988, Spring). Beyond stigma: Visibility and self-improvements of persons with congenital limb deficiencies. *Journal of Social Issues, 44*, 95–116.

Hull, J. D. (1987, February 2). Slow descent into hell. *Time*, p. 26.

Lasch, C. (1984). *The culture of narcissism: American life in an age of diminishing expectations.* New York: W. W. Norton.

Mobily, K. J. (1983). Quality analysis in therapeutic recreation curricula. *Therapeutic Recreation Journal, 17*(1), 18–25.

Murphy, J. F. (1980). An enabling approach to leisure service delivery. In T. L. Goddale & P. A. Witt (Eds.), *Recreation and leisure: Issues in an era of change* (pp. 197–210). State College, PA: Venture Publishing.

National Federation of the Blind. (1985). *Rising expectations on the part of the blind status report.* Washington, DC.

Newsweek. (1987, January 12). A family down and out. P. 44.

O'Morrow, G. S. & Reynolds, R. P. (1989). *Therapeutic recreation: A helping profession.* (3rd ed.) Englewood Cliffs, NJ: Prentice-Hall.

Raab, E., & Lipset, S. M. (1980). The prejudiced society. In M. Wertheimer (Ed.), *Confrontation: Psychology and the problems of today* (pp. 135–145). Glenview, IL: Scott, Foresman.

Riley, B. (Ed.). (1987). *ATRA: Evaluation of therapeutic recreation through quality assurance.* State College, PA: Venture Publishing.

Schleien, S., Olson, K., Rogers, N., & McLaferty, M. (1985). Integrating children with severe handicaps into recreation and physical education programs. *Journal of Park and Recreation Administration, 3*(1), 50–66.

Social Issues and Health Care Review. (1988). New Products and Technology, *3*(2), 18–20.

SZASZ, T. (1988, March 14). Homelessness is not a disease. *USA Today, 119*, 28.

TEAFF, J. D. (1985). *Leisure services with the elderly.* St. Louis: C. V. Mosby.

Time. (1987, December 28). A job but no place to live. p. 27.

USA Today. (1988, February 5). Making life more livable. *118*, 4.

Author Index

Subject Index